A POWER TO TRANSLATE THE WORLD

RE-MAPPING THE TRANSNATIONAL
A Dartmouth Series in American Studies

SERIES EDITOR
Donald E. Pease
Avalon Foundation Chair of Humanities
Founding Director of the Futures of American Studies Institute
Dartmouth College

The emergence of Transnational American Studies in the wake of the Cold War marks the most significant reconfiguration of American Studies since its inception. The shock waves generated by a newly globalized world order demanded an understanding of America's embeddedness within global and local processes rather than scholarly reaffirmations of its splendid isolation. The series Re-Mapping the Transnational seeks to foster the cross-national dialogues needed to sustain the vitality of this emergent field. To advance a truly comparativist understanding of this scholarly endeavor, Dartmouth College Press welcomes monographs from scholars both inside and outside the United States.

For a complete list of books available in this series, see www.upne.com.

David LaRocca and Ricardo Miguel-Alfonso, editors, *A Power to Translate the World: New Essays on Emerson and International Culture*
Melissa M. Adams-Campbell, *New World Courtships: Transatlantic Alternatives to Companionate Marriage*
Elèna Mortara, *Writing for Justice: Victor Séjour, the Kidnapping of Edgardo Mortara, and the Age of Transatlantic Emancipations*
Rob Kroes, *Prison Area, Independence Valley: American Paradoxes in Political Life and Popular Culture*
Etsuko Taketani, *The Black Pacific Narrative: Geographic Imaginings of Race and Empire between the World Wars*
William V. Spanos, *Shock and Awe: American Exceptionalism and the Imperatives of the Spectacle in Mark Twain's* A Connecticut Yankee in King Arthur's Court
Laura Bieger, Ramón Saldívar, and Johannes Voelz, editors, *The Imaginary and Its Worlds: American Studies after the Transnational Turn*
Paul A. Bové, *A More Conservative Place: Intellectual Culture in the Bush Era*
John Muthyala, *Dwelling in American: Dissent, Empire, and Globalization*
Winfried Fluck, Donald E. Pease, and John Carlos Rowe, editors, *Re-Framing the Transnational Turn in American Studies*

DAVID LaROCCA AND
RICARDO MIGUEL-ALFONSO, EDITORS

A POWER TO TRANSLATE THE WORLD

New Essays on Emerson and International Culture

DARTMOUTH COLLEGE PRESS
HANOVER, NEW HAMPSHIRE

Dartmouth College Press
An imprint of University Press of New England
www.upne.com

Manufactured in the United States of America
Typeset in Sabon by Integrated Publishing Solutions, Grand Rapids, Michigan.

Library of Congress Cataloging-in-Publication Data

A power to translate the world : new essays on Emerson and international culture / edited by David LaRocca and Ricardo Miguel-Alfonso.
pages cm. — (Re-mapping the transnational : a Dartmouth series in American Studies)
Includes bibliographical references and index.
Summary: "This work is an edited collection tracing the global impact of Emerson's thought" — Provided by publisher.
ISBN 978-1-61168-828-3 (cloth : alk. paper) — ISBN 978-1-61168-829-0 (pbk. : alk. paper) — ISBN 978-1-61168-830-6 (ebook)
1. Emerson, Ralph Waldo, 1803–1882—Criticism and interpretation. 2. Emerson, Ralph Waldo, 1803–1882—Influence. 3. Emerson, Ralph Waldo, 1803–1882—Public opinion. I. LaRocca, David, 1975– editor. II. Miguel-Alfonso, Ricardo, editor. III. Title: Emerson and international culture.
PS1638.P69 2015
814´.3—dc23 2015011818

5 4 3 2 1

An individual man is a fruit which it cost all the foregoing ages to form and ripen. The history of the genesis or the old mythology repeats itself in the experience of every child. He too is a demon or god thrown into a particular chaos, where he strives ever to lead things from disorder into order. Each individual soul is such, in virtue of its being a power to translate the world into some particular language of its own; if not into a picture, a statue, or a dance,—why, then, into a trade, an art, a science, a mode of living, a conversation, a character, an influence.

—Ralph Waldo Emerson, "The Method of Nature"

CONTENTS

A POWER TO TRANSLATE THE WORLD

DAVID LAROCCA AND
RICARDO MIGUEL-ALFONSO

INTRODUCTION: THINKING THROUGH INTERNATIONAL INFLUENCE

AS OF A POINT of inspiration and provocation, we have adopted from Emerson's "The Method of Nature" the phrase "a power to translate the world" as the title of the present volume. When followed by our gloss of a subtitle, the interpretive work of this collection of new essays is off and running: what is the relationship between translation and the international, between some such world we are said to share and the culture(s) that claim(s) to inhabit it? Moreover, in a book series that signals its allegiance to the concept of the transnational, how are we to handle that term's fealty or filial relation, if any, to the act or art of translation? In some form or fashion, these questions preoccupy the contributors gathered here, who each in his or her own way—through close readings of diverse texts, by the application of myriad means of exegesis—aim to provide some orientation to the quick conceptual muddle one might otherwise come to in adducing the relationships between translation, the transnational, the international, and influence.

By way of Emerson's cue that "[e]ach individual soul" is "a demon or god thrown into a particular chaos, where he strives ever to lead things from disorder into order," we have collectively, and humbly, undertaken to track and trace the peculiarities of how, specifically, "a power to translate the world" may culminate "into some particular language of its own"—perhaps most intriguingly, into influence as such. With Emerson's tropes and figures in mind—beginning strikingly with translation itself—we may approach the manner, methods, and modes by which a writer or artist's coaxing of reality from chaos to order, from abstract concept to concrete form, may not reside strictly within his private company but may by turns, over time, radiate to the expanded surface of our stony rounded sphere, simply called the world—or resonate through those vast interior realms we may refer to as worlds. How others live with Emerson's influence, and as the cases here illustrate, how such cohabitation renders new forms of translation, yields at once an encounter with evidence and a mystery that defies an easy account of what we read. Emerson has a "particular language" of his own, and it is to the influential effects of that language on others—beyond America's borders—that we turn our attention; we also reverse our orientation in order to assess some ways in which lines written by non-Americans came to affect Emerson's thought, his language. Such an interrelationship provides a context for our shared inquiry.

Recovering the International for the Transnational Age

In a literal sense, American studies includes American literature and American philosophy; in a practical or professional sense, it would be better to say the three fields bear relation to one another, though the nature of their intimacy is a perpetual American question. As American studies has undergone what has been, and continues to be, described as a "transnational turn," a reader may wonder what happens when unexpected innovations and long-standing preoccupations of that field are brought into conversation with the inheritance of American letters as they are known in literature and philosophy.[1] In short, what happens to American literature and American philosophy when those national domains are oriented to a global context? In the present volume, we have collected a series of thoughtful responses to this question, each of which is inflected by the particular disciplinary and subdisciplinary expertise of its author. By and large, these investigations take place within the preoccupations, forms, and definitions familiar to American departments of English; in other portions of this book, these undertakings are complemented by contributions from philosophers, poets, creative writers, and critics, who bring their own—sometimes overlapping, sometimes distinctive—interests and cues for interrogation.

As the current volume's presence in Re-Mapping the Transnational: A Dartmouth Series in American Studies suggests, we endeavor to contribute a new valence to the ongoing deliberation over what series editor Donald E. Pease describes as "the impact of transnational perspectives on American studies."[2] Assessing that effect in this collection, however, will occur primarily within the jurisdictions of American literature and American philosophy, and in the present case more particularly, through an assessment of Ralph Waldo Emerson's reading from beyond the borders of a land that in the year of his birth expanded with, and was redefined by, the Louisiana Purchase—and even more prominently, the reading of Emerson's work by others beyond American borders, in countries around the world. One question that underwrites the volume, then, is: To what extent does the transnational turn in American studies find credence and expression in the global reading of American literature and American philosophy in the figure and form of Emerson's prose?

A first observation comes in the very subtitle of our volume—namely, that it promises a close look at Emerson and *international* culture. Why not, if only for the sake of consistency, *transnational* culture? The work of a contemporary writer can legitimately, and it would appear, usefully be caught up in the developments of the transnational in a way that Emerson and his contemporaries cannot. We find evidence of this propitious effect in astute readings of Philip Roth and Richard Powers, among other authors, both of whom have written contemporaneously with the radical, transforming, and unsettling effects of "the transnational turn."[3] Meanwhile, back in the nineteenth century—figured either as the period in which Emerson read in the works of writers from other nations, or as the locus from which writers read Emerson after his time—we are undeniably implicated in an era defined more by nation building and the formation and retention of national identity (as the brief allusion to the Louisiana Purchase is meant to invoke, if only glancingly) than faced with an era, such as our own, in which we are increasingly encouraged to consider the movement or even erasure of borders and boundaries, and to dwell in the seemingly endless and evolving liminal spaces that emerge as a result. As Pease notes, "when used as a noun, the transnational refers to a condition of in-betweenness (the 'trans'), and to a behavioral category that imputes the traits of flexibility, non-identification, hybridity, and mobility to agents of conduct" (4). Thinking across time, the notion of the "transnational" in the nineteenth century might have seemed a euphemism for colonialism: (imperial/parent) nations conquering and redefining other (colonized/child) nations and lands in or on their own terms. Now, in the twenty-first century, as if in a profound gesture to rewrite history, those same national borders have again come under question. They are shown to be assigned, contestable, fiat barriers—and are, tragically, a regular aspect of the conditions for war making. Again Pease clarifies: "The transnational differs from the international in that it forecloses the possibility that either nation in the transaction will remain self-enclosed and unitary. In transnational formations, identities, things, finances, and places are not bound by national identifications and investments" (5).

Thus, for those who speak of or think about the international, there abides something crucial, something stable, about the persistence of self-enclosure and unity, even in the face of internal development and the effects of outward forces. Referencing the concept of "American exceptionalism" necessarily lays heavy weight on the signifier "American," and yet, a transnational reading of the term can quickly divest it of potentially problematical political insinuations (for example, rabid, unchecked imperialist agendas; corrosive jingoism; and the like) by noting that the essential character of the concept—that a people can write themselves into existence as a polis—can be successfully implemented *anywhere* willing spirits arise to embrace it.[4]

While the international cannot anticipate the transformative effects of the transnational, the latter term—which Pease calls a "volatile transfer point," "mobile category," and "promiscuous signifier" (4, 5, 6)—may very well accommodate all of our discourse in this volume about the international, since it has the expansive power to incorporate what we say. Our hope and our aim is that our remarks here find pertinence in the emerging, insightful, but also turbulent debates that define transnational studies as such. Yet it would be an act *avant la lettre* to impose the "transnational" (as we are coming to understand and define it) on Emerson's nineteenth century—either in terms of him as a reader, or of those who read his work. Thus, the animated movement and meaning of the "and" in the subtitle of the book—a conjunction meant to highlight Emerson's status as a national (American) author who read widely the work of non-Americans *and* the reading of Emerson's (American) writing by a world of readers beyond his shores.

The "international" may now, for us, seem either quaint or naive, a holdover from an outmoded outlook (perhaps one, not ironically, overcome, displaced, or otherwise absorbed by the transnational), and thus an odd anachronism. But for Emerson and his age, the international was the cutting edge of cultural and intellectual sophistication—a bold antidote to provincialism and an antagonist to stultifying isolation. It was an achievement, and often a novelty, to read in the literature from another land. Emerson was, for example, among the first readers in America to have in hand English translations of Confucius and Mencius, Hafiz and Saadi, as well as myriad contemporary writers from European countries along with fresh renderings of classic works from Greece, Rome, and the ancient Levant. The exchange, the engagement—the "inter-" of the international—was a conceptual thrill: a mode of time travel, an enriching form of ethnological exploration and experiment (often without leaving the comforts of Concord, or at least the confines of America), and the occasion for unexpected discoveries of common ideas and disparate approaches to them. Far from an embarrassment, an experience of the international was an indication of accomplishment, a mark of one's capacity to move (literally or conceptually) across lands, borders, and often ossified habits of mind. At the time of his death in 1882, Emerson was the most well-known American man of letters in the world. This could be recognized as international literary celebrity, not a transnational acclaim, since it was crucial to that celebrity—or more properly, to his writing—*that* he was an American.

Emerson, after all, did not write about North American philosophy, but American. He was not preoccupied with contributions from Canadian or Mexican writers (finding pertinence in Canada and Mexico only in their political significance as territories adjacent to the United States, and therefore as affecting its constitution as a nation-state), and neither was he attentive to the many distinctive works from Central America and the Caribbean. His was a nationalistic-centric thinking, and it was perpetually conducted in relationship with the nationalisms of other thinking—British, German, French, Spanish, Italian, Swedish, among others—and also the radiating, multiform, provincial identities of the Greek, Roman, Persian, and Chinese empires. As Emerson noted in his journal, with characteristic precision and comprehensiveness, "That idea which I approach & am magnetized by,— is my country" (*JMN* 9:66). Across the ocean, and years earlier, but in a similar atmosphere of nationalistic consciousness we find Thomas Carlyle, who, when he came to write a preface to his compendium of translated works by German authors—*German Romance* (1827)—anticipated that his English-speaking audience might wonder after the relevance of the *Germanness* of the prose. Did the national character of the author matter for good or ill to the texts he presented? Was his admitted difference (from, say, an English author) itself a catalyst to shared insight, or was it neutralizing, or even a liability, lending credence to alienation and further entrenching cultural difference? Carlyle admonished his readers: "One thing it will behove him not to lose sight of: They are German Novelists, not English ones; and their Germanhood I have all along regarded as a quality, not as a fault. . . . Every nation has its own form of character and life; and the mind which gathers no nourishment from the everyday circumstances of its existence, will in general be but scantily nourished."[5]

Emerson's habits of reading from the literatures and philosophies of other lands, along with Carlyle's commendation to respect the distinctiveness of national character in the formation of its literatures and philosophies, illustrates how the pre-transnational age supplies instances of *inter*national, not transnational, engagement. As the American Emerson picked up Scottish Carlyle, so Scottish Carlyle read the American Emerson; these are but two instances of the presence and effect of textual and authorial identity as we find it in the nineteenth century. And thus while Emerson is, along with a few other of his New England neighbors, nearly synonymous with the transcendentalist, he is not part of our contemporary shift to the transnational. It would be pleasurably fortuitous if we could line up all the trans-words—transcendental, transnational, transatlantic, translation, even transgender—and claim them as a match set. Instead, we have the difficult task of tracing and parsing the differences that obtain between them.

While there is reason to be cautious about swapping terms, one for the other, all these terms are, it would seem, under negotiation—calling out for our interpretative assessment. For example, if one wished to temper Emerson's outlook (such as we might name it a transcendental nationalism or nationalistic transcendentalism), or adapt it—even, as one is wont to say here, *translate* it—to our current setting, one would do well to consider Johannes Voelz's notion of Emerson as an "organicist nationalist."[6] If Emerson was invoked as a "hypercanonical" figure of American identity—in modes similar to Franklin and Jefferson, or Melville and Whitman—and thus used as a bulwark to defend (and expand) that identity, it is also worth appreciating, Voelz notes, "how cunningly he opened up possibilities of identification and solidarity beyond the temporal and spatial confines of the nation."[7] In this light, consequently, Emerson is not a starched and stale remnant of a bygone era, but a thinker whose words call forth a new series of adaptive interrogations, through which we may see our own present-day—increasingly transnational—scenario with greater depth and enhanced clarity.

So, in the midst of the allusions to and affiliations with the transnational made apparent in this volume, we wish to keep open a case for the recovery, retention, reintegration, reinvigoration, reimaging, and reapplication of the well-worn, perhaps old-fashioned, term: the international. For it seems, in our opinion, that the use of this term in the context of these essays sheds promising light on the significance of the transnational in its current form and for its future potential—both intellectually and practically. Moreover, we see productive lines of affinity between what may be deemed the spirit of contemporary transnationalism and the notion of cosmopolitanism as forwarded by Kwame Anthony Appiah—but readily traceable to the ancient Cynics and Stoics.[8] Both concepts aim to complicate and unsettle our inherited faith in borders, in established communities, in native/other dichotomies, in self-formation and self-description, and they do so, in part, by invigorating our perception of the often invisible facets of social ontology that contribute to systemic oppression, discrimination, inequality, and intolerance. But even then, Appiah ends up favoring a "rooted" cosmopolitanism, an emphasis that reminds us of the ineluctable importance of place, of context, of affiliation—one could even plausibly add, of the nation or the national.[9] Thus, for our purposes, we retain the term "international" for its theoretical efficacy, not as a nostalgic recovery, and still less as a mere provocation; we do not aim to present the term (again, or anew) as if in a curmudgeonly bid for conceptual ossification. Quite the contrary, we have found, and hope our readers will too, that thinking through the international stimulates promising effects in the nature and definition of the transnational, and by relation, the cosmopolitan; contributes to the onward movement of the experiments with the transnational that occur on and off the page; and makes evident the degree to which our humble terminological defiance in keeping track of the international—and its long history of usage—enriches and enlarges our thinking about the transnational.

One way to recognize why we retain the term "international"—and not as an affectation—resides in the way the *inter-* (or "the between") is a more fitting figurative gesture for the life and work of Emerson—both as a reader and as the creator of texts read by others—than the *trans-* (or "the across"). We are looking here fundamentally at exchanges and influences, at the "between" of cultures: where they meet, how they overlap, infiltrate, infect, make allergic, colonialize, and so forth and not how they dissipate or erase characteristics of identity for persons, texts, and nations. For a time, within recent memory, it seemed that the word "multicultural" was deployed as an intermediary term, resting somewhere between the inter/national and the transnational—a concept used when difference was deemed important in part because it was often suppressed by colonizing forces or otherwise eclipsed by a competing identity (especially one that possessed asymmetrical political, educational, and economic power). The multicultural as such involved the recovery and acknowledgment of difference. But now, and increasingly, there is a movement toward the erasure of difference itself—part of the wave of factors we identify in discussions of the postracial and posthuman as well as the postnational, all of which appear to provide substrates for the advancing currents of globalization. The de facto prevailing spirit of this trend anoints the logic of hybridization, layering, mixture, and mash-up, as well as the conjectured reinscription of continua across time, place, and species. Difference is dissolved and reconstituted into novel, unprecedented forms; if traits can be traced, they are parcels and semblances, not totalities; if sources are identified, they are but manifestations of evidence for a case against pure descent. It is precisely, then, in the tension between the international and globalization—antagonists with respect to the reality and significance of national identity, and its potential difference from other national identities—that we are reminded how far we are from nineteenth-century moral, ethnological, and political thinking, and also, perhaps strangely, how important it is to remain conscientious of this temporal and conceptual distance.

We may observe how, among other options, the reinscription of the international into the conversation within American studies—and including debates in American literature and American philosophy about the status of works aligned or identified as importantly national in character (for example, [American] transcendentalism as a literary movement and [American] pragmatism as a philosophical one)—either intensifies the contrast between outlooks and regimes or leaves us confounded by the similarities that obtain for the international and the transnational. Johannes Voelz posits, for example, in "Utopias of Transnationalism and the Neoliberal State," that "[r]ather than asking whether and to what degree transnational formations constitute successful moments of resistance against nationalism, American exceptionalism, and (neoliberal) imperialism," we should consider "the interdependencies between what is commonly called globalization from above (neoliberal global corporatism) and globalization from below (anti-imperial flows of culture across national boundaries). . . ." Thus, while critics have studied, and lauded, the degree to which "transnationalism celebrates the disruption of celebratory nationalist narratives and recovers a world that putatively flows across boundaries," we ought, suggests Voelz, to be on guard: "If we divest ourselves of the urge to interpret the transnational as resistant and subversive, and instead examine the links as well as the fissures between both dimensions of globalization [i.e., from above and from below], we realize that cultural studies of transnationalism need to address a set of questions that differs quite radically from the questions we are fond of asking in American studies."[10]

One of the several questions we may have to ask, one that is "rarely even considered," Voelz suggests, is "whether cultural transnationalism (understood as the border-crossing flow of cultures and peoples, and secondarily also of goods) may have a function in the realignment of the nation-state under the conditions of neoliberal globalization" (356).[11] Voelz's critique amounts to something like a counterreformation in thinking about the transnational, especially insofar as that term—and its invocations and applications—has been understood to overcome or transcend the international (and its correlates, such as exceptionalism, imperialism, colonialism, and the steady retention of difference in the definition of national and authorial identity). Consequently, Voelz illuminates those features and traits that suggest how the transnational is interrelated and interdependent with the dominating forces of late-capitalist globalization and may not, as we read it, be a term that is serviceable to all contexts of contemporary literary and philosophical (as well as political, legal, and economic) critique (356–57).

The transnational, in Voelz's orienting analysis, encourages us to treat identity as movable and unmoored—something that can safely survive passage across the sea without being bruised by the journey. In this respect, the transnational is antagonistic to the act and the immediate, intimate labor of translation, for the latter is always a process of engagement with concrete instances of language and their possible accommodation to another language. The transnational—either as a concept, or perhaps better, as an innuendo—might prompt or promote the idea that something that exists here can exist there without loss or difference, without harm to the idea or to the culture in which it arrives and implicates itself (or even the culture it left behind). The notion—or observation—that translation is not fully cooperative with transnational impulses, whether intentionally, constitutionally, or inadvertently, highlights at least one productive aspect of international identity, namely, the extent to which *dialects* contribute to national characteristics. Far from equating a language with a country (as in French = France), regional dialects—which are also informed by race, gender, class, religion, education, economy, moral commitments, political allegiances, the effects of diaspora, and so forth—add further points of defiance to any notion of a supervening "French" language that could, in turn, be translated "into" an identifiable and uniform "English" language. The nuances of these observations are the daily bread of various centers for translation studies, such as at Barnard College and the University of Texas at Dallas, and in the journal edited by Peter Conners, *Translation Studies*. The breadth and depth of these scholarly undertakings in the process—including the enframing categories and practices—of translation lend authority and assurance to Voelz's critique of the transnational-as-we-know-it, and provide a context (political, philosophical, historical, linguistic) in order to assess how, or whether, the transnational ought to be figured in discussions of translation. At last, the transnational is itself a term in need of definition and translation. Fortunately, the assembled contributors to this volume have generated thoughtful, informed vignettes on these matters—all of the writers undertaking the inherent and formidable challenge of assessing fugitive terms by way of the analysis of literary identity, written prose, and intellectual influence.

An Interpretation of Influence

As the notions of identity and origin are germane to the foregoing discussion of the international and the emerging effects of the transnational on those notions, we must also consider how influence is understood—both in Emerson's time and in our own—as a theory of a process and also as a description of a specific kind of phenomenon. If, for example, boundaries retain their metaphysical reality, and that formation is coupled with the physical demarcation of territories (the inside and the outside, and also the margins, the overlaps, and the contested spaces), so influence is said, in some important sense, to be traceable. Following after Carlyle, invoked earlier, we might identify the occasions when an English reader took up the German novel and how that reading changed the course of his or her subsequent writing. Likewise, libraries, bibliographies, and annotations stimulate and reinforce interpretive associations between texts across borders—such as when we discover how Herman Melville, already at work on *Moby-Dick* in 1850, bought a copy of Carlyle's *German Romance*. Here, among so many other places, the reading list, the work-under-development, and the national identities of the authors writing and being written about come into play as a conglomeration of interpretable moments that find expression in the subsequently created texts.

Almost as an accident, then, we are reminded how our habits of reading along nationalistic lines implicate our interpretations with imposed borders and boundaries. As we see in Carlyle, and elsewhere, any discussion of ideas with a robust awareness of international engagement will involve speaking territorially, even somatically. Thus, for example, we can take note how the international (more than the transnational) has about it the nature of *intercourse,* where two bodies (parents, parent-texts) engage to form a third body (a child, a text-as-offspring). Compare this scenario with the evolution of transnational identity, or even more literally, the *transgender,* which involves a single body going across a threshold, a liminal space, a boundary or border to the effect of inhabiting a new identity—not a temporary identity, but a once-and-for-all crossing over to a new domain. Thus, intercourse and transnational/transgender identity are structurally and somatically different.

In this light, consider how Nietzsche, Maeterlinck, Huidobro, and Gandhi—all of them distinctively, perennially identified by reference to their national traits—read Emerson, and thereafter yielded new, hybridized literary forms and approaches to philosophical and literary thinking. (One pauses here to keep pace with the implications of such metaphors, since biological hybrids—the intermingling of different species—are often found to be sterile, whereas the intercourse these readers undertake are plainly and impressively generative.)[12]

Meanwhile, by contrast, we might take the case of Henry James—who moved to England in 1876 (a handful of years before Emerson died)—as a case of a transnational crossing over that is more in keeping with the formal or constitutive attributes of the transgender. Over time, James—in his person and as an author—shifted allegiances to the identity, bearing, and outlook of an Englishman. However, James's conversion culminates, paradoxically enough, with a gesture of nationalistic pride, as he sought the formal instantiation of British citizenship (which occurred within the year before his death)—a final and official declaration of loyalty to his adopted country in the midst of the Great War, coupled with a protest of America's refusal to join the war effort. The paradox of James's transnational shift, then, leaves the lingering impression that the values and virtues of one nationality over/against another in fact reintroduce and reentrench the importance of national identity. Consequently, James's (apparently) transgressive transatlantic movement may, all told, merely be counted as another case where nation-state borders matter for the constitution of personal identity (and by extension literary identity—for in what sense can we claim Henry James is an English writer?).[13]

And, to be sure, an analogous paradox occurs for transgender identity, since whichever "side" of the split or segment of the spectrum is pursued, the new status almost naturally, we might say, must invigorate the definitions and differences of the adopted sex. Put more tersely, the transgender person does not, as it were, remain in a *perpetual* state of negotiation with respect to sexual identity but aims to achieve a novel and permanent location for sexual reference; we can contrast this with the logic of transvestitism (an outmoded term that has now been replaced by "cross-dressing"), which finds a person alternating between gender-normed territories. While the transvestite employs dress to cross back and forth, the transgender person seeks permanent reassignment through "transitioning" (and thus alters individual status, not merely by means of temporary vestments but also, in many cases, through legal alteration, such as name changing, and physical or medical transformation; depending on conditions, transsexual may be the preferred term). With the expression of transvestitism, then, we note the provisional shift from one state to another, and may use verbs with a continuous aspect ("crossing back and forth"), while of the transgender and transsexual, the perfect aspect better captures the permanent transition from one position to another ("has crossed"). Admittedly, Judith Butler and Kate Bornstein complicate this account by questioning whether a transsexual can be described as a "man" or a "woman," but rather "must be approached through active verbs that attest to the constant transformation which 'is' the new identity, or indeed, the 'in-betweenness' that puts the being of gender identity into question."[14] Perhaps the theorizing of the term "genderqueer"—a signifier that refuses a strict male/female dichotomy, and thereby stands in contradistinction to the implied dualism that defines the potentiality of both the transgender and the transsexual—may be invoked to address what Butler calls, now famously, "gender trouble." Still, the binary, bifurcating terms of the female and male, the feminine and masculine, may be more necessarily demarcated (and even reinforced) by gender nonconformity and through acts of gender re-description—as opposed, say, to the sexual identifiers of the willingly androgynous, where *ambiguity* is chosen over discrete heteronormative gender specification.

In the wake of such concerns, the reading of literary and philosophical texts takes on a different cast, depending on how we describe the impact of a reader's being influenced by an author from another country. Would we be prone, even obliged, to describe Nietzsche's, Maeterlinck's, Huidobro's, or Gandhi's writerly output as somehow *Americanized* because they were careful readers, quoters, and integrators of Emerson's thought? Or do we prefer to see their national identities reinforced by their willingness or desire to read beyond native works? When enumerating our options for defining influence—one writer on another, one text on another—we wish to recommend the metaphor of translation that resides in the title of our volume, a quotation drawn directly from Emerson, as featured in the epigraph. The beauty as well as the conceptual rigor of Emerson's use of the term helpfully orients us *also* to the literal nature—or rather, the methods and practices—of translation.

Consider as a conspicuous recent engagement on this front, Barbara Cassin's *Dictionary of Untranslatables*, which is at once a tour de force of intellectual curiosity marshaled to glorious effect, and a reminder—or even a revivification—of the arts of lexicography, philology, rhetoric, and comparative language studies.[15] Its many gathered authors and editors, focusing on Latin, Greek, and select European languages, take up a terminological exploration—dictionary-style—and thus contribute meaningful excurses on the diverse, sometimes complementary, sometimes contradictory, almost always revelatory ways in which scholars have been borrowing, transforming, and reapplying concepts for millennia. Our volume does not aim solely for this word-based sleuthing and essaying, though to be sure, specific words and concepts as presented by Emerson do occupy the minds and the commentaries of his international readers—and the critics at work here. The present collection also finds our scholars conjecturing about broader kinds of inquiries—often within the conceptual milieu of a given period or historical context, and sometimes by seeking comprehension about the ideas that animate a given scene of reading, translation, or incorporation through a more text-centric analysis. Here, then, you will find philosophically, religiously, and literarily inflected versions of etymology, ethnography, and what might be named metaphysical anthropology.

Taking up influence-as-translation (the preferred and most prominent mode for understanding influence in the present case) instead of influence-as-cause, reinstates the crucial presence and transformative effects of the reader/translator, bringing along all of the identities he or she inhabits and inherits. Thus, instead of drafting a linear, causal line between a reader, his chosen text, and his subsequent work (for example, Nietzsche's reading of Emerson's writing, followed by Nietzsche's writing that follows after—both temporally and in terms of intellectual affinity—his reading in Emerson), we imagine a continual process of translation between reader/translator and incarnations of writing. Eschewing a once-and-for-all model of direct causation and direct relationships, we consider the more peculiar but also more plausible scene involving the ongoing rhizomatic effects of reading. This picture or portrait allows us to including everything from book-in-hand readings and annotations to memes, and even the more intangible but still relevant phenomenon of an unsourced idea—one we might speak of as being "in the background" or, as Emerson puts it, "the ideas of the time are in the air, and infect all who breathe it"—a kind of idea commonly left unattributed, unclaimed, or anonymous, since it is not traceable or verifiable in the same way as a written work.[16]

In this respect, our approach to translation may find company, if we are lucky, with the illuminating studies of Emily Apter, in *Against World Literature: On the Politics of Untranslatability* and Brent Hayes Edwards, in *The Practice of Diaspora: Literature, Translation, and the Rise of Black Internationalism.* Apter helpfully complicates our comfort with the notion of "world literature," and thus upsets our confidence in speaking of a (unified or singular) world. In the wake of Apter's study, as in her contributions to the *Dictionary of Untranslatables,* our rituals of affirmed—or affirmable —definitiveness in translation are interrupted, perhaps beginning with the very notion of the "world" (as seen in Apter's book title, and by way of Emerson's "The Method of Nature," in our own). Consequently, everything from *Weltliteratur* to *Weltanschauung,* from Heidegger's being-in-the-world to Emerson's power-to-translate-the-world is open to doubt and realignment. Likewise, Edwards attends to the peculiar imbrication of language and translation as they find purchase in the national, international, and transnational; in his study, these are figured along the lines of race, exile, and artistic expression. Edwards's "vagabond internationalism"—meant to depict a "transnational flotsam community"—may as well serve to describe the movements, ambiguities, and unresolved elements at work in any study that takes up the transnational in conjunction with the labor of translation.[17] These transatlantic communities-in-motion (whether in person or on paper) serve to intensify the stakes of Appiah's rooted cosmopolitanism, reminding us, in part, of Simone Weil's social and spiritual entreaty in *The Need for Roots.*

Appiah expresses impatience with the terms "globalization" and "multiculturalism," even as Weil was anticipating their substantive impact on the nature of human inhabitation of the world—both as individuals and as communities (of individuals).[18] So, Appiah's "rooted cosmopolitanism" might be understood—though Appiah himself does not develop this line—as a response to Weil's concern with the ever-expanding phenomenon of, as she says, "uprootedness" within modern civilization. She is particularly attentive to the double-bind of allegiance to a nation (since one's country can be a source or means for rootedness, but also—in her analysis of France, for instance—a justification for contempt and thereby alienation from the national collective). With even a glimpse of the historical evolution of the time, our knowledge of antisemitism in France during World War II must, for example, frame and inform any reading of the concatenation Jewish and French. Even, as it were, *internal* to a given culture, there may arise crises and conflicts of identities and allegiances (chosen and contingent). In the light of Weil's writing—and personal experiences—her account of uprootedness stands in haunting relation to the phenomena of diaspora and the experience of forced exile from one's nation (but also including, it would seem, ejection from *within* the prevailing borders of the country).

National identity can be variously an asset as well as a liability, depending on the moment of reception, but perhaps more vexingly, it can simply be a distraction—as if it always retains the power to divert attention from some lower, smaller, or otherwise less comprehensive entity doing work as its representative. To be sure, Emerson wrote "The American Scholar," but from a distance—or even as a form of caricature—he *became* this figure (or one among many) in the minds of Americans, and in time, for some of his readers abroad. Of course, "Emerson's ideas," so far as they can be attributed, were not always linked to him or derivable from him—perhaps instead being caught up in the legacies of Thoreau or Whitman, or even Hawthorne and Melville. (One cannot overlook the peculiar, sometimes pernicious, effects of misquotation—a problem that occurs within the same language, even *before* such words might be erroneously translated into another language—as we find it in the work of authors as diverse and foreign to one another as Ayn Rand and J. M. Coetzee.)[19] And when "Emerson's ideas" are claimed on his behalf—named as his, for instance, on account of an intentional or accidental mimicry of his speech—we might occasionally resist, seek out confirmation by reference to source material, and discover that those ideas are not—or do not seem to be—his after all; in short, we observe that attribution never guarantees fidelity, for attribution must necessarily involve interpretation, which in the case of an international audience reading across languages, also entails translation. Hence the legitimate and usefully agitating brouhaha over "untranslatability."

The very resistance of languages to be translated "fully" or in all instances, effectively, may be a contributing factor that hampers, or even precludes, the legitimate attribution of sources (for example, so that a reader can trace from whom he or she derived ideas) and thereby a prod to the manner by which authored ideas enter the ether, as it were anonymously. As Emerson told us, even Plato quoted from his predecessors, but by now we may have simply lost track of the lineage of authorship and influence. We may even be gullible enough to believe we thought of something on our own—something unthought of before! "When we are praising Plato," writes Emerson, "it seems we are praising quotations from Solon, Sophron and Philolaus."[20] So, with issues of translation, we must add problems of remembering and forgetting what has come before, and the difficulty of knowing that we do not know (not just as a Socratic puzzle, but also a practical one, namely, knowing who has said *before* what we are trying to say now, or being at a distance from work that remains inaccessible for one reason or another—lost in the library, or lost behind the opaque screen of a "foreign" language).

Still and so, those apparently vague and insubstantial moments of conceptual impact—noted above as "in the air"—can have sustained influence on those who breathe them, take them in, and incorporate them into new work. While direct evidence of reading shall remain the hallmark of our critical attention to influence (a process that requires disciplined practices of close reading and translation), we can also remain open and receptive to possibilities where the influence of a text appears even if the writer has not, as it were, read it; in such cases, we might draw an analogy to biological phenomena such as (anonymous) osmosis, and at other times, more mysteriously, to something like an occult happening that exceeds our capacity for tracing discrete elements, histories, and connections.

As a brief case study of the foregoing phenomenon, consider Stanley Cavell's account of the way Martin Heidegger ends up being a reader of Emerson. How did this unexpected scene come about? Heidegger read Nietzsche, who, in turn, of course read Emerson. Yet it is in the nature of Nietzsche's status as a mediator for—or translator of—Emerson's work that Cavell draws a conspicuous conceptual connection between the German philosopher and his American antecedent. In *Emerson's Transcendental Etudes,* Cavell contends, with rapt and reasoned interest in the implications of such a claim: "So the similarity of Emerson to Heidegger can be seen as mediated by Nietzsche, and this will raise more questions than it can answer. As to the question of what may look like the direction of influence, I am not claiming that Heidegger authenticates the thinking of Emerson and Thoreau; the contrary is, for me, fully as true, that Emerson and Thoreau may authorize our interest in Heidegger."[21] Cavell's justification for such an apparently anachronistic or temporally inverted narrative is based on Cavell's understanding or depiction of influence—again, not one of direct and traceable causes so much as verified by a series of engagements of close readings of texts—which is registered partly in his account of reading Heidegger's lectures on Nietzsche, delivered between 1936 and 1940: "Emerson's presence in Nietzsche's thought as Heidegger receives it—in certain passages of Nietzsche that Heidegger leans on most heavily—is so strong at certain moments that one has to say that Nietzsche is using Emerson's words; which means that Heidegger in effect, over an unmeasured stretch of thought, is interpreting Emerson's words" (213). The fantastical qualities of Cavell's treatment, however, render a sober reconfiguration of influence as such (directionally, causally, conceptually), namely, that: "Nietzsche is not 'influenced' by Emerson but is quite deliberately transfiguring Emerson, as for the instruction of the future" (213). Here Cavell's term "transfiguring" —allowing for the theological allusions and pedigree of the verb—is a partner to our notion of "translation," which is itself always a conjuring of meaning (one is tempted to say, spirit as well as sense) from one realm of life in language to another.

The notion of influence-as-translation is further enhanced in this case because we have come to recognize the odd ways in which Heidegger's high profile and philosophical respectability, especially among Europeans and later among Americans (admitting, without pause, the moral crisis that plagued—still plagues—his reputation owing to his affiliation with the Nazis), had a directly positive impact on Nietzsche's habilitation in the United States.[22] When Heidegger's writing became part of the vanguard of Continental philosophy to appear in North America, including his extensive remarks on Nietzsche (as prominently reflected in his four-volume study), Nietzsche's work itself was regularly castigated for its alleged contribution to, or more perversely, authorization of Nazi thinking—another illustration of the impact of one's theory of influence. In what sense was Nietzsche made responsible not for what he wrote but for what his readers thought he wrote? So, as Cavell says he is "continuing to follow out the consequences of finding in Emerson the founding of American thinking—the consequence, for example, that his thought is repressed in the culture he founded" (194), we can reflect on the above narrative in which, by turns transfigurative and otherwise translated, Heidegger—by way of reading Nietzsche who read Emerson—enhanced Nietzsche's credibility in America, which in another turn, came to make prominent Emerson's contribution to Nietzsche's thinking. By a form of association, Nietzsche's admiration for his American "soul-brother" inscribes or perhaps reauthorizes Emerson's philosophical legitimacy, thereafter reawakening in readers the perception of Emerson's qualities as a thinker and his work's pertinence to philosophy in America—the founding of its thinking.[23] And so, an unexpected circle is drawn in which Emerson is given back, in some fashion, to "the culture he founded" by, of all people, Heidegger.

If, as Cavell suggests, Heidegger's reading of Nietzsche's writing involved, in part, "interpreting Emerson's words," then we have one picture of influence-as-translation (or transfiguration), and if we allow that Heidegger's positive impact on Nietzsche's reputation in America created the conditions for a renewal of interest in—and respect for—Emerson's writing, then we have another, complementary picture of influence-as-translation. In the latter case, we are tempted to say that Heidegger-by-way-of-Nietzsche allowed Emerson's "rejected" or otherwise neglected thoughts to "come back to us with a certain alienated majesty."[24]

The End of National Culture?

Cavell's transatlantic intellectual history, as rehearsed briefly above, gives some credit to the notion that an idea may be the more proper element of our attention, and the personality of its author a secondary aspect: local, contingent, and caught up in the politics and priorities of her time. Ideas may, in an important sense, transcend the person, and by extension, exceed or obviate the national as a category for definition or as a cause for crisis. (Perhaps we simply want to call these ideas *for* human beings, not of them or by them?) Thus Heidegger recognizes something in Nietzsche where, by turns, transformations, transfigurations, and translations, Nietzsche is said (not by Heidegger but by Cavell) to derive from Emerson. In this proximate scenario, we stumble upon a case that might be more broadly described as exhibiting something like the notion of a common culture of ideas. And it would be the business of the critic—of whatever disciplinary training and aspiration—to study this culture. Again, the very term "culture" would have to find its resonance beyond a particular national identity or territorial location and instead become a generic term for the matter at hand wherever and whenever one wished to think through ideas. And so we find ourselves asking what a *transnational* culture could be, that is, as a culture that has diminished its allegiance to and reliance on national traits. Hence the double sense of the *end* of national culture, where we are at once solicitous for terms that define (or is it defend?) the properties and proprieties of countries, and at the same time, cautiously rehearse what may be the dissolution of faith in fixed identities (national and otherwise) in favor of the volatile and inconstant circumstances of the dawning transnational age.

As we think through *international* influence, however, we do so through the work of readers of texts—often critics, who are possessed of "creative power" of a certain sort. In all this, we are reminded how the international helps to focus and place in relief the clarifying form of the native and the foreign as we, as it were, first encounter them, rudimentarily: the origin and the other. In short, the term "national" suggests that we are not to be so sure that something—a thought, a theory, a picture of reality—is "ours" after all. Or put the other way, that what is "theirs" (other-than-ours) may be something we are capable of generating on our own should the conditions be sufficiently propitious and our powers sufficiently garnered for the task. As Matthew Arnold writes in "The Function of Criticism at the Present Time": "Don't let us trouble ourselves about foreign thought; we shall invent the whole thing for ourselves as we go along."[25] In this endogenous mood, Arnold is clearly not worried about remembering what has been said before by (foreign) others, much less dedicated to searching the stacks to confirm authorial attribution. Rather, Arnold's is an aspirational sentiment given credence by his view of criticism undertaken in what he conceives to be its best form. Yet, he is just as willing, readily so, to admit that these conditions do not exist, say, in England in 1864, and so he articulates what may be recognized as a more commonsensical view of the virtues of looking beyond one's borders for ideas:

> By the very nature of things, as England is not all the world, much of the best that is known and thought in the world cannot be of English growth, must be foreign; by the nature of things, again, it is just this that we are least likely to know, while English thought is streaming in upon us from all sides, and takes excellent care that we shall not be ignorant of its existence. The English critic of literature, therefore, must dwell much on foreign thought, and with particular heed on any part of it, which, while significant and fruitful in itself, is for any reason specially likely to escape him. (49)

Arnold finds one of the great legitimating ideas that animates—and sustains—our interest in the international. By even suggesting a distinction between a native thought and a foreign one, and by extension the notions of nationally derived, sanctioned, and protected linguistic, literary, and philosophical identity, he liberates the reader or critic to read beyond his borders, and thereby to see what is contained within them. The inner and outer, the near and far, the familiar and foreign, are all most potently drawn before our attention.

Arnold rehearsed his agenda for critics—for the kind of criticism he wished to see them undertake in their criticism—as "*a disinterested endeavor to learn and propagate the best that is known and thought in the world*" (50, italics in the original). (For more on this line of Arnold's thinking, see K. L. Evans's essay in the present collection.) And so at the very heart of Arnold's conception of criticism is a recognition of its *international* labors, that it must be conducted in full view of the world's letters and ideas. Thus, he exhorts critics to "at all events endeavor, in dealing with [the mass of current English literature], to try it, so far as they can, by the standard of the best that is known and thought in the world" (50). Quite reasonably, Arnold says that the ascertainment of any such perception of "the best that is known and thought in the world" would have to derive from learned knowledge of the foreign, of the texts beyond those found in one's immediate vicinity, outside the language of one's native fluency. And so Arnold concedes that "one may say, that to get anywhere near this standard every critic should try and possess one great literature, at least, besides his own; and the more unlike his own, the better" (50).

Yet there is more, since Arnold's path for criticism does not culminate in a robust art of studies in comparative literature—though it suggests a long period of that work—but presses forward beyond the international to what we may recognize as a nascent form of transnationalism. In the denouement of his essay, Arnold concludes with a vision of criticism beyond borders—that is, criticism where "the best that is known and thought in the world" is not determined based on the country of origin but on the quality of the ideas it issues forth. The critic's discernment, then, would cease to be localized or nationalized (or for that matter, personal and delineated by reference to the author's identity), and instead be aimed at determining the vigor and nature of thought on its own terms, and in relation to an evolving global standard:

> But, after all, the criticism I am really concerned with,—the criticism which alone can much help us for the future, the criticism which, throughout Europe, is at the present day meant, when so much stress is laid on the importance of criticism and the critical spirit,—is a criticism which regards Europe as being, for intellectual and spiritual purposes, one great confederation, bound to a joint action and working to a common result; and whose members have, for their proper outfit, a knowledge of Greek, Roman, and Eastern antiquity, and of one another. Special, local, and temporary advantages being put out of account, that modern nation will in the intellectual and spiritual sphere make most progress, which most thoroughly carries out this programme. (50–51)

Which is to say, that the nation that most boldly humbles itself in its inquiry into "the best that is known and thought" in *other nations* will be the best positioned to offer the kind of criticism that Arnold thinks is worthy of the name, worthy of our attention, and worthy into posterity.

Why Emerson Now?

Once we understand that our critical standards and tools are many times contingent and that criticism is best practiced as a relational (and now global) activity, it is perhaps the moment to answer the two main implicit questions a reader may pose to the creators of a volume such as this: Why Emerson? And why now?

Of course, the general philosophical preoccupation of this volume—that is, to explore how a (national, and subsequently international) writer has acquired a transnational status—can be extended to many American writers of the nineteenth century (as well as before that era and after it). And while it is true that Emerson is without a doubt the most prominent and famous American intellectual of his time, probably the most authoritative and respected American voice of the whole nineteenth century, it is also true that other writers enjoyed equal (or nearly equal) literary renown—Poe, Whitman, Melville, Thoreau, Dickinson, Fuller, and Hawthorne, among others come readily to mind. Even as many of these writers also deserve the same consideration and study from an international perspective, we can at least note that some of them—perhaps most prominently, Poe and Whitman—have received serious attention on this front. Choosing Emerson is not, for us, however, just a matter of his celebrity and centrality in the American literary and philosophical canon, but rather part of a conceptual strategy that enframes and enriches each phase of the present series of investigations. Because of the highly metaphoric nature of his language, the elasticity and adaptability of his ideas, and his decidedly international vision, Emerson has rendered himself a particularly apt transmitter of "influence" inside and outside the United States.[26] The presence of his philosophy and poetics has been, since the 1830s, constant and pervasive in the shifting of cultures (and subcultures), and the elapsing of time-periods and punctuating upheavals that have come to constitute an endlessly evolving American society. By way of a broad, promiscuous global readership, his work has also proved to be a crucial node in the matrix of national, literary, and philosophical identities in many countries around the world. To study Emerson as an *American* writer also reveals, in part, how the United States became an international cultural, intellectual, and political force; as Franklin and Jefferson are part of the very synapses of American consciousness, so Emerson has been digested into its circulation.

Yet even as Emerson has endured as a "representative man" of the so-called American Renaissance, he appears—especially in the proceedings of this volume—as both an icon of and a medium for a humanistic vision of the world that transcends frontiers. As one might expect, Emerson's kind of national identity antagonizes national identity as such. If we find him trying to find terms and conditions for American identity—"when the sluggard intellect of this continent will look from under its iron lids and fulfill the postponed expectation of the world"—we also, in the same breath, find him standing in relation to humanity across time and space. For "the world" to have expectations of America, which the latter has disappointed (and likely *continues* to disappoint), America must, in some sense, know itself as a nation. And yet, the appeal to "the world" subtly intimates that it might be a unity unto itself—distinct from America—a realm that America might one day join. The paradox remains steadfast into our own day—in these hours when this new series of twenty-first-century essays were conceived—namely, whether America must be itself as a nation in order to achieve itself beyond national characteristics. The spirit of inquiry into and after such a paradox in the following pages animates reflection at once on the pertinence of Emerson's significance for his nation, and his relevance for the history of thought in non-American nations—and also, on a third register, where the national and international provide a common ground for what might be described as a global civilization—that unrehearsed, unpredictable, uncanny phenomenon we cautiously approach under the appellation "transnational."

The question "why now?" is perhaps easier to answer. Not only do we live in an era of unprecedented globalization in which frontiers—physical and ideological—have proved questionable, if not occasionally pernicious; nowadays, it is also an imperative that we explore authors and their works as belonging to a general network (transatlantic, transpacific, transhemispheric) that makes national insularity untenable. The recent developments, not only in literary studies but also in sociological theory and even politics, force us (willingly or not) to look at contextual conditions more than we have done thus far, and with a more comprehensive, ecumenical vision. We can no longer consider ideas as isolated from the historical moment and the place where they emerge, nor can we study them without taking into account their circulation throughout time and space and the intellectual and ethical transformations that this movement implies. To do otherwise would mean to think of authors and nations as self-encapsulated entities without projection or effect outside themselves. Emerson's philosophy, as suggested, contradicts and contests such an outmoded vision, and surprises us with its capacity to keep tempo with the pace of the *au courant*.

These are admittedly theoretical questions, but there is another, more practical concern: how do we get a sense of the kind of work that has been achieved, and also catch a glimpse of work that lies ahead—unrealized, as yet unfathomed? It is always daunting to take stock of the totality of a given field or subfield—especially ones such as these with dynamic and diverse literatures—yet it may be helpful to seek out clues to where we stand. Depending on scholarly temperament, one might pursue the prominent positive examples (as signs of work completed, perhaps also as work that does not demand new interventions or reassessments), or one might choose to identify those works that have set *other* worthy agendas. Perhaps to round things out, it would be helpful to do a bit of both, for we see differently what is possible in relation to tradition (and its celebrated works) and the prospects for an as-yet-determined future scholarship.

By way of the interventions in this collection, the authors aim to extend and reconfigure the parameters of Emerson scholarship, even as they acknowledge the rich extant literature and avail directions for further research. Here path-making also comes with the discovery, as it should, of new scenes and specimens; naturally, all of them stand in need of interpretation. While it is true that the relevance of Emerson beyond U.S. borders has been a subject of study since at least Frederic Ives Carpenter's *Emerson and Asia* (1930), it is also true that there seems to be a certain (self-imposed? disciplinary?) limitation on scholarship when it comes to studying his work from a more genuinely *global* point of view. In fact, despite the inventive and eclectic range of geographical and conceptual regions explored between these covers, it becomes apparent that still other lands beckon our study: what of Emerson in Africa? In modern India? In Oceania and the Antipodes? Or for that matter, what about the uses of Emerson by America's neighbors in Canada and Mexico? A volume such as the present one must be at once prismatic and provisional, but it could be said to do some service not just by the subjects it tackles but also by those it glances but cannot yet grasp.

Until very recently, much of the published work on Emerson as an international figure has confined itself to his relevance in three main places: England, Germany, and Asia.[27] A conspicuous amount of impressive and rewarding work has been dedicated to these realms, to be sure, and we have simultaneously benefited from it and also not hesitated to encourage contributors to retain a focus on these classical loci of interest as they revisit these regions, which yield perennial enrichment. As readers and inheritors of Emerson's impact abroad, there are still many elemental and unexplored issues within this field of inquiry that continue to solicit and secure our fascination. Yet, by expanding the scope of investigation, and seeking out new authors, texts, and terrains—as we do in the present collection—the established research repertoire is not eclipsed but aggrandized. Thus, contributors return to England, Germany, and Asia—with awareness of prior research—to expose and explore areas deserving new or renewed critical analysis (see especially the chapters on a more varied European descent by Elbert, Habich, and Friedl; on British political economy by Gougeon; and taking up Emerson's presence in China and Japan by Saito, Dolan, Wey, and Foust). Whether in the nineteenth or the twentieth centuries, and into this next young century, Emerson's interaction with these locales and literati remains essential for giving a fair and, so far as it is possible, informed account of his role in the history of ideas.

However, depending on the work one happens upon, the impression is sometimes made that beyond these distinctive geographical regions (and their formidable literary and intellectual traditions) Emerson's influence is muted, if not missing entirely. Sporadically emitted flares—alerting us to a project in need of articulation and engagement—can be found in the contemporary literature.[28] And we can take the measure of these works—what they achieve and what they summon us to pursue further—yet it remains dangerous to presume knowledge of the intended purview of a given program of research. What can be said, for example, when it is noticed that neither the *Cambridge Introduction to Ralph Waldo Emerson* (ed. Joel Porte and Saundra Morris, 1999) nor the *Oxford Historical Guide to Ralph Waldo Emerson* (ed. Joel Myerson, 2000) include any reference to, let alone a sustained reflection on, what kind of influence Emerson had outside the United States (not even to the aforementioned England, Germany, and Asia)? In his valuable *Ralph Waldo Emerson in Europe: Class, Race, and Revolution in the Making of an American Thinker* (2012), Daniel Koch's appointed mandate rightly should have kept him bound by the Continent, yet he still reduces "Europe" mostly to France (or more particularly, revolutionary Paris of 1848), and he then crosses the Channel to focus on England and Scotland. In the crowd of august contributions to *Ralph Waldo Emerson in Context* (ed. Wesley T. Mott, 2013), a veritable taxonomy of core themes are addressed, yet attention beyond America remains prominently focused, again, on Europe, Britain, and Asia. Even the chapter on Europe is mostly limited to France and Germany because, as its author Jan Stievermann declares, Emerson's lack of interest in Spain, Portugal, northern Europe, and eastern Europe was due to "cultural and personal biases, and the limits of Emerson's linguistic competence."[29] Yet Emerson's lack of interest in these regions, for whatever reason, does not forestall or forsake the possibility—and often the reality—that interest in *Emerson's* work percolated out of these same regions, and others besides. We have learned much from reading what Emerson read in world literature, and what he thought about it—from the *Iliad* to the *Bhagavad Gita*, from the *Qur'an* to the *Heimskringla*, from Hafiz and Saadi to the *Analects* of Confucius—so now we add to these beneficent facts the pursuit of learning from world literature's reading of Emerson.[30]

Although all of the immediately aforementioned books are admirable on their own terms—and very helpful as orienting introductions to broad movements of thought as well as guides to topics of specialized study—these works illustrate, in part, how we still lack a global approach to Emerson that is worthy of the name. If more examples of truncation and ellipsis are needed, they can be readily adduced: for instance, Emerson's significance for the literature and philosophy of Latin America is still largely neglected (except for the renowned work of José Martí)—even though some of the first Spanish translations of Emerson's work appeared in Mexico and Argentina. Walt Whitman has been already studied in that context, but nothing (or next to nothing) has been said about how important Emerson was for the nationalist political and literary movements of nineteenth-century Latin America through the Spanish translation of his works. Given our praise and appreciation of the labors exhibited in the existing scholarship, it should be evident that our point here is neither to malign illustrious books for their lacunae, nor to belabor the evidence of those gaps; we hope, rather, to justify the impetus for the present undertaking and to stimulate readers' interest in its capacity to complement and ameliorate the wider literature on the tandem subjects of Emerson's incorporation of international culture and his effect on international culture.

Consider, in this vein of a recomposition and a broadening of the scope of our shared inquiry, how Emerson's ardent interest in the Persian mystics and the spiritual teachings of Sufism takes on a new tenor when his voice finds company in contemporary Middle Eastern–*American* literature (as we learn in the chapter by Roger Sedarat). Such a connection suggests that the pollinations of thought in the pages that follow trace actual as well as indirect—auspicious but also largely unarticulated—moments of international propagation. Think also of how Kahlil Gibran was presented with Maurice Maeterlinck's *The Treasure of the Humble* as an introduction to the European literature of the time. That gift seems fitting until it is contended that the book "owes more to the everyday streets of Concord than the rarefied salons of Paris." If Gibran's reading is "really thirdhand Emerson," then it should give us pause and stir intrigue to find that *The Prophet* "remains the all-time best-selling book in America"—at least for its publisher.[31] Emerson read widely. And Emerson was read widely—even when readers did not know it was he! As with Heidegger, so with Gibran.

The contributors to the present collection, therefore, attempt to offer a further step in the direction of a more actively articulated, more fully formed global assessment of Emerson's conceptual and intellectual significance (especially to non-American readers of his work). We hope, in what has been said and in what follows, to have demonstrated that there remains for Emerson scholarship an eminent—and expansive—terrain worthy of wide survey and penetrating exploration. The Near East and the Far East, for instance, as addressed in the pages to come, offer old ground to excavate for new and rewarding discoveries. Likewise, some significant byways and brambles of English and European thinking—Arnold, Henry James, Maeterlinck, and Rilke—receive fresh readings along with work gathered from disparate domains, among them, Huidobro in Chile, Ghandi in India, a range of Jewish readers, as well as the vanguard of Middle Eastern–American literature. And our lead essayist, Donald Pease, offers a unique and compelling line of continuity between Emerson and the forty-fourth president of the United States, Barack Obama.

New Essays for a New Era of Inheritance

No discipline of thinking is immune from the radical, rushed process of dynamic global transformations in everything from the political and territorial status of nation-states to the prompts of instantaneous digital newsfeeds. The volatility implied by the aggressive alterations in identity—both for nations and persons—may be read as an intriguing coda to eras when definitions were more rigid and slow to change, if not seemingly immutable. If there is now no reliable rubric for seeing who can change more or faster, or even for the better, there is—in often undeniably startling relief—the dizzying fact of change itself and what it portends about the prior state, its transition, and its emergent form. It is from within this context that we—as writers and readers—encounter the modest but deliberate work from the contributors to this volume, who aim, in their own ways, to study the significance of nationality and influence at a time when both phenomena have yielded dilemmas that pulsate through the currents of contemporary culture. What is the meaning of America—and its literature and philosophy—in an age that contests the national as a bona fide description (and defense) of identity? What is the use of tracing influences when the very notions of origin, intention, and even cause and effect are put in doubt, or simply bracketed, and thus treated as negotiable terms? We believe the present series of new essays will afford some salutary input on these and related questions—questions that solicit our vigilant response and catalyze our enduring curiosity because they direct us to dilemmas that are at once perspicuous and pervasive. If we are individually and collectively to possess and effectuate a power to translate the world, we are duly rewarded to begin with Ralph Waldo Emerson—as writer, as representative mind, as theorist of American identity, and as provocateur to settled opinions on the home front and on farther shores.

Notes

1. See Winfried Fluck, Donald E. Pease, and John Carlos Rowe, eds., *Re-Framing the Transnational Turn in American Studies* (Hanover, NH: Dartmouth College Press, 2011).

2. Pease, "Introduction: Re-mapping the Transnational Turn," in ibid., 2. Subsequent references to Pease's introduction will be cited parenthetically in the text by page number.

3. See Ulla Haselstein (chap. 1), Laura Bieger (chap. 8), and John Carlos Rowe (chap. 13), in Fluck et al., *Re-Framing the Transnational Turn in American Studies*.

4. See Donald E. Pease, *The New American Exceptionalism* (Minneapolis: University of Minnesota Press, 2009).

5. Thomas Carlyle, *German Romance*, in Henry Duff Traill, ed., *The Works of Thomas Carlyle*, 30 vols. (1896; Cambridge: Cambridge University Press, 2010), 21:4. Originally published in 1827.

6. Johannes Voelz, *Transcendental Resistance: The New Americanists and Emerson's Challenge* (Hanover, NH: Dartmouth College Press, 2010), chap. 6.

7. Ibid., 205.

8. Kwame Anthony Appiah, *Cosmopolitanism: Ethics in a World of Strangers* (New York: W. W. Norton, 2006), xiv.

9. Kwame Anthony Appiah, *The Ethics of Identity* (Princeton, NJ: Princeton University Press, 2007), chap. 6 passim.

10. Johannes Voelz, "Utopias of Transnationalism and the Neoliberal State," in Fluck, Pease, and Rowe, *Re-Framing the Transnational Turn in American Studies*, 357, 370, 357. Subsequent references to this work will be cited parenthetically in the text by page number.

11. Voelz continues, parenthetically: "(characterized by the whole gamut of the rise of the transnational corporation, the emergence of global governance regimes, and the structural reorganization of the nation-state by such measures as deregulation, the concentration of power in the executive branch, the outsourcing of executive functions, and the limiting of citizenship rights)" (356).

12. For more on metaphors of reading—including the generativity that follows in the form of writing—see David LaRocca, *Emerson's English Traits and the Natural History of Metaphor* (New York: Bloomsbury, 2013).

13. As we press toward a more inclusive, international inquiry into Emerson's literary and philosophical fate and fortune, it is very worth noting—and drawing in—the pronounced and penetrating segment of contemporary scholarship devoted to the more circumscribed domain of transatlanticism, including these representative works: Samantha Harvey, *Transatlantic Transcendentalism: Coleridge, Emerson, and Nature* (Edinburgh: Edinburgh University Press, 2013); Kevin Hutchings and Julia Wright, eds., *Transatlantic Literary Exchanges, 1790–1870: Gender, Race, and Nation* (Burlington, VT: Ashgate, 2011); Susan Manning and Andrew Taylor, eds., *Transatlantic Literary Studies: A Reader* (Baltimore: Johns Hopkins University Press, 2007); and Eve Tavor Bannet and Susan Manning, eds., *Transatlantic Literary Studies, 1660–1830* (Cambridge: Cambridge University Press, 2012).

14. Judith Butler, *Gender Trouble: Feminism and the Subversion of Identity* (New York: Routledge, 2007), xii (from the 1999 preface). Originally published in 1990.

15. Barbara Cassin, ed. *Dictionary of Untranslatables: A Philosophical Lexicon* (Princeton, NJ: Princeton University Press, 2014).

16. Emerson, "Uses of Great Men," in *Representative Men* (1850), in *The Complete Works of Ralph Waldo Emerson*, ed. Edward Waldo Emerson, Concord ed., 12 vols. (Boston: Houghton Mifflin, 1903–4), 4:25–26.

17. Brent Hayes Edwards, *The Practice of Diaspora: Literature, Translation, and the Rise of Black Internationalism* (Cambridge, MA: Harvard University Press, 2003), 198.

18. Appiah, *Cosmopolitanism*, xiii.

19. See Ayn Rand, *Philosophy: Who Needs It* (New York: Signet, 1984). J. M. Coetzee, *Elizabeth Costello* (New York: Penguin, 2003).

20. Emerson, "Plato; or, The Philosopher," in *Representative Men* (1850) in *The Complete Works of Ralph Waldo Emerson*, 4:42.

21. Stanley Cavell, *Emerson's Transcendental Etudes*, ed. David Justin Hodge (Stanford, CA: Stanford University Press, 2003), 16–17. Subsequent references to this work will be cited parenthetically in the text by page number.

22. Another German, Walter Kaufmann, an émigré who extensively and expertly translated Nietzsche's work, was also a significant factor in the restatement of Nietzsche's prominence in the canon of philosophical study among Americans at midcentury.

23. See David LaRocca, "The Education of Grown-Ups: An Aesthetics of Reading Cavell," *Journal of Aesthetic Education* 47, no. 2 (Summer 2013): 109–31.

24. Ralph Waldo Emerson, "Self-Reliance," in *The Complete Works of Ralph Waldo Emerson*, 2:45–46.

25. Matthew Arnold, "The Function of Criticism at the Present Time," in *Culture and Anarchy and Other Writings*, ed. Stefan Collini (Cambridge: Cambridge University Press, 1993), 43.

26. See Lawrence Buell, *Emerson* (Cambridge, MA: Harvard University Press, 2003), 325–34; and Barry Tharaud, ed., *Emerson for the Twenty-First Century: Global Perspectives on an American Icon* (Newark: University of Delaware Press, 2010), 33–55.

27. Focusing, for example, on what Nan Z. Da calls "books on Emerson/China synergies," we may glean a sense of the depth and range of work devoted to this subset of research on Emerson and Asia. In Da's helpful bibliography, she adduces the following titles: K. V. Raghupathi, *Emerson's Orientalism* (New Delhi: Prestige Books, 2007); Frederic Ives Carpenter, *Emerson and Asia* (New York: Haskell House, 1930); and Qian Mansu, *Ai Mo Sheng he Zhong Guo: Dui Ge Ren Zhu Yi de Fan Ying* [Emerson and China: Reflections on individualism] (Beijing: SDX and Harvard-Yenching Academic Library, 1996). Da continues: "Books such as Arthur Christy's *The Orient in American Transcendentalism: A Study of Emerson, Thoreau and Alcott* (New York: Columbia University Press, 1932); *The Asian Legacy and American Life* (New York: Greenwood Press, 1968); and Arthur Versluis's *American Transcendentalism and Asian Religions* (Oxford: Oxford University Press, 1993) have argued that the appropriation of orientalism and Asian religions became the condition of possibility for a particular version of American transcendentalism." See Nan Z. Da, "Emerson, China, and the Uses of Literature," *J19: The Journal of Nineteenth-Century Americanists* 1 (Fall 2013): 285–313, esp. n. 13. See also Yoshio Takanashi, *Emerson and Neo-Confucianism: Crossing Paths over the Pacific* (New York: Palgrave Macmillan, 2014).

28. See, for example, Wai Chee Dimock and Lawrence Buell, eds., *Shades of the*

Planet: American Literature as World Literature (Princeton, NJ: Princeton University Press, 2007); and Tharaud, *Emerson for the Twenty-First Century*.

29. Jan Stievermann, "Europe," in Wesley T. Mott. ed., *Ralph Waldo Emerson in Context* (Cambridge: Cambridge University Press, 2014), 31.

30. Luminous, enduring, and influential examples of what non-American readers thought of Emerson's work can be found in David LaRocca, ed., *Estimating Emerson: An Anthology of Criticism from Carlyle to Cavell* (New York: Bloomsbury, 2013).

31. See in this volume, David LaRocca, chap. 6, n. 35.

[I]

EMERSON BEYOND BORDERS IN HIS TIME

[1]

DONALD E. PEASE

THE ANTI-SLAVE FROM EMERSON TO OBAMA

READINGS OF EMERSON HAVE normatively assumed the form of variations on the theme of the crisis precipitated by conflicting interpretations of Emerson's attitude toward questions of social reform. The interpretations through which Emerson has been institutionalized within the United States literary canon have isolated a depoliticizing transcendentalism and a politicizing social reformism as perennial yet antagonistic predispositions within his writings.[1] The divisive antagonisms that are perceptibly at work within Emerson's collected essays have also occasioned an ongoing contestation among his critics and interpreters over whether Emerson the Transcendentalist or Emerson the Social Reformer should predominate.[2]

Emerson encouraged contradictory readings of his work when he refused to consolidate the heterogeneous personifications of his project into a coherent identity. Rather than making them cohere, Emerson placed the persona of the Reformer, through whom he advanced powerful demands for social change, in a relationship of antagonistic cooperation with the persona of the Transcendentalist, who was averse to limit thinking to questions of social reform.

Emerson called the structural performative that was the source and the outcome of the unending tension between these two figurations of address "self-reliance": "The virtue in most request is conformity; self-reliance is its aversion" (*CW* 2:29). Emerson described the truth process through which he obtained access to this figure with the following formulation, "I shun father and mother and wife and brother when my genius calls me" (*CW* 2:30–31).

Whether Emerson's interpreters have analyzed the relationship between the Transcendentalist and the Reformer as enabling paradoxes or as disabling contradictions has depended on whether they assumed that Emerson's essays should exercise a political or a strictly literary efficacy. At the conclusion of the twentieth century, critics argued that Emerson's essays constitute examples of the "ideology of liberal dissent" that underwrites U.S. liberal individualism. According to Sacvan Bercovitch, perhaps his most astute reader, even in dissenting from specific cultural arrangements, Emerson, under this description, was required to conform to the transindividual liberal order whose institutions he would reform: "The appeal of Emersonian dissent lies in an extraordinary conjunction of forces: its capacity to absorb the radical communitarian vision it renounces, and its capacity to be nourished by the liberal structures it resisted. It demonstrates the capacity of the culture to shape the subversive in its own image, and thereby, *within limits,* to be shaped by the radicalism it seeks to contain."[3]

When Bercovitch proposed that the Emersonian legacy is to be understood as indistinguishable from the discourse of liberal individualism, he presupposed that what Emerson called self-reliance is interchangeable with the self-positing possessive individual who was the constitutive subject of the discourse to which Emerson's interpreters made it conform. But what Emerson referred to as "my genius when it calls me" achieved effects that were independent of the processes of identification, interpellation, and internalization associated with liberal institutions.

Although "my genius" could not be said to exist without such an addressee, Emerson's speakers did not produce the call, nor did they represent their calling as a recognizable social identity. The speakers' provocatives instead bore witness to influxes of creative power that could neither be fully generated by, nor wholly assimilated to, subjective consciousness. Genius introduced a constitutive division into the speaker's subjectivity that disallowed the possibility of any unified identity. Insofar as this influx of creative power penetrated in depth without depending on the mediations of the speaker's own representations, it compromised the autonomy of the speaker's will. But in so doing, "my genius" also undermined liberalism's conception of the possessive individual as its subject.

Because there was no social identity that "my genius" could take up that was not dependent on an already instituted social role, the self-reliance that genius effected was inherently nonsubstantial and lacking in positive content. As a generalized aversion to all taken-for-granted paradigms of social subjectification, self-reliance resulted in a subtraction from the order of things rather than a development within them. Unlike the primary integer within any already existing discourse into which recent critics have interpellated him, the speaker of Emerson's public address did not possess an identifiable social role, nor did it come into possession of a recognizable private identity.

The speaker's stirring injunctions opened up pathways leading from the world of signification into the realm of Emersonian provocation. They did so through instructions that recommended dispossession from established institutions rather than self-development within them. As an inflooding of power that could not be integrated within the existing order, "my genius when it calls me" deprived its addressees—no matter whether Emerson the Reformer or Emerson the Transcendentalist—of their social personhood—"I shun father and mother and wife and brother when my genius calls me."

It is because they were produced through the self-reliance that their utterances reproduced that the speakers of Emerson's essays could not be integrated into a coherent authorial identity. Through their relaying of serial acts of response to the call of genius, the speakers of Emerson's essays might instead be described as constituting a transindividual structure of self-dispossession that produced subject effects that were independent of Emerson's individual agency. What holds the discontinuous speakers together within this transindividual structure is the structure of aversion to which the speaker of "Self-Reliance" committed the entire relay of Emersonian provocations. The pledge—to dissociate from all social relations—constituted the governing performative that interconnected the speakers of Emerson's essays.

Emerson correlated freedom with the abandonment of the already represented world. And he construed the relationship between the speaker called to enunciate an Emersonian provocation and "my Genius" to entail the inauguration of a wholly new world. Neither the speaker of the provocation nor "my Genius" were part of the already created world. The speaker's lacking a part in the already instituted order inspired him to evoke a new order through his acts of provocation. In refusing to accommodate his thinking to the prevailing order of signification and in refusing to identify with a mandated social role, Emerson construed himself as included within the social order as what was extrinsic to its conditions of belonging. When Emerson resigned from the ministry, he imagined the place he opened up through his refusal to perform the Passover to have been subtracted from the given order.[4]

As a part of the world that had no part in the order of things, the speaker called forth by "my Genius" inhabited this extraneous space. Emerson found a literal historical referent for this place that lacked a place in the given order in the institution of slavery. Emerson's scene of writing and the institution of slavery were comparable insofar as both of these extraneous places described parts of the world that had no part in the order of things. As a modality of existence that was, like Emerson, unintegratable within the symbolic order, but unlike Emerson, could not *turn* that lack of accommodation into the power of constituting an alternative, the slave materialized an exception to the given sociopolitical order.

Emerson understood slavery to be a precondition for his thinking. Now when I claim that Emerson's project presupposed the negative positioning of slavery, I mean that claim to be understood quite literally: as the materialization of an otherwise unrepresentable, nonsocial space that divided persons from nonpersons, citizens whose lives were understood as worthy of re-presentation from figures represented as lacking presence, and persons whose deaths society officially mourned from those it constructed as already dead, slavery demarcated a social limit for the negation of limitation.[5]

Because slavery represented the completion of the negation to which, according to Emerson, all already instituted forms tended, slavery revealed the nothingness at the heart of the already constituted order. A slave—and for Emerson this term was not restricted to persons actually enslaved—named that category of person whose interests were identical with property. As the limit to freedom internal to every person, the slave disclosed the constitutive split dividing the transcendental "I am God in nature" from the empirical "I am a weed by the wall" aspects of the Emersonian enunciative doublet (*CW* 2:182). Slavery, that is, named the condition of negation persons passed through in learning to desire the power to transfigure that condition (the desire of freedom).[6] When transposed into Emerson's figures of thought, the disclosure of this interior absence aroused the negative capacity to turn away and initiate the Emersonian exercise Stanley Cavell has called "aversive thinking."[7]

The Anti-Slave

Emerson usually left the figure who inhabited the space in between the desymbolization of the symbolic order and the emergence of the different social order to which genius called him out of his thinking. Emerson encountered the figure of thought through which he called forth the alternative to the already constituted world as an actually existing historical figure in the following passage from his address on the "Anniversary of the Emancipation of the West Indies": "So now, the arrival in the world of such men as Toussaint, and the Haytian heroes, of the leaders of their race in Barbadoes and Jamaica, outweigh all the English and American humanity. The anti-slavery of all the world is dust in the balance before this: is a poor squeamishness and nervousness; the might and right are here: here is the anti-slave: here is man: and if you have man, black or white is an insignificance" (*AW* 31).

The event that occasioned his remarks stands as a benchmark in Emerson's literary career. In 1844, members of the Concord Female Anti-Slavery Society persuaded Emerson to give a talk in Concord celebrating the tenth anniversary of the emancipation of the slaves in the British West Indies. At their invitation, Frederick Douglass came to Concord to speak at the celebration alongside Emerson. Thoreau, Hawthorne, and Margaret Fuller were in the audience. Many Concord residents strongly opposed the observance; William Lloyd Garrison described their attitude in the *Liberator:* "The doors of every Church in the town were barred against the advocates of universal emancipation and they were compelled to resort to the court house."[8]

Emerson's address was marked by a kind of rhetorical bilingualism. In the opening twenty pages, he traversed the historical narratives, signposts, and commonplaces of the semiotic field of the anti-slavery movement so as to draw predictable moral lessons. What he advocates practically is drawn from the long history of British emancipation, whose itinerary he tracks in the changes in British case law from 1777 to 1834. The hard and time-consuming work of these legal decisions eventually resulted in a revolution in the slave owners' moral economy: "It was shown to the planters that they, as well as the negroes were slaves; that although they paid no wages, they got very poor work; that their estates were ruining them, under the finest climate; and they needed the severest monopoly laws at home to keep them from bankruptcy. The oppression of the slave recoiled upon them" (*AW* 21).

The intense subjectivity that takes Emerson up when he encounters Toussaint and the "Haytian heroes" breaks the link with the progressive history he has been telling. If the law produced the legal fiction of the slave, Toussaint incarnated the anti-slave as the condition for its transformation. This eventful turn replaces the geography of legality with an achronic scene in which the audience proleptically achieves the collective aim of the antislavery movement. Emerson's figuration of the anti-slave instantiates an intervention in Alain Badiou's sense that the truth of this speech act constitutes a subject out of the event of its enunciation.[9]

The Colonial Relation

As the geographical distance between Haiti, Jamaica, and Concord, Massachusetts, disappeared into the tropes of Emerson's 1844 address, the figure of the anti-slave also dramatically illuminated the connections between the colony and the metropole, the contradictory imbrication of American liberty and race slavery in the Anglo-American Atlantic world, which Anthony Bogues has called the "colonial relation."[10]

Slavery and colonial rule significantly differed from the enterprises within global modernity in that they did not condition the formation of modern subjects. Colonized subalterns were excluded from the processes of subjectivization underpinning citizen formation. As technologies of domination, colonial violence and racial slavery deployed apparatuses that seized and mastered bodies through practices of brute force that operated in as well as on the flesh. Colonial violence was intended to break and destroy, to remove possibilities and act immediately upon the person through the body. Forcibly excluded from the subjected/subjecting processes of civil subjectivization, colonial subalterns and slaves were constructed as civilly dead subjects.[11]

But how could Toussaint, the anti-slave, oppose the colonizer's structures of power within any cognitive-political terrain other than one introduced by the colonizer? In the aftermath of successful colonial revolts, Toussaint and ex-slaves and colonial subalterns could not simply take up preexisting positions within a disciplinary society whose social norms were structured on their generalized exclusion. Had they done so, they would have subjectivized the technologies of violence responsible for their abjection. The freedom practices of the anti-slave differed from the liberal practices of freedom structured on subaltern absence insofar as they emerged through the creation of forms of life that could not be integrated within the political horizon of Western humanism.[12]

As the constitutive outside of the colonial order they overturned, the (anti)slaves were excluded from formal categories of Western radical political theory. Emerson represented the anti-slave as the inaugural event of a new epoch in world history. The Haitian Revolution was not merely an extension of the European revolutionary movement. No one could have imagined that Toussaint and the Haitian slaves, who had been excluded from the ontological and epistemological terrain, could have become the protagonists of a collective revolution. This great emancipatory event disrupted the dominant global order of things. Since it was enacted by persons who had no part in the existing order of things, it changed the relationships between what was thought to be possible and impossible, introduced different configurations of, and new questions for, human societies.

It was in Haiti that human freedom and equality appeared in their most radical and universal forms and were sustained in the face of violent opposition from the dominant political and economic power of the day. Susan Buck-Morss has explained the singular universality of this event with admirable precision: "It is in the discontinuities of history that people whose culture has been strained to the breaking point give expression to a humanity that goes beyond cultural limits. And it is in our empathic identification with this raw, free, and vulnerable state that we have a chance of understanding what they say. Common humanity exists in spite of culture and its differences. A person's nonidentity with the collective allows for subterranean solidarities that have a chance of appealing to universal, moral sentiment, the source today of enthusiasm and hope."[13]

As the figure the speaker desired to engender at the limit in between these two orders—the order of signification and the order of Emersonian provocation—the anti-slave did not belong either to the preexisting social order or to the Emersonian alternative. The "experience" of the limit internal to the Emersonian provocation but external to its accomplishment, the anti-slave existed prior to as well as after the performative acts through which Emerson retroactively instituted his symbolic identity. The crisis that this figure effected in the speaker did not simply reanimate one or the other of the personifications (the Transcendentalist, the Reformer) of "Self-Reliance." The anti-slave effected a crisis within the transindividual discourse through which these antagonistic positions were regulatively opposed to one another. Rather than taking up an abstract universal position, elevated above the conflict (normatively associated with the transcendentalist), the speaker achieves universality by way of fully identifying with a singular partisan position—the one that within the space of the conflict stands for the universal perspective of what Emerson calls "higher law."

The Anti-Slave from Structural Performative to Structuring Impasse: Barack Obama's Rift

Although it appears to be a substantive, the anti-slave is at once the effect and outcome of the actions it performs. As the agency embodying the structural performative that Emerson calls self-reliance, the anti-slave can change the coordinates of the entire symbolic order. But when it remains within the already constituted order, the anti-slave can also structure an antinomy that sets up the redemptive messianic figure who would liberate from an oppressive slave past and a threatening figure who would exact vengeance for the past.

But insofar as it exists at the site of the structuring antagonism—the distinction between colonial and global modernity—the anti-slave can also function as a symptom of the post-racial fantasies that sustain the impasses it renders visible. In the following passage from his 1998 autobiography, *Dreams from My Father: A Story of Race and Inheritance,* Barack Obama recalls his mother's reaction to the colonial relations film *Black Orpheus* to exemplify the racial fantasies he entered political life to supplant:

> The storyline was simple: the myth of the ill-fated lovers Orpheus and Eurydice set in the favelas of Rio during carnival, in Technicolor splendour, set against scenic green hills, the black and brown Brazilians sang and danced and strummed guitars like carefree birds in colourful plumage. About halfway through the movie I decided I'd seen enough, and turned to my mother to see if she might be ready to go. But her face, lit by the blue glow of the screen, was set in a wistful gaze. At that moment I felt as if I were being given a window

> into her heart, the unreflective heart of her youth. I suddenly realised that the depiction of the childlike blacks I was now seeing on the screen, the reverse image of Conrad's dark savages, was what my mother had carried with her to Hawaii all those years before, a reflection of the simple fantasies that had been forbidden to a white, middle-class girl from Kansas, the promise of another life: warm, sensual, exotic, different.[14]

This revelation took place in 1982, when his mother, while visiting Obama during his student years at Columbia University, asked him to accompany her to a showing of the movie at a theater in Greenwich Village. Rather than sharing his mother's enchantment with *Black Orpheus,* her twenty-year-old son discerned in the film's depiction of blacks the contradictory representations—a redemptive messianic figure and a colonial savage—that the figure of the anti-slave had effected in his mother's gaze.

In *Dreams from My Father,* Obama diagnosed the antithetical, racialized images populating his mother's optical unconscious as having resulted from contrary but interdependent tendencies informing the political imaginaries of the majority of U.S. citizens. In *The Audacity of Hope,* Obama described the black messiah/black terrorist complex as the two sides of the racist antinomy that structured the history of race relations in the United States. This complex of antithetical representations also regulated what it was considered possible and impossible for African American political leaders to desire.

The film *Black Orpheus* presupposed the anti-slave imaginary that Barack Obama thought monopolized the field of racial representation. *Black Orpheus* also displayed the recalcitrant racial complex he wanted to change. Instead of repudiating this structuring antinomy, Obama's presidential campaign presupposed the system of racialized images he found depicted in *Black Orpheus.* Unlike the protagonist of Marcel Camus's film, however, Obama ran as at once the effect and the limit to these structuring antitheses. Obama considered the black messiah/black terrorist complex a structural racist antinomy that could not be historically surpassed. As the horizon that embraced and held the new rules and norms that Obama produced from within its framework, this structuring antinomy constituted the non-progressive backdrop for the changes Obama aspired to introduce into the political order.

An event that took place during the Democratic primaries supplied then Senator Barack Obama with the occasion to exploit the ineluctable tie binding African American leaders to the black messiah/black terrorist complex. From January through March 2008, right-wing political commentators published selected passages from sermons delivered by Jeremiah Wright, Obama's pastor in Chicago's Trinity United Church of Christ, as proof that the man whose sermons had inspired Obama to write *The Audacity of Hope* was in fact an anti-American terrorist. Rather than defending Reverend Wright or castigating his opponents, Obama delivered a speech on March 18, 2008, at the National Constitution Center in Philadelphia titled "A More Perfect Union," which turned the controversy surrounding his pastor into an example of the recalcitrant contrariety that had haunted race relations in the United States since the New World slavery.

Obama described the controversy as a "racial stalemate" that represented "the complexities of race in this country that we've never really worked through—a part of our union that we have yet to perfect." After locating the basis for the nation's racial division in the United States Constitution, Obama reasserted the "impossible" desire animating his presidential run as undergirded by the conviction that in "working together we can move beyond some of our old racial wounds, and that in fact we have no choice if we are to continue on the path of a more perfect union."[15]

This speech permitted Barack Obama to construct a position within the social symbolic order—the rift in its perfectible union—that enabled him to represent his extraordinary desire as if it were a universal political responsibility. Instead of remaining subject to these antithetical images, Senator Obama suspended their rule by positioning himself within the breach between these antagonistic representations and expressing his intention to achieve a "more perfect union" through them. Obama also ran his presidential campaign from this unprecedented political space. But in aspiring to make a more perfectible union out of resolutely antagonistic partisans, Obama could not wholly identify with either one of the parties in dispute. He occupied the strange position of being simultaneously more than and less than the constituencies through whom he aspired to render the union more perfectible. He was more than one of the antagonists because he could not perform as one of the factions he aspired to unify, and render their union *more* perfectible; less than one because that act had to be subtracted from the political order whose union he would render more *perfectible*.

During his first term, the incompatible representations that antagonistic political constituencies assigned President Obama oscillated between the opposite poles of the aforementioned racial antinomy. At the one extreme, Obama's political supporters characterized him as the most inspired of the nation's sovereign leaders; at the other extreme, his political antagonists cast him as one of mankind's accursed. In these antithetical formulations, the extimate belonging of President Obama as the sovereign head of state sat in uncanny proximity to the intimate non-belonging of President Obama as what Giorgio Agamben has called *homo sacer*.[16]

Obama's fluctuation between the positions of the sovereign and the *homo sacer* enabled him to deploy both of the positions within the structuring racist antinomy—the venerated black messiah/black terrorist—to his political advantage. He reworked the seemingly endless oscillation between these antagonistic images into the energies animating the momentum of his political movement.[17] By representing the desire for change in terms of his effort to achieve a "more perfect union," he ratified an understanding of history as a series of impasses. Barack Obama may have represented his presidential campaign as a truly "transformative moment," a change whose time had come, but he did not align his political aspirations with a belief in the progress of American history. Rather than achieving a perfected union within and through the progressive unfolding of a historical *telos,* the antinomy within which Obama operates discloses the nonprogressive traumatic impasses that progressive history perforce disavows.

The transformative moment of Obama's election and the structuring racist antinomy that should have rendered it impossible did not converge to form a post-racial American society. They instead collided into one another. But the strategies whereby Obama brought the "what has been" informed by an enduring racist logic together with the "now" of his election brought the vicious circle informing this racist antinomy to a standstill. Every moment of Obama's presidential movement also reestablished the antagonism that reimposed the racial divide.

In occupying this rift in between antagonistic positions and permanently striving for a more perfect union, Obama took up a site that envisioned American history as an accumulation of stalemates. He characterized the project he undertook from within this location as making "a way out of no way." But the only way out of the structuring impasses that the anti-slave inscribed in the symbolic order requires a reanimation of the radical imagination that Toussaint L'Ouverture—and Ralph Waldo Emerson—embodied.

Notes

1. I elaborate on this reading in "'Experience,' Antislavery, and the Crisis of Emersonianism," in Branka Arsić and Cary Wolfe, eds., *The Other Emerson* (Minneapolis: University of Minnesota Press, 2010), 131–66.

2. Cary Wolfe has attempted to dampen, if not resolve, the contentious arguments among Emerson's legatees with the observation that the schism between Emerson the Transcendentalist, "trying to make his break and his peace with the religious tradition," and Emerson the Reformer, "who was intent on ameliorating conditions in Jacksonian America, was not to be healed simply by redirecting attention from one side of this antagonism to the other." Cary Wolfe, "Alone with America: Cavell, Emerson, and the Politics of Individualism," *New Literary History* 25 (1994): 137.

3. Sacvan Bercovitch, *The Rites of Assent: Transformations in the Symbolic Construction of America* (New York: Routledge, 1993), 304.

4. I spell out the textual rationale for this claim in "'Experience,' Antislavery, and the Crisis of Emersonianism," 146–51.

5. I elaborate on this formulation in "'Experience,' Antislavery, and the Crisis of Emersonianism."

6. For a different understanding of Emerson's attitude toward the questions of race and slavery, see Cornel West, *The American Evasion of Philosophy: A Genealogy of Pragmatism* (Madison: University of Wisconsin Press, 1987), 9–41. West alludes to Ralph (Waldo) Ellison's observation that blackface minstrelsy and Emersonian self-reliance were historically contemporaneous and socially interactive cultural agencies. According to Ellison, it was their assumption of a blackface mask that permitted Emerson's self-made men to construct an open future as the other to a socially immobilized negro past. When they donned this mask, Emerson's self-reliant individuals dissociated from their previous identities—which they projected onto the nonidentity of the black mask.

7. Stanley Cavell elaborates on what he means by "aversive thinking" in "Aversive Thinking: Emersonian Representations in Heidegger and Nietzsche," *New Literary History* 22, no. 1 (Winter 1991): 129–60.

8. Quoted in Larry J. Reynolds, *Righteous Violence: Revolution, Slavery, and the American Renaissance* (Athens: University of Georgia Press, 2011), 3.

9. See Alain Badiou, *Being and Event*, trans. Oliver Feltham (New York: Continuum, 2005).

10. For an insightful discussion of colonial relation in the context of the technologies of empire, see Anthony Bogues, *Empire of Liberty: Power, Desire, and Freedom* (Hanover, NH: Dartmouth College Press, 2011), 9–38.

11. I elaborate on this claim in "The Crisis of Critique in Postcolonial Modernity," *boundary 2* 37, no. 3 (2010): 179–205.

12. Ibid.

13. Susan Buck-Morss, *Hegel, Haiti, and Universal History* (Pittsburgh: University of Pittsburgh Press, 2009), 132.

14. Barack Obama, *Dreams from My Father: A Story of Race and Inheritance* (New York: Three Rivers Press, 2004), 123–24.

15. For the full text of Obama's speech, see *Wall Street Journal*, http://blogs.wsj.com/washwire/2008/03/18/text-of-obamas-speech-a-more-perfect-union.

16. For a brilliant description of the role the proximity of the sublime and desecrated bodies of the sovereign played in fashioning the fiction of the "king's two bodies," see Eric Santer's remarkable *The Royal Remains: The People's Two Bodies and the Endgames of Sovereignty* (Chicago: University of Chicago Press, 2011).

17. Anthony Bogues called my attention to the ways in which the oscillation between the positions of the sovereign and that of *homo sacer* could become the means of under-

standing the formation of a subaltern political movement. This dynamic underpins his analyses of the ethics of living together in his magisterial new book, *Empire of Liberty: Power, Desire, and Freedom.* For an analysis of the relationship between state fantasy and governmental rule, see Donald E. Pease, *The New American Exceptionalism* (Minneapolis: University of Minnesota Press, 2009).

[2]

DAVID M. ROBINSON

EMERSON, THE INDIAN BRAHMO SAMAJ, AND THE AMERICAN RECEPTION OF GANDHI

I

EMERSON'S INITIAL REACTION TO the spiritual traditions of India was less than welcoming. Assigned the task of presenting a poem on "Indian Superstition" for the Harvard College exhibitions during his senior year, he delivered a work that Robert D. Richardson, Jr., unsparingly described as "a jejune, xenophobic, condescending, even racist overview of Indic mythology from the vantage point of European Christianity."[1] Richardson's description of the poem will not seem overly harsh to most modern readers, but the poem's real significance lies in the implicit suggestion of the assignment itself: Western religious traditions must somehow come to terms with the ancient religions of Asia. As Richardson noted, Emerson "would later come to admire" the Hinduism that he criticized in "Indian Superstition" (16).[2] This Emersonian affirmation of the place of Hinduism and other world religions in developing a post-Christian spirituality contributed to a transcultural reconception of religion in the nineteenth century, with important intellectual and political consequences. The "Emerson" of this chapter is, in this sense, not only the Concord essayist, but a marker for a strand of American religious thinkers, including Unitarians, transcendentalists, and Free Religionists, whose dialogue with Indian religions evoked a desire for religious syncretism to which important post-Hindu reformers associated with the Brahmo Samaj movement responded.[3] This dialogue, which I hope to sketch in broad strokes here, eventually set the stage for the American reception of Mahatma Gandhi in the early twentieth century.

II

Interest in Indian religious culture had been alive in New England since the late eighteenth century, and as Alan D. Hodder has shown, it intensified dramatically when a crucial Hindu reform figure, Rammohun Roy, "founder of the Hindu Renaissance and the father of modern India," began to seek a dialogue with liberal Christianity.[4] Rammohun found affinities with William Ellery Channing's tolerant and forward-thinking theology and was also impressed with the reform-centered ministry-at-large of Channing's colleague Joseph Tuckerman. Could a meeting of the minds between Hindus and Christians evolve from the antidogmatic spiritualism of Channing's sermons and Tuckerman's early version of the social gospel? This would remain, as we will see, a recurring question in India and New England throughout the nineteenth century.

Rammohun's intellectual foundation was monotheism, and his adherence to a God of unity was a crucial element in his vision of both social and religious reform. A conception of the one God also enabled his efforts to establish a productive dialogue with Christianity. In his *Precepts of Jesus* (1820), Rammohun assembled excerpts from the four Gospels, with translations into Bengali and Sanskrit, and an introductory essay presenting Jesus as a wise teacher of a "simple code of religion and morality" that was "admirably calculated to elevate men's ideas to high and liberal notions of one God."[5] He distinguished the moral precepts of Jesus from other aspects of Christian theology, insisting that a canon of ethical principles could function usefully apart from any entanglements with doctrinal controversy. Refusing to enter the wilderness of Christian theological dispute, he argued that ethical principles are "beyond the reach of metaphysical perversion, and are intelligible alike to the learned and the unlearned."[6] He was disposed to embrace the moral principles of Jesus, but not the theology of Christianity.

Unitarians welcomed *The Precepts of Jesus* but were not wholly aware of its implications for Rammohun's efforts to return what he considered a corrupted Hinduism to its originating God. Channing and Tuckerman had developed what he understood as a reformed Christianity, the principles of which he hoped to establish within Hinduism. Rammohun's mastery of the English New Testament, and his use of it as a tool for both Hindu revival and for the defense of Hindu traditions against British rule, suggest the complexities of his "hybrid" subject position as a colonized intellectual. As Homi Bhabha's incisive account of the Hindu reception of the English Bible in the nineteenth century has shown, iterations of colonial authority can both erase and enable strategies of resistant identity in the experience of the colonized.[7] Rammohun's use of a Unitarian Jesus to deepen cross-cultural religious dialogue, advance reform within Hinduism, and shield Indians against missionary pressure to convert, is a telling example of what Hodder has described as "opposition by assimilation," a practice that his successors would creatively adapt.[8] Developing from Rammohun's work was a lineage of cosmopolitan spirituality, grounded in Hinduism and tempered by the transmuted Christianity of Channing, Emerson, and Theodore Parker.[9] This emerging religious identity, receptive to Western religious insight yet determinedly Indian, was institutionalized by Rammohun in the Brahmo Samaj (Society of God). As a reform-oriented religious association, the Brahmo Samaj had appeal to Indians in search of alternatives to Hinduism and Christianity. In a similar way, a post-Christian Emersonian spirituality, drawing on Hinduism and other world religions, bolstered slipping believers in Europe and America who were struggling for new religious footing during the Victorian crisis of faith.[10]

III

Struggling with dangerously poor health and wavering about his vocational destiny as a minister, Ralph Waldo Emerson received a letter from his Aunt Mary Moody Emerson on May 24, 1822, which celebrated the conversion of a "learned Hindu" to "xianity from his own researches." "He studied much in the Vades," she explained, and "found that in antient times his religion was purer & better than now." He eventually became "a fixed Unitarian, and an enthusiastic admirerr of the high toned philosophy and morals of our blessed Master!"[11] Mistaken though she may have been about Rammohun's conversion, her reaction was typical of many New England Unitarians, who felt that the narrative strengthened their position against their Calvinist adversaries. She parlayed the news, as Phyllis Cole has noted, into a lesson on metaphysics that anticipated her nephew's full embrace of monistic idealism in the 1830s.[12] "At bottom of the histories and incarnations [in Hinduism]," she explained, "is often the doctrine of the universal presence & agency of One God." A month later she sent him "a sweet morsel of Hindu poetry," a partial transcription of Sir William Jones's "A Hymn to Narayena," which centers on the idea of the one-ness of the all-encompassing spirit and the mind that apprehends it: "One only Being knows."[13] This philosophy held that all things were ultimately spirit, and materiality an illusion. "Their philosophy is as it respects matter the same as Berkliasm you know," she noted (*MMEL* 157). Mary Moody Emerson's understanding of Hinduism as an iteration of ancient idealist and monistic traditions thus explained Rammohun's reformist opposition to polytheistic versions of Hinduism and connected his thought with the absolute idealism of George Berkeley. This philosophy, she believed, would protect her nephew from the suffocating materialism of Locke. Working through these ideas himself, Emerson would eventually concur with her.

Emerson did not begin to absorb the connection between Hindu mythology and idealism for another decade, when he encountered, in Richardson's words, "[Victor] Cousin's brilliant short treatment of the argument between Arjuna and Krishna" in his *Cours de l'histoire de la philosophie* (114–15). What burned hottest in this text for Emerson was Krishna's declaration that "a perpetual and eternal energy has created all which you see and renews it without cessation."[14] This avowal captured the paradox of the eternal unity and the ceaseless energy and productivity of the cosmos, principles that he would strive to reconcile throughout his career. In "Self-Reliance" he made it clear that the autonomous "self" he championed was in fact enabled by a larger energy, and that "the ultimate fact" was "the resolution of all into the ever blessed ONE" (*CW* 2:40). While his Aunt Mary had hoped that idealism would protect him from Locke, she did not anticipate that his pursuit of it would lead him into the post-Christian spirituality of transcendentalism. His brilliantly evocative and notoriously slippery term, the "Over-soul," a concept with Neoplatonic roots, best encapsulated his qualified theism and preserved the ultimate monism of his philosophy. Emerson did not wholly exclude a concept of "God" but limited it to a depersonalized and disembodied source of energy. "The soul knows no persons" (*CW* 1:82), he declared in "The Divinity School Address." This gradual comprehension of the interwoven concepts of monistic idealism and incessant transition is the essential narrative of Emerson's intellectual development in the 1830s. "What is popularly called Transcendentalism among us, is Idealism," he would later declare, "Idealism as it appears in 1842" (*CW* 1:206). As his transcendentalism became clearer, he also became more captivated by its affinities with Hinduism.[15]

Emerson recognized that his new approach to religion emerged in an era in which the foundations of Christianity seemed to give way. "We live in a transition period," he wrote in 1860, "when the old faiths which comforted nations, and not only so, but made nations, seem to have spent their force" (*CW* 6:110). The exploration of Hinduism and other Asian religions by the transcendentalists thus had a significant cultural impact in the later nineteenth century, as Asian religious concepts, symbols, and forms of worship offered an alternative spirituality in modern American culture.[16] Disaffected Unitarians of the 1870s and 1880s formulated the loose confederation of "Free Religion" and established *The Radical* and *The Index* as venues for their new theology.[17] "Radical" though they may have been in some respects, these new religious ideas were closely tied to the study and assimilation of the world's ancient religions, which both undermined the assumption of Christian exceptionalism and authorized conceptualizations of a shared human quest for the divine. Samuel Johnson, the Free Religionist who studied the Asian religions most deeply, initiated his three-volume series of *Oriental Religions and Their Relation to Universal Religion* with a study of India. That volume carried an epigraph from Emerson.[18] Working against the deeply ingrained prejudice that non-Christian religions were heathen and unenlightened, Johnson described his research as "a contribution to the Natural History of Religion" that would illuminate "the Universality of Religious Ideas, as illustrated by the Ancient Faiths of the East." In all religions, he wrote, "the one spiritual nature, that makes possible the intercourse of ideas and times and tribes, must have found utterance in some eternally valid form of thought and conduct."[19]

IV

There was a simultaneous advance of kindred religious theories in India after the death of Rammohun in 1833. Fading during the later 1830s, the Brahmo Samaj was revitalized by Debendranath Tagore, who saw Rammohun's Hindu-grounded monotheism and emphasis on ethical culture as a solution to his own crisis of religious identity and as a way forward for colonized India. He reestablished the association as an influential cultural institution in a modern India struggling to emerge from British colonial rule.[20] His successor, Keshub Chandra Sen, championed a sweeping theory of religious unity that melded the figure of Jesus with the originating spiritual authenticity of Hindu revelation. Rabindranath Tagore, the 1913 Nobel laureate in literature, became the most widely recognized spokesman in the West for the imaginative power of the Brahmo tradition. As David Kopf has argued, the Brahmos "played a crucial role in the genesis and development of every major religious, social, and political movement in India from 1820 to 1930" and "were the pioneers of liberal political consciousness and Indian nationalism."[21]

Debendranath's recovery of Rammohun's monotheistic legacy is clearly evident in his *Brahmo Dharma* (1850), a compilation of the religious tenets and moral principles of the Brahmo Samaj loosely drawn from the *Upanishads*. It opens with an avowal of one God, universally available to humans of all places and times. "The divine fire of the knowledge of God is hid in the hearts of all human beings. The consciousness of the infinite goodness of God is written in ineffaceable letters in the souls of all men."[22] In the early-twentieth-century translation of this text, God is called "Brahman, the Reality, the Lord of us all" (2), the "Almighty Supreme God" (2), the "one Eternal God" (2), and "the supreme Soul" (6), terms that emphasize the unitary, undivided nature of God. He is also called "infinite, all-pervading, indwelling" and "the Bliss" (3), emphasizing his permeating spiritual presence in the material world—a God who is "unseen, unembodied, unspeakable, uncontained" (7). The Brahmo God clearly has a close affinity with what Emerson speaks of as "that Unity, that Over-soul, within which every man's particular being is contained and made one with all other" (*CW* 2:160). For Debendranath and his adherents, this unified but "indwelling" God was empowering in two quite different ways. The unity of God was a rejection of Hindu polytheism but also a reclamation of the Hindu religious roots that challenged Christian missionary attempts to "convert" Hindus. "Is your God this God?" the *Brahmo Dharma* seems to say to those who would bring a new gospel.

Within a decade of Debendranath's enunciation of these principles, the Brahmo Samaj was infused with the new intellectual and organizational energy of his protégé and eventual successor, Keshub Chandra Sen, an astute and eloquent apostle of religious syncretism, whom Kopf has termed "probably the most innovative, charismatic, and influential religious reformer in nineteenth-century India."[23] More Westernized than Debendranath, Keshub and his protégé Protap Chandra Majumdar were influenced by Charles A. Dall's 1855 revival of earlier American Unitarian missionary efforts in India.[24] Keshub developed a powerful religious discourse on Hindu-Christian exchange, cooperation, and tolerance. He later launched the "New Dispensation" movement, which aspired to bring about a fusion of the world's religions.[25]

Keshub's linguistic fluency and his grasp of both Hindu tradition and Christian theology enabled him to develop a nuanced perspective on a central division between the two faiths, Christology. He revered and proclaimed Jesus, but did so on terms that were clearly Indian. Describing the many sectarian efforts to win him over during his 1870 lecture tour of Great Britain, he wryly compared that nation to "a vast market" in which "every sect is like a small shop where a peculiar kind of Christianity is for sale." He responded with his own question: "Think you that I have no Christ within me?" He resisted the presumption that Christ was "always their Christ," and would not accept what was not theirs to give.[26] He claimed instead an Asian Christ, whose origins and principles spoke directly to India. In his 1866 lecture "Jesus Christ: Europe and Asia," a pivotal text in the religious history of colonized India, he reconfigured the religious message of the West, making his Asian Christ a foundation for a merging of European and Asian religious civilizations.[27] "I am a Brahmo," Keshub declared, and "I cherish the profoundest reverence for the character of Jesus, and the lofty ideal of truth which he taught and lived" (3). While he attested to the "supernatural moral heroism" (18) of Jesus, he reminded his audience that "my convictions" differ from "the orthodox opinions of popular Christianity."

The religious and political strands of the lecture converged on a vision of a reborn India, newly empowered by its embodiment of the moral power symbolized in his Asian Christ. "I rejoice, yea, I am proud, that I am an Asiatic," he declared. "And was not Jesus Christ an Asiatic?" (33). This is the moment in which Keshub seized the most sacred element of British authority for India itself. "Christianity was founded and developed by Asiatics, and in Asia. When I reflect on this, my love for Jesus becomes a hundredfold intensified," he proclaimed. "I feel him nearer my heart, and deeper in my national sympathies" (33). In linking Jesus to Indian "national sympathies" Keshub turned the address into a rallying cry for national pride, solidarity, and above all, determination to persist in a long and difficult work of national recovery. He located the strength for this struggle in the "supernatural moral heroism" (18) of Jesus, who exhibited a "grandeur of which Asiatic nature is susceptible" (34). His "meekness" was the source of his power, "that deep serenity of soul, that extraordinary self-possession, which is never ruffled by provocation and insult, and is above resentment" (39). Keshub's Asiatic Jesus prefigured in a remarkable way the nonresistance principles of India's eventual liberator, Gandhi: "Surely, if a Native could learn charity from brutal violence, and meet provocation with forgiveness instead of anger, his victory would be complete, while his oppressor would lie vanquished amid shame and ignominy and public execration" (40). Such powerful meekness, Keshub urged, must confront "those who delight in vengeance, and boast of their muscular Christianity," which is "unworthy of the Christian name" (41).

Keshub thus skillfully entwined theological issues with the political circumstances of India in ways that both protested British oppression and searched for a nonconfrontational and nonviolent way forward. He called attention to the abuses of the British missionaries and directly condemned the racist hostility of elements of "the European community in India . . . who not only hate the Natives with their whole heart, but seem to take a pleasure in doing so" (22). Even so, Keshub reflected "with grateful interest on the day when the British nation first planted their feet on the plains of India" and provided "deliverance from oppression and misrule, from darkness and distress, from ignorance and superstition" (20).

Keshub's delicate balance of accommodation and resistance make the lecture a revelatory example of hybrid discourse in the postcolonial sense, particularly in its suggestion of the ways that European actions and attitudes often generated an uncertainty that undermined their presumed colonial authority. "The ambivalence at the source of traditional discourses on authority," Homi Bhabha observed, "enables a form of subversion, founded on the undecidability that turns the discursive conditions of dominance into the grounds of intervention."[28] Keshub's presentation of a recognizably Hindu

Jesus morally disarmed the British, turning their own source of authority against them. Keshub was not, however, an overtly revolutionary figure. In fact, four years after the delivery of "Jesus Christ: Europe and Asia," he made a celebrated lecture tour of England and was even introduced to Queen Victoria. The Asian Christ that he preached was, he believed, a figure of reconciliation, a man who was the vehicle of an all-embracing faith capable of unifying Hinduism and Christianity.

The fervor for nonsectarian harmony and the concomitant political edge of Keshub's thinking would intensify in the 1870s and 1880s, leading to his New Dispensation movement, an attempt to institutionalize the process of religious fusion and propagate its message of religious concord among the world's people. Its claims were grand and its vision all-encompassing. "If the New Testament follows the Old in the line of logical sequence, the New Dispensation follows as necessarily as the Old Dispensations that have gone before it."[29] Through the principle of "Sympathy" these earlier dispensations would be surmounted, their differences absorbed into a larger comprehensive truth. Notably, this harmony would be the product of the Asian, specifically Indian, absorption of European Christianity. Keshub summoned "ancient India to come into modern India with all her *rishis* and saints" and instigate a "transfiguration" not only of India but of the world. "How by *yoga* one nation becomes another! How Asia eats the flesh and drinks the blood of Europe! How the Hindu absorbs the Christian; how the Christian assimilates the Hindu!" (25).[30] His language evoked the Christian rite of communion, but the image of India violently devouring colonizing England was a powerful political subtext that spoke volumes about the increasingly unquiet India of the 1880s. Keshub's command to his readers, ostensibly a plea for moral discipline grounded in the example of Christ, was also quite provocative: "India! absorb England. Asia! assimilate Christian Europe" (26).

Keshub died in 1884, before his New Dispensation movement could have a significant impact. But his bold refashioning of Christianity's central figure was further developed and more widely disseminated by his protégé Protap Chandra Majumdar in *The Oriental Christ* (1883), a detailed portrait of "the prophet of the East, the sweet Jesus of the Galilean lake, whom we still see in our hearts."[31] An important link between American Unitarians and India after Keshub's death, Majumdar made his debt to his mentor clear in a lengthy introductory essay that traced the stages of Keshub's developing Christology. Majumdar's Oriental Christ possessed the same powerful "meekness" as Keshub's Asian Christ, a "voiceless uncomplaining calmness" (182) during his crucifixion that confirmed his "perfect self-control" and his "deep divine sympathy" (184). It was his sympathy, Majumdar wrote, that "was magical in its power of transforming" (185).

Majumdar's more detailed portrait of Keshub's Jesus emphasized his compassionate embrace of others. This deep empathy for his fellow men and women, Majumdar wrote, rendered him an image of "universal humanity" (33), who embodied less the divine than the ideal human. He was thus grounded in India's deeply rooted philosophical heritage, an expression of the monotheistic idealism at the heart of the Brahmo Samaj theology. "Keshub speaks of Christ as the prince of idealists. And his religion is spoken of as extreme idealism. And it is in this idealism that India has a hold on the real nature of Christ and Christianity" (34). Published in Boston the year after the death of Emerson, *The Oriental Christ* secured for its American readers the connective strands between Indian Brahmo religious universalism and Emersonian post-Christian spirituality. "The East has always been the home of idealism" (34), Majumdar wrote, confirming Emerson's conviction that transcendentalism was a new iteration of idealism and that "Europe has always owed to oriental genius, its divine impulses" (CW 1:80).

V

In 1895, when the prominent American Unitarian minister Jabez T. Sunderland visited India during his sabbatical travels, he met Majumdar and other Indian Brahmos. With that visit, the American view of colonized India began to change direction substantially.[32] Sunderland considered himself "a radical of the Theodore Parker and Emerson type," and he came to India with relatively sympathetic views of differing religious systems, while still holding a belief in the exceptional authority of Christianity. He returned with memories of a Pauline conversion experience on the question of colonialism. He afterward became, in Alan Raucher's words, "the most persistent American propagandist for India."[33] Among his many experiences, he was most deeply moved by a conversation with a group of Indian university students who shared their ambitions and vocational struggles with him and emphasized the insuperable barriers they faced because of continuing British rule. Holder of a long pastorate in the university town of Ann Arbor, Michigan, Sunderland was sensitive to the plight of these "keen-minded, earnest fellows, all of them desirous of making something worth while of their lives, and all ambitious to serve their country."[34] To these young men, the only opportunities open to the educated Indian were "low positions—too low to be accepted by Englishmen." And they carried a stiff requirement: "all persons permitted to occupy these positions must give up their patriotism and their manhood, keep out of politics, be loyal to the alien Government, that is, must not criticize it nor advocate any reforms, be docile servants and satellites of their British lords" (189–90). Even though the signs of colonial rule must have been apparent to Sunderland throughout his visit, he remembered this as the experience that caused the scales to fall from his eyes. "That afternoon," he recounted, "I realized as I had never done before how bitter, bitter a thing it is for educated young men, in whose breasts burn the fires of patriotism as true and holy as was ever felt by any Englishman or American, to know that they have no country." He saw with clarity men whose nation "has been taken by force, and is held in subjection by the sword of a foreigner!" (190).

Sunderland's encounter was magnified in significance, as Paul E. Teed has noted, "because it took place in the midst of the 1895 meeting of the Indian National Congress," an organization that became a seedbed for Indian nationalism. These proceedings were "a revelation" for Sunderland (60–61). Through his Brahmo Samaj contacts, Sunderland was invited to speak at one of the sessions, a rarity for a non-Indian, and "embraced congress politics," which were deeply distrusted by British authorities, "as a major force for progress" (60–61). His advocacy for Indian nationalism began on his return to the United States and reached a peak of public prominence with his 1908 *Atlantic Monthly* essay, "The New Nationalist Movement in India," a trenchant argument that Britain had, with great damage, exercised "irresponsible power" in India.[35] Disabusing his American readers of the idea that British rule in India was benign, as in Canada, Sunderland described "virtually a slave empire" (528), marked by the stark economic oppression of a desperately impoverished populace. The Indians faced a system of governance "that keeps the majority of the entire population on the very verge of starvation even in years of greatest plenty" (529–30). The British compounded this oppression with taxes "more than twice as heavy as [those paid by] the people of England and three times as heavy as those of Scotland" and with a salt tax that remained "well-nigh prohibitive to the poorer classes" (531). The enormous costs of the colonial governmental infrastructure and the control of commerce by British companies furthered the damage by maintaining the flow of "a vast stream of wealth" (533) from India to England.

Sunderland's essay was a significant contribution to a growing anti-imperialist discourse in America at the turn of the century, a period in which progressive organizations such as the Anti-Imperialist League, the American Union against Militarism, the National Civil Liberties Board (later the American Civil Liberties Union), and the India Home Rule League of America were springing up in response to American imperialistic adventures in the Philippines and elsewhere. Sunderland himself had a hand in the 1907 founding of the Society for the Advancement of India, and he later served in prominent roles in the Home Rule League of India.[36] Entering the orbit of these progressive reform groups through his Indian nationalist activity, Sunderland gained a valuable ally in a fellow Unitarian minister, John Haynes Holmes, author of an influential work on pacifism, *New Wars for Old* (1916), that grew out of his opposition to the American entry into World War I. Holmes exemplified the development of the social gospel in the early twentieth century and played an important role in the founding of both the NAACP and the ACLU.[37] To Holmes, the war represented a moral crisis for Western civilization as a whole. In 1920, Holmes and Sunderland coauthored an essay in which they applied the principles of nonviolence to the crisis in India, arguing that British repression, rather than containing Indian unrest, was "driving India toward revolution, and violent revolution." Britain's self-defeating tactics thus had the disastrous effect of sanctioning and replicating violence. "Repression gives the example, sets the pace, for the use of violence," they argued, invoking Emerson's principle that "force can only bring us force, as hate brings hate."[38]

Holmes was pulled into Indian nationalist politics largely through Sunderland's influence, but in 1918 he found a further bond with India in an essay by the British scholar and reformer Gilbert Murray.[39] Murray addressed the kind of postwar disillusion with world peace efforts that Holmes had experienced, but he cautioned that "we must not delude ourselves into believing that the path of the human soul or conscience when protesting against the world is a safe path, or a path that must in the end lead to victory." Indeed, the "protesting soul" may experience "suffering and humiliation" and even "end in defeat" (196). The soul's only course was to "carry its own corpse," as Murray put it, to clear itself of the "entangling chains" of the body, and "get rid of desire and ambition, and hatred and even anger, and think of nothing but what it wills as right" (196). The idea of the "right" must take precedence over the material needs of the body, Murray argued, linking ascetic devotion to the practice of political activism. His example of such a self-liberated "protesting soul" was Gandhi, whose early leadership of the Indian community in South Africa he depicted as a victory won "by a policy of doing no wrong, committing no violence, but simply enduring all the punishment the other side could inflict until they became weary and ashamed of punishing" (201).

Murray's words struck Holmes with a compelling impact, and he would look back on this revelation of Gandhi's ideas and presence as life-changing. "In my extremity I turned to Gandhi, and he took me in his arms, and never let me go," Holmes would recall in 1949. "Away across the globe he cared for me, and taught me, and reassured me."[40] Holmes's emotionally charged language drew from a deep tradition of Christian hymnody and conversion narratives, and clearly linked Gandhi with Jesus as a savior figure. Gandhi's authority was, for Holmes, beyond that of reason and proof. Indeed, he described this Gandhian revelation in Emersonian terms: "an intuition of the soul rather than any persuasion of the mind" (29).

The first fruit of this revelation was Holmes's influential proclamation of a new savior for the desperately lost Western world, delivered in a 1921 sermon titled "Who Is the Greatest Man in the World Today?"[41] The sermon addressed the "vast experience of disillusionment" that resulted from the outbreak of the war, in which "a whole philosophy of life had collapsed as suddenly and disastrously as the international relations in which we had put our trust" (*My Gandhi,* 23). Holmes declared that the victors of the war were now "being tested by the challenge of peace—by the great problem as to how to use a victory after it had been won. And it is just here, in this most rigorous of all tests, that these leaders of the nations failed" ("Greatest Man," 151). The failure of moral leadership that had produced the war continued, Holmes felt, in the diplomacy that followed. Holmes accepted the fact that European civilization had failed and that some new alternative for moral leadership had to be found. "I turn away, therefore, from the storm of the Great War, and from the men who rode that storm to power and place," Holmes wrote, "and I look elsewhere for that man who impresses me as the greatest man who is living in the world today" ("Greatest Man," 151). Murray's Gandhi was that man, and he carried a striking resemblance to the Asian Christ of Keshub and Majumdar in his uncompromising dedication to "the doctrine of non-resistance, which he calls 'the root of Hinduism'" ("Greatest Man," 169). Through this principle, Gandhi gained the forbearance and the powerful meekness that made him a liberator to others. Despite imprisonment, being "set upon by raging mobs, beaten into insensibility, and left for dead, . . . nothing shook his courage, disturbed his equanimity, exhausted his patience, or poisoned his love and forgiveness for his foes" ("Greatest Man," 170).

Hearing Murray's and Holmes's descriptions of Gandhi in the light of the Asian Christ of Keshub and Majumdar, it may seem as if some prophecy had been made and fulfilled. But it is more germane to recognize that Murray, Holmes, Keshub, and Majumdar were all enunciating versions of the concept that spiritual law eventually overcomes material obstructions—an idea that Gandhi was applying to British colonial rule. Gandhi was, like Rammohun, Keshub, and Majumdar, a hybrid figure. Trained in British law and loyal to his colonial rulers during World War I, he nevertheless strategically turned the other cheek in his battle for justice by employing the political principle of noncooperation.[42] He was receiving the English Bible and the English code of laws and putting them to unanticipated uses against English imperialism. Closely following Murray, Holmes argued that

Gandhi executed these principles and "won the victory" in South Africa, an "astonishing illustration of a battle won by doing no wrong, committing no violence, but simply enduring without resentment all the punishment an enemy can inflict" ("Greatest Man," 170). Holmes's pacifist hero was both a moral idealist and a successful tactician and leader, and his efforts against British colonial oppression were "a revolution different from any other of which history has knowledge." While it was "a movement directed straight and hard against English rule in India," it was remarkable in that "there is mingled no hatred against English people," and, most important, it "has no place for force or violence of any kind" ("Greatest Man," 171). Gandhi "is insistent, however, that non-resistance is not only right but expedient," Holmes explained. "It is the one sure way of attaining a triumph that will endure," because it arises from the unassailable strength of moral principle: "In advocating this policy of non-violence, Gandhi takes pains to emphasize that he is not doing this because Indians are weak. On the contrary, he commends non-violence just because India is so strong and thus so well able to meet the hazards involved" ("Greatest Man," 171).

A recognizable incarnation of Keshub's meek but powerful Jesus, Holmes's Gandhi seemed to foretell the inevitably victorious work of justice. Holmes quotes Gandhi's declarations that "India has a mission for the world" and that "my religion . . . has no geographical limits," statements that prophetically underlined the potential influence of his ideas in Europe and America ("Greatest Man," 172). Holmes's advocacy of Gandhi helped keep him in the public mind in America as a moral alternative to the deeper failures of Western civilization.[43] Holmes made Gandhi the defender of an ideal, and the living presence to whom progressive thinkers might attach Emerson's ever-renewing assurance that "there is victory yet for all justice; and the true romance which the world exists to realize will be the transformation of genius into practical power" (*CW* 3:49).

Notes

1. Robert D. Richardson, Jr., *Emerson: The Mind on Fire* (Berkeley: University of California Press, 1995), 8–9. Subsequent references to this work will be cited parenthetically in the text by page number.

2. Other valuable accounts of the development of Emerson's understanding and embrace of Indian religions include Lawrence Buell's section on "The Asian Difference" in his *Emerson* (Cambridge, MA: Harvard University Press, 2003), 169–98; and Alan D. Hodder's "'The Best of the Brahmans': India Reading Emerson Reading India," in Barry Tharaud, ed., *Ralph Waldo Emerson: Bicentenary Appraisals* (Trier: Wissenschaftlicher Verlag Trier, 2006), 171–201. On early New England interest in Asia, see Kenneth Walter

Cameron, *Emerson's "Indian Superstition" with Studies in His Poetry, Bibliography, and Early Orientalism* (Hartford, CT: Transcendental Books, 1977), 6–8.

3. On the origins of the Brahmo Samaj, and the impact of its founder Rammohun Roy on the New England Unitarians, see Spencer Lavan, *Unitarians and India: A Study in Encounter and Response* (Boston: Skinner House, 1977), 32–72; David Kopf, *The Brahmo Samaj and the Shaping of the Modern Indian Mind* (Princeton, NJ: Princeton University Press, 1979), 3–41; Alan D. Hodder, "Emerson, Rammohan Roy, and the Unitarians," in Joel Myerson, ed., *Studies in the American Renaissance 1988* (Charlottesville: University Press of Virginia, 1988), 133–48 (quotation from 134); and Srinivas Aravamudan, *Guru English: South Asian Religion in a Cosmopolitan Language* (Princeton, NJ: Princeton University Press, 2005), 37–44. I follow Kopf in the spelling of Rammohun Roy's name and that of other Indian figures in this chapter.

4. Hodder, "Emerson, Rammohan Roy, and the Unitarians," 134. Hodder shows the importance of Rammohun's emergence in bringing Emerson to "initiate a gradual though thorough-going re-evaluation of Indian thought and culture" (135).

5. Rammohun Roy, *The Precepts of Jesus* (London: The Unitarian Society, 1824), xvi–xviii. This is a reprint of the 1820 Calcutta edition, with a preface by Thomas Rees, secretary to the British Unitarian Society, supplemented by Rammohun's three *Appeals to the Christian Public,* which respond to Trinitarian critic Joshua Marshman's attacks. Available on Google Books. For analysis of the impact of *The Precepts of Jesus,* see Kopf, *The Brahmo Samaj,* 3–15; and Hodder, "Emerson, Rammohan Roy, and the Unitarians," 137–38.

6. On Rammohun's focus on moral principle as the key to religion, see James N. Pankratz, "Rammohun Roy," in Robert D. Baird, ed., *Religion in Modern India* (New Delhi: Manohar, 1981), 172–73. Pankratz explains that "Rammohun's rationalistic theism provided him with a hermeneutic by which to evaluate critically his own tradition and Christianity" (174).

7. Homi K. Bhabha, "Signs Taken for Wonders: Questions of Ambivalence and Authority under a Tree outside Delhi, May 1817," in *The Location of Culture,* 2nd ed. (London: Routledge, 2004), 145–74. In Bhabha's examples, the English Bibles distributed by British missionaries were accepted by Indians but rarely put to their intended use. By contrast, the scholar and linguist Rammohun read the Bible more deeply than the British cared to hear.

8. Hodder, "'The Best of the Brahmans,'" 197. In considering the reception of Emerson in India, Hodder has reminded us "that at no point can this story be separated from the larger colonial situation" (179). On Rammohun's resistance to Christian conversion efforts, see Lavan, *Unitarians and India,* 57–58. On the deep religious opposition to Rammohun's work from within India, see Aravamudan, *Guru English,* 40–41.

9. As Kopf explains, Keshub Chandra Sen developed a close relationship with Charles Dall, an American Unitarian missionary in India, and "through Dall's efforts, thousands of copies of the complete works of Channing, Emerson, and Parker were circulated

among the Brahmos" (*The Brahmo Samaj,* 16). Dall also influenced Keshub's disciple Protap Chandra Majumdar.

10. As Buell notes, citing the example of Charles Eliot Norton, Emerson's unorthodox spirituality could also be corrosive to religious faith (*Emerson,* 185).

11. *The Selected Letters of Mary Moody Emerson,* ed. Nancy Craig Simmons (Athens: University of Georgia Press, 1993), 152. Hereafter cited as *MMEL*. See also Hodder, "Emerson, Rammohan Roy, and the Unitarians," 133–39, for a fuller explanation of the Unitarian interest in, and perception of, Rammohun.

12. Phyllis Cole, *Mary Moody Emerson and the Origins of Transcendentalism: A Family History* (New York: Oxford University Press, 1995), 169–70. Further quotations from this text will be cited parenthetically as *MME*.

13. Sir William Jones, *The Poems and Life of Sir William Jones* (London: Suttaby and Evance; and Baldwin, Cradock, and Joy, 1818), 163–68. Available on Google Books. See Cameron, *Emerson's "Indian Superstition,"* 17, and Hodder, "Emerson, Rammohan Roy, and the Unitarians," 141–43, for a discussion of the perceived connections between idealism and Hinduism.

14. Victor Cousin, *Introduction to the History of Philosophy,* trans. Henning G. Lindberg (Boston: Hilliard, Gray, Little, and Wilkins, 1832), 72. Emerson first read Cousin in 1831 in the original French edition of 1827. But he became familiar with this English translation, which was influential in New England.

15. For the text of "The Over-Soul," see CW 2:157–75. On the origins and development of Emerson's Over-soul concept, and the three phases of Emerson's absorption of Hindu thought, see Hodder, "'The Best of the Brahmans,'" 180–88. Buell notes that "only in the 1840s did Asian religion become a really serious interest" for Emerson (*Emerson,* 173).

16. Among the many studies of transcendentalism and Indian religions, see Arthur Christie, *The Orient in American Transcendentalism* (New York: Columbia University Press, 1932); Russell B. Goodman, "East-West Philosophy in Nineteenth-Century America: Emerson and Hinduism," *Journal of the History of Ideas* 51 (October–December 1990): 625–45; Arthur Versluis, *American Transcendentalism and Asian Religions* (New York: Oxford University Press, 1993); and Alan D. Hodder, *Thoreau's Ecstatic Witness* (New Haven, CT: Yale University Press, 2001), 174–217.

17. For the history of the Free Religion movement, see Stow Persons, *Free Religion: An American Faith* (New Haven, CT: Yale University Press, 1947). For its impact on American religious culture, see Leigh Eric Schmidt, *Restless Souls: The Making of American Spirituality* (San Francisco: HarperCollins, 2005); and David M. Robinson, "'The New Epoch of Belief': The *Radical* and Religious Transformation in Nineteenth-Century New England," *New England Quarterly* 79 (December 2006): 557–77.

18. See Versluis, *American Transcendentalism and Asian Religions,* 259–60. On Johnson's work on Asian religions, see Versluis, 248–69; and Carl T. Jackson, "The Orient in Post-Bellum American Thought: Three Pioneer Popularizers," *American Quarterly* 22

(Spring 1970): 67–81. Johnson drew his epigraph from Emerson's poem "The Problem": "Out from the heart of nature rolled / The burdens of the Bible old; / The litanies of nations came, / Like the volcano's tongue of flame, / Up from the burning core below, / The canticles of love and woe."

19. Samuel Johnson, *Oriental Religions and Their Relation to Universal Religion: India,* 3rd ed. (Boston: James R. Osgood, 1873), 1, 4.

20. See Kopf, *The Brahmo Samaj*, 188–93, on Debendranath's crisis of identity and early religious and intellectual development, and idem, 101–28, on his contributions, along with those of his successors Keshub Chandra Sen and Protap Chandra Majumdar, in cultivating "the Brahmo Puritan ethic" (114), and negotiating the complex task of embracing "progressive Western values" (101) while maintaining an Indian identity. Kopf argues that the Brahmos of the mid-nineteenth-century "became the forerunners of modern India" (102). On Debendranath's restoration of the Brahmo Samaj in Rammohun's image, see Brian A. Hatcher, "Remembering Rammohan: An Essay on the (Re-) Emergence of Modern Hinduism," *History of Religions* 46 (August 2006): 66–75.

21. Kopf, *The Brahmo Samaj,* xiii.

22. [Debendranath Tagore], *Brahmo Dharma*, trans. Hemchandra Sarkar (1928; rpt., Calcutta: Sadharan Brahmo Samaj, 1992). Subsequent references to this work will be cited parenthetically in the text by page number. As Sarkar explains in his introduction, "The entire contents of the first part of the Brahmo Dharma are from the Upanishads. But [Debendranath] has taken them from different places; and in the process he has frequently torn them away from their contexts and even sometimes distorted them and pieced them together to suit his purpose." This rewriting was wholly intentional, his object being "an original book" that was "one organic whole" (iii–iv, v).

23. David Kopf, "Neo-Hindu Views of Unitarian and Trinitarian Christianity in Nineteenth-Century Bengal: The Case of Keshub Chandra Sen," in Arvind Sharma, ed., *Neo-Hindu Views of Christianity* (Leiden: E. J. Brill, 1988), 106. For an insightful discussion of Keshub's development and career, see Aravamudan, *Guru English,* 44–53.

24. See Lavan, *Unitarians and India,* 81–130. Dall himself was a moderate Unitarian who strongly identified with Christianity and tried to win over both Keshub and Majumdar. But he also became, with Keshub's help, the first non-Indian Brahmo. He was a conduit for tracts and collected editions of Unitarian authors such as Channing, Emerson, and Parker.

25. As Kopf recounts, Debendranath recognized Keshub's eloquence and organizational energy, and made him a close inmate of the Tagore household for a period, but became uncomfortable with his willingness to engage Christianity. But in the mid-1860s, they parted ways, causing a schism in the Brahmo Samaj that left Keshub to take leadership in 1866 and remake it in his own direction (Kopf, *The Brahmo Samaj*, 253–64). For details on Keshub's search for a universal religion, see Aravamudan, *Guru English,* 49–51.

26. *The Brahmo Somaj: Keshub Chunder Sen in England*, 3rd ed. (Calcutta: Brahmo Tract Society, 1897), 252–53. Quotations from this text will be cited parenthetically by page number.

27. Keshub Chandra Sen, "Jesus Christ: Europe and Asia," in *Keshub Chunder Sen's Lectures in India* (London: Cassell, 1901), 1–47. Available on Google Books. Quotations from this text will be cited parenthetically by page number.

28. Bhabha, "Signs Taken for Wonders," 160.

29. Keshub Chunder Sen, "We Apostles of the New Dispensation [A Lecture by Keshab Chandra Sen]" (Calcutta: Bidhau Press, 1881), 18. Available on Google Books. Located in the Andover-Harvard Theological Library, Harvard University: Andover-Harv. Theol Pamph. BL 1265.S4 Z92. Further quotations will be cited parenthetically by page number. See Kopf, *The Brahmo Samaj*, 264–86, for a detailed account of the history of Keshub's New Dispensation movement.

30. Keshub's use of the concept of yoga may reflect the influence of Ramakrishna, whose more mystical version of reformed Hinduism had enormous influence in late-nineteenth-century India—and through his pupil Swami Vivekananda, also had a powerful impact in Europe and the United States. See Kopf, *The Brahmo Samaj*, 264–68, on the influence of Ramakrishna on Keshub.

31. P. C. Mozoomdar, *The Oriental Christ* (Boston: George H. Ellis, 1883), 45. Further quotations will be cited parenthetically by page number. See Buell, *Emerson*, 191–96, on Majumdar's important role in "the Indianization of Emerson" (196); and Hodder, "'The Best of the Brahmans,'" 193–98, for a discussion of Majumdar's knowledge of Emerson's works and his use of Emerson in his defense of Asian religious traditions. Aravamudan analyzes Majumdar's success, and his inner struggles, in the role of "an Eastern guru for a Western audience" (*Guru English*, 52–53).

32. See Lavan, *Unitarians and India*, 143–45, on Sunderland's earlier ministry and theological positions. His visit to India is analyzed in Paul E. Teed, "Interfaith Encounter and Religious Pluralism: J. T. Sunderland's Mission to Brahmo Samajes of India, 1895–96," *American Studies* 50 (Spring–Summer 2009): 51–69.

33. Alan Raucher, "American Anti-Imperialists and the Pro-India Movement, 1900–1932," *Pacific Historical Review* 43 (February 1974): 86.

34. Jabez T. Sunderland, *India in Bondage*, rev. ed. (New York: Lewis Copeland, 1932), 189. Further quotations will be cited parenthetically by page number.

35. Jabez T. Sunderland, "The New Nationalist Movement in India," *Atlantic Monthly* 102 (October 1908): 528.

36. See Raucher, "American Anti-Imperialists," 85–89, on the Indian nationalist movement's connections with other anti-imperialist and progressive organizations. See Lavan, *Unitarians and India*, 171–76, on Sunderland's work for Indian nationalism, including his roles in the Society for the Advancement of India and the Home Rule League of India.

37. John Haynes Holmes, *New Wars for Old* (New York: Dodd, Mead, 1916). For Holmes's roots in the social gospel movement and his ministerial career, see David M. Robinson, *The Unitarians and the Universalists* (Westport, CT: Greenwood Press, 1985), 136–39 and 277–78.

38. John Haynes Holmes and J. T. Sunderland, "Repression—Road to Revolution," *Young India* 3 (July 1920): 160–62. The quotation is attributed to Emerson's "Politics," and while it is consistent with the argument of that 1844 essay, I have as yet been unable to locate the exact quotation in Emerson's writings.

39. Gilbert Murray, "The Soul as It Is, and How to Deal with It," *Hibbert Journal* 16 (January 1918): 191–205. Further quotations from this text will be cited parenthetically by page number. As Lavan noted (*Unitarians and India,* 174–75), both Holmes and Sunderland spoke at the 1918 meeting of the India Home Rule League, an event that represented Holmes's entry into the Indian nationalist movement.

40. John Haynes Holmes, *My Gandhi* (New York: Harper and Brothers, 1953), 9. Further quotations from this text will be cited parenthetically by page number and title.

41. John Haynes Holmes, "Who Is the Greatest Man in the World Today? [part 1]," *Unity* 87, no. 10 (May 5, 1921): 151–53; and "Who Is the Greatest Man in the World Today? [part 2]," *Unity* 87, no. 11 (May 12, 1921): 169–72. Further quotations from Holmes's sermon will be cited parenthetically by page number as "Greatest Man."

42. For an enlightening discussion of Gandhi's practice and description of the doctrine of noncooperation, see Sean Scalmer's chapter "At War over Words" in his *Gandhi in the West: The Mahatma and the Rise of Radical Protest* (Cambridge: Cambridge University Press, 2011), 73–104. Scalmer focuses on the difficulties of translating Gandhi's term "satyagraha" as an expression of his political philosophy and tactics, and Gandhi's own effort to find a suitable English term for the principle underlying his efforts. For a description of Gandhi's impact on the American pacifist movement in the early twentieth century, see Leilah C. Danielson, "'In My Extremity I Turned to Gandhi': American Pacifists, Christianity, and Gandhian Nonviolence, 1915–1941," *Church History* 72 (June 2003): 361–88.

43. For an excellent overview of the American reception of Gandhi, see Lloyd I. Rudolph, "Gandhi in the Mind of America," in Lloyd I. Rudolph and Susanne H. Rudolph, eds., *Postmodern Gandhi and Other Essays: Gandhi in the World and at Home* (Chicago: University of Chicago Press, 2006), 92–139.

[3]

MONIKA M. ELBERT

TRANSCENDENTALIST TRIANGULATIONS: THE AMERICAN GOETHE AND HIS FEMALE DISCIPLES

> In *Faust*, we see the redeeming power, which, at present, upholds woman, while waiting for a better day, in Margaret.
>
> —Margaret Fuller, *Woman in the Nineteenth Century* (1845)

AT A TIME IN America when women were trying to find their voice within society and to find an author who would speak to their needs, it is interesting that a male author, Goethe, and his *Faust* drama play such a pivotal role in the imagination of women writers. In some ways, they have co-opted Goethe's material (and especially the suffering but redemptive Gretchen/Margaret figure), if only to muse upon new roles or possibilities for women in the future.[1] One can focus on Margaret Fuller (the American "Margaret" of sorts) and Louisa May Alcott to explain how the changing attitudes toward a man-made history (especially toward the "great man" in history) figured in their feminine and spiritual rewriting of history—and to a new definition of womanhood. This reconsideration or reconfiguration gives rise to an interesting triangle, with Goethe at its apex, and Fuller and Alcott becoming unwitting sisters. Or, even more tantalizingly, Goethe was the spiritual stand-in for the real-life intellectual crush Fuller and Alcott had—which was on Emerson. It is a study of reciprocities: Goethe can be seen as the Germanic forerunner to Emerson—and the Germanic Bettina sets a precedent for his two disciples, Margaret Fuller and Louisa May Alcott, in their contemplations about finding a voice in the transcendentalist community. This chapter will deal with the evolving concepts of gender (especially women's roles) from Goethe to Emerson and then from Emerson to Fuller and Alcott, with Emerson being the man in the middle. This is not simply the story of two women's adoration of the master writer, but an entire culture's. Several years after Emerson's death in 1882, the legacy of both Emerson and Goethe lived on in Bronson Alcott's beloved Concord School of Philosophy, which sponsored a series of lectures on Emerson in 1884 and on Goethe in 1885.

At the apex of this derivative triangle is Fuller and Alcott's hero worship of Emerson, who actually shared the passion for Goethe (though initially less enthusiastically than Fuller) or promoted Goethe in his relationship to both women.[2] Emerson finally warms up to Goethe so much that he renounces the American prejudice against his carnality to include him as a man of genius in the final essay of his *Representative Men* (1850), where he lauds Goethe's "manly mind, unembarrassed by the variety of coats of convention with which life had got encrusted, easily able by his subtlety to pierce these and to draw his strength from nature, with which he lived in full communion."[3] Both Goethe and Emerson appear at times to be paternalistic types who were rather cool and aloof intellectual figures (much in the vein of Goethe's Faust, and like Faust and Mephistopheles figures in Alcott's *A Modern Mephistopheles*). In several letters to Emerson, Fuller alludes to Emerson's coldness (Emerson acknowledges as much) and aloofness, just as in her preface to her translation of Eckermann's *Conversations with Goethe* (1839), she describes her momentary dissatisfaction with Goethe: "I . . . have been disturbed by his aversion to pain and isolation of heart."[4] But Fuller is finally convinced that Goethe holds the key to spiritual reform in men, and she praises him in her famous 1841 essay in *The Dial* (perhaps responding to Emerson's negative remarks about Goethe in his earlier 1840 *Dial* essay): "One is ashamed when finding any fault with one like Goethe, who is so great."[5] Indeed, she enumerates the ways in which women have saved men's souls in Goethe's works: "Faust, bent upon reaching the centre of the universe through the intellect alone, naturally, after a length of trial, which has prevented the harmonious unfolding of his nature, falls into despair" but then finds salvation in act 2 in Gretchen (Margaret). In Goethe's novel *Wilhelm Meister,* the male protagonist is enlightened by several women who are wiser than he: the kind and domestic Teresa, the "sage and beneficent Natalia" (25), and finally the spiritually enlightened, mystical, and "celestial" Macaria. Of the latter, Fuller asserts, "we recognize that no thought is too religious for the mind of Goethe" (27). In Goethe's play *Iphigenia,* the female protagonist redeems men, so Fuller claims, "by a woman's reliance on the voice of her innocent soul" (41).

Significantly, Fuller gravitated toward the spiritual side of Goethe, whereas for Emerson, "Goethe knew too much of himself . . . and there was too much of the personal and private in his work."[6] In many of Fuller's letters to Emerson, there are numerous references to Goethe and his work, as she tries, like one of Goethe's female protagonists, to get to the soul of Emerson by practicing her own form of feminine self-reliance. Even in one of her reviews of Emerson's essays, Fuller clamors for a softer side of Emerson: "Here is, undoubtedly the man of ideas, but we want the ideal man also; want the heart and genius of human life to interpret it, and here our satisfaction is not so perfect." Essentially, she is calling for a feminized, more intuitive Emerson: "We could wish he might be thrown by conflicts on the lap of mother earth, to see if he would not rise again with added powers."[7] This return to "mother earth" will entail an appreciation of woman's redemptive power, as Goethe will see it with Faust's redemption through the Mothers in the second part of the drama, and which Emerson, after Fuller's death, will finally intuit in his famous lecture, titled "Woman."

For her part, Louisa May Alcott records indebtedness to Emerson for introducing her to Goethe: in her journals, she writes, "R.W.E. gave me Goethe's works at fifteen, and they have been my delight ever since. My library consists of Goethe, Emerson, Shakespeare, Carlyle, Margaret Fuller, and George Sand."[8] Intriguing (in the context of this chapter) it is that she brings together Goethe, Emerson, and Fuller in this passage. The girlhood crush on Emerson seems to be inscribed in various places in Alcott's journal and in her writing, as in *Moods* (1864), where the motto from Emerson's essay "Experience" begins the book: "Life is a train of moods like a string of beads; and as we pass through them they prove to be many colored lenses, which paint the world their own hue, and each shows us only what lies in its own focus." It is telling that if Alcott ascribes moodiness to her characters Sylvia and Warwick in *Moods,* Emerson himself describes these moods as moments of despair when enlightenment seems transitory or evanescent. In "Experience," he exclaims, "Once I took such delight in Montaigne, that I thought I should not need any other book; before that, in Shakespeare; then in Plutarch; then in Plotinus; at one time in Bacon; afterwards in Goethe; even in Bettine; but now I turn the pages of either of them languidly, whilst I still cherish their genius" (*CW* 3:33). In fact, Emerson, on the occasion of writing "Experience," has been unmoored (no pun intended, in the context of Alcott's *Moods*) by the passing of his beloved son. The evanescence is captured in his essay as well as in Louisa May Alcott's novel *Moods*—as Emerson forfeits his identity as Moor to become the warring Warwick, in Alcott's eyes.

Though critics have come to view Warwick in Alcott's *Moods* as the embodiment of Thoreau, I tend to see Warwick, the despairing fighter for the rights of man, never content with the moment, but always looking forward to another passionate cause, to be Alcott's rendition of Emerson. There is a depressive quality to Warwick, one that Emerson articulates in his essay "Experience"—an ever-striving Faustian tone: "There is no power of expansion in men. Our friends early appear to us as representatives of certain ideas, which they never pass or exceed" (*CW* 3:33). While Sarah Elbert finds Warwick the embodiment of Thoreau ("an American Rochester modeled on Henry David Thoreau"),[9] I find him to be more like Emerson, who cannot get close to anyone without feeling the need to withdraw. Also, Alcott might have felt that Emerson would be her ideal reader, as she starts with one of his epigraphs, a ploy that did indeed prompt Emerson to agree to read the manuscript.[10] Bronson Alcott proudly exclaimed that "Emerson must see this. Where did you get your metaphysics?" (*LLJ*, 125). In the novel, too, Warwick is the writer of prose, and Moor is the poet, which makes me think that the logical Warwick is more like the rational Emerson than the dreamy Thoreau.[11]

With Louisa's appreciation of Emerson as a brilliant mind and a kind of surrogate father for her daydreamer transcendentalist father, she might also be following in the tradition of hero worship promulgated by Bettina von Arnim. We can all recall the moment when Louisa May Alcott envies her sister Anna the kiss he gave her at her wedding: "Mr. Emerson kissed her; and I thought that honor would make even matrimony endurable, for he is the god of my idolatry, and has been for years."[12] Alcott is most intense in her adoration when she says she tried to follow in the tradition of Bettina von Arnim, to have a correspondence with Emerson; Bettina von Arnim was best known for her intimate letters to Goethe (then in his late fifties), ultimately called *Goethe's Correspondence with a Child* (1835; English ed., 1837), though Bettina was in her early twenties and fabricated or embellished much of the material. Alcott describes her own infatuation with Emerson in great detail:

> My romantic period began at fifteen, when I fell to writing poetry, keeping a heart-journal, and wandering by moonlight instead of sleeping quietly. About that time, in browsing over Mr. Emerson's library, I found Goethe's "Correspondence with a Child," and at once was fired with a desire to be a Bettine, making my father's friend my Goethe. So I wrote letters to him, but never sent them; sat in a tall cherry-tree at midnight, singing to the moon till the owls scared me to bed; left wild flowers on the doorstep of my "Master," and sung Mignon's song under his window in very bad German. (*LLJ* 57)

She added that she ultimately revealed her childhood crush to the aging Emerson, and he remained for her the inimitable "Master":

> Not till many years later did I tell *my* Goethe of this early romance and the part he played in it. He was much amused, and begged for his letters, kindly saying he felt honored to be so worshipped. The letters were burnt long ago, but Emerson remained my "Master" while he lived, doing more for me,—as for many another,—than he knew, by the simple beauty of his life, the truth and wisdom of his books, the example of a great, good man, untempted and

unspoiled by the world which he made better while in it, and left richer and nobler when he went. (*LLJ* 57)

Interestingly, on this occasion she actually equates Emerson with Goethe and herself with the young Bettina—a kind of triangulation that seemed popular in Concord. As Bruce Charlton notes, "Emerson engaged in a scintillating correspondence with the young intellectual and poet Caroline Sturgis that was explicitly modelled on Bettina-Goethe; Fuller reviewed and translated passages from the *Correspondence;* then a generation afterwards Louisa May Alcott found Emerson's copy of Bettina when browsing in his library, and—in emulation—composed many passionate yet platonic (unsent) letters to the middle-aged philosopher, and made romantic gestures such as leaving anonymous flowers on his doorstep."[13] This brings in the Fuller connection again: Fuller translated some of the *Correspondence* (between Bettina von Arnim and Goethe) and started but did not complete a full translation of *Die Günderode.*[14]

But Alcott's connection to Emerson was not finally erotically charged, in the way Fuller's relationship to Emerson appeared to be; clearly, she was just a child who had played with the Emerson children. She did indulge in hero worship, when, for example, her father gave her a picture of Emerson on her twenty-eighth birthday. In fact, Emerson seems like a good version of the father she probably wanted, someone who could stave off poverty because he was fiscally responsible. Alcott mentions Emerson's generosity when her father was in financial straits: "Father had four talks at Emerson's; good people came, and he enjoyed them much; made $30. R. W. E. probably put in $20. He has a sweet way of bestowing gifts on the table under a book or behind a candle-stick, when he thinks Father wants a little money, and no one will help him earn. A true friend is this tender and illustrious man" (*LLJ* 125). He was also a good mentor, as he gave her transcendentalist advice about writing: "But Emerson says 'that what is true for your own private heart is true for others.' So I wrote from my own consciousness and observation and hope it may suit someone and at least do no harm" (*LLJ* 162). And if Emerson did not feel safe expressing anything but paternalistic admiration for women, he was quite warm in his expression of sympathy—or in relation to male friends, like Bronson Alcott. Emerson received the telegram that Louisa's sister May had died, and he offered comfort to Louisa, whom he found home alone: "He was much moved and very tender. I shall remember gratefully the look, the grasp, the tears he gave me; and I am sure that hard moment was made bearable by the presence of this our best and tenderest friend" (*LLJ* 324). When Emerson died, Alcott recorded the exact time in her journal and again drew parallels between Emerson and Goethe:

> Mr. Emerson died at 9 P.M. suddenly. Our best and greatest American gone. The nearest and dearest friend Father has ever had, and the man who has helped me most by his life, his books, his society. I can never tell all he has been to me,—from the time I sang Mignon's song under his window (a little girl) and wrote letters *a la* Bettine to him, my Goethe, at fifteen, up through my hard years, when his essays on Self-Reliance, Character, Compensation, Love, and Friendship helped me to understand myself and life, and God and Nature. Illustrious and beloved friend, good-by! (*LLJ* 345)

My suggestion then is that both Alcott and Fuller can imagine themselves in the role of the adoring correspondent (Bettina) with Emerson, and like Bettina and Günderode, they almost become sisters in arms—or sister spirits, who first try to locate hope for women in a benevolent paternal model, but who then relinquish the need for a father figure in creating a sisterhood. So the move is from the hero worship in Bettina's letters to Goethe in *Goethe's Correspondence with a Child* to a more salient type of female emancipation as typified in the equally idealized bond between Bettina and Günderode, in *Die Günderode* (1840). These two texts were translated by Fuller. Emerson himself wrote about the ideal woman in Bettina von Arnim (another triangle of sorts), as he records in a journal entry and letter (*JMN* 7:228; *L* 3:77): "Wonderful Bettina! . . . we are indebted to her for the most remarkable book every written by a woman. She is a finer genius than George Sand or Mme. De Staël, more real than either, more witty, as profound & greatly more readable. And where shall we find another woman to compare her with" (Letter to John F. Heath, August 4, 1842). How about in Fuller, who became Emerson's best audience (as he would reveal, upon her death, with those unsavory words about losing his audience; *JMN* 11:258)! It seems then that the ghost of Bettina is filtered through the illustrious minds of Concord and Boston to conjure up an image of feminine strength and/or veneration of male genius. But if the young Louisa was more like Bettina, then Fuller, because of her proximity in age, proved to be more of a threat to Emerson's sense of decorum and privacy. As Christina Zwarg noted, Emerson felt the sexual energy in his correspondence with Fuller and took on the role of another Goethe character in his relationship with her: "Though fully aware of Fuller's power to influence his thought, Emerson played Tasso to her Princess [based on her translation of Goethe's *Tasso*] while she was alive, haunted by false threats of seduction and captivity." Fuller apparently was aware of her allure: she could "easily see how her influence over Emerson was being acknowledged allegorically through his praise for Bettina von Arnim."[15]

It is a well-known fact that, early in her life especially, Fuller indulged in a type of Goethe worship, which she sometimes transferred to Emerson. Many of her writings discuss or focus on Goethe: these include her letters, her 1834 translation of Goethe's *Torquato Tasso;* the preface to her translation of Eckermann's *Conversations with Goethe* (1839); her important 1841 essay on Goethe in *The Dial; Woman in the Nineteenth Century* (1845); her *Memoirs* (as collected by Emerson as well as by Julia Ward Howe); and another version of the Goethe essay in her brother's collection of her writings, *Life Within and Without,* published posthumously (1859). Fuller writes about Goethe's art and philosophy in glowing terms and singles out *Faust* as his best dramatic work (followed by the novel *Wilhelm Meister*). She sees both Goethe and his protagonist Faust as strong men who can move history; she shares the Romantic attitude of her day that strong men/individuals (like Goethe, Emerson) move history and that history cannot move humanity. This belief in the great, active man is an idea shared by Emerson in "Self-Reliance," where he proclaims, "An institution is the lengthened shadow of one man" (*CW* 2:35), and his discussion of "great men" in *Representative Men* pays homage to such figures. Emerson's collection of great men ends with his discussion of Goethe. Margaret Fuller responded quite positively to Goethe's belief in the power of one individual, as he is the "great apostle of individual culture."[16] Fuller juxtaposes Fourier's group mentality with Goethe's individualistic belief system: Fourier believed that "better institutions . . . will make better men," whereas "Goethe expressed, in every way, the other side. If one man could present better forms, the rest could not use them till ripe for them" (*WNC* 74). This latter view that she attributes to Goethe, "As the man, so the institution" (*WNC* 74), accords with Fuller's idea that politics would not change woman's condition, but that personal enlightenment would. And she does look ahead to the strong, heroic mother figure (Virgin Mary archetype) as a redemptive figure for womankind, at the end of her treatise *Woman in the Nineteenth Century,* just as Goethe had looked toward "the Mothers" in *Faust,* part 2, as agents of change.

In some ways, Fuller praises Goethe's Faust for all the wrong reasons; eager to show how Faust is edified, indeed redeemed, by women, she denies his exploitation of woman: she makes it appear as if woman were here to serve or to teach man, to show him his higher self. That was certainly the role of American women at the time Fuller was writing: to act as the selfless helpmeet in the culture of domesticity. However, on another level, Fuller is able to transcend the restrictions of male history-making. She tries to spiritualize what Goethe had intellectualized: she asserts that "Goethe was not what is called a spiritual writer," and in another place she accuses Goethe of being aristocratic and not caring about the people. Similarly, Fuller accuses Faust of an overdeveloped intellect, condemning him for his self-serving "modern necromancy," which she sees as a poor substitute for spirituality. In the end, Fuller envisions the perfect specimen of humankind as a combination of female and male traits. After she states that "Goethe always represents the highest principle in the feminine form. Woman is the Minerva, man the Mars," Fuller calls for a reconciliation of male and female, intellect and emotion ("There is no wholly masculine man, nor purely feminine woman"), but curiously here she sees Goethe privileging the wise female over the traditionally warriorlike male. She also realizes, like Goethe, that woman might be the source of this social progress, as she evokes Goethe's notion of the strong woman: "In this country is venerated, wherever seen, the character which Goethe spoke of as an Ideal: 'The excellent woman is she, who, if the husband dies, can be a father to the children.'"[17] She likens the wise Minerva to the Gretchen protagonist in *Faust*. In her essay on Goethe for *The Dial* (extracts of which she includes in WNC), she celebrates Gretchen's redemptive power (for man) without seeming to be aware of the repercussions for woman in her role as man's helpmeet: "As in the Faust, the purity of Gretchen resisting the demon always . . . is announced to have saved her soul to heaven; and in the second part, she appears, not only redeemed herself, but by her innocence and forgiving tenderness hallowed to redeem the being who had injured her."[18] Fuller explains that Margaret is related to the Great Mother figure, the savior figure who does appear in various guises in her work, especially in the conclusion of *Woman in the Nineteenth Century,* with Fuller's prototype of the Virgin Mary.

In her various writings on Goethe, Fuller also writes about the redemptive power of woman:

> In *Faust* we see the redeeming power, which, at present upholds woman, while waiting for a better day, in Margaret. The lovely little girl, pure in instinct, ignorant in mind, is misled and profaned by man abusing her confidence. To the Mater *Dolorosa* she appeals for aid. It is given to the soul, if not against outward sorrow; and the maiden, enlightened by her sufferings, refusing to receive temporal salvation by the aid of an evil power, obtains the eternal in its stead.
>
> In the second part, the intellectual man, after all his manifold strivings, owes to the interposition of her whom he had betrayed, *his* salvation. She intercedes, this time, herself a glorified spirit, with the Mater *Gloriosa*. (WNC 74–75)

Immediately before this section, Fuller gives credit to Goethe for being so favorably influenced by women in his life (his mother, his sister, his benefactresses, his female sources of inspiration): so that "from his poetic soul, grew up forms new and more admirable than life has yet produced, for whom his clear eye marked our paths for the future" (*WNC* 74). Fuller also goes into a description of many of Goethe's female characters in order to show his noble intention. And she praises Goethe for the type of androgyny espoused by characters such as his Mignon and Theresa, who "wear male attire when they like, and it is graceful for them to do so" (*WNC* 77). Fuller also remarks on the power of the two strongest women in Goethe's *Wilhelm Meister* (one of Emerson's and Fuller's favorite novels) to effect change: "In the Macaria, bound with the heavenly bodies in fixed revolutions, the centre of all relations, herself unrelated, he expresses the Minerva side of feminine nature. . . . Mignon is the electrical, inspired, lyrical nature" (*WNC* 76). She does, in fact, translate Goethe's Macaria into her Minerva and Mignon into the feminine Muse as prototypes for women to follow. In fact, she lauds Goethe for creating women so strong and individualistic that they can become equals to husbands: "In all these expressions of Woman, the aim of Goethe is satisfactory to me. He aims at a pure self-subsistence, and a free development of any powers with which they may be gifted by nature as much for them as for men. They are units, addressed as souls. Accordingly, the meeting between Man and Woman, as represented by him, is equal and noble" (*WNC* 76). Later, Fuller will employ this idea about marriage when she calls for "units before union."

In her essay "The Great Lawsuit" (the forerunner to *Woman in the Nineteenth Century*), Fuller feigns an apology that she has overused Goethe: "I tire every one with my Goethean illustrations," but then she corrects herself and says she is driven to do so, and she transforms Goethe into her ideal man: "Goethe, the great mind which gave itself absolutely to the leadings of truth, and let rise through him the waves which are still advancing through the century, was its intellectual prophet."[19] She maintains that she promotes Goethe as a thinker because of his understanding of "the prospects and wants of women." Unfortunately, in making Goethe her hero, at least early in her career, she turns a blind eye to his real-life escapades with women and does not write about the many hearts he broke along the way while learning from women; in that way fiction imitated life for Goethe in *Faust* in the use/abuse of Margarete, who was ultimately his savior. And even though Fuller had favorite female authors, Goethe remains one of her favorite authors, ironically promoting a feminist cause. According to Julia Ward Howe, a devotee of Fuller's and a follower of certain transcendentalist thinking, Fuller "mentions among the women whom she considered helpers and favorers of the new womanhood, Miss Edgeworth, Mrs. Jameson, and our own Miss Sedgwick. Among the writers of the other sex, whose theories point to the same end, she speaks of Swedenborg, Fourier, and Goethe."[20] Of the male authors, Howe feels that Goethe left the strongest impression on Fuller: "The world-wise Goethe everywhere recognizes the presence and significance of the feminine principle; and, after treating with tenderness and reverence its frailest as well as its finest impersonations, lays the seal of all attraction in the lap of the 'eternal womanly.'"[21]

Emerson was at times jealous of Fuller's passion for Goethe, or he begrudged her the admiration she felt for Goethe. In fact, he was somewhat ambivalent about Goethe's genius: he collected portraits and statues of Goethe, but a household cat was also named "Goethe."[22] In his 1840 essay for *The Dial*, "Thoughts on Modern Literature," Emerson critiques Goethe, ironically, for his egotism and coldness (which Fuller accused Emerson of having): "No man was permitted to call Goethe brother. He hid himself, and worked always to astonish, which is an egotism."[23] His feelings toward Fuller are also marked by such ambivalence, sometimes in conjunction with her admiration for the poet. Anecdotes about Fuller initiating discussion at her Conversations present her as an impassioned, dramatic speaker; though not always positive, these reports are emotionally charged. Fuller as an orator had a type of magnetic aura that Emerson called "Mother power," a quality that Fuller would later use to her advantage in her discussion of the empowered woman.[24] Emerson complains of her arrogant tone, but behind the venom, we feel that he is envious; shortly after attacking her speaking ability, Emerson maligns her choice of authors, almost jealous that she had taken Goethe as her mentor: his "mind had been her teacher, and, of course, the place was filled, nor was there room for any other. She had that symptom which appears to all the students of Goethe—an ill-dissembled contempt of all criticism on him which they hear from others, as if it were totally irrelevant."[25]

Though Emerson called her conversation "the most entertaining" in America, paying her the dubious compliment that "her powers of speech throw her writing into the shade" (*JMN* 8:369), he was petrified by the intimacy of her letters. For all his babbling about friendship (the meditations in his letters to Margaret served as a springboard to his essay "Friendship" in 1842), Emerson was a rather cold and distant man; no one, not even his wife Lidian, could get close to him.[26] Early on in Emerson's relationship with Fuller, he admits that he wants to avoid the circles of conversation; he is terrified by her offering of friendship: "Sarah Margaret Fuller writes me that she waits for the Lectures seeing well after much intercourse that the best of me is there. She says very truly; and I thought it a good remark which somebody repeated here from S.S. [Samuel Staple] that I 'always seemed to be on stilts.' It is even so. Most of the persons whom I see in my own house I see across a gulf. I cannot go to them nor can they come to me. Nothing can exceed the frigidity and labor of my speech with such" (*JMN*

7:301). Emerson seems to be proud of his inability to give or to share in the conversational game of friendship. What happened to the potentially liberating correspondence, the written form of conversation, that Fuller offered him? Why did he back off from what Thomas Wentworth Higginson saw as an exhilarating correspondence: "Franker and truer letters never went from woman to man"?[27]

After Fuller's death, Emerson tries to make sense of his earlier relationship with her and attempts to describe the rationale behind his withdrawal from her: "I believe I fancied her too much interested in personal history. . . . She studied my tastes, piqued and amused me, challenged frankness by frankness, and did not conceal the good opinion of me she brought with her, nor her wish to please. She was curious to know my opinions and experiences. Of course, it was impossible long to hold out against such urgent assault."[28] The turning point in their relationship had come when Fuller recognized that the best and most private part could be found in his essays but not in his letters to her. In a most scathing letter of September 29, 1840, Fuller talks about how he has disappointed her by not offering her the clue to the "labyrinth" of her being: "How often have I left you despairing and forlorn. How often have I said, this light will never understand my fire; this clear eye will never discern the law by which I am filling my circle."[29] Emerson answers this attack on his lack of sensitivity with a rather stuffy apology, accusing her of luring him into her circles: "I ought never to have suffered you to lead me into any conversation or writing on our relation, a topic from which with all persons my Genius ever sternly warns me away" (*L* 2:352). He reproaches her for being less than reasonable, for removing the firm "foundation of everlasting friendship," the "solid good" of what he perceived as their friendship. Again, he remains obtuse while Fuller invites him to partake of her intuitive language, to understand her "crying for the moon": he dismisses her with the retort, "There is a difference in our constitution. We use a different rhetoric. It seems as if we had been born and bred in different nations. You say you understand me wholly. You cannot communicate yourself to me. I hear the words sometimes but remain a stranger to your state of mind" (*L* 2:353).[30] It would not be surprising if Margaret's translation of Eckermann's *Conversations with Goethe* was less anguishing than her actual conversations with Emerson, and that her translation of a true testament of friendship, *Die Günderode* (1842), written shortly after Emerson's stoical essay on "Friendship," would prove more liberating.

It is no wonder, either, that Fuller feels more in touch with Emerson in his library, when he is out for the day, than with Emerson in person: "I like to be in the library when you are out of it. It seems a sacred place. I came here to find a book, that I might feel more life . . . but there is so much soul here [in the library] that I don't need a book. When I come to yourself, I cannot receive you, and you cannot give yourself; it does not profit" (*L* 2:234). Emerson sees friendship in the abstract, like books in the library: "I do then with my friends as I do with my books. I would have them where I can find them, but I seldom use them. We must have society on our own terms, and admit or exclude it on the slightest cause" (*CW* 1:126). For Fuller, reciprocity was necessary; according to J. F. Clarke, in the construction of Fuller in her *Memoirs,* "Margaret's constancy in friendship caused her to demand it in others, and thus she was sometimes exacting." But the picture of Margaret fabricated by the male cohort of memoirists also denies her the power of the Sage of Concord: "Those who know Margaret only by her published writings know her least; her notes and letters contain more of her mind; but it was only in conversation that she was perfectly free and at home."[31]

Various critics have noted Emerson's lack of warmth toward Fuller and have gone so far as to suggest that, for her, Goethe was the real source of inspiration. In an 1833 letter to James F. Clarke (another male letter correspondent who did not understand her), Fuller declares an intense affinity with Goethe: "We cry, 'help, help,' and there is no help—in man at least. How often have I thought, if I could see Goethe, and tell him my state of mind, he would support and guide me! He would be able to understand me. . . . He would have wished to see [in] me what Nature intended."[32] Emerson would never understand Fuller's deep connection to Goethe, which made her feel compelled to justify her position on Goethe in a letter to Emerson: "I do not consider him from that point of view you wished me to take. I do not go to him as a guide or friend but as a great thinker, who makes me think, a wonderful artist who gratifies my tastes."[33] We do not have Emerson's letter explaining the "point of view" he took,[34] but we do know that Fuller defended Goethe's "religion or morality" and had recently sent him a copy of her translation of Goethe's "Eins und Alles," which most certainly affected Emerson's thinking in his own poem "Each and All."

Frederick Augustus Braun, in his study of Fuller and Goethe, declares that because Emerson could not fathom her emotional depths, "Emerson was never her 'spiritual father,' and that he never exercised on her inner life anything like an overpowering influence." Braun goes on to explain: "The fundamental thought in her doctrine was, as in that of Goethe, the harmonious development of the *whole* being, the heart as well as the mind."[35] But I feel that Fuller ultimately had a softening effect on Emerson, much like the power of Minerva, or that of the redemptive Gretchen, or the influence of the Mothers in *Faust II.* And maybe Emerson, like Faust, was edified after the death of his Gretchen. Writing in his journal shortly after Fuller's death, Emerson likens the greatness of her mind to the greatness of her heart, and he even compares Fuller to Goethe—not directly but by appealing to the words of their friend Elizabeth Hoar: "'Her heart, which few knew, was as great as her mind, which all knew'—what Jung Stilling [a friend of Goethe's] said of Goethe, E.H. says of Margaret; and, that she was the largest woman; & not a woman who wished to be a man."[36]

Emerson gave his famous speech "Woman" in 1855, five years after Fuller's death, and I can sense her ghost in his words. His declaration that women are of the same substance as men resounds with Fuller's earlier work in *Woman in the Nineteenth Century,* where she referred to Goethe as showing woman's particular power. Emerson, though, refers to Plato, not Goethe, in his lecture: "Plato said, Women are the same as men in faculty, only less in degree. But the general voice of mankind has agreed that they have their own strength; that women are strong by sentiment; that the same mental height which their husbands attain by toil, they attain by sympathy with their husbands. Man is the will, and Woman the sentiment" ("Address at Woman's Rights Convention" *LL* 2:19). This echoes Goethe's vision of womanhood that informed Fuller's discussion, but it is unfortunate he uses Plato instead of Goethe in making his case. Emerson does appeal to woman's special genius in her oracular or spiritual power, which he sees as the touchstone of civilization: "Her gifts make woman the refiner and civilizer of her mate. Civilization is her work (*LL* 2:17)." This section of "Woman" resounds with Fuller's similar meditations on women's special power: "The spiritual tendency is toward the elevation of woman, but the intellectual, by itself, is not so. Plato sometimes seems penetrated by that high idea of love which considers man and woman as the twofold expression of one thought. But then again Plato, the man of intellect, treats woman in the republic as property, and in the 'Timæus' says that man, if he misuse the privileges of one life, shall be degraded into the form of a woman" (*WNC* 60). One notes here that Fuller offers a corrective that Emerson forgets—that Plato had his own gender-biased views of women. And so it is unfortunate that Emerson cannot evoke the name of Goethe in his famous lecture for women's emancipation. One of Alcott's early biographers, Ednah Cheney, in her lecture "Das Ewig Weibliche," delivered at the Concord School of Philosophy, appealed to Goethe's understanding of woman: "How earnestly he sought to understand Woman's life from her own stand-point."[37] Cheney feels that Goethe really understood woman's soul and that "he always recognized the value of Woman's own life in relation with, but not simply as supplementary to, that of man."[38] It is perhaps to Fuller's credit that Emerson softens his view of Goethe. In Emerson's 1840 essay "Thoughts on Modern Literature," for *The Dial*, Emerson sees Goethe as limited "as the poet of the Actual, not of the Ideal." And he laments further, "Yes, O Goethe! but the ideal is truer than the actual."[39] However, by 1850, in his essay "Goethe; or, the Writer," the final essay of *Representative Men,* Emerson gives Goethe a backhanded compliment: "What distinguishes Goethe for French and English readers is a property which he shares with his nation,—a habitual reference to interior truth."[40] It is a quality, he says, that Americans could not appreciate, and he ultimately attacks Goethe and Napoleon for being realists.[41] I would argue that Goethe's sense of "interior truth" is the same quality that Fuller shared and led to her progressive vision of activism.

Fuller, ever aware of and participating in contemporary reform movements, foresaw a better day when the androgynous enlightened person, like the feminized (softened) Faust of part 2, who strove for the eternal feminine, would be able to move history positively and to liberate humanity from the burden of conventional thought. Ultimately, though part of the male Romantic movement,[42] Fuller, nonetheless, constructs the feminized version of a man's Faust: she feels that Mephistopheles and Faust can be reconciled, as she celebrates the redemptive power of woman (as helpmeet to men) and the progressive vision of man's perfectibility through androgyny. Such androgynous gender roles were further explored, later, by Alcott.

Louisa May Alcott, writing several decades after Fuller, no longer believes in the possibility of having one man or woman redeem the world; she definitely did not clamor for a new Virginia who would be the savior of American women in Fuller's conclusion to *Woman in the Nineteenth Century.* Nor does she espouse woman's renunciation (Gretchen's) as an exemplary way for her women to behave. Indeed, as a realist writer, she sees history moving men, so that all humanity is trapped, men and women alike. She, too, was involved in a type of Goethe adoration, as noted already. At the impressionable age of fifteen, Alcott was given by Emerson a set of Goethe's works and later proclaimed that they have "been my delight ever since." In 1877, Alcott published one of her darkest (and not well-received) novels, *A Modern Mephistopheles,* which caught the spirit of her age. So dark it was that the anonymously published work was not readily associated with Alcott. Edna Cheney, the early biographer of Alcott, notes that from Goethe's Romantic text, Alcott has made a commonplace, too realistic tale: "The circumstances are in a romantic setting, but still they are prosaic; and tragedy is only endurable when taken up into the region of the ideal, where the thought of the universal rounds out all traits of the individual. In Goethe's *Faust,* Margaret is the sweetest and simplest of maidens; but in her is the life of all wronged and suffering womanhood" (*LLJ* 293). I would agree that Alcott's new Margaret (in the shape of Gladys) is also representative of "all wronged and suffering womanhood," but she is far removed from the ideal that Goethe captures in the second part of *Faust,* where Gretchen is nearly beatified. Cheney might have it right when she says that Alcott's realism gets in the way of her portrayal of Goethe's Margarete, a realism far removed from her children's fiction: "The realism which is delightful in the pictures of little women and merry boys is painful when connected with passions so morbid and lives so far removed from joy and sanity" (*LLJ* 293). Alcott later would wonder what "dear old Concord" and especially Emerson would have thought about her forays into the dark tales of passion.[43]

Clearly, Alcott was influenced by Goethe in her rewriting of the Faust conflict, and she says as much in a journal entry: that her final novella, *A Modern Mephistopheles,* had been simmering in her brain ever since she had reread *Faust* the previous year (1874). Goethe's strong influence is also apparent in the epigraph, which reads, "The Indescribable, / Here it is done: / The Woman-Soul leadeth us / Upward and on!" Again, we see the significance of a woman's ability to transform the men around her through her spiritual and maternal qualities. In fact, if the novel *Work,* published in 1873, four years prior to this later one, shows the positive effect of work on a woman's growth, *A Modern Mephistopheles* shows the deleterious nature of work on both genders, and I am wondering if Emerson's warning about "Fame" in the poem of the same name (1824) motivated Alcott to write *A Modern Mephistopheles:*

> He pays too high a price
> For knowledge and for fame
> Who sells his sinews to be wise,
> His teeth and bones to buy a name,
> And crawls through life a paralytic
> To earn the praise of bard and critic. (*CW* 9:622)

This poem epitomizes the Faustian striver of Goethe's *Faust,* part 1 (1808), and though it is from his juvenilia, Emerson will clearly show the folly of putting too much of oneself into a soulless job in his essay "The Transcendentalist." Alcott shows how the work-world conspires to destroy man's/woman's souls, and that we are all entangled in this web. In her previous novel, *Work,* Alcott goes back to an idea of Carlyle's, more in touch with the New England background that informed the Puritan work ethic, as she takes her introductory epigraph from Carlyle: "An endless significance lies in work; in idleness alone is there perpetual despair." To do her mother justice, a mother who worked herself into illness because of the dreamer transcendentalist father, she dedicates *Work* to her: "My Mother, whose life has been a long labor of love, this book is gratefully inscribed by her daughter." It may be possible that she is taking transcendentalist men like her father,

Bronson, and her father's best friend, Emerson, to task for their overreliance on the working woman behind the scenes. In any case, if we look at the Emerson-Thoreau dynamics in *A Modern Mephistopheles,* as we did above in *Moods,* the Mephistopheles character who is the mentor to Faust sounds somewhat like a diabolically charged Emerson, with Faust being Thoreau, and the disappointment Emerson felt him to be. In his eulogy of Thoreau, he expresses that disappointment: "he seemed born for great enterprise and for command; and I so much regret the loss of his rare powers of action, that I cannot help counting it a fault in him that he had no ambition" (CW 10:429).

In this later novel, *A Modern Mephistopheles,* Alcott no longer believes that the strong individual of Goethe's Romantic philosophy could effect social change. (She reverts to Carlyle's and Fourier's idea that men are only as good as their institutions, and not Goethe's idea that institutions are the only as good as the individual man.) Thus, though there is sympathy for Gladys, the new version of Margaret, who dies after giving birth to a child, there is also sympathy for the two men (stuck in stereotypical gender roles) who unwittingly love and destroy her. Jasper Helwyze, the modern Mephistopheles, turns into a demon when the woman he loves, Olivia, shuns him and abandons him. Olivia, the modern equivalent of the pimplike Martha in *Faust,* initially also forsakes the charge of her surrogate daughter, Gladys/Gretchen—but then learns the meaning of real sisterhood/motherhood in opposing Helwyze's plans—and is thus redeemed. Helwyze vents his anger on a poor, aspiring, young writer, Felix Canaris, who, though he likes to write, has more ambition than talent. He sells his soul to Helwyze, who acts as his patron and finally even writes his books—which become best-sellers. In his boredom and bitterness, Helwyze orchestrates a plan: Canaris, who is indebted to him for his public acclaim, must seduce the young, innocent Gladys and marry her. This marriage, made, or at least, contracted, in hell, turns out to be the demise of all the characters. No one seems master of himself: the girl, who has known poverty all her life and who has been tyrannized by her father early on, is obsessed with work (so as to "resist temptation," like a good descendant of the Puritans), and she tries to inculcate Canaris with a Protestant work ethic by inspiring him to write; Helwyze cannot reconcile himself with work; Olivia becomes the nurse of a dying and perverse Helwyze; and Canaris tries to avoid work, even though the lesson he learns from his dying wife is that he must work: his declaration of independence from Helwyze is that he will find "any honest work" he can. Finally, Helwyze, Mephistopheles's counterpart and the usurper of power, after falling in love with Gladys, the woman he attempted to destroy, makes a gloomy confession, "So much for playing Providence! . . . Goethe could make Satan as he liked; but Fate was stronger than I, and so comes ignominious failure. Margaret dies, and Faust suffers, but Mephistopheles cannot go with him on his new wanderings."[44] Thus, the devil (Helwyze) is tortured by knowing he will not be reconciled with Gladys in heaven, but the Faust figure (Canaris) feels that she has proven to be his redemption on earth and they will be reunited in heaven. In this world of unstable relationships, we find helpless creatures driven by their economic situations into an abyss of self; there are no easy resolutions or reconciliations—only an intrusive work world and a sense of inadequacy that comes from unfulfilling labor. Man, woman, and even the modern Mephistopheles are defeated by the diabolical economy. Yet, perversely, even if there is no spiritual reconciliation between male and female, as Fuller envisaged, there is a common enemy against which all can conspire, and that is the enervating and debilitating nature of modern work, which severs any link between the material and the spiritual. Gladys does become the apotheosis of Fuller's Madonna here, the woman who will teach the men how to live with a higher purpose, though she dies shortly after her newborn son dies. In a negative and subtle way, Alcott suggests a reconciliation between Faust, Margaret, *and* Mephistopheles. But both Fuller and Alcott also question the idea of authorial originality and of social change in their reworking of the Faust myth. And they are aware of authorial permeations and permutations. Alcott's version of the Faust myth offers "a significant critique of patriarchal (dis)order and art: it is a disturbing allegory of the author's attempt to dispel the influence of patriarchy and to substitute for it a matriarchal creativity that could harmonize the illicit and the legitimate, the private inclination and the public good."[45]

I think it telling that in an 1884 periodical essay by one "S. R.," titled "A Legend of Good Women," the writer gives a historical account of famous American women and then ends her essay with a cast of female characters who were influenced by the great Emerson and who believed in his intellectual powers. Among those she mentions are the Peabody Sisters, Elizabeth Hoar, Sarah Clarke, and Sarah Bradford (later, wife of Samuel Ripley). Fuller, she quotes, is known to have praised Emerson as her principal benefactor: "his influence has been more beneficial to me than that of any other American, and . . . from him I first learned what is meant by the inward life." The essay ends, though, by asserting that the women in Emerson's life actually fostered his own development. Citing from Goethe's last scene glorifying woman in *Faust,* the author juxtaposes Emerson with Goethe: "Doubtless, if the beloved sage of Concord has spoken in the same spirit [as these adoring women], we would surely see that while he thus helped onward the life of the spirit for these disciples, he also found with Goethe: 'Das Ewig-Weibliche / Zieht uns hinan' [The eternal feminine leads us on]." And appropriately, the 1884 critic concludes, "Upward and onward is the influence of Good Women," thereby forging a place for the women who, one hundred years later, would become part of the American Renaissance canon, and allowing us to see male and female writers in conversation with each other: collaborators, not rivals.[46] If Fuller was looking ahead to a life where women could speak out true feelings in the marketplace, Alcott certainly was able to be more honest with her emotions, even if veiled under the guise of gothic thrillers. But perhaps most heartening was Emerson's final summation of Fuller; many years after her death, he would reminisce about her warmly, acknowledging that she was the centripetal force in the Concord movement, the heart of the Concord circle of sages: "Margaret with her radiant genius and fiery heart was perhaps the real center that drew so many and so various individuals to a seeming union" (*JMN* 16:22). And with that I hear the ghost of Goethe's Margarete being resurrected and saving another thinking man's soul.

Notes

1. Helen Druxes, in her study of the Faust myth, considers gender issues as part of the problematics underlying Goethe's rewriting of the story and its impact on nineteenth-century readers: "That Goethe found the feminine principle necessary to the successful recuperation of the Faustian quest indicates a dawning awareness of the *male* hero as problematic." See Helen Druxes, *The Feminization of Dr. Faustus* (University Park: Pennsylvania State University Press, 1993), 2.

2. Actually, Fuller performed a great service to the transcendentalist community by introducing Goethe to them through her translation of Eckermann's *Conversations with Goethe* (1839). Though Goethe was not initially favorably received by the lagging Puritanical mindset of New England, Thomas Carlyle's positive reviews of Goethe's *Faust* and especially of *Wilhelm Meister* and his translation of the latter made the portrait of Goethe more amenable to Emerson. Though my focus is on Emerson's female audience here, one can see that the exchange between Emerson and Carlyle also made Emerson reconsider his previously negative assessment of Goethe. Fuller's numerous translations included Goethe's *Tasso*. After Emerson read Fuller's version of Eckermann's *Goethe*, he was much reconciled and thanked her: "The translating of this book seems to be a beneficent action for which America will long thank you. The book might be called—Short way to Goethe's character—so effectually does it scatter all the popular nonsense about him, & show the breadth of common sense which he had in common with every majestic poet, & which enabled him to be the interpreter between the real & the apparent worlds" (June 7, 1839; *L* 201–2).

Although Emerson did not meet Goethe in person, his older brother William, studying for the ministry but without much conviction, had met Goethe in Weimar. Supposedly, Goethe advised him that he could still have doubt and be a minister—to separate the private from the public man, even if he had little faith in what he was preaching. Apparently, William had a type of crisis, and when he returned to America, he relinquished his dreams of being a minister, and moved to New York, where he became a lawyer. See Evelyn Barish, *Emerson: The Roots of Prophecy* (Princeton, NJ: Princeton University Press, 1989), 161–63.

Before Fuller persuaded him otherwise, Emerson actually held the earlier image of Goethe largely in contempt: "The Goethe of the 'vicious egoism' and 'velvet life,' the man-of-the-world and the courtier, the aristocrat, and above all, Goethe the lover" (Frederick B. Wahr, *Emerson and Goethe* [Ann Arbor, MI: George Wahr, 1915], 94). In an early journal passage, Emerson has a very negative impression of Goethe after reading *Wilhelm Meister*: "all-sided, gifted, indefatigable student as he is," he seemed only "to be only another monad . . . bestirring himself immensely to hide his nothingness, spinning his surface directly before the eye to conceal the universe of his ignorance (*JMN* 4:298). In one of his later essays, Emerson seems to embrace the idea that Goethe is the representative artist, a type of Over-soul, who draws from the world around him, as he quotes from Goethe, "What would remain to me if this art of appropriation were derogatory to genius? Every one of my writings has been furnished to me by a thousand different persons, a thousand things: wise and foolish have brought me, without suspecting it, the offering of their thoughts, faculties and experience. My work is an aggregation of beings taken from the *whole* of Nature; it bears the name of Goethe." Ralph Waldo Emerson, "Quotation and Originality," in *The Complete Works of Ralph Waldo Emerson*, ed. Edward Waldo Emerson, Centenary ed., 12 vols. (Boston: Houghton Mifflin, 1903–4), 8:200.

3. Ralph Waldo Emerson, "Goethe; or, the Writer," in *Representative Men* (1850), in *The Collected Works of Ralph Waldo Emerson,* ed. Joseph Slater et al. (Cambridge, MA: Harvard University Press, 1987), 4:156.

4. Margaret Fuller, translator's preface to Johann Peter Eckermann's *Conversations with Goethe in the Last Year of His Life* (Boston: J. Munroe, 1839), xxi. Compare also Alcott's ultimate knowledge about Emerson's coldness. She writes to her father, after reading Emerson's memoirs (published after Emerson's death), that she is disappointed: "he did not keep his word and tell all the long & strong friendship between himself & you. He said he would, but he left it undone, & I am *very* sorry, for he understood you best of all men . . ." (October 13, 1887). See *The Selected Letters of Louisa May Alcott*, ed. Joel Myerson et al. (Boston: Little, Brown, 1987), 321.

5. Margaret Fuller, "Goethe," *The Dial* 2, no. 1 (July 1841): 30. Subsequent references to this work will be cited parenthetically in the text by page number.

6. Wahr, *Emerson and Goethe*, 97.

7. Margaret Fuller, "Emerson's Essays," in *Margaret Fuller, Critic: Writings from the New-York Tribune, 1844–1846*, ed. Judith Mattson Bean and Joel Myerson (New York: Columbia University Press, 2000), 5.

8. Louis May Alcott, *Louisa May Alcott: Her Life, Letters, and Journals*, ed. Ednah D. Cheney (Boston: Roberts Brothers, 1889), 398. Hereafter cited parenthetically as *LLJ*.

9. Sarah Elbert, introduction to *Moods*, by Louis May Alcott (New Brunswick, NJ: Rutgers University Press, 1999), xxx.

10. Ibid., xi.

11. Larry Reynolds would agree with Sarah Elbert's designation of the characters, as he believes that Moor is the "idealized portrait of Emerson" (Larry J. Reynolds, *Righteous Violence: Revolution, Slavery, and the American Renaissance* [Athens: University of Georgia Press, 2011], 135). Reynolds feels that the character of Moor in the novel "resembles the public Emerson of the 1840s," but "it does not capture the bellicose [more political] Emerson of the late 1850s" (135–36). To emphasize the difference between Moor and Warwick, "Alcott obviously drew upon an earlier version of her 'master,' perhaps adding a portion of her father's mildness as well" (136). I personally do not see anything terribly poetic about Emerson is this context. Reynolds believes that Warwick "is a heightened version of Thoreau as he appeared in the wake of John Brown's raid" (136).

12. Louisa May Alcott, *The Journals of Louisa May Alcott*, ed. Joel Myerson and Daniel Shealy (Boston: Little, Brown, 1989), 99.

13. Bruce G. Charlton, "Editorial Preface to the English Translation of *Goethe's Correspondence with a Child*, by Bettina von Arnim (1837)," http://hedweb.com/bgcharlton.

14. See Margaret Fuller, trans., *Günderode*, by Bettina von Arnim (Boston: E. P. Peabody, 1842).

15. Christina Zwarg, *Feminist Conversations: Fuller, Emerson, and the Play of Reading* (Ithaca, NY: Cornell University Press, 1995), 85, 86.

16. Margaret Fuller, *Woman in the Nineteenth Century*, ed. Larry J. Reynolds (New York: Norton, 1998), 73. Hereafter cited parenthetically as *WNC*.

17. Margaret Fuller, "The Great Lawsuit: Man *versus* Men. Woman *versus* Women," *The Dial* 3 (July 1843): 40.

18. Fuller, "Goethe," 26. Fuller would later change her view about the balancing of the sexes in her own *Woman in the Nineteenth Century*, where the equation is shifted to "Man partakes of the feminine in the Apollo, woman of the Masculine as Minerva." Thus, she is able to feminize the concept of the higher-level male, as she envisions the perfect specimen of mankind to partake equally of male and female traits. Earlier she had talked about woman embodying the Muse and the Minerva, but she trades off the passive female side (Muse, inspiration for males) for the strong-thinking Minerva.

19. Fuller, "The Great Lawsuit," 46.

20. Julia Ward Howe, *Margaret Fuller (Marchesa Ossoli)* (Boston: Roberts Brothers, 1883), 154.

21. Ibid.

22. Wahr, *Emerson and Goethe*, 79.

23. Ralph Waldo Emerson, "Thoughts on Modern Literature," *The Dial* 2 (October 1840): 153.

24. Meg McGavran Murray, *Margaret Fuller: Wandering Pilgrim* (Athens: University of Georgia Press, 2008), 119.

25. Ralph Waldo Emerson, "Books," in Ralph Waldo Emerson, William H. Channing, and James F. Clarke, eds., *Memoirs of Margaret Fuller Ossoli* (1852; rpt., New York: Burt Franklin, 1972), 1:243.

26. Joel Porte, ed., *Emerson in His Journals* (Cambridge, MA: Harvard University Press, 1982), 214.

27. Thomas Wentworth Higginson, *Margaret Fuller Ossoli* (Boston: Houghton Mifflin, 1884), 67.

28. Emerson et al., *Memoirs of Margaret Fuller Ossoli*, 202–3.

29. Margaret Fuller, *The Letters of Margaret Fuller*, 6 vols., ed. Robert N. Hudspeth (Ithaca, NY: Cornell University Press, 1983–94), 2:159.

30. Emerson was so terrified of the intimacy Fuller offered him that even in his private obituary to her, about "losing his audience," he is paranoid about the secrets she might have gathered in her correspondence: "When I heard that a trunk of her correspondence had been found & opened, I felt what a panic would strike all her friends, for it was as if a clever reporter had gone underneath a confessional & agreed to report all that transpired there" (*JMN* 11:258). He seemed troubled by her power to "draw out of people their last secret" (*JMN* 11:256).

31. J. F. Clarke, "Friendship," in Emerson et al., *Memoirs of Margaret Fuller Ossoli*, 1:78.

32. Fuller, *Letters*, 1:182.

33. Fuller, *Letters*, 1:288.

34. Fuller, *Letters*, 1:182n2.

35. Frederick Augustus Braun, *Margaret Fuller and Goethe* (New York: Henry Holt, 1910), 143.

36. Joel Porte, ed., *Emerson in His Journals* (Cambridge, MA: Harvard University Press, 1982), 414 (July–August 1850).

37. E. D. Cheney, "Das Ewig-Weibliche," in *The Life and Genius of Goethe: Lectures at the Concord School of Philosophy*, ed. F. B. Sanborn (Boston: Ticknor and Co., 1886), 225.

38. Ibid., 224, 225.

39. Emerson, "Thoughts on Modern Literature" 156, 155.

40. Emerson, "Goethe, or the Writer," 4:161.

41. In criticism of Emerson/Goethe, there is a tendency to avoid the woman question; see, for example, the otherwise comprehensive study by Gustaaf Van Cromphout, *Emerson's Modernity and the Example of Goethe* (Columbia: University of Missouri Press, 1990). Although Joseph C. Schöpp has written about Fuller's connection to Goethe, he focuses on Goethe's idea of the "daimon" or creative genius and only takes up "Goethe's and Fuller's notion of woman as a creative force" on the last few pages of his essay. Schöpp's essay is "Playing the Eclectic: Margaret Fuller's Creative Appropriation of Goethe," in *Margaret Fuller: Transatlantic Crossings in a Revolutionary Age*. Charles Capper and Cristina Giorcelli, ed. (Madison: University of Wisconsin Press, 2007), 38.

42. Frederick Augustus Braun makes the case that Fuller was more like Goethe than like the other male transcendentalists, insisting that Goethe was her intellectual master and parent. See Braun, *Margaret Fuller and Goethe*, 146.

43. Elbert, introduction to *Moods*, xxx.

44. Louisa May Alcott, *A Modern Mephistopheles* (1877; rpt., New York: Bantam, 1995), 203, 205.

45. Rena Sanderson, "*A Modern Mephistopheles*: Louisa May Alcott's Exorcism of Patriarchy," *American Transcendental Quarterly* 5 (1991): 41–55.

46. S. R., "A Legend of Good Women," *Friends' Intelligencer,* February 9, 1884, 40, 52.

[4]

LEN GOUGEON

EMERSON, GREAT BRITAIN, AND THE INTERNATIONAL STRUGGLE FOR THE RIGHTS OF THE WORKINGMAN

LIKE OTHER TRANSCENDENTALISTS, Ralph Waldo Emerson had a deep respect for the dignity of labor.[1] In 1837, he delivered his famous address "The American Scholar" to the graduating class at Harvard, wherein he offered what some consider to be a proto-Marxian critique of the alienation felt by American workers.[2] Whether Marxian in nature or not, Emerson's belief in the importance of the American laborer permeates his works. As one critic recently observed, "from early to late," Emerson's writings offer "a sustained hymn in praise of labor."[3] His outspoken opposition to slavery was driven, in part, by this commitment to the dignity of free labor. His visit to revolutionary Europe in 1847–48 would open his eyes to the global dimensions of the problem. The result was an enduring allegiance to the international cause of the workingman.

Emerson believed that the alienation of the American laborer derived from the fact that both laborers and employers failed to acknowledge and embrace the divinity that abides in every person. This divine force, which Emerson sometimes called the "Over-soul," imparts dignity to every individual regardless of class, caste, or race. In the current state of society, this divinity has been suppressed. The result is the objectification and alienation of labor and social fragmentation. Thus, in "The American Scholar" Emerson observes, "Man is metamorphosed into a thing, into many things. The planter . . . is seldom cheered by any idea of the true dignity of his ministry. . . . The Tradesman scarcely ever gives an ideal worth to his work. . . . The priest becomes a form; the attorney, a statute-book; the mechanic a machine; the sailor, a rope of a ship" (CW 1:53). Emerson's answer to this alienation is to assert "the doctrine that man is one." Within this unity there is equality. One of the important signs of recent progress in this regard, Emerson believed, is "the movement which effected the elevation of what was called the lowest class in the state," and he encourages his listeners to "embrace the common" and to "explore and sit at the feet of the familiar, the low" (*CW* 1:65, 67). For Emerson and other transcendentalists, labor is a necessity for both physical and moral health: "I hear therefore with joy whatever is beginning to be said of the dignity and necessity of labor to every citizen. There is virtue yet in the hoe and the spade, for learned as well as for unlearned hands. And labor is everywhere welcome; always we are invited to work . . ." (*CW* 1:61–62).

Later, in his lecture "Reforms" (published in *The Dial* in February 1841), Emerson outlines his "doctrine of labor," which held that "the labor of society ought to be shared by all and in a community where labor was the point of honor the vain and the idle would labor." If this should happen in America, "slavery would fall into the pit" (*EL* 3:264). For Emerson, the dignity of manual labor is the foundation of a democratic republic. It is through honest labor that even the lowliest earns the right to participate in the political process. The result, ideally, is a political and economic balance of power between the rich and the rest. As Emerson observed in his 1844 essay "Politics," "When the rich are outvoted, as frequently happens, it is the joint treasury of the poor which exceeds their accumulations. Every man owns something, if it is only a cow, or a wheelbarrow, or his arms, and so has property to dispose of" (*CW* 3:121). Unfortunately, as Emerson was increasingly aware, in America there was a very large class of persons who were excluded from both political and economic equality because, in fact, they owned nothing, not even their own bodies. These were, of course, the slaves.

Emerson was convinced that negro slaves shared in the same divinity as all other human beings. Therefore, they were entitled to the same rights.[4] "Democracy/Freedom," he recorded in his journal, "has its root in the Sacred truth that every man hath in him the divine Reason." That is "the equality & the only equality of all men," and "because every man has within him somewhat really divine therefore slavery is the unpardonable outrage it is" (*JMN* 4:357). The reform of American society, Emerson believed, would be brought about through the influence of this divinity, whose presence within every rational being manifests as "moral sentiment."[5] He was convinced that moral and material progress go hand in hand. Thus, as he observed in an early antislavery address, the economic prosperity of the South would actually be better served "by placing the negro nation on a fair footing, than by robbing them" because "it is cheaper to pay wages, than to own the slave" (*AW* 8). Emerson's commitment both to the abolition of slavery and the rights of the workingman grew considerably throughout the decade of the 1840s. He came to see these causes as interrelated. The conditions endured by the Irish railroad workers in Massachusetts, he told Thoreau in 1843, were not that different from the "negro driving" of the South (*L* 7:558). Both groups were the victims of dehumanizing exploitation.[6]

In 1847–48, Emerson traveled to England for an extensive lecture tour. What he experienced there would lead to increased efforts to achieve social justice for the poor and oppressed on both sides of the Atlantic. At the time of his visit, as Daniel Koch points out, "Emerson was among the most widely read living authors in Britain."[7] He was also, as Clarence Gohdes contends, "the American author who probably exerted the greatest influence on the intellectuals of the British isles."[8] Emerson's popularity extended from the high to the low. His lectures consistently attracted large crowds, both in literary London and in the working-class districts of the north. Although he did not lecture there, Emerson's writings were also generally well-known in revolutionary France.[9]

Emerson was deeply affected by his European experience. Although he spent most of his time lecturing in England, he did manage a visit to revolutionary Paris in May 1848. While there, he sat in on meetings of the National Assembly and attended various gatherings of the Free Trade Club and the Barbès Club, where political radicals and workingmen called for social justice under a democratic government. These experiences had a significant impact on Emerson's social consciousness.[10] When he returned to England, it was as if his eyes had been newly opened. He became more sensitive to the enormous class disparity of English society, which now appeared in sharp contrast to the democratic environment of New England as well as revolutionary France. While in England, Emerson attended sessions of the House of Lords and the House of Commons, as well as meetings of the radical Chartists. The Chartist movement was the world's first independent movement for the rights of the working class. The group had been formed in 1838, and its "People's Charter" called for six specific reforms: voting by secret ballot, universal male suffrage, annual Parliaments, equal electoral districts, no property qualifications for members of Parliament, and payment of members. During Emerson's stay in England, the Chartists were agitating for greater working-class representation in government. He attended a Chartist gathering on March 9, 1848, called to celebrate recent events in France. During this time, there were Chartist demonstrations in London almost every day. Although he was at first disturbed by what seemed to be the random violence and lack of leadership evidenced in these demonstrations, eventually Emerson came to sympathize with the cause and felt that English scholars and poets should support the Chartists' demands for greater liberty.[11] He observed in his journal, "I fancied, when I heard that the times were anxious & political, that there is to be a Chartist revolution on Monday next, and an Irish revolution in the following week, that the right scholar would feel,—

now was the hour to test his genius. His kingdom is at once over & under these perturbed regions. Let him produce its Charter now, & try whether it cannot win a hearing, & make felt its infinite superiority today, even today" (*JMN* 10:310–11). But the Victorian sages remained silent.

During his lecture tour in England, Emerson had the opportunity to speak with Chartist leaders. On the night before a huge demonstration in London (April 10, 1848), Emerson met Thomas Cooper, a Chartist with some reputation as a workingman's poet.[12] Cooper had recently spent two years in prison because of his involvement in radical protests. He and Emerson met at a gathering outside London at the home of one of Emerson's English friends. In their meeting, Cooper was impressed by Emerson's congenial personality, and the two were apparently comfortable with one another. The following day they walked to London together. Cooper later remarked that Emerson was "the only American in whose company I ever felt real enjoyment." Their long conversation focused on "Religion, Politics, [and] Literature—ours and America's." Cooper also noted that Emerson "seemed eager to learn all he could, and willing to communicate all he could."[13]

Earlier, on March 7, 1848, Emerson had attended a Chartist meeting in London. He wrote to his wife, Lidian, that the assembly "was crowded, and the people very much in earnest." It is these activists, Emerson felt, that "give body & terror to the demands made by the Cobdens & Brights, who agitate for the Middle Class. When these are satisfied," he believed, "the universal suffrage & the Republic will come in" (*L* 4:34–35). Among the featured speakers at the meeting was Ernest Jones. At this time, Jones was associated with Karl Marx and Friedrich Engels, and he openly supported their social reform agenda. Like Emerson, he appreciated the importance of "physical force" in the pursuit of reform.[14] He also enjoyed a reputation as "a poet of Chartism" In his addresses, he routinely attacked aristocratic privilege and the oppression of the working class.[15]

Emerson's sympathy for English workingmen was no doubt reinforced by such meetings, as well as his experience in Paris where "physical force" was demonstrated daily. In a long letter to Lidian, he described the excitement of the place, where he witnessed "streets full of bayonets, and the furious driving of the horses dragging cannon towards the National Assembly." He also noted that he found "the clubs the most interesting—the men are in terrible earnest. The fire & fury of the people, when they are interrupted or thwarted, are inconceivable to New England . . . and every body suppose to have a pistol in his pocket." Emerson was also impressed by "the deep sincerity of the speakers who are agitating social not political questions, and who are studying how to secure a fair share of bread to every man, and to get the God's justice done through the land . . ." (*L* 4:73–74).

These French demonstrations for the rights of the workingman affected Emerson's perception of the plight of English laborers. In his journal he notes, "I have been exaggerating the English merits all winter, & disparaging the French. Now I am correcting my judgment of both, & the French have risen very fast" (*JMN* 10:327). He also began to perceive a sharp contrast between democratic New England and aristocratic Old England. "In England," he noted, "every man is a castle. When I get into our first class cars on the Fitchburg Road [in Massachusetts], & see sweltering men in their shirt sleeves take their seats with some well drest men & women, & see the very little difference of level that is between them all, . . . [I] imagine the astonishment that would strike the polished inmates of English first class carriages, if such masters should enter & sit beside them. . . ." Because of this, Emerson concludes, "it is not fit to tell Englishmen that America is like England. . . . England is the Paradise of the first class; it is essentially aristocratic. . . . In England, every man you meet is some man's son; in America, he may be some man's father" (*JMN* 10:329).

This growing awareness of British class consciousness undoubtedly enhanced his sympathy for the Chartists. It also made him increasingly critical of the British literary class. Earlier, in 1839, Thomas Carlyle had written a lengthy essay on "Chartism," a copy of which he sent to Emerson. In it, he showed little sympathy for the movement, recommending education for some and emigration for others. In Carlyle's view, surplus British laborers could be a valuable export commodity. "The stupid black African man brings money in the market," he observed, "the much stupider four-footed horse brings money:—it is we that have not yet learned the art of managing our white European man!"[16] Emerson responded with telling restraint. He advised Carlyle, "We seemed to have a right to an answer less concise to a question so grave & humane. . . ."[17] After almost a decade, however, the sardonic sage remained unmoved. He, along with John Ruskin, Matthew Arnold, and other elites of the Victorian literary class refused to support the lowly Chartists, despite the fact that they thought of themselves as progressive liberals. To Emerson, their passivity was a severe disappointment.

> The writers are bold & democratic. The moment revolution comes, are they Chartist & Montagnards? No, but they talk & sit with the rich, & sympathize with them. Should they go with the Chartist? Alas they cannot: These have such gross & bloody chiefs to mislead them, and are so full of hatred & murder, that the scholar recoils;—and joins the rich. That he should not do. He should accept as necessary the position of armed neutrality abhorring the crimes of the Chartist, yet more abhorring the oppression & hopeless selfishness of the rich. . . . (*JMN* 10:325–26)

Emerson also became more critical of the aristocrats who were uncaring toward the poor and oppressed. In his lecture "Natural Aristocracy," composed primarily while he was in Manchester, Emerson maintained that "the upper class should be distinguished by merit; any class not so distinguished ceases in fact to be the upper." The privileged elite have an obligation to serve others who are less fortunate. If these "perfumed gentlemen" fail to do so, Emerson asserts, "and instead go about to set ill examples and corrupt them, who shall blame them if they shoot him in the back or burn his barns, or insult his children. . . . Not I."[18]

When he returned to America, Emerson threw himself into the antislavery movement with renewed vigor. In lectures and addresses throughout the 1850s, a time of increasingly violent clashes between pro- and antislavery factions, he was reminded of the Chartists and their struggle, an association made by reformers on both sides of the Atlantic. William Lloyd Garrison, for example, after his trip to England in 1840, reported in the *Liberator* that "the Chartists in their struggle for emancipation are the abolitionists of the United States." Expatriated Chartists would later join forces with abolitionists in the United States, while Chartists in England lent their support to antislavery groups there.[19]

Emerson's pursuit of social justice became an international crusade as a result of his European experience. He came to realize that the cause of equality and free labor in democratic America was the cause of equality and free labor everywhere. This insight is nowhere more evident than in two lectures he gave repeatedly to American audiences following his return. In the first, titled "England" (December 5, 1848), he states, "In drawing these sketches, I am well aware there is a dark side of England, I have not wished to expose." He then goes on to describe the stark contrast between the "colossal wealth" of some and the "hideous pauperism" of the many that he witnessed in England. Thus "fair, ruddy, well-educated bodies go attended by poor, dwarfed, starved, short-lived skeletons." Such a painful disparity suggests to Emerson that "there are two Englands;—rich, Norman-Saxon, learned, social England,—seated in castles, halls, universities, and middle class houses of admirable completeness and comfort, and poor Celtic, peasant, drudging, Chartist England, in hovels and workhouses, cowed and hopeless." But at the moment, this dismal reality is not his primary subject. "I only recognize this fact, in passing," he states. "It is important that it be stated. It will not help us now to dwell on it" (*LL* 1:205). A month later, in a lecture titled "London" (January 3, 1849), Emerson repeated basically the same statement, but this time he added an important line. Just as there are "two Englands," he says, "Freedom in America has developed two Americas—, one white and exclusive; and the other, black and excluded

. . . it is important that it be stated;—it will not help us now to dwell on it" (LL 1:218). Throughout the new decade, however, Emerson would have a good deal to say about this cruel disparity. The cause of the Chartists was not markedly different from that of the American slave. Indeed, it was the cause of oppressed workingmen everywhere.

Not surprisingly, Emerson came to see a relationship between British materialism and American slavery. Thus, in an address attacking the infamous Fugitive Slave Law in 1854, he associates Great Britain's failure to support the liberal European revolutions of 1848 with that nation's apparent enthrallment to material gain. "The Anglo-Saxon race is proud and strong but selfish," he asserts. "They believe only in Anglo-Saxons. Greece found it deaf, Poland found it so, Italy found it so, Hungary found it so. England goes for trade, not for liberty. . . . The like torpor," he adds, "exists here throughout the active classes on the subject of domestic slavery and its appalling aggressions" (AW 86), hence their apparent willingness to tolerate this immoral but profitable abomination.

Emerson's most extensive treatment of the defects of English society came in 1856. *English Traits,* a study of English history and social character, was largely the result of his extended visit there. In this work, Emerson emphasizes the cultural differences between England and America, especially as they relate to the role of labor and the condition of the workingman. This difference is largely a matter of class structure. "The English dislike the American structure of society," he points out, "whilst yet trade, mills, public education, and chartism are doing what they can to create in England the same social condition." Emerson further observes that in England, as in the American South, the upper class maintains a "monopoly of political power." The result is that the privileged live in "the paradises of the nobles, where the live-long repose and refinement are heightened by the contrast with the roar of industry and necessity, out of which [they] have stepped aside" (CW 5:85, 103). In England, as in the American South, the common man (or slave) labors while the privileged indulge themselves with the comforts of leisure and prosperity.

Emerson recalled the Chartists in other significant ways. When the *Atlantic Monthly* was established in 1857 as the voice of American progressivism, it found an appreciative readership on both sides of the ocean.[20] Not surprisingly, Emerson was asked to contribute to the first issue. One of the items he submitted was "The Chartist's Complaint," a poem that he had first drafted during his stay in England.[21] In the piece, he makes explicit the painful divide between laborer and aristocrat in this presumably civilized and progressive nation by drawing a vivid picture of the "two Englands" that he had alluded to in his earlier lectures. One "Chill and wet, unlighted, mean," which is the laborer's England; the other consists of "the rich man's wood and lake . . . [a] planted isle where roses glow" (*CW* 9:430–31). The question implied is, how long will the people tolerate this cruel disparity?

Emerson's interest in social justice and the plight of the laborer, both in America and England, grew more prominent as the nation lurched from one crisis to the next throughout the violent decade of the fifties. The outbreak of the American Civil War and the British reaction would crystallize his opinion of the limitations of British character and elicit severe criticism of the once-admired "mother country."

The struggle in America between the aristocratic slave owners of the South and the democratic Unionists of the free North resembled the struggle in England, where the heirs of the Chartists and their liberal supporters continued to press for the enfranchisement of the workingman. The workingmen of England had always looked to the United States as a compelling example of the ability of the common man to exercise self-rule.[22] When the Civil War erupted, British reaction reflected this divide, with British liberals, especially Chartists and Trade Unionists, supporting the Union cause and British conservatives (mostly the upper class) tacitly supporting the Confederacy.[23] One of the most vociferous British supporters of the Union cause, Philip Foner notes, was the fiery Chartist radical who had so impressed Emerson, the reformist poet Ernest Jones.[24]

In the United States, transplanted Chartists like George Julian Harney would also promote the Union cause to both British and American audiences. Harney, who in the 1840s and 1850s edited the official Chartist journal, the *Northern Star,* emigrated to Boston in 1863. Shortly after his arrival, he became the American correspondent for the British *Newcastle Weekly Chronicle.* From this position, in the words of one historian, Harney was able to carry on "the tradition of Chartist internationalism" by promoting "a strong transatlantic war effort in favor of the North." Like Emerson, Harney was convinced that the Union cause was the cause of the workingman.[25]

Most conservative British intellectuals and writers were inclined to support the South in the struggle. One of the major reasons for this was their fear that a truly democratic America would reinforce the notion that the common man could and should have a voice in governance. Goldwin Smith, for example, who held a chair in history at Oxford University, wrote to his friend, Boston liberal Charles Eliot Norton, in November 1863 that "the aristocracy are against you almost to a man. The great capitalists are against you, and they have done a good deal to give a wrong tone to the City and to the London Press." But he also notes that "the great mass of the intelligent lower classes are on your side. This has been the case at least since the great issue between Free Labor and Slavery was fairly tendered; you could hardly expect that it should be so before."[26] Norton responded to this situation in an editorial published by the New England Loyal Publication Society in May 1863, where he attacked "the aristocrats in England" and maintained that the success of the Union cause means "the success of democracy everywhere; it is the success of equal rights, of free institutions, of free and well paid labor, of individual independence all the world over."[27]

Emerson saw the war in exactly these terms. Early on, he made a strong argument for the dignity of labor in a popular, pro-Union lecture titled "American Civilization," which was later published in the *Atlantic Monthly* (April 1862). In this defining document, Emerson maintains that the war was being fought to establish the dignity of free labor everywhere. He insists that "the division of labor . . . is nothing but a large allowance to each man to choose his work according to his faculty, to live by his better hand," and he condemns the South as a place "where the laborer is not secured in the earnings of his own hands,—where suffrage is not free or equal."[28] Such a society, he asserts, "is, in all these respects, not civil, but barbarous, and no advantages of soil, climate, or coast can resist these suicidal mischiefs" (506). The same could be said of England. Emerson here castigates any culture that denigrates rather than honors labor. The "labor of each for all," he asserts, "is the health and virtue of all beings. ICH DIEN, *I serve,* is a truly royal motto. And it is the mark of nobleness to volunteer the lowest service. . . . Nay, God is God because he is the servant of all." Slavery denies the divine quality of labor. It consists of the "stealing of men and setting them to work,—stealing their labor, and the thief sitting idle himself" (507).

Like their British counterparts, the arrogant and idle aristocrats of the South, Emerson insists, are on the wrong side of history. They "have endeavored to reverse the natural sentiments of mankind, and to pronounce labor disgraceful, and the well-being of a man to consist in eating the fruit of other men's labor." This is a gross violation of a natural law that is the very foundation of a civilized state. For an honorable man, labor is "the visible sign of his power; and to protect that, to secure that to him, . . . is the object of all government. There is no interest in any country so imperative as that of labor; it covers all, and constitutions and governments exist for that,—to protect and insure it to the laborer." To deny this invites chaos. For such madness there is "no solution but servile war" (507). Ultimately, justice will be done. The slaves of the South will be liberated, and their equality and the dignity of their labor acknowledged. "Emancipation is the demand of civilization," Emerson declares. It "puts every man in the South in just and natural relations with every man in the North, laborer with laborer" (509).

On January 1, 1863, Lincoln issued his Emancipation Proclamation, declaring all slaves in rebellious states to be "forever free." Although the measure was limited in scope and of questionable legality to some, Emerson was delighted. For him, the principle behind the act was far more important that its immediate effect. In his journal he declared that the war was now clearly being fought to vindicate "the rights of man" (*JMN* 15:293). In "The President's Proclamation," published in the *Atlantic* in November, Emerson insisted that the measure was based on "grand human principles" that were "representative of mankind, standing for all nationalities," thus affirming that universal human rights by their very nature are not subject to national boundaries or distinctions of class, caste, or race (*AW* 130).

Reaction to the proclamation in England was predictable. The conservative elites attacked it with a passion, while the working class saw it as an affirmation of their cause.[29] The August 1863 issue of *Macmillan's Magazine* carried a brief satirical squib by Carlyle titled "Ilias (Americana) in Nuce" (the American Iliad in a Nutshell), in which "Paul and Peter," representing the South and the North, attempt to beat each other's brains out because one "hires servants for life" and the other hires servants "by the month or the day." The piece clearly showed that Carlyle's views had not evolved much since 1839. For him, black or white, servants are servants. Whether you call them slaves or not is immaterial. This comparison was made explicit just months later in a popular, conservative British journal. While unwilling to approve the institution of slavery openly, British conservatives often argued that slaves were better off under a paternalistic institution where they could be "guided" to perform useful labor. In the eyes of some at least, the same was true of the British workingman. An anonymous 1864 article in the *Saturday Review*, "Slaves and Labourers," offers the following observation:

> In the Southern States, both the wealth and the civilization of the community depend largely on the enforced labour of the negro population. . . . In England too, it may be said . . . that society rests on the existence of a vast population born to do mean things, born to perform the rudest labour, and engaged in nothing else from birth to death. England is the government of a minority, resting on the subjection of a majority forced by circumstances to fulfill all the coarser tasks and more repulsive duties of the human race. And in both England and the South, the political system which prevails rests on facts, not on theories. The South says that it is absurd to talk of treating the negroes as on an equality with the white race, because, as a matter of fact, they are not on an equality.

This principle of natural inequality is especially relevant in England "when a sweeping Reform Bill is proposed. . . ." "It is absurd," the writer argues, "to suppose that the rude British hind can be made fit to vote by giving him a vote." In fact "the British Constitution very sensibly provides that he shall be governed by his betters. Thus the governing classes in England speak, and . . . a Southerner would not recognize in it any great difference from much that he has heard at home."[30]

New England liberals were outraged by Carlyle's insult and the attitude of the British ruling class, generally. Emerson responded with biting criticism of both in an address titled "Fortune of the Republic." In this highly political address, Emerson once again invokes the example of the Chartists and proclaims that their vision, while not yet a reality in England, will soon find fulfillment in a reunited and free America.

This was a critical time for the Union. War weariness was gripping the North, and there were many who were prepared to accept peace at any price, even the toleration of slavery. In Emerson's view, this spirit of accommodation amounted to a tacit acceptance of the South's undemocratic and aristocratic pretensions and principles. As such, it reflects a pernicious European, and specifically British, influence in America. "I call this spirit a remainder of Europe, imported into this soil," notes Emerson. "To say the truth, England is never out of mind. Nobody says it, but all think and feel it. England is the model in which they find their wishes expressed, not, of course, middle-class England, but rich, powerful and titled England" (AW 140). As Emerson had observed during his visit in 1847–48, and later noted in *English Traits* (1856), the British social and political model, like the South's, emphasizes aristocratic privilege along with the exploitation of the laborer. As Emerson says of England, "Never a lofty sentiment, never a duty to civilization, never a generosity, a moral self-restraint is suffered to stand in the way of a commercial advantage. In sight of a commodity, her religion, her morals are forgotten" (AW 141). Recalling his experience there, he asserts that "England is Chinese in her servility to wealth, and to old wealth. Hence the discovery in 1848,—that Paris was the capital of Europe; Paris and not London. . . . [T]he liberty of London was selfish and mixed, a liberty quite too much drenched in respect for privileges, cast-iron aristocracy and church hierarchy" (AW 141).

Emerson remained convinced that the intellectual and literary class in England was complicit in maintaining this noxious and undemocratic elitism.[31] Thomas Carlyle stands as a prime example of this failing. Emerson's criticism here is sharp and personal. Instead of challenging the status quo, as he once did, Carlyle has obviously been co-opted by it. "Even her [England's] ablest living writer," Emerson asserts, "a man who has earned his position by the sharpest insights, is politically a fatalist. In his youth he announced himself as a 'theoretical sansculotte fast threatening to become a practical one.' Now he is practically in the English system, a Venetian aristocracy, with only a private stipulation in favor of men of genius" (AW 141). Unlike the cynical Carlyle, Emerson sees the current American struggle as destined to bring about "the extinction of slavery," which will be one of the major "triumphs of humanity" (AW 143). This grand victory is possible because Lincoln has embraced the notion that a true democracy reflects the will of the people and the spirit that informs that will. "In America," Emerson observes, "the government is acquainted with the opinion of all classes, knows the leading men in the middle class, knows the leaders of the humblest class." This is strikingly different from England and the rest of Europe, or even America while the South dominated. "Not such,—far from such," Emerson notes, "—is England, France, and Austria: and, indeed, not such was America under previous administrations" (AW 144). Indeed, by comparison, the elitist politics of Europe remain essentially "Feudal" and the "six demands of chartism," have still not been granted in England, while "they have all been granted here to begin with," at least in the free North (AW 144). When the Union triumphs, America will supersede England as the world's most progressive democracy, as the last vestiges of aristocratic influence are purged from the national character and the dignity of the workingman is universally acknowledged.

The victory that Emerson predicted in 1863 became a reality in 1865. This triumph of the common man reinforced the liberal cause in England, where the political descendants of the lowly Chartists were finally able to persuade Parliament to pass the Reform Act of 1867, substantially expanding the franchise for the first time since 1832. And with this the progress of democracy continued on both sides of the Atlantic.

Notes

1. Len Gougeon, "Transcendental Politics and Economics," in Joel Myerson, Sandra Petrulionis, and Laura Dassow Walls, eds., *The Oxford Handbook to Transcendentalism* (New York: Oxford University Press, 2010), 139ff.

2. See Richard Grusin, "'Put God in Your Debt': Emerson's Economy of Expenditure," *PMLA* 103, no. 1 (1988): 37; and David Herreshoff, *The Origins of American Marxism from the Transcendentalists to De Leon* (New York: Pathfinder Press, 1967), 18.

3. Neal Dolan, *Emerson's Liberalism* (Madison: University of Wisconsin Press, 2009), 114.

4. Paul Boller, *American Transcendentalism, 1830–1860: An Intellectual Inquiry* (New York: G. P. Putnam's Sons, 1974), 137.

5. See T. Gregory Garvey, "Emerson's Political Spirit and the Problem of Language," in T. Gregory Harvey, ed., *The Emerson Dilemma: Essays on Emerson and Social Reform* (Athens: University of Georgia Press, 2001), 15; and Len Gougeon, *Emerson & Eros: The Making of a Cultural Hero* (Albany: State University of New York Press, 2007), 159–91.

6. Other abolitionists saw the same connection with regard to exploited textile workers, and they condemned equally "The Lords of the Lash, and the Lords of the Loom." See Richard H. Abbott, *Cotton and Capital: Boston Businessmen and Antislavery Reform, 1854–1868* (Amherst: University of Massachusetts Press, 2009), 22.

7. Daniel Koch, *Ralph Waldo Emerson in Europe: Class, Race and Revolution in the Making of an American Thinker* (London: I. B. Tauris, 2012), 23.

8. Clarence Gohdes, *American Literature in Nineteenth-Century England* (Carbondale: Southern Illinois University Press, 1944), 145.

9. Daniel Koch has recently located more than 250 British and French newspaper and journal articles about Emerson and his English lecture tour (*Ralph Waldo Emerson in Europe*, 9).

10. Larry J. Reynolds, *European Revolutions and the American Literary Renaissance* (New Haven, CT: Yale University Press, 1988), 33ff.

11. See Koch, *Ralph Waldo Emerson in Europe*, 130; and Len Gougeon, "Emerson and the British: Challenging the Limits of Liberty," in "Liberty Ltd.: Civil Rights, Civil Liberties, and Literature," Brook Thomas, ed., special issue, *REAL: Yearbook of Research in English and American Literature* (Berlin: Gunter Narr Verlag, 2006), 179–213, 181ff.

12. Robert D. Richardson, Jr., *Emerson: The Mind on Fire* (Berkeley: University of California Press, 1995), 451; Koch, *Ralph Waldo Emerson in Europe*, 130.

13. Thomas Cooper, *The Life of Thomas Cooper, Written by Himself* (London: Hodder and Stoughton, 1879), 312.

14. For Emerson on the use of physical force, see my "Militant Abolitionism: Douglass, Emerson, and the Rise of the Antislave," *New England Quarterly* 85 (December 2012): 622–57.

15. Koch, *Ralph Waldo Emerson in Europe*, 127, 96; Philip Foner, *British Labor and the American Civil War* (New York: Holmes & Meir, 1981), 71–72.

16. Thomas Carlyle, *Chartism*, 2nd ed. (London: James Fraser, 1840), 108.

17. Ralph Waldo Emerson, *The Correspondence of Emerson and Carlyle*, ed. Joseph Slater (New York: Columbia University Press, 1964), 266.

18. Quoted in Koch, *Ralph Waldo Emerson in Europe*, 151, 154.

19. See Douglas B. A. Ansdell, "William Lloyd Garrison's Ambivalent Approach to Labour Reform," *Journal of American Studies* 24, no. 3 (December 1990): 404–5; Owen R. Ahston and Joan Hugman, "George Julian Harney, Boston, U.S.A., and Newcastle upon Tyne, England, 1863–1888," *Proceedings of the Massachusetts Historical Society*, 3rd ser., 107 (1995): 170–71; and Ray Boston, *British Chartists in America, 1836–1900* (Totowa, NJ: Rowman and Littlefield, 1971), 84.

20. See Ellery Sedgwick, *The Atlantic Monthly, 1857–1909: Yankee Humanism at High Tide and Ebb* (Amherst: University of Massachusetts Press, 1994), 5; and James C. Austin, *Fields of "The Atlantic Monthly": Letters to an Editor, 1861–1870* (San Marino, CA: Huntington Library, 1953), 31.

21. M. A. de Wolfe Howe, *The Atlantic Monthly and Its Makers* (Boston: Atlantic Monthly Press, 1919), 24.

22. Boston, *British Chartists in America*, 14; Eugenio F. Biagini, *Liberty, Retrenchment and Reform: Popular Liberalism in the Age of Gladstone, 1860–1880* (Cambridge: Cambridge University Press, 1992), 70.

23. R. J. M. Blackett, *Divided Hearts: Britain and the American Civil War* (Baton Rouge: Louisiana State University Press, 2001), 120; Gougeon, "Emerson and the British," 191.

24. Foner, *British Labor and the American Civil War*, 72.

25. Ahston and Hugman, "George Julian Harney," 166, 177–78.

26. Goldwin Smith, "The Letters of Goldwin Smith to Charles Eliot Norton," *Proceedings of the Massachusetts Historical Society* 49 (October 1915): 106, 107.

27. Records of the Loyal Publication Society, Boston Public Library.

28. Ralph Waldo Emerson, "American Civilization," *Atlantic Monthly* (April 1862): 503. Subsequent references to this work will be cited parenthetically in the text by page number.

29. Blackett, *Divided Hearts*, 230–31.

30. Unsigned, "Slaves and Labourers," *Saturday Review* (January 16, 1864): 72.

31. It should be emphasized that Emerson did not indict all British writers and intellectuals. John Stuart Mill, Elizabeth Gaskell, Arthur Clough, and others offered strong support for the Union cause, for which Emerson was very grateful.

[5]

ROBERT D. HABICH

AN "EXTEMPORE ADVENTURER" IN ITALY: EMERSON AS INTERNATIONAL TOURIST, 1832–1833

I

AN INVETERATE TRAVELER BY profession whose exhausting lecture schedule kept him on the road for much of his working life, Ralph Waldo Emerson was an international traveler only three times: from 1832 to 1833, when he visited continental Europe and Great Britain following the death of his wife Ellen and his resignation from Boston's Second Church; from 1847 to 1848, when he lectured in England and Scotland and briefly visited revolutionary Paris; and finally from 1872 to 1873, when his daughter Ellen took him to Europe and North Africa to recuperate emotionally after the burning of their house. But of these three international trips, it was during his first one that Emerson best fit the definition of a tourist: a "temporarily leisured person who voluntarily visits a place away from home for the purpose of experiencing a change."[1] The 1847–48 lecture tour was mostly business, his itinerary arranged by his friend from Manchester, the newspaper publisher Alexander Ireland.[2] Similarly, his last European visit was largely arranged by Ellen, who shepherded her weary father from country to country. The story of that last trip is essentially told through Ellen's letters home, with Emerson himself capable of writing little.[3]

In his first tour, however, Emerson is at once the most spontaneous in his itinerary, the most self-consciously touristic, and the most open and revealing in his reactions to new cultures. As the editors of Emerson's *Collected Works* point out, his first European journey "was a genuine awakening for Emerson; no amount of previous reading or inherited lore had prepared the otherwise provincial American for the intellectual or artistic wonders he would encounter throughout his journey, and especially in Rome and Florence and their environs, where he witnessed Italian antiquity and the Italian Renaissance in an entirely new light" (*CW* 10:584). Energetic and curious, writing almost every day, Emerson was excited by the prospects of new experiences and at the same time skeptical and self-conscious as an American confronting for the first time the realities of a deep cultural past.

Though he insisted he harbored "no churlish objection to the circumnavigation of the globe, for the purposes of art, of study, and benevolence" (*CW* 2:46), Emerson had his suspicions about tourism. On the one hand, based on his own experience during his first transatlantic crossing, he subscribed to the nineteenth-century faith in the therapeutic value of traveling. In his 1838 lecture "Prudence," he praises sea voyages as "sanative to exhausted bodies and anxious minds" because they bring about a "total revolution of habits, actions, spectacles and company" (*EL* 2:324). On the other hand, on personal principle, Emerson was unenthusiastic about the idea of travel for its own sake, no doubt part of a generalized opposition to idleness ingrained in his Yankee heritage. In a passage from "Self-Reliance" (1841) that anticipates Thoreau's impatience in *Walden* with those who roam the globe to "count the cats in Zanzibar,"[4] Emerson famously dismissed traveling as a "fool's paradise," a pointless attempt at self-development that actually brought travelers farther from the truth they were seeking: "He who travels to be amused, or to get somewhat which he does not carry, travels away from himself, and grows old even in youth among old things." "The superstition of Travelling," Emerson charged, was symptomatic of "a deeper unsoundness affecting the whole intellectual action" (*CW* 2:46). Being a tourist, in other words, could make you well or make you old, but it could also make you crazy. Like his writing about tourism, Emerson's own encounters with other cultures were ambivalent, sometimes contradictory, and difficult to reconcile with his later philosophy. Few critics, in fact, have tried, perhaps because his reactions to his cultural encounters run so opposite to the developing idealism and liberality expressed in his essays and lectures.[5] If there is some accounting for Emerson's experience as a tourist, it must surely come from elsewhere than the transcendentalism that would later define his thinking. Approaching his 1832–33 tour from the perspective of tourism theory offers an illuminating explanation of his international experiences; and the time he spent in Italy—self-contained, culturally rich, and productive of the fullest record of his attitudes—was the most revealing of the tour.

Emerson set sail for Europe on Christmas day, 1832. It had been a momentous year, emotionally and vocationally, for the young, relatively unknown minister. Still reeling from the loss of his wife Ellen Tucker, who had died of tuberculosis in 1831, he resigned from Boston's Second Church in October 1832, an act of principle that freed him from the ceremony of historical Christianity but threw him back upon the vocational anxieties that had beset him for most of his adult life. His actual itinerary during his first tour was largely a matter of health and happenstance. Suffering during the autumn from what might have been dyspepsia, a condition likely exacerbated by the stresses of the past year, he was advised by his physician to travel for his health. He originally planned to visit his brother Edward, who was then undergoing treatment for tuberculosis in Puerto Rico, but at the last minute Waldo changed his mind; the brig *Jasper* was in Boston harbor, preparing to sail for the Mediterranean, and despite the captain's reservations about Emerson's frail health, he joined four other passengers on his first voyage abroad.[6] Though he had been borrowing books on Italy before his trip, he seems to have given little forethought to what he would do once he got there. Emerson's definition of his own role as tourist is revealing. He would be, he told his brother William, an "extempore adventurer" in Europe (*L* 1:359).[7]

After a five-week crossing that unexpectedly restored Emerson's physical health, the *Jasper* arrived in Malta on February 2, 1833. Emerson waited out a two-week quarantine aboard ship before exploring the ancient city of Valetta, then sailed to Sicily, and finally to the Italian mainland, arriving on March 12 in Naples, where he struck out on his own. First impressions were significant. He thought Naples a beautiful place, but complained about the rain; he called it in a letter home "a very large boisterous disagreeable city" (*L* 1:367). After three weeks in Naples, he headed north for a month in Rome and then north again for another month in Florence (*JMN* 4:169). From Florence he traveled to Venice ("a city for beavers," he called it [*JMN* 4:186]) and Milan; then he crossed the Alps into Geneva, made his way to Paris, and thereafter to England, Scotland, and home again. All told, in 1833 Emerson spent about six months in continental Europe and Great Britain, fully half of them in Italy.[8]

Albert J. von Frank accurately notes a pattern in Emerson's interests during this first European tour: in Italy, art and architecture; in France, science; and in England, literature.[9] If Emerson's itinerary is fairly predictable—Robert Richardson characterizes it as a traditional Grand Tour in reverse[10]—his reactions to Italy were far more complex. He was distrustful of the people he met, sometimes with good reason. An easy mark for disreputable guides and for thieves, who once picked his pocket twice in the same day, Emerson lamented the "swarming, faithless, robber population" overtaking Naples (*JMN* 4:143) and the lack of "plain good manners & sensible people" in Rome (*JMN* 4:154). He attended a papal audience and found it "millinery & imbecility" (*JMN* 4:153), though he was swept away by the grandeur of St. Peter's Basilica; he enjoyed the opera in Florence but found the entr'acte ballerinas "nearly ideotic" (*JMN* 4:171). At his most sentimental, Emerson comes off as a gullible naïf; at his most xenophobic, he anticipates what would in the twentieth century be called the Ugly American. Alternately awestruck, indifferent, mean-spirited, enthusiastic, jingoistic, ethnocentric, and finicky, Emerson the tourist is a puzzle to us, and a very un-Emersonian one at that.

We should not ignore the biographical circumstances that contributed to some of his contrariness. He was just thirty years of age, alone and abroad for the first time, unemployed, and a widower. Meeting up with congenial American travelers could elevate his spirits; rainy weather and solitude led him, not surprisingly, to feel blue and homesick. "I hate travelling," he wrote his brother William one soggy day in Naples, just a few weeks into his Italian tour. "Happy they that sit still! How glad I shall be to get home again" (*L* 1:370). Richardson explains Emerson's erratic behavior abroad largely in terms of personality, his loneliness and self-doubts warring against the stimulation of new sights, new ideas. But there is a coherence to Emerson's responses that defies the randomness of weather and companionship and equally defies explanation by his incipient transcendentalism, which would burst forth three years after his Italian tour in the ringing generalizations of *Nature*: openness to experience, joy in the present moment, and an original, integrative relation between the self and the world. None of these philosophical ideals seems very evident in the turmoil and criticism that characterize his three months in Italy. To be sure, because Emerson privileged progress and movement as central activities to the development of the self, the literal transgressing of boundaries and the broadening knowledge of other cultures gesture toward Emerson's larger, lifelong "construction and reconstruction of [his] identity," as Jason Berger has recently argued.[11] But Emerson's specific, impassioned, and contradictory responses to Italy perhaps deserve more focused explanation. We will be more successful in understanding Emerson's reactions if we bring to bear some of the insights of tourism research, a window into Emerson's behavior that literary scholars have been slow to recognize.[12] Oddly enough, we have never thought to explain Emerson the tourist in touristic terms. Concentrating on his first Italian tour, this chapter will first examine Emerson's culture shock as he confronts a cultural present, then explore his relationship to the cultural past as a representative American, and finally examine how he transforms these touristic behaviors into literary productions, especially his lectures on Italy.

II

The term "culture shock" has filtered into common parlance as defined by Merriam-Webster's: "a sense of confusion and uncertainty sometimes with feelings of anxiety that may affect people exposed to an alien culture or environment without adequate preparation." In tourism theory, however, culture shock is a process, not a state of mind. First developed in the mid-1950s by the anthropologist Kalervo Oberg, who was studying the ways missionaries adapted to host cultures in sub-Saharan Africa, it came to be applied to international students abroad (in the 1960s), business people engaged in international trade (1970s), then finally to tourists in the 1980s.[13] The process of culture shock for foreign visitors is almost always described in four stages: (1) initial euphoria, (2) irritation and hostility, (3) gradual adjustment, and (4) adaptation.[14]

We can use those stages to map Emerson's emotional itinerary during his first European trip. The first stage of culture shock is "initial euphoria." Though he was never especially demonstrative about his emotions, Emerson was aware of his own limited experience and excited about the prospects of broadening travel. He first touched European soil in Malta and recorded ambling through the old town of Valletta, which he and his companions toured with pop-eyed wonder. As he put it in his journal, it made him feel "green & juvenile" to act so giddy (*JMN* 4:116). He explored Malta and Sicily with vigor and delight, his journals recording a frenetic daily schedule of sightseeing. It was a strange new world, but initially he embraced it. In his journal he wrote confidently, "I am a full believer in the doctrine that we always make our own welcome" (*JMN* 4:68).

But his early enthusiasm soon gave way to the second stage of culture shock, "irritation and hostility," during his time in Naples and Rome, where he recorded his diatribes about beggars, his weariness with ruined antiquities, his studied indifference to local sights. In part, his irritation may have resulted from what people in the field call "museum fatigue" or what travelers know more colloquially as "ABC syndrome" ("another bloody castle"). But there is more to Emerson's testiness than a tiring sensory overload; in his complaints Emerson explores what it means to consume another culture, pointing out the relative value of antiquities and foreign culture to newcomers like himself versus their everyday uses for residents. In Sicily, for instance, he spent hours seeking out the Arethusa fountain, mythical home of the nymph who was transformed into a spring to escape the courtship of the sea god Alpheus. To his distress, he found it tucked away in a back alley; "I abhor to tell" he wrote in his journal, "[that] the fountain was bubbling up in its world renowned waters within four black walls serving as one great washing tub to fifty or sixty women who were polluting it with all the filthy clothes of the city" (*JMN* 4:125). This discovery was representative of many of his disappointments in Italy. As David Justin Hodge points out, much of Emerson's disenchantment derived from his firsthand exposure to the Roman Catholic Church, whose rituals increased his sense of foreignness.[15] The minister whose resignation affirmed his doubts about a single sacrament must have been overwhelmed by the ubiquity of rite and ceremony. He tended to value the sites of antiquity but detest their present occupants; as he told his brother William, it was old Italy he came to see, not new (*L* 1:368).

As he traveled from Naples to Rome, and then to Florence, however, Emerson's attitude shifted to what Fred E. Jandt calls "gradual adjustment," the third stage of culture shock. He seems to have realized that his own rigid expectations and cultural blinders were at least partially to blame for his discontent. In a metaphor he would later use in his essay "Circles," he wrote in a letter home that the traveler "is perpetually disappointed" because his dreams "are always flying before him—never realized" (*L* 1:371). Emerson's attitudes were changing; he was becoming less judgmental. If Romans were as beggarly as Neapolitans, he thought Rome had the compensation of an abiding artistic culture. He visited the sculpture gardens at the Villa d'Este in Tivoli and gushed at the combination of nature and antiquity that he found there: "such trees, such walks, such fountains, such grottoes, such adornments" (*JMN* 4:165). By the time he left Rome he could say flatly, "I am glad I came" to "this venerable old egg shell of nations, institutions, arts, [and] religions. . . . So splendid a spectacle which grows ever upon the eye & upon the mind ought not to be hid" (*L* 1:379). As Rome was an improvement over Naples, so he found Florence an improvement over Rome. Despite the heat and what he considered its inferior architecture, Florence had "[g]ood streets, industrious population, spacious well furnished lodgings, elegant & cheap Caffés, the cathedral & the Campanile, the splendid galleries and no beggars" (*JMN* 4:167–68). He stayed near the Santa Maria Novella piazza, just steps from the Duomo and not far from the bustle of the Arno, the Uffizi, and the Pitti Palace. Now two months into his Italian tour, he was immersing himself in Italian life. "[I]n order to see what is worth seeing & especially who is worth seeing in each city," he wrote a friend in the United States, travelers need to "go into society a little. Now no man can have society upon his own terms. If he seek it, he must serve it too" (*JMN* 4:178).

Emerson spent more than a month in Florence, Venice, and Milan before leaving for Switzerland on June 11, 1833, but no sooner had he left Italy than he began to miss it. He told his brothers Charles and William how "sad was I to find that in crossing the Alps I had left forever behind me that antiquated historical expression which belongs to Italian towns & to none others" (*L* 7:215). Paris he found too modern and industrial, poorer in the arts, more like New York or Liverpool (*L* 1:387–88). In the terminology of tourism theory, Emerson had reached the fourth stage of culture shock:

"adaptation." Jandt associates adaptation with biculturalism, "the ability to function in both cultures."[16] Emerson wasn't quite there yet. But he was developing a double-consciousness, at once cognizant of his place as a cultural outsider and sympathetic with the perspective of his European hosts, "whose avocations I interrupt by my letters of introduction [and who] accuse me by their looks for leaving my business to hinder theirs" (*JMN* 4:79). And he longed to be back in Rome and Florence, "whose glory is departed or departing" (*L* 7:215), antique cities that he now saw as victims of a crass and unappreciative present.

III

Almost from the beginning of his first European tour, Emerson steeled himself against the possibility of appreciating his new cultural contact with what Philip Nicoloff calls "a policy of skeptical resistance" (*CW* 5:xvi) and Robert Weisbuch, "a fully sophisticated cultural strategy . . . to reach for a decisively different, distinctly American maturity."[17] On his first sight of continental Europe, as the *Jasper* sailed through the Strait of Gibraltar, Emerson spied the tiny villages tucked against the hills of southern Spain and grumbled in his journal, "Is not a hut in America a point that concentrates as much life & sentiment as a hut in Europe?" (*JMN* 4:113). It was a petulance that erupted on occasion for the rest of his trip. On his voyage home, he noted in his journal that while Italy and the United States may have different names for the same things, "[w]hat matter whether this hill & yon green field be called Garofalo, Terni or Ipswich & Cape Cod. Let the soul once be fully awake & its thought is so much that the place becomes nothing" (*JMN* 4:320). In a famous reaction to Naples, he wrote, "[W]hat if it is Naples, it is only the same world of cake & ale—of man & truth & folly. I won't be imposed upon by a name. . . . Who cares? Here's for the plain old Adam, the simple genuine Self against the whole world" (*JMN* 4:141). For the remainder of his 1833 trip Emerson occasionally lapsed into boilerplate comments about European immorality and Yankee virtues that strike us today as almost laughably naive and self-consciously nativistic. To Abel Adams he wrote that the worth of travel is a renewed appreciation for home. "The way to learn to value America its churches its government its manners & all is to come hither," he wrote from Florence on May 28. Religious liberals will prize their home even more when they see the "unbelief & loosest morals" of Italy (*L* 1:384–85). As he waited to sail from Liverpool, he rhapsodized in his journal, "I am thankful that I am an American as I am thankful that I am a man" (*JMN* 4:81), and when at last he was at sea, he wrote, "This morn I saw the last lump of England receding without the least regret" (*JMN* 4:236). Place may indeed have meant nothing to him at certain times—surely an odd comment for a tourist to make—but a journal entry late in his 1833 trip suggests that much of this early skepticism was posing, the self-conscious posturing of a representative American abroad. Instead of complaining, he now counseled himself, "Be cheerful. What an insane habit is this of groping always into the past months & scraping together every little pitiful instance of awkwardness & misfortune" (*JMN* 4:77). Up again, old tourist, he seems to say.

If Emerson's resistance to new cultural contact sometimes smacks of self-dramatization and studied patriotism, his reflective philosophizing about his position as tourist raises other questions as well. To what extent is he enacting the role of the American abroad? And—especially in the letters—to what extent is he saying what his homebound correspondents expected to hear? As we will see, he was working out his later lectures on Europe in the "storehouse" of his journals, and so his experimentation with voice and stance may be nothing more than an exercise in drafting. However, it may also be part of another pattern of touristic behavior. As Shirley Foster has argued, nineteenth-century Americans abroad struggled to respond to historical sites without relinquishing their republican ideas of American independence and superiority.[18] To do so, Foster maintains, "they implemented discursive strategies enabling them to establish their own agency and to challenge or subvert the domination of literary cultism and the commodification of an inherited aesthetic" (176). These strategies included the imaginative remaking of tourist sites to create less culturally threatening versions of European antiquity—a process Foster calls "imaginative enhancement" (177)—and self-mockery as a way of acknowledging their own naïveté, which Foster calls "knowing iconoclasm" or "anti-tourism" (188).

Undoubtedly all tourists reconstruct their experience according to their knowledge, politics, and emotional needs, and in his "imaginative enhancement" of his foreign encounters Emerson may only have been more skillful than the average visitor. To cite just one example of his deft construction of touristic experience: he coarsely dismisses Rome's "beggarly Italians" (*JMN* 4:154) but writes breathlessly about a charming flower girl he met in Florence, "the fair Erminia," who gave away her flowers if she couldn't sell them (*JMN* 4:175–76). Emerson could hardly have failed to notice the inconsistency here, that beggars in Rome were repulsive and scheming but those in Florence were fair and generous. As if to underscore his own self-mockery, Emerson notes wryly that *his* meetings with Erminia "always cost me a crazie," one-twelfth of a Tuscan lire (*JMN* 4:175). The picture of a gangly American half-smitten with a waiflike beggar girl calls up all the stereotypes of the innocent sucker abroad; the name "Erminia"—"weasel" in Italian—reinforces the irony.

Emerson as "anti-tourist" carries even richer and more rhetorical associations. If Emerson was ambivalent at times about the culture he encountered, he was equally uncertain about his role as a cultural consumer, an attitude that manifests itself in a complicated series of personae. Chief among these is the parochial scholar desperate to escape his native culture. Even before he left Boston, for instance, he wrote to his brother William with self-deprecating humor, "I am a-weary of my helpless hopeless arm chair[.] I gain nothing, I rot ever, & have a keen appetite for the stimulus of Gods charitable air" (*L* 1:360). He returned to the image several months later, this time spinning it positively in a letter to his friend George Sampson. "I found sincere people at home—why did I not stay there? Well I rue my fault & will hasten back & grow old, if God please, in my chimney corner amidst my own friends" (*L* 1:378). The persona of the hermit-scholar allows Emerson at once to confess his own provincial attitudes and at the same time to demonstrate his awareness of the pose itself. He was clearly no homebound pedant. But the pose is useful in establishing the ironic stance Emerson found necessary to mediate his concomitant admiration for, and criticism of, European culture. And it provides some of Emerson's most endearing and humorous evidence of his self-consciousness as a tourist. To his sister-in-law Susan Haven Emerson, William's wife, he grumbles about Naples's soggy weather and shifty natives, then undercuts his complaints with knowing self-deprecation. "Now do not think the fault is mine. I am very easy to please," he confides to Susan. "Since I landed at Malta I hardly pass a monastery but I ask them on what terms they will receive me for life." He joked that he needed only "calm civil people, warm weather, a fine prospect, a few books & a little coffee" (*L* 1:367). But in fact those creature comforts were often what he despaired of finding in Naples; the persona was sometimes uncomfortably close to the truth. Juxtaposing his self-conception as the "extempore adventurer" against the persona of "the plain old Adam, the simple genuine Self against the whole world" (*JMN* 4:141) allows him to criticize himself and his new surroundings simultaneously. A caricature of his own parochialism, Emerson the "anti-tourist" is free to assess Europeans and their culture from behind the protective shield of American innocence.

IV

Within months of his return, Emerson was already at work on two lectures about his first European tour, titled simply "Italy," that he began presenting in early 1834.[19] The first covers his travels from the time he left Palermo for

Naples through his departure from Rome; the second chronicles his experiences in Florence, Venice, and Milan. The fact that only his Italian experience found its way into lecture form confirms its importance to him. We are well aware of the influence of Emerson's time in Paris on the development of his manifesto *Nature* (1836). Much less is known about these earlier public presentations, lectures that capture in subtle ways the transformation of touristic experience to literary form.

Though the manuscripts of these two lectures are extant, the editors of Emerson's *Early Lectures* chose not to print them, citing their close resemblance to parallel passages in the journals.[20] Only the opening paragraph of the first lecture and the closing paragraph of the second are reproduced in *Early Lectures,* along with parallel passages in the notes. It may have made commercial sense to avoid duplicating large sections of the journals, but the scholarly justification bears some scrutiny, for a collation of the manuscript lectures on Italy reveals some significant differences from the passages in the *JMN*. Some of these differences are not surprising for an author transforming private experience into public expression. Chief among these are the omissions from the lectures of some of the personal anxieties called up by Emerson's touristic encounters. In Venice, for example, he meditates in his journals about the effect of geographical isolation enforced by the canals. "I pity the people [of Venice]," he writes on June 2, 1833, "who are not beavers, & yet are compelled to live here." His feelings for Venetians are then universalized to all those who are "estranged from truth & love, from Him who is truth & love," and finally personalized in a shocking episode of self-loathing that is notably (and understandably) omitted from his lectures: "Sometimes I would hide myself in the dens of the hills, in the thickets of an obscure country town[,] I am so vexed & chagrined with myself,—with my weakness, with my guilt. Then I have no skill to live with men. . . . It seems to me, no boy makes so many blunders or says such awkward, contrary, disagreeable speeches as I do. In the attempt to oblige a person I wound & disgust him. I pity the hapless folks that have to do with me" (*JMN* 4:74).

Elsewhere, too, Emerson omits or mutes his emotional responses. Though he retains in the lectures his diatribe against the "imbecility" of papal ceremony, for instance, he leaves out his sneering comments about "beggarly Italians." And surprisingly, he deletes his rhapsody over the beauty of Tivoli. In place of these emotional moments are changes that reinforce the persona of a traveler calmly insistent on his own convictions. For example, in the lectures he omits the journal passage mentioned above, in which he vows to meet his host culture halfway: "no man can have society upon his own terms. If he seek it, he must serve it too." The omission removes a key statement about Emerson's flexibility in adjusting to new experiences. Other changes reinforce the narrator's national agenda. In "Italy I," describing the papal procession on Palm Sunday, he adds "This pomp does not satisfy Americans," a sentence that does not appear in the journals. In addition, he omits from the lectures his journal entry about Gibraltar ("Is not a hut in America a point that concentrates as much life & sentiment as a hut in Europe?") and a similar one about Garofalo ("[w]hat matter whether this hill & yon green field be called Garofalo, Terni or Ipswich & Cape Cod"), passages that made him seem puzzlingly unresponsive to the very cultures he had come to see. The effect of these omissions, together with the other changes in the lectures, is to create a narrative presence that is individualistic without being emotional, principled but not intolerant.

Emerson's labored construction of his persona in the Italy lectures suggests that he struggled to balance his personal reaction as a tourist with his public role as an interpreter and reporter of his international experience. It is a struggle that seems to run from beginning to end of the Italy lectures—*if* we have only the beginning and the end to go by. In the opening paragraph of the first lecture and the closing paragraph of the second—the only text from the Italy lectures reproduced in *Early Lectures*—Emerson apologizes for his lack of sophistication, first claiming to be nothing more than "an American traveller" and lastly presenting himself as something of a Jamesian center of consciousness, "simply a spectator [who] had no ulterior objects" (*EL* 1:89–90). Taken by themselves, those two claims would seem to argue for quite different speakers, a traveler burdened with national baggage versus an unaffiliated onlooker who simply records all he sees. But given the other changes he made in the transition from journal to lecture, Emerson may in fact have been linking national identity with fairness and objectivity (the lack of "ulterior objects") in an attempt, albeit not very successful, to redefine the character of the American tourist along more democratic and tolerant lines: open to cultural experience but choosy with his praise, responsive to the beauty of foreign culture but restrained enough to be trustworthy, all the while principled in his indictment of moral weaknesses. No longer a tourist on foreign soil, Emerson in the Italy lectures develops a narrative persona that mirrors what Foster calls the "knowing iconoclasm" of the "anti-tourist," undercutting both his own authority and his reverence for the sites he visited.

V

Emerson's experience in Italy, like his letters, journals, and lectures, betrays the earnestness and struggles of a young writer and the naïveté and self-conscious dramatization of a first-time traveler. Philip L. Pearce cautions against the "sin of homogenisation" in tourism research, the temptation to assume more uniformity of experience than we know to be the case.[21] Certainly the warning is an apt one for a writer like Emerson, who consistently praised inconsistency and whose powers of expression were unarguably superior to that of most other international travelers. But in his first international cultural contact, Emerson resembles a much larger group of tourists, then and now, who mistake their shared experience of culture shock for something unique to themselves. Perhaps it was hard for Emerson to admit that in significant ways his touristic responses made him just like anyone else. It is hard for Emerson scholars to see that, too. Emersonians are quite comfortable applying other structures to Emerson's early experience—the process of grieving in "Experience" and "Threnody," for instance, or the process of mystical transcendence in *Nature*. But social sciences are different from literary studies; the former measure broad patterns and typicalities, while Emerson scholarship tends—to put it mildly—toward viewing Emerson as exceptional. Is he interesting because he differs from the norm or because he conforms to it? Literary studies have tended to stress the first, his difference; tourism theory tends to value the second, his sameness. Though it cuts the wake of most Emersonian criticism, there is merit to that second position: put bluntly, sometimes Emerson thinks and acts just like everybody else does—a gently heretical perception that, to me at least, does nothing to diminish the times when he does not. Analyzing Emerson's Italian tour through the lens of tourism theory destabilizes his exceptionalism in productive, if unconventional, ways.

Notes

1. Valene Smith, *Hosts and Guests: The Anthropology of Tourism*, 2nd ed. (Philadelphia: University of Pennsylvania Press, 1989), 1.

2. For an excellent discussion of Emerson's 1847–48 tour, see Daniel Koch, *Ralph Waldo Emerson in Europe: Class, Race and Revolution in the Making of an American Thinker* (London: I. B. Tauris, 2012), which establishes Emerson's disappointment with Brook Farm and the Mexican-American War in 1847 as inaugurating a period of "despair, confusion, and melancholia" over the efficacy of "organized resistance" (15, 31).

3. On March 18, 1873, Ellen Emerson reported to Lidian Emerson that she had seen no improvement in her father: "His hands are as cold & numb as ever, he remembers no better, he feels the same inability to write even the smallest note." Ellen Tucker Emerson, *The Letters of Ellen Tucker Emerson*, 2 vols., ed. Edith E. W. Gregg (Kent, OH: Kent State University Press, 1982), 2:68.

4. Henry David Thoreau, *Walden*, ed. J. Lyndon Shanley (Princeton, NJ: Princeton University Press, 1971), 322.

5. Evelyn Barish in her art book *Emerson in Italy* (New York: Holt, 1989) considers the 1833 Italian tour a "spiritual journey on which he aimed consciously to achieve what he called 'the Anointed eye'—that is, a vision open to the universe and its grace" (4). In *Emerson: The Mind on Fire* (Berkeley: University of California Press, 1995), Robert D. Richardson, the best of Emerson's biographers, explains it largely in terms of post-traumatic self-discovery and healing. Gigliola Nocera in "Journeys of the Body and Pathways of the Mind: R. W. Emerson's Europe," in Giorgio Mariani et al., eds., *Emerson at 200: Proceedings of the International Bicentennial Conference* (Rome: Aracne Editrice, 2004), 95–104, relies heavily on Richardson.

6. Ralph L. Rusk, *The Life of Ralph Waldo Emerson* (New York: Scribner's, 1949), 170.

7. Emerson claimed in the first chapter of *English Traits* (1856), "I suppose if I had sifted the reasons that led me to Europe," that his motivation was to meet Coleridge, Wordsworth, Landor, De Quincey, and Carlyle (*CW* 5:1).

8. Emerson's itinerary is fully detailed in Richardson, *Emerson: The Mind on Fire,* 131–50, and Rusk, *Life of Ralph Waldo Emerson,* 168–97.

9. Albert J. von Frank, *An Emerson Chronology* (New York: G. K. Hall, 1994), 77.

10. Richardson, *Emerson: The Mind on Fire*, 133.

11. Jason Berger, "Travel," in Wesley T. Mott, ed., *Ralph Waldo Emerson in Context* (New York: Cambridge University Press, 2014), 50.

12. A rich branch of social science, tourism research has significant economic consequences. Tourism is a growth industry worldwide, outperforming recessions and "directly responsible for 5% of the world's GDP, 6% of total exports and employing one out of every 12 people in advanced and emerging economies alike," according to the United Nations World Tourism Organization. See the United Nations World Tourism Organization, "International Tourism to Reach One Billion in 2012," http://media.unwto.org, accessed November 1, 2012.

13. Philip L. Pearce, *Tourist Behaviour: Themes and Conceptual Schemes* (Clevedon, UK: Channel View Publications, 2005), 129.

14. Fred E. Jandt, *Intercultural Communication: An Introduction*, 2nd ed. (Thousand Oaks, CA: Sage, 1998), 287–88. In "Culture Shock: Adjustment to New Cultural Environments," *Practical Anthropology* 7 (1960): 177–182, Kalervo Oberg's terms for the four states are similar: "honeymoon," "hostility," "recovery," and "adjustment."

15. David Justin Hodge, *On Emerson* (Belmont, CA: Wadsworth, 2003), 21.

16. Jandt, *Intercultural Communication*, 288.

17. Robert Weisbuch, "Post-Colonial Emerson and the Erasure of Europe," in Joel Porte and Saundra Morris, eds., *The Cambridge Companion to Ralph Waldo Emerson* (New York: Cambridge University Press, 1999), 193.

18. Shirley Foster, "Americans and Anti-Tourism," in Nicola J. Watson, ed., *The Literary Tourist: Readers and Places in Romantic and Victorian Britain* (Basingstoke, UK: Palgrave Macmillan, 2007), 175–83. Subsequent references to this work will be cited parenthetically in the text by page number.

19. Emerson apparently gave these lectures several times in 1834, in New Bedford and later Concord and possibly Boston. For details, see *EL* 1:87–88. The manuscript lectures are part of the Ralph Waldo Emerson Memorial Association deposit, Houghton Library, Harvard University, call numbers bMS Am 1280.194 (4) and (5) and are quoted here with the kind permission of the Houghton Library and the Ralph Waldo Emerson Memorial Association. I am grateful for the help of my research assistant Jerrica Dowling, who expertly transcribed the lectures.

20. Perhaps the editors of the *Early Lectures*, working only with Edward Waldo Emerson's less complete 1909–14 edition of the *Journals*, did not fully appreciate the differences between the private and public texts. The fourth volume of the *Journals and Miscellaneous Notebooks*, where most of Emerson's Italian material resides, was forthcoming when volume 1 of the *Early Lectures* was published in 1959 and would not appear until five years later.

21. Pearce, *Tourist Behaviour*, 18.

[II]

EMERSON AND GLOBAL MODERNITY

[6]

DAVID LAROCCA

"ETERNAL ALLUSION": MAETERLINCK'S READINGS OF EMERSON'S SOMATIC SEMIOTICS

"A Gesture, a Sign, a Look, a Word"

IN HIS INFLUENTIAL, FIELD-DEFINING study, *The American Renaissance,* F. O. Matthiessen claims that Ralph Waldo Emerson's "extension of the meaning of the inner life relates him to the dominant strain in modern art that leads from Hawthorne through the younger James to Proust, from Poe through the symbolists to Eliot."[1] And as Stanley Cavell has shown classical Hollywood's indebtedness to Emerson's thinking, and P. Adams Sitney has demonstrated an evident lineage of Emersonian poetics in the tradition of American avant-garde filmmaking, so we—as Matthiessen suggests—might consider anew Emerson's influence on the European movement in arts and letters known as Symbolism. Emerson's effect is also attested to by William K. Wimsatt, Jr. and Cleanth Brooks, who addressed Emerson's place in the history of literary criticism—featuring him between Coleridge and Melville—in a section titled "Symbolism."[2] Though the critics retain what seems a grudging respect for Emerson's influence as a reader of literature (referring to "the somewhat rhapsodic language in which Emerson habitually expressed himself[,]" in "high-pitched and evangelistic essays," a condescension regularly found among that generation of critics),[3] they nevertheless emphasize his capacity for symbolic thought—especially how he, like many of his illuminating American contemporaries, were "starved after two hundred years of the Puritanical attenuation of symbolism."[4] Wimsatt and Brooks cite Emerson from "The Poet," where he contends, in a mode anticipating the ordinary language philosophy of J. L. Austin that "Words are also actions, and actions are a kind of words" (CW 3:6).[5] Thereafter, Wimsatt and Brooks conclude that "there can be no doubt that Emerson has to be accounted one of the forerunners of the conception of literature as symbolic form."[6] As Emerson writes, and as they deploy in support of their assessment of his pertinence: "We are symbols and inhabit symbols."[7]

In a European context, one of the primary innovators of Symbolism was Maurice Maeterlinck (1862–1949), a writer, poet, essayist, playwright, and Nobel Laureate who was also an enthusiastic reader and interpreter of Emerson's work.[8] In fact, Arthur Bartlett Maurice reminds us that Maeterlinck was in his own time referred to, by James Huneker among others, as "The Belgian Emerson."[9] And we find him depicted, more broadly, as the "European Emerson."[10] As Maurice writes: Maeterlinck's "feeling for Emerson had become such that he wrote an Introduction to the Essays of the American that had been translated into French by I. Will."[11] When Hamilton Osgood came to read the "preface" to *Sept essais d'Emerson* (1894), he "found [it] to be so sympathetic, so appreciative, and withal so imbued with Emerson's purest and highest thought, that a desire to lay it, in our own tongue, before American readers became instant and forcible"—and he thus hurried to supply an English translation of his own.[12] In the wake of a brief character sketch of Maeterlinck written by Jules Huret, Osgood concludes how it is "of extreme interest to observe how much Maeterlinck is influenced by Emerson, with whom, perhaps, he is as familiar, as is any other European *litterateur.*"[13] In his foreword to his English translation of *On Emerson, and Other Essays,* Montrose Jonas Moses presumes his audience's familiarity with the work of Maeterlinck's American predecessor: "And while reading Maeterlinck's essay on his avowed master and greatest influence, it will be noted how completely and how unconsciously Emerson's thoughts have been assimilated by Maeterlinck."[14] The year before, Moses published a monograph—*Maurice Maeterlinck: A Study* (1911)—in which he says repeatedly that Emerson was Maeterlinck's "greatest influence"—having cited Maeterlinck's claim to this effect as his principal evidence.[15] Even with Maeterlinck's own self-analysis in place—his own willing admission of adoration and adoption of Emerson—critical appraisals by others, on the influence of one author on another, could hardly be more widespread, more in agreement, and in many cases, more hyperbolic.

After graduating from the University of Ghent, Maeterlinck spent time in Paris, where he met members of the emerging Symbolist movement, including Auguste Villiers de L'Isle-Adam. Subsequently, Maeterlinck wrote plays—full of fatalism and mysticism—that proved essential to the Symbolist outlook: *Les sept princesses, L'intruse, Les aveugles, Pelléas et Mélisande, Alladine et Palomides, Interieur,* and *La mort de Tintagiles.* Even his accessible and engaging *The Life of the Bee* (1901) seems a natural history of potent symbolic significance—not unlike Virgil's *Georgics* (c. 29 BC), Charles Butler's *The Feminine Monarchie* (1609), and Bernard Mandeville's *The Fable of the Bees* (1705/1714)—though, in his own estimation, the most "kindred matter" is work on the subject by Jules Michelet and Ludwig Büchner.[16]

Perhaps not surprisingly, given his interest in the clade Anthophila, Maeterlinck later wrote a volume titled *The Intelligence of Flowers* (1907).[17] After moving to Paris, where he lived until 1906, Maeterlinck published his first volume of *Essays* and *Aglavaine et Sélysette.*

It would be much too ambitious to conduct an inquiry into the many ways that Emerson's thought might be said to inform Symbolism broadly construed—principally because it was a dilated, decades-long movement in several fields of creative expression—and the inquiry would still be too expansive if constricted to Maeterlinck's specific contributions to the movement. In the present chapter, therefore, I focus on the much more circumscribed and modest project of conducting an investigation into a signature instance of Maeterlinck's direct engagement with Emerson's work, namely, his essay on Emerson from *The Treasure of the Humble* (1897).[18] If my work on this one further dimension of Emerson's contribution to international culture remains speculative—merely suggestive—it will at least have the virtue of being text-based, underwritten by a close reading of this signature essay by Maeterlinck, quintessentially titled "Emerson."

Conceptually intrigued by the metaphorical implications of the marionette theater for live actors—that humans are but puppets on the strings of fate—Maeterlinck innovated stage dialogue to create what he called "static drama," a notion he explained in "The Tragical in Daily Life" [Le tragique quotidien (1896)] (also featured in *The Treasure of the Humble*)—an account that went on to influence the Symbolist movement more generally. Katherine Biers has taken up her own study of Emerson's influence on theater—in her case, treating Maeterlinck as a medium through which Emerson shaped the thought of Susan Glaspell, "the innovative modernist feminist playwright who helped set the terms for American dramatic modernism."[19] Biers underscores, as she says, "the fact that Maeterlinck's Symbolist techniques were deeply indebted to Emerson's concept of the 'oversoul,' and [Maeterlinck's] characterization and dialogue onstage sought to approximate the inconstant authorial character embedded in the shifting tropes and moods of Emerson's essays. Emerson's ideas were profoundly altered as they returned to American shores on Glaspell's stage, taking on a new and unexpected life as feminist theatre."[20] The structure and patterns of reading, creation, and transmission predicated of Emerson-by-way-of-Maeterlinck-to-Glaspell should feel familiar to anyone who has followed the now century-long critical inheritance of Emerson's influence on Nietzsche and Nietzsche's subsequent effect on Europeans (including those who transformed American thinking), and directly on American writers. The literature on this tandem topic is formidable, and it is not insignificant that Biers makes much of Nietzsche's substantive contribution to Glaspell's work.[21]

Biers, a theorist of drama, helpfully glosses the significance of Maeterlinck's theatrical innovation:

> "Static theater" is devoted to portraying the subliminal and unconscious developments that permeate everyday life, rather than major events in the lives of heroic figures. Via this paradoxically non-dramatic, antitheatrical theatre, reliant often on gesture rather than words, Maeterlinck offers a revolutionary break with stage naturalism, with the nineteenth century's well-made play, and also with the exclusive emphasis on a disembodied theatre of reading put forward by many Symbolists. Maeterlinck's focus on the "quotidian" instead gives pride of place to the portrayal of states of boredom, anxiety, and—above all—waiting, all downplayed in traditional drama. This theatre of situation rather than action had a profound influence on twentieth-century drama, one that is, perhaps, clearest in the absurdist, existentialist dramas of Beckett.[22]

To rectify what appears to be scholarship that acknowledges Maeterlinck's interest in Emerson "only in passing," Biers directs her attention to the way "Maeterlinck's manifesto [viz., "The Tragical"] takes up and transforms the Emersonian Over-soul for the project of both a dramatic Symbolism and a dramatic Platonism, turning it into the 'true tragic element of life' that can serve as the essence of a distinctively modern drama."[23] Biers raises the stakes of Maeterlinck's incorporation of Emersonian ideas by extrapolating Maeterlinck's impact on the dominant dramatic trends at the fin de siècle and into the early twentieth century. And so, for Biers, "It seems reasonable, therefore, to conclude that it was as a result of reading Emerson that Maeterlinck was able to reconceive theatre, in the 1890s, as a state of waiting for an event that never arrives. Given the profound influence his techniques had on later playwrights, it is, thus, Emerson, as much as Nietzsche, who can be understood as the philosophical father of avant-garde theatre."[24]

As a complement to Biers's research on Emerson's perhaps unexpected—and largely inconspicuous—impact on American and European avant-garde theater, I here offer an initial and supplementary salvo on the lines of resemblance between Emerson and Maeterlinck, including the linguistic artifacts that may be cited as evidence when tracing the adoption of prominent ideas for static theatre, and more broadly in exegetical prose and critical writing. For instance, a reader familiar with Emerson's "iron string" and "iron necessity" ("Self-Reliance"), "iron wire" ("Experience"), "iron links of Destiny" ("Montaigne; or, the Skeptic"), and "iron leaf" ("Fate") may be intrigued by Maeterlinck's application of fatalistic concepts and images to the dramatic stage. Meanwhile, three of the essays in *The Treasure of the Humble*—on Emerson, Novalis (1772–1801), and the Flemish mystic

John of Ruysbroeck (1293/4–1381)—became an independent volume—*On Emerson, and Other Essays*—when the work was translated into English by Montrose J. Moses in 1912.[25] The chapter on Emerson reflects Maeterlinck's fascination with interpretable objects and Emerson's unique role in emphasizing the symbolic nature of existence, and the predicates we use to describe it. Maeterlinck admired Emerson as someone who has "succeeded in fixing some few of the eternal allusions which we encounter at every instant in life, in a gesture, a sign, a look, a word,—in silence and in the events which surround us."[26] It will become evident just how crucial allusion (eternal or more provisional) is to Maeterlinck, and how deeply he appreciated Emerson's capacity for prompting it through his use of tropes, signs, and symbols, and also quite crucially in his account of the semiology of everyday life, for example—as just one example—in his rhetorical question "What is a farm but a mute gospel?" (*CW* 1:26). And Maeterlinck himself transposed and translated the idea: "There remains only the life of the every day, and yet we cannot live without greatness."[27] Upon approvingly quoting this line, and those that enframe it in "Maeterlinck's Philosophy of Life," John Dewey noted, "it is a grateful thought that Maeterlinck has learned so much of Emerson."[28] "That Dewey was in turn an admirer of Maeterlinck," Stanley Cavell relates, "is more likely to be unfamiliar, and initially to be even less plausible"—and adds, knowing something of Dewey's philosophical temperament—"In a sense it seemed implausible to Dewey."[29]

Cavell offers an elucidatory clinic on the varieties of reading, influence, and incorporation when he tells us about Dewey's reluctance to paraphrase Maeterlinck. As if postulating a repressed psychoanalytic reason for this unwillingness, Cavell hypothesizes, "What's the matter? . . . I have to assume, from Dewey's own fervent essay on Emerson,[30] that he recognizes the extraordinary paraphrasing of Emerson in Maeterlinck's prose," and then concludes with uncanny perspicacity, "that the figure Dewey is more significantly confessing his inability to paraphrase is Emerson."[31] For those who care, or are attuned to it, Cavell provides another instance in which a European writer of tremendous eminence—Nietzsche is the principal lead of this affair in other remarks by Cavell—as it were gives back American thoughts to America. That is, as with Nietzsche, so now with Maeterlinck, while American audiences have variously struggled to appreciate work by Emerson—what Cavell calls "a sequence of repressions of Emerson's thoughts by the culture he helped to found"[32]—they do, by turns, find it appealing when Emerson is read by others, perhaps especially Europeans. A reader may wonder what this reading of an American by a non-American amounts to. Does it register an indirect authorization of Emerson's prose, giving us reason and putting us at risk for receiving Emerson anew on the home front, yet laced with an "alienated majesty"? This tradition of reception appears alive and well in the recent engagements with Emerson made by Jacques Rancière, for example, in his masterwork, *Aisthesis: Scenes from the Aesthetic Regime of Art,* where the French scholar—having already admitted his awareness of Maeterlinck's love of Emerson[33]—conducts his own critical examination of Emerson's work, principally, "The Poet," and is still very much in harmony with Maeterlinck's attunement to symbolism and the everyday:

> Emerson thus exceeds the thought of the author from whom he borrows his idea of the poet as creator of symbols, namely, Carlyle. For the latter, the symbols of the spiritual world present in the natural order were to be found in flags, banners and standards, in works of art, examples of heroic characters and the vestimentary parade of dandies. For Emerson, the symbols of the spiritual world can be found everywhere. The task of the poet is to awaken this potentiality of speech, this potential of common experience of a spiritual world, slumbering in every list of words, as it is in the array of objects, and the deployment of prosaic activities.[34]

And so Emersonian "turns" of thought (as Cavell variously describes them), or thinking that is "transfigured" (in Emerson's parlance), continue to emerge from European minds and pens.[35] Rancière's critical estimation provides another instance of this habit of inheriting Emerson's writing; and in his savvy gloss, we can appreciate Rancière's shrewd comparison between Carlyle's "heroic" and Emerson's "prosaic," a contrast that gives shape and urgency to Maeterlinck's attraction to the American's reconception of figuration and symbolization.

The notion of Maeterlinck's readings of Emerson, then, arrives with a double sense: Maeterlinck's reading of Emerson's writing and Maeterlinck's interpretation and transformation of that writing in his own literary and dramatic efforts. While I cannot, and do not aim to, explore the full extent to which Emerson can be said to have inspired or otherwise contributed to aspects of Maeterlinck's ideas and their subsequent development in the Symbolist movement, I will highlight those specific lines of affinity—metaphors, analogies, themes, concepts, problems, responses, and of course, allusions—that Maeterlinck himself mentions in this essay; to substantiate the direct reading, I will also look to a few substantive and exemplary lines from Emerson that reinforce one's impression that Maeterlinck and his Symbolist contemporaries were justified in finding useful, complementary, generative ideas expressed in Emerson, and drawing upon them in their own creative work.

The direct instances (namely, from the essay "Emerson") may be sufficient for generating an informed yet discreet engagement with Emerson's effects on Maeterlinck's thinking and writing (for example, in his contribution to Symbolism and the European Symbolist movement as they have been defined). I begin simply by asking how Maeterlinck's essay "Emerson"—what might be called a report on his abiding admiration of the American writer, an esteem reflected both by imitation and by an overt analytical act of interpretation—shows an understanding of the terms Maeterlinck himself highlights in the short piece (namely: symbol, gesture, look, sign, silence, and word, among others) and how Maeterlinck would have read these terms and concepts in Emerson (that is, by a Belgian contemporary who was twenty-years-old when Emerson died in 1882). A close reading of Maeterlinck's essay on Emerson will naturally draw us back to the work by Emerson that Maeterlinck was reading closely. Emerson's *Nature,* "The Poet," "Plato; or the Philosopher," and "Fate" appear to contain ideas consanguineous with Maeterlinck's conceptual sensibilities and preferences.

But, as is common with Emerson's oeuvre, familiar terms and ideas permeate his work, so remarks of especial pertinence to Maeterlinck may yet be sussed and sourced in writing by Emerson that Maeterlinck may not have read, therein making points of affinity more generic and less forensic; still Maeterlinck's perception of a sentiment in one location does not forbid us from finding compelling points of association from other occasions. We cannot, of course, *prove* that Maeterlinck read these specific works of Emerson (though there is strong evidence that he did read widely in Emerson), nor do I suppose we would need to in order to make the plausible assertion that there are important moments of resemblance or resonance between the prose of the American essayist and his Belgian acolyte. Thus, my aim in the present investigation is to exhibit some sense of their shared metaphors, allusions, intellectual preoccupations, and ways of describing reality. Since Emerson antedated Maeterlinck, and we know Maeterlinck read Emerson, there may be a temptation to ascribe a causal relationship; but that need not be drawn or defended to enjoy filiation and lines of suggestion—the moments when Maeterlinck appears to sometimes directly and often obliquely engage ideas that Emerson would have found familiar, would have recognized as his own or as sympathetic to his own. Indeed, Maeterlinck's own practice of alluding to Emerson's work suggests his close reading of the American writer even as Maeterlinck's artful prose—incorporating ideas and influences from others along the way—reinforces his capacity for distinctive thought.

As aids to my reflection in this subfield of Maeterlinck studies, and the sub-subfield of Maeterlinck's readings of Emerson, I have benefited from the many aforementioned, cited, and authoritative contemporary studies, as well as works in the longer history of research, including Richard Hovey's introduction—"Modern Symbolism and Maeterlinck"—to his translated collection, *The Plays of Maurice Maeterlinck* (1896);[36] Henry Rose's *Maeterlinck's Symbolism* (1910)—which includes a fascinating link to Emanuel Swedenborg (1688–1772), a figure of shared interest for both Emerson and Maeterlinck; and Rose's subsequent book, *On Maeterlinck: or Notes on the Study of Symbols* (1911). Two further book-length studies proved crucial: Mary Ellen Macdonald Clark's *Maurice Maeterlinck: Poet and Philosopher* (1915), and Miroslav John Hanak's *Maeterlinck's Symbolic Drama: A Leap into Transcendence* (1974). Articles of an earlier vintage on Maeterlinck further supplemented and informed my inquiry, including research by William Lyon Phelps, George R. MacMinn, Benjamin Mather Woodbridge, Gust L. Van Roosbroeck, and Paul Revere Frothingham.[37] All of these appraisals provide robust accounts of the shape and tenor of Maeterlinck's thought, including his symbolism, and thus offer highly useful interpretive interventions, and enriching historical perspectives, that have substantiated my effort to identify points of resemblance between Emerson's understanding of symbol, gesture, look, sign, silence, and word and Maeterlinck's account of these notions as featured in his essay. (It is also abundantly clear that further speculative ventures might be conducted by others who possess nuanced language facility between the English and French texts *and* also enjoy a familiarity with both Maeterlinck and Emerson's work—that, indeed, would be a sub-sub-subfield!) As it is when trying to appreciate how non-English speakers admire and appropriate Emerson's work (often read in translation, not in Emerson's original English)—as we find in cases from Nietzsche, Proust, Musil, Rilke, and Borges, among others—so it is an admitted liability of the present study that I have limited fluency in French. As a result, even a close reading of Maeterlinck's work will be based on English translations, such as they are, and therefore must somewhat qualify my interpretive claims for the original French texts and their Belgian author.[38] Translations, we come to find, for better and for worse, are readings in themselves, and so readers must hope that the indispensable intermediary agent can catch and cast the sense of his or her source material and the spirit of its author.

Symbolism has been said to begin with Charles Baudelaire's *The Flowers of Evil*—and as Baudelaire was also a reader of Emerson, he made occasional overt references to his American contemporary.[39] Symbolism in Baudelaire and thereafter is often described as emphasizing the gothic component of Romanticism (which in itself may prompt our attention to Edgar Allan Poe's influence on Baudelaire). By and large, though, Symbolists were keen to find language that acknowledged the mystical and ineffable aspects of human life, often coupled or complemented by a keen appreciation of fate and mortality. And so much of the Symbolist's written work—no doubt related to the visual poetics and genre iconography of Symbolist painters—was framed by overt use of metaphorical language, often intended to communicate difficult things indirectly. To the extent that Emerson's work may also be described in similar terms, we may glean an initial and immediate sense of his pertinence to the Symbolists of the second half of the nineteenth century and into the twentieth. My intention is to elucidate one aspect of this development by focusing on Maeterlinck's reading of and commentary on Emerson, trying along the way to emphasize those key conceptual insights that Maeterlinck may have adopted and adapted in his own work—so essential to Symbolism.

"Mystical Accomplices"

Human linguistic expression seems predicated on the forgetfulness of its symbolic nature. To the question: "What is a word?" Nietzsche responded, "It is the copy in sound of a nerve stimulus. But the further inference from the nerve stimulus to a cause outside of us is already the result of a false and unjustifiable application of the principle of sufficient reason."[40] Glossing his description, Nietzsche adds that the "creator [of language] only designates the relations of things to men, and for expressing these relations he lays hold of the boldest metaphors."[41] Nevertheless, though we are forgetful that metaphors are invented and imposed, it is a convenience—often an activator to thought and its capacity for being shared—that we become oblivious to the metaphors and analogies that underwrite thinking. Thus, a paradox looms, for anyone who wishes to express ideas, namely, that—to forward thoughts, to invent with or through language—one must rely on those very same images of which one is prone to ignore or dismiss, or simply cannot see. Emerson appeared untroubled by the figurative qualities of language and thus regularly undertook to exhibit his thinking with the aid of "the boldest metaphors," both as concealers and revealers, and according to a logic that conceptually animated and oriented them to his chosen subjects. We see this in the circular/circulating structure of "The Over-Soul," which invokes Platonic and Plotinian ideas; in the ebb and flow, the cause and effect, the homeostasis of "Compensation"; and even in the description of posture in his most well-known concept and celebrated essay, "Self-Reliance." There are many factors that draw one writer to another, and the present study is inflected, even saturated, by the consideration of such speculations, but it appears evident that Maeterlinck found in Emerson a view of language that managed at once to remain conscious of the governing force of its symbols while simultaneously mobilizing them to creative effect. Emerson was cognizant of the particular signs he deployed without becoming self-conscious about their contribution to a larger point. And so, as a sentence is composed of words, and paragraphs of sentences, and essays of paragraphs, so Emerson would build from disparate iconic elements something with a constitutive force that transcended the limitations of the individual parts. With some measure of self-reflexivity, he marshaled language to the aid of his linguistic creation by remaining humble before its sublimely symbolic character. In the years following his reading of Emerson, Maeterlinck himself would become the most prominent proponent of the new intellectual outlook known as Symbolism. My task here, then, briefly and again speculatively, is dedicated to a consideration of the extent to which Maeterlinck may have drawn inspiration for Symbolism from his appreciation and appropriation of Emerson's writing. Keeping in mind the broad sweep of scholarship on this subject, noted above, I turn to the single, short piece that Maeterlinck wrote titled "Emerson."

Even Maeterlinck's essay itself is an allusion—as Emerson is first quoted at midpoint, and then only invoked by name very late in the work; that structure, in its constituent forms and attributes, resembles Emerson's habit of using the name of a historical figure as the title for an essay—only to find the figure making a late appearance in the exegesis (consider, for example, the lengthy, anonymous wind-up to explicit reference in the essays that constitute *Representative Men*). But what is Maeterlinck doing with his allusion here: referring to an unnamed but known, familiar source, attested to by the title; paraphrasing Emerson, as if giving a lesson in Emerson's thought by rehearsing it in Maeterlinck's own words; or, pushing beyond paraphrase, to some further version of Emerson's thought that contains an *explanation* of its significance while also attempting to capture several of its key tenets? Even as we readers take our cue and orientation from the initial remark by Novalis (which is reinvoked midway, as if to remind us of our conceptual coordinates and the allusions and associations they are meant to inscribe), and even as we acknowledge Maeterlinck's aim to follow after Emerson's response to Novalis's insight, we are held in suspension: watching as Maeterlinck conducts a metacritical investigation of Emerson. That is, as Maeterlinck addresses what can be called Emerson's somatic semiotics—the way we read bodies as texts—Maeterlinck positions himself in relation to Emerson's person and prose. We are given a lesson in reading while reading.

Seeing as Glancing

As with Saint Augustine's parable of language acquisition in the *Confessions,* and the correction of that view by Ludwig Wittgenstein in the *Philosophical Investigations,* Maeterlinck introduces us to a scene not of adolescent speaking but of adolescent seeing—more particularly to seeing as a form of discernment: "The child that meets me will not be able to tell his mother what he has seen; however, as soon as his eyes have sensed my presence, he knows all that I am, all that I have been, all that I shall be" (EE 362). So the child cannot *say* what he sees, and yet he has undergone an intuitive—naive, preliterate—encounter with an interpretable object. "As soon as the child's glance," Maeterlinck continues, "has met mine,—my face, my attitude and the infinite which surrounds them and of which they are the interpreters,—he knows what to cling to" (EE 362). Here we are reminded of Emerson's similar attention to the striking, penetrating perceptual capacities not so much of *studying* other bodies, other faces, but of merely glancing at the them: "the cabman is phrenologist so far," he writes in "Fate" (CW 6:5).[42] And this talent for quick insight continues into adulthood, notes Maeterlinck, as "that man who knocks at my door expends, at the very moment he greets me, as many marvelous spiritual treasures as the prince whom I have wrested from death. I open to him, and in an instant he sees at his feet, as though from the height of a tower, all that takes place between two souls" (EE 362).

The glance—as a metonym or fraction of the acts of the eye-apparatus—is, we might say, part of this organ's capacity for gesture. The glance "speaks" in the place of things being (literally) said. Maeterlinck notes: "[A friend] has said many profound things of his soul; but in that small time which divides a glance that pauses from a glance that vanishes, I have learned all that he could never say" (EE 363). Or in a similar defeat of words, he writes: "What their mouth utters signifies nought besides what their presence declares" (EE 363). In Emerson, writing in 1864, a couple of years after Maeterlinck's birth, we find: "The attitude, the tone, is all. Let our eyes not look away, but meet. . . . A just feeling will fast enough supply fuel for discourse, if speaking be more grateful than silence. . . . Don't *say* things. What you *are* stands over you the while, and thunders so that I cannot hear what you say to the contrary" (CW 8:52).

The Expressive Body

Maeterlinck, like Emerson, and as later, Freud, has an appreciation for the power of the unintentional, the improvised, and the accidental. Of course, none of them think these are unplanned—rather just that they become manifest while their causes (often) remain insufficiently revealed: "In our eyes two identical destinies saluted each other and loved each other," writes Maeterlinck (EE 363). In "The Transcendentalist," Emerson affirmed: "Man owns the dignity of the life which throbs around him, in chemistry, and tree, and animal, and in the involuntary functions of his own body" (CW 1:206). And

Maeterlinck, still dwelling on the textual riches of the glance, writes: "On the other side of our involuntary emotions, we lead a marvelous life, still, very pure, and very certain, to which our hands are outstretched, our eyes which are opened, and our unexpected glances which meet, make continual allusion. All our organs are the mystical accomplices of a superior being; and it is never a man,—but a soul that we have known" (EE 363).

For Emerson, the body is inhabited by the spirit (as he says in "The Poet," "We were put into our bodies" [CW 3:3]), and so the body's organs (inner and outer, apparent and hidden) are the instruments by which the spirit makes itself known. For this reason, "[a]ll goes to show that the soul in man is not an organ" (CW 2:161), but rather that organs are conduits for expression. Or as Emerson construes it, "the soul, whose organ [what we might conventionally call 'the body'] he is, would he let it appear through his action, would make our knees bend" (CW 2:161).

The Elusive Allusive

Maeterlinck underscores and elaborates on Emerson's somatic semiotics by directing attention to the meaningfulness of the signs and allusions made by the human body in action: "the infinite which is moved by the opening of an eyelid, by the bending of the head, and by the closing of a hand." And yet, because these signs become commonplace or are dismissed as inadvertent, even irrational or beyond the control of conscious deliberation, "We live so far from ourselves that we are ignorant of nearly everything that occurs at the horizon of our being" (EE 364). One's appearance, subtle facial movements, posture, "the form and the gait of the body" (CW 1:67), the sounds of breathing, the pitch or tone of voice, the impression of a caress or handshake, the steady concentration of a trained eye, all contribute to one's perhaps preconscious or unconscious reading of another's assessment. We may want to borrow the colloquial phrase and simply call this a kind of body language.[43] As Maeterlinck admonishes: "Raise your eyes, see what you are, see what you do" (EE 364). And: "This glance exchanged in the dark; these words which had no meaning at the foot of the mountain—see what they become and what they signify further" (EE 364). Counterintuitively, in the midst of his regular invocation of glancing and glimpsing and seeing, Maeterlinck illustrates his point about the somatic nature of expression through a parable of *blindness* (and the attendant *in*capacity of words to compensate for the loss of sight): "Are we not like unto a man who has lost his eyesight during the first years of his childhood? He has seen the endless spectacle of beings. He has noted the sun, the sea, and the forest. Now and always, these marvels are ever-present in his make-up; and should you speak of them, what will you be able to say to him, and what will your poor words be beside the glade, the tempest, and the dawn which still live in the depths of his spirit, and are made part of his flesh?" (*EE* 364). Maeterlinck orients us, like Emerson, to remember that "there remains to us only our daily life"—and yet "in spite of everything, your life is incomprehensible" (*EE* 365). You must live because there are no hours without innermost miracles and without ineffable significance. You must live because there is not an act, there is not a word, there is a not a gesture which escapes inexplicable claims in a world "where there are many things to do and few things to know" (*EE* 365).

On account of the body's perpetual, unheeded expressiveness, there is no such thing as concealment: "Hides his thoughts!" Emerson exclaims in response to the notion that a philosopher might withhold his ideas from the world, "Hide the sun and moon. Thought is all light, and publishes itself to the universe. It will speak, though you were dumb, by its own miraculous organ. It flows out of your actions, your manners, and your face" (*CW* 1:116). Yet the fleshy exposure does not yield understanding, as Maeterlinck picks up the spirit of Emerson's remark: "And though they speak through their glances, their hands, their faces, and their assembled presence, they shall ever be ignorant of what they have said" (*EE* 362). Expressiveness, then, is not necessarily coordinate with intelligibility. In this way, the body's speech—its gestures, glances, and somatic allusions—is perhaps more akin to a Mosaic scene of encounter with divine dictation. There are numerous points in Emerson's work, and in Maeterlinck's brief essay, when there appear anticipations of key features in Emmanuel Levinas's thought—namely, his focus on the face of another, or the other, as the portal for "a relation with the Transcendent": "The dimension of the divine opens forth from the human face."[44] Maeterlinck says that Emerson shows us how in "two passers-by who accost each other, he has made us see the countenance of God who smiles with the countenance of God" (*EE* 366). Moreover, and more immanently, "what we do, this can itself be read on our face" (*EE* 365).

Emerson was, on his own merits, a committed theorist of facial expression—especially attentive to the figure of the face as an illuminating intermediary between the inmost and the outmost, the private and the public, the internal intention and the outward expression, the eternal and the ephemeral. Partly, we might conjecture that his interest and his sustained comments on physiognomy owe something to the popular pseudoscience of phrenology; and if those studies did not earn his affirmation of their scientific credibility, he remained attentive to their appeal for analogical force. Phrenology was an analysis and taxonomy of fixed, structural forms of the skull (and thus, not incidentally, was perceived as a formidable indicator of fate), whereas a reading of the human face, in the study of physiognomy, was an art of interpreting the changes and alterations of an evolving, environmentally and emotionally responsive facial topography (and thus, importantly, not a study of personal fate so much as a bold conjecture about the meaning of *internal* states as they find expression in the form of external arrangements of one's countenance—as if, we might say, like Orson Welles, that film, in photographing the face, photographs thought). For it is in the refinements of line and movement that reading a face—and its animated features—takes its cue. And unlike phrenology, with its implication of accessibility only to highly trained specialists, we are all certified and credentialed in the practiced, but often unacknowledged, habit of reading faces—as Emerson notes: "We are all physiognomists and penetrators of character" (CW 6:119). "We doubt not a man's fortune may be read . . . in the lines of his face, by physiognomy."[45]

From *Nature* in 1836 and "Literary Ethics" in 1838 to "Behavior" (the sixth chapter of *The Conduct of Life*) in 1860 and elsewhere and in between, we can glean and marvel at Emerson's protracted attention to human physiognomy's crucial role in our engagement with one another. "What [a person] is engraves itself on his face" (CW 2:92). "Every act of the man inscribes itself in the memories of his fellows and in his own manners and face" (CW 4:151). "Nature tells every secret once. Yes, but in man she tells it all the time, by form . . . face and parts of the face" (CW 6:90). "The face and eyes reveal what the spirit is doing" (CW 6:94). These sustained references to the face—its capacity for legibility—is of a piece with his broader claims for the symbolical character of the human body, and beyond that—to the symbolic forms that reside in nature more generally.

"A Mute Gospel"

As Emerson wrote of the symbolic character of life in his prose and poetry from early to late, and through a broad range of direct and indirect invocations, there is reason to believe that no matter where Maeterlinck may have read in Emerson's work, he would have likely encountered some form or variation on the notion—perpetually emphasized and reevaluated by Emerson—that the human body (aside from its capacity for speech, for mark-making, for the uses of language) is symbolical and expressive. In "Behavior," for example, the human figure itself assumes the capacity for articulation, description, and multiform communication: "The tell-tale body is all tongues" (CW 6:94). And later, in "Works and Days," Emerson trades the organic metaphor for the mechanistic and instrumental: "The body is a meter" (CW 7:79). And these analogies are matched also in Emerson's consideration of wild nature as well as human agricultural interventions, as he asks in *Nature*, "What is a farm but a mute gospel?" (CW 1:26). The farm, like the human body, is a sign-set (a site for or of signs), and is similarly silent—a crucial attribute of Maeterlinck's recurrent appreciation of the nonverbal, preliterate nature of physical forms such as the eye and face and body. Maeterlinck, perhaps so formidably attuned to the ubiquity of symbols in humans and in nature, often appeals to a bewilderment that stuns to silence. If we know, we know by the penetrating power *beyond deduction*. Our words often live at odds with our bodies (including our desires, intentions, and aspirations), and thus regularly contradict and undermine our constitutional and emotional tenor. Maeterlinck's insight strikes deeper than the cliché that one may say what one does not mean, or that one speaks against one's own interests; rather, the very attempt at linguistic or logical articulation seems to interfere with somatic expression—as if cognitive ordering were always well ahead of or well behind the expressive intelligence of the human face and body, and its subtly deployed features and nuanced forms. Thus, by association, if there be a legitimacy to the farm's eloquence—its capacity for a kind of "speech" that renders its divine message in the prose of crop lines instead of stanzas—so also can we find meaning in the limbs of the human body in motion, and the lineaments of the human face in its expressive movements. Aside from audible speech—that is, in silence, in the gesture, in the glance—we are ourselves rich texts awaiting attentive, perceptive readers.

Many readers are familiar with what might be taken as the seed-terms of Emerson's approach to reading bodies as texts—so described here as his somatic semiotics—namely, lines from his first book: "Nature is the symbol of spirit" (CW 1:17). "Every natural fact is a symbol of some spiritual fact" (CW 1:18). Yet, the founding thoughts of this founding book continue to appear in later works, such as in "The Poet": "Things admit of being used as symbols because nature is a symbol" (CW 3:8). Ever a critic of arid system-making, foolish consistency, and vacant logical reductions, Emerson was instead convinced that "a good symbol is the best argument" (CW 8:7)—in short, that one's system or logic, one's reason, could be most artfully achieved by means of trope and taxonomy, by analogy and association.[46] Exercising just such a concatenation of elements, "[w]e learn nothing rightly until we learn the symbolical character of life."[47] And that "[a]s a power [poetry] is the perception of the symbolic character of things and a treating them as representative" (CW 8:14). Thus "[t]he power of the poet is . . . in using every fact in Nature . . . as a fluent symbol."[48] So if we need a name to assign to this reader of somatic semiotics, we could do worse, in Emerson's schema, than to call him or her, the poet.

The moral is overt but not obvious, for it is the poet who renders the world obliquely, who has a sense and an appreciation for indirection, innuendo, and yes, allusion (eternal or otherwise). The poet is literate and lives in the milieu of letters, but he or she is not literal. The interpretation of logic holds the philosopher's attention, and the confessions of the soul, the psychologist's and the priest's; the grammarian checks for the propriety of usage, and the historian scans for accuracy of event and account. But the poet? The poet attends to the symbolical character of things, and as Emerson wrote in "Plato; or, the Philosopher," "All things are symbolical" (CW 4:38).

"We Are Symbols and Inhabit Symbols"

The poet has a proper field of labor, since, as Maeterlinck says: "Man is eager for explanations. His life must be shown to him. He rejoices when he somewhere finds the exact interpretation of a small gesture which he has been making for some twenty-five years. Here on earth there is no trivial gesture" (EE 366). The poet—or the reader of somatic semiotics—becomes the student of such small gestures (their form, their context, their relationship to other small gestures) and the wider patterns of life that provide a context for their reception. Maeterlinck is sure that few see more than what lies idly, apparently in view: "Here, it is the man and nothing more" (EE 366). In our everyday, commonplace, quotidian lives, "[h]e is not arbitrarily exalted; he is merely nearer us than usual. It is John who prunes his tree; it is Peter who builds his house; it is you who speaks to me of the harvest; it is I who give you my hand. But we are so situated that we touch the gods, and we are astonished by what we do. We did not know that all the forces of the soul were present; we did not know that all the laws of the universe were about us, and we turn dumbfounded, like people who have seen a miracle" (EE 366).

We return to Maeterlinck's postulation that *doing* and *knowing* are distinct, perhaps incompatible. And we should reserve any presumption that because the poet addresses the symbolical character of life that he or she knows more than those who stand dumbfounded. Perhaps the poet, like the rest of us, can be reassured by small achievements of reading, brief moments of interpretive insight, and remain humble in the face of the expansive totality of meanings that present themselves to the student of nature. Thus, where there is attentiveness, there need not be comprehension; the attention is the readerly achievement, even with its limitations and liabilities of insight. Maeterlinck concludes that "Emerson has come to affirm simply this equal and secret grandeur of our life. He has encompassed us with silence and with wonder. He has placed a shaft of light beneath the feet of the workman who leaves the workshop" (EE 366). And thus may we retain the humility that attends silence and wonder while observing that the poet never leaves his or her workshop. For him, for her, all things are symbolical.

Maeterlinck offers a summation of Emerson's rare contribution to our thinking about the symbols that surround us and the symbols that we are: "There are not many who have shown us that man is greater and more profound than man, and who have thus succeeded in fixing some few of the eternal allusions which we encounter at every instant of life, in a gesture, a sign, a look, a word,—in silence and in the events which surround us" (*EE* 362). In these direct remarks on Emerson's achievement, and in his more varied appropriations and transformations of Emerson's writing, Maeterlinck appears to appreciate the side of Emerson that creates—often as if to retain or recover what was becoming lost—a mood of wonder, a dwelling in mystery and the mystical, a fondness for what remains unknown and inscrutable, often even or especially in our immediate encounter with signs and symbols. Emerson said that "in the woods we return to reason and faith," and in an essay dedicated to the topic of destiny, "Fate," he conjures the world of his forefathers for further consideration: "Our Calvinists, in the last generation, had something of the same dignity. They felt that the weight of the Universe held them down to their place. What could they do? Wise men feel that there is something which cannot be talked or voted away,—a strap or belt which girds the world" (*CW* 1:10; also *CW* 6:3). That bind, though, was the condition for a kind of exaltation in the enigmas that abound, pervading our thoughts and imaginations, our prayers and our reveries. Emerson cultivated a sober quietism at the periphery of human existence, aimed to find a limit to reason's dictates, like Kant, so that we might sit merely in astonishment of merely being at all, or as he figured the relationship between attention and explanation: "Man does not stand in awe of man, nor is his genius admonished to stay at home, to put itself in communication with the internal ocean, but it goes abroad to beg a cup of water of the urns of other men. We must go alone. I like the silent church before the service begins, better than any preaching" (*CW* 2:41).

Is it the poet's work, or our own, to fathom two senses of "eternal allusion," that is, without succumbing to a skepticism that would pun the phrase and make it eternal *illusion*? First, there is the interminable, unending flow of reference that defines allusion—how one sign calls out to another, claims an association behind, below, or beyond itself; and secondly, there is the humbling fact that allusions are caught up in our destinies as bodies—in this context, as somatic symbols—and thus are, despite their abundance and accumulation, also subject to fate. Therefore, allusions are at once endlessly proliferating, and also poised for human perception, definition, and account.

We are left to negotiate, after Emerson, after Maeterlinck, the correlation between the allusion of symbols (what they are, refer to, and mean) and the registration of our ignorance about them. Maeterlinck seems to have appreciated that Emerson presented a picture of our human condition as an ongoing negotiation of these terms, ever onward, in consideration of the fatal forms our bodies take—enfleshed, fragile, and defined by a perpetual cycling of the inner and outer, the deep and profound coursings of vital energies and their expiration, along with the superficial signs that bubble up—either to obey or betray them on the face, in a glance.

The present chapter, both for its brevity and its methodology, embodies an allusion to Emerson's work and Maeterlinck's reading of it. The results thus necessarily call attention to the *conditions* of any hermeneutics of experience, any attempt to read the signs of life while being them and inhabiting them; in this regard, as Emerson and Maeterlinck appear committed to soliciting in their readers, such remarks—even if they summon the potency and depth of insight afforded by the glance—must concomitantly remain suggestive, prospective, poised with anticipation. Thus, as readers of Emerson and of Maeterlinck's readings of Emerson, we may catch a steady, if quick glance at their avowed or otherwise abiding connection; perhaps, in reading these gestures, these superficial and representative signs, we will know more—or more rightly—than if we set about to study the connections anatomically, forensically, causatively, deductively. In this altered spirit, defined as it is by an earned respect for the mystical and coupled with a sober faith in that which exceeds easy comprehension, we may glean that a hallmark method of or for thinking in Emerson, and later Maeterlinck, is the harvest of first impressions: as the "cabmen is phrenologist so far," so are we given sufficient reason here to consider that a line of life and affinity obtains between the American and the Belgian Emersons.

Notes

1. F. O. Matthiessen, "In the Optative Mood," from *American Renaissance: Art and Expression in the Age of Emerson and Whitman* (Oxford: Oxford University Press, 1941), in David LaRocca, ed., *Estimating Emerson: An Anthology of Criticism from Carlyle to Cavell* (New York: Bloomsbury, 2013), 440. This collection hereafter cited as EE. Michael Murphy, for example, tell us that Proust read Emerson in Émlie Montégut's translation of *Essais de philosophie américaine* (1851), and later came to read *Sept essais d'Emerson* (1894, trans. I. Will), which was prefaced by Maeterlinck (*Proust and America* [Liverpool: Liverpool University Press, 2007], 68). Moreover, "Proust's early admiration for Maeterlinck is well known" (67n2).

2. William K. Wimsatt, Jr. and Cleanth Brooks, *Literary Criticism: A Short History* (1957; rpt., New York: Vintage, 1967), chap. 26.

3. Ibid., 585–86. For more on Emerson's troubled inheritance by the New Critics and Southern Agrarians, who were, by and large, impatient with his prose, see "A Conversation among Critics," the introduction to *EE*, 1–25, esp. 9–13.

4. Wimsatt and Brooks, *Literary Criticism*, 586.

5. For more on words as actions, see J. L. Austin, *How to Do Things with Words* (Cambridge, MA: Harvard University Press, 1962); Stanley Cavell, *Emerson's Transcendental Etudes*, ed. David Justin Hodge (Stanford, CA: Stanford University Press, 2003); and David LaRocca, *Emerson's English Traits and the Natural History of Metaphor* (New York: Bloomsbury, 2013), esp., chap. 3, sec. 7; chap. 8, secs. 4–5; and chap. 13, secs. 11–12.

6. Wimsatt and Brooks, *Literary Criticism*, 585. To support their claim, Wimsatt and Brooks cite Charles Feidelson, Jr., *Symbolism and American Literature* (Chicago: University of Chicago Press, 1953), esp. 119–35.

7. Wimsatt and Brooks, *Literary Criticism*, 587; Emerson, *CW* 3:12.

8. An early assessment of Maeterlinck's reading of Emerson was offered by George R. MacMinn, "Emerson and Maeterlinck," *Sewanee Review* 24 (July 1916): 265–81.

9. See the introduction by Arthur Bartlett Maurice to Maurice Maeterlinck's *The Miracle of Saint Anthony* (New York: Dodd, Mead and Co., 1918), 33, 40.

10. Paul Revere Frothingham, "The Mysticism of Maeterlinck," *Harvard Theological Review* 5 (April 1912): 251, 255.

11. Arthur Bartlett Maurice, introduction to Maurice Maeterlinck, *The Miracle of Saint Anthony*, 18.

12. Hamilton Osgood, "Maeterlinck and Emerson," *Arena* 15 (1896): 563–73. This publication also contains Maeterlinck's preface in an English translation by Osgood, a piece that was reprinted—in a new translation—as the first of three essays in *On Emerson, and Other Essays*, trans. Montrose J. Moses (New York: Dodd, Mead and Co., 1912)—the other two being on Novalis and Ruysbroeck—and, more recently, using the Moses translation, in *EE*, 362–66. Osgood relates that the translation of Emerson's writing into French, *Sept essais d'Emerson* (1894), which Maeterlinck prefaces, was made by Mademoiselle Mali, whose nom de plume was I. Will; this attribution is also corroborated in the foreword to *On Emerson, and Other Essays* by Montrose J. Moses (9), and in an essay by Richard Langham Smith, "Aimer ainsi: Rekindling the Lamp in *Pelléas*," in Elliot Antokoletz and Marianne Wheeldon, eds., *Rethinking Debussy* (New York: Oxford University Press, 2011), 86.

13. Osgood, "Maeterlinck and Emerson," 565.

14. Moses, *On Emerson, and Other Essays*, 11.

15. Montrose Jonas Moses, *Maurice Maeterlinck: A Study* (New York: Duffield and Co., 1911), 13, 203, 291.

16. Maurice Maeterlinck, *The Life of the Bee*, trans. Alfred Sutro (1901; rpt., New York: Dodd, Mead and Co., 1908), 7.

17. Maurice Maeterlinck, *The Intelligence of Flowers* (New York: Dodd, Mead and

Co., 1907); rpt., *The Intelligence of Flowers*, trans. Philip Mosley (Albany: State University of New York Press, 2008).

18. Maurice Maeterlinck, *The Treasure of the Humble*, trans. Alfred Sutro (New York: Dodd, Mead and Co., 1897), 95–119.

19. Katherine Biers, "Stages of Thought: Emerson, Maeterlinck, Glaspell," *Modern Drama* 56 (Winter 2013): 457.

20. Ibid., 458.

21. See early studies by Stanley Hubbard, *Nietzsche und Emerson* (Basel, 1958); and Eduard Baumgarten, *Das Vorbild Emersons in Werk und Leben Nietzsches* (Heidelberg, 1956); but also, especially the more recent—and better-known—work of Stanley Cavell, *Emerson's Transcendental Etudes*, ed. David Justin Hodge (Stanford, CA: Stanford University Press, 2003); David Mikics, *The Romance of Individualism in Emerson and Nietzsche* (Athens: Ohio University Press, 2003); George Stack, *Nietzsche and Emerson: An Elective Affinity* (Athens: Ohio University Press,1992); and Jennifer Ratner-Rosenhagen, *American Nietzsche: A History of an Icon and His Ideas* (Chicago: University of Chicago Press, 2012). Biers, "Stages of Thought," references only the last contributor in this list (471n3), and therefore seems to underfund what could be a double argument for Emerson's influence on Glaspell by way of *two* prominent European thinkers, viz., Nietzsche and Maeterlinck. Biers is clearly aware of Glaspell's close reading of Nietzsche—"Intertextual approaches to Glaspell's oeuvre, however, have generally neglected the importance of a broader development, inspired in large part by Friedrich Nietzsche" (458), so it may be worth pointing up Emerson's influence on the German as well as the Belgian thinker. See also David Justin Hodge, "Una traduzione transatlantica: Fato e libertà in Emerson e nel giovane Nietzsche" [Transatlantic translation: Young Nietzsche writing toward Emerson], in Sergio Franzese, ed., *Nietzsche e L'America* (Pisa: Edizioni ETS, Nietzscheana Saggi 2, 2005), 83–105.

22. Biers, "Stages of Thought," 463. She cites Maeterlinck, "The Tragical" (in *The Treasure of the Humble*, 106); and Katharine Worth, *The Irish Drama of Europe from Yeats to Beckett* (Atlantic Highlands, NJ: Humanities Press, 1978).

23. Biers, "Stages of Thought," 470; Maeterlinck, "The Tragical," 99. Of those who note the interest "only in passing," Biers cites May Daniels, *The French Drama of the Unspoken* (Edinburgh: Edinburgh University Press, 1953); and Bettina Knapp, *Maurice Maeterlinck* (Boston: Twayne, 1975).

24. Biers, "Stages of Thought," 471.

25. See note 38 below for selected remarks by William Lyon Phelps on Moses's translation of Maeterlinck's *Emerson, and Other Essays*. The year before his translation of Maeterlinck appeared, Moses's book *Maurice Maeterlinck: A Study* was published (1911).

26. Maurice Maeterlinck, "Emerson," in EE, 362.

27. Osgood's translation of Maeterlinck's preface, in "Maeterlinck and Emerson," 571.

28. John Dewey, "Maeterlinck's Philosophy of Life," in *The Middle Works: 1899–1924*, vol. 6: *1910–1911; Journal Articles, Book Reviews, Miscellany in the 1910–11 Period,*

and "How We Think," ed. Jo Ann Boydston (Carbondale: Southern Illinois University Press, 1978/2008), 133. First published in *Hibbert Journal* 9 (1911): 765–78, later reprinted as "Maurice Maeterlinck" in *Characters and Events*, ed. Joseph Ratner (New York: Henry Holt, 1929), 1:31–44. This line, from the Osgood translation (1896), is also quoted by Edward M. Colie as an illustration of Maeterlinck's reading—and comprehension—of Emerson, in his introduction to Maeterlinck's collection of essays, *The Buried Temple* (New York: Dodd, Mead and Co., 1910), xi.

29. Stanley Cavell, *A Pitch of Philosophy: Autobiographical Exercises* (Cambridge, MA: Harvard University Press, 1994), 168.

30. Cavell refers here to John Dewey, "Emerson—The Philosopher of Democracy" (*EE* 291–96).

31. Cavell, *A Pitch of Philosophy*, 168.

32. Cavell, *Emerson's Transcendental Etudes*, 222. See also 60–61, 66, 171–72, 205, 222.

33. See Jacques Rancière, *The Aesthetic Unconscious* (Cambridge: Polity Press, 2009); first published as *L'inconscient esthétique* (Paris: Éditions Galilée, 2001), 40n11.

34. Jacques Rancière, *Aisthesis: Scenes from the Aesthetic Regime of Art*, trans. Zakir Paul (New York: Verso, 2013), 60. In a footnote, Rancière directs our attention to Carlyle's *Sartor Resartus* (1833–34), where the "theory of symbols is notably developed in Book III, Chapters 3 ('Symbols'), 7 ('Organic Filaments'), and 10 ('The Dandiacal Body')."

35. Cavell, *Emerson's Transcendental Etudes*, 168, 227. Emerson, "The American Scholar," in *The Complete Works of Ralph Waldo Emerson*, Concord edition (Boston: Houghton Mifflin, 1903–4), 1:96. To be sure, there are startling moments of Emerson's influence outside of Europe, for example, as found in Iwano Homei's "Oyomei to Emason" [Wang Yangming and Emerson, 1910], and *Shimpiteki hanju shugi* [The principle of the mystic demi-animal, 1906], which, as Yoshio Takanashi tell us, "describes a philosophy he termed 'demi-animalistic momentalism.' Influenced by Western mystics, including Emerson, Maeterlinck, and Swedenborg, Iwano rejected a dualistic view of life—including the drawing of such oppositions as flesh and soul, and subjectivity and objectivity—and instead emphasized the instinctive, nonrational element in humanity." Yoshio Takanashi, *Emerson and Neo-Confucianism: Crossing Paths over the Pacific* (New York: Palgrave Macmillan, 2014), 33–34. Perhaps it is a holdover from what Emerson termed in "The American Scholar" our "apprenticeship to the learning of other lands" (namely, Europe and the ancient Mediterranean) that we may be less surprised by the admiration and use of Emerson's work by non-Europeans. There is, as Cavell has contended, a long tradition of condescending to Emerson in America—"that he was hardly capable of consecutive thought, let alone capable of taking on Descartes"—a habit that is perhaps exacerbated by the proposal, or firsthand admission, that European writers love and esteem his work, and have made it their own through close reading and interpretation (Cavell, *Emerson's Transcendental Etudes*, 85).

From another direction, we may consider David Weir's account of the peculiarities of F. Holland Day's tutorship of Kahlil Gibran, author of *The Prophet* (1923). As Weir says of *The Prophet*, "calling his work secondhand is really quite generous, since to consider his work closely is to enter a *mise en abîme* of belatedness almost comic in its ramifications" (*Decadent Culture in the United States: Art and Literature against the American Grain, 1890–1926* [Albany: State University of New York Press, 2008], 175). As Weir notes: "In sum, there are large cultural ironies at work in Day's choice of Maeterlinck as Gibran's introduction to fin-de-siècle European literature, because *The Treasure of the Humble* owes more to the everyday streets of Concord than to the rarefied salons of Paris" (176). And Weir adds: "If Gibran is secondhand Maeterlinck, that means he is really thirdhand Emerson; and if Emerson is really secondhand Hegel (or secondhand Hinduism), that means Gibran is so far removed from anything like originality he appears, paradoxically, original—at least to those with no awareness of the outworn tradition from which he emerged" (177). Once again, it would appear that America is given back Emerson by some interpretation beyond its borders, and in the case of Gibran, with a sort of embarrassing lack of conscientiousness about its debt to Emerson (however many layers of remove we may claim for his work). How striking and odd, then, to discover that *The Prophet* "remains the all-time best selling book in America" (177).

Weir locates the source of this stratospheric claim in *Kahlil Gibran: His Life and World* (1998) by Jean Gibran and Kahlil Gibran. In her *New Yorker* article "Prophet Motive," Joan Acocella says, "Since its publication in 1923, *The Prophet* has sold more than nine million copies in its American edition alone" (January 7, 2008). Given that single volumes by J.R.R. Tolkien and J. K. Rowling have sold more than 100 million copies, it seems hard to reconcile Jean Gibran's attestation. Looking back to *Kahlil Gibran*, however, the implication may be that it was the best-selling book *at the time of its appearance*, in America. Or perhaps we can rely on Waïl S. Hassan's helpful qualification: "In the U.S. today, Gibran is the best-known Arab American writer. . . . His work, *The Prophet* (1923), remains Alfred Knopf's best-selling title ever, having sold over eight million copies and been translated into more than fifty languages (*Immigrant Narratives: Orientalism and Cultural Translation in Arab America and Arab British Literature* [Oxford: Oxford University Press, 2011], 60).

36. David Weir writes: "Hovey had traveled to Europe and gotten to know Verlaine, Mallarmé, and Maeterlinck, eventually becoming Maeterlinck's principal English translator. . . . Hovey more than anyone else was responsible for the American fascination with the Belgian symbolist that led to additional translations of Maeterlinck's work" (*Decadent Culture in the United States*, 176).

37. William Lyon Phelps, review of *On Emerson, and Other Essays* by Maurice Maeterlinck, trans. Montrose J. Moses, *North American Review* 197, no. 688 (March 1913): 429–30. George R. MacMinn, "Emerson and Maeterlinck," *Sewanee Review* 24 (July 1916): 265–81. Benjamin Mather Woodbridge, "Maeterlinck and the Spirit of Belgium," *Books Abroad* 8 (October 1934): 381–83. Gust L. Van Roosbroeck, "Rosetti and Mae-

terlinck," *Modern Language Notes* 34 (November 1919): 439–41. Frothingham, "The Mysticism of Maeterlinck," 251–68.

38. William Lyon Phelps registered scathing comments on Moses's translation of Maeterlinck's *On Emerson, and Other Essays*: "[W]hy should one of the greatest stylists of France, the country where prose style comes nearest perfection, be served up by a writer ignorant of every law of his own language? . . . The [translation of the] book is quite scandalously bad. The translation is so often wrong, deliberately contradicting the meaning of the author, that it misleads the reader even as to the substance of the thought; while the translator's knowledge of, and sense for, English are so lacking that one of the most exquisite writers appears in a garb of such hideous and awkward language—even when it is not totally ungrammatical as to entirely misrepresent him." See William Lyon Phelps, "*On Emerson, and Other Essays* by Maurice Maeterlinck," 429–30.

39. See, for example, the excerpts in EE 135–36.

40. Friedrich Nietzsche, "On Truth and Lies in a Nonmoral Sense," in *Philosophy and Truth: Selections from Nietzsche's Notebooks of the Early 1870s*, trans. Daniel Breazeale (Atlantic Highlands, NJ: Humanities Press, 1979), 81.

41. Ibid., 82.

42. See also my *Emerson's English Traits and the Natural History of Metaphor*, esp. chap. 1, sec. 19 and chap. 4, passim.

43. Aside from analogical connections to literary and philosophical prose, even the literal sense of a "body language"—as a grammar or text that emerges from an expressive body—offers a rich site for further investigation. For instance, consider the difference between a choreographed dance that *alludes* to physical violence and a perpetrated act of violence—thus the power of fiction versus a claim from historical events. Significant portions of work, for example, by Marina Abramović, Matthew Barney, Mikhail Baryshnikov, Pina Bausch, Merce Cunningham, and Robert Lepage involve the performance of the human body as the focus, if not the totality, of the artistic exhibition. For more on reading bodies as texts, see David LaRocca, "Performative Inferentialism: A Semiotic Ethics," *Liminalities: A Journal of Performance Studies* 9 (2013): 1–26.

44. Emmanuel Levinas, *Totality and Infinity: An Essay on Exteriority*, trans. Alfonso Lingis (Pittsburgh: Duquesne University Press, 1969), 78; see also sec. III.A, "Sensibility and the Face," and sec. III.B, "Ethics and the Face," 187–93, 194–219.

45. Ralph Waldo Emerson, "Demonology," in *The Complete Works of Ralph Waldo Emerson*, 10:10.

46. For a more lengthy study of this claim, see my *Emerson's English Traits and the Natural History of Metaphor*; for analogy, see esp. chap. 3, sec. 17, and pp. 9, 11–12, 14, 29–30, 43–44, 50, 123, and 166.

47. Emerson, "Education," in *The Complete Works of Ralph Waldo Emerson*, 10:132.

48. Emerson, "Art and Criticism," in *The Complete Works of Ralph Waldo Emerson*, 12:300.

[7]

HERWIG FRIEDL

EMERSON IN GERMANY, 1850–1933: APPRECIATION AND APPROPRIATION

Emerson in Germany: A Survey

THE GERMAN CRITICAL ENCOUNTER with Emerson's writing and thinking began in the 1850s, notably and most influentially with three predominantly appreciative essays by Herman Grimm.[1] The publication of collections of Emerson's essays in translation and of sophisticated interpretations of his works continued through the 1920s. During that period, four histories of American literature provided the German reader with cultural backgrounds and literary contexts of Emerson's works: In 1866, Karl Brunnemann introduced Emerson and the transcendentalists as elegant, if not necessarily original, writers who overcome the dogmatic style of colonial American literature; Eduard Engel's literary history—first published in 1883 and in print through the early 1920s—compared Emerson, the idealist in Concord, with Goethe in Weimar, with Nietzsche as aphoristic thinker, and (favorably) with Carlyle; in 1891, Karl Knortz, the man who tried to introduce Nietzsche to his fellow Americans in the 1880s, stressed Emerson's Puritan ethics and his affinity with Asian mysticism and the monist speculations of Boehme and Schelling; and the most sophisticated of these literary histories was the 1913 study by Leon Kellner, Zionist and Jewish Austrian professor of English (and American) philology at the University of Czernowitz/Chernivtsi (today in Ukraine). Kellner emphasized the difference in Emerson's appropriation of German idealism from the positions of Channing and Alcott and saw in him an affinity with Whitman; most important, though, Kellner understood the later Emerson as an evolutionist in the intellectual company of Goethe, Oken, St. Hilaire, Agassiz, and Darwin.[2]

The decades between 1890 and 1910 were witness to the most varied, intense, and original analyses of Emerson's writings by German literary and cultural critics, theologians, and philosophers. Within that time span, the Emerson Centennial of 1903 occasioned at least thirty mostly appreciative essays in journals and newspapers all over Germany and Austria. The eulogy by Professor Heinrich Brömse, philologist and prolific editor of medieval and modern Low German texts, may serve as a representative example: he argued that even though Emerson received important suggestions from Kant, as a critic of traditional metaphysical speculation, and from Goethe, in matters of natural evolution, his true distinction is the reconciliation of a skepticism inspired by Montaigne and an authentic mystical intuition. The first decade of the twentieth century was also a time of major analyses of Emerson's religious philosophy. In 1906, Josef Sauer wrote a theologically well-informed interpretation of the gradual emergence of Emerson's dynamic pantheist vision. Sauer (1872–1949), a Catholic priest, liberal theologian, professor at the University of Freiburg, and Heidegger's predecessor (1932–33) in the office of Rektor (president) of that university, Sauer generously elucidated the liberating dimensions of Emerson's nondenominational pantheism. Sauer's Protestant counterpart was the chief pastor of Esslingen, Johannes Herzog, whose book on Emerson's theology concentrated on the ultimate compatibility of the practical, existential dimension of Emerson's institutional criticism of the church and the unshakeable basis of his mystical faith, which made him the Meister Eckhart of the nineteenth century.[3]

Even though the number of publications abated somewhat during the decade of World War I, major contributions to Emerson studies appeared again during the 1920s. An outstanding example from that decade is the profound book-length study of Emerson's oeuvre by Paul Sakmann, editor of anthologies of French Enlightenment writers and a Social Democratic member of the Württemberg parliament after 1919. On the basis of the journals and the published works, Sakmann understood Emerson as the ultimate and necessary product of Protestant nonconformity, as skeptical mystic, as a philosopher of nature who integrates Spinoza, Rousseau, Goethe, and Schelling and prepares the way for Nietzsche and modern naturalism. Sakmann's most original contribution may well be that he read essays like "Manners" as treatises on art, on the dynamic, vital, and literal art of human conduct.[4]

At the end of the Weimar Republic and with the ascendancy of the fascist Nazi regime in 1933, significant critical response to Emerson in Germany stopped almost completely. As a critical summa of German research on Emerson, as a kind of coda, and, at least implicitly, as an elegy commemorating past achievements, Julius Simon's thorough, meticulous, and highly informative doctoral dissertation published in 1937, *Ralph Waldo Emerson in Deutschland (1851–1932)*, summarized eighty remarkable years of Emerson criticism and Emerson studies in Germany and in German-speaking countries.[5] Significantly, Simon's critical survey ends with the year before Hitler's usurpation of power and thus marks the end of a tradition that is by now largely forgotten but worthy to be remembered, resuscitated, and reactivated. After the political, cultural, and moral catastrophes of the Third Reich and World War II, German Emerson studies were resumed again around 1950 in the context of mostly American critical perspectives such as New Criticism. Only since the 1980s have German scholars regained a more independent, "original relation to the universe" of Emerson's thought in the writings of Thomas Krusche, Olaf Hansen, Manfred Pütz, Dieter Schulz, Joseph C. Schoepp, Herwig Friedl, and Johannes Voelz; but that is another story.[6]

The story of the significant tendencies in the appreciation and appropriation of Emerson's thinking between 1850 and 1933, which I would like to reconstruct and tell here, is the story of positioning Emerson in national, transnational, and transhistorical fields.[7] This story will unfold in only approximately chronological sequence, focusing on selected major critics and representative critical points of view. It opens with an introductory presentation of the earliest and trendsetting German response to Emerson. This is followed by sketches of the way Emerson criticism was embedded in national, international, and transnational—as well as historical—horizons or contexts within which important German-speaking cultural critics, public intellectuals, philologists, and philosophers perceived Emerson's significance.

The history of reception of a major writer and thinker is an integral part of cultural and literary history, as Winfried Fluck reminds us: "The cultural history of literary texts thus cannot be separated from their varying uses in the act of reception; it is a history of second narratives. Literary history and the history of reception cannot be separated."[8] In the case of an international or transnational history of the reception of Emerson, the "history of second narratives"—as distinguished from the primary narrative of the history of the works considered independently—must be understood as contributing to the literary and cultural history of the United States and of Germany. Such a history could also be written as a North Atlantic or as a truly global sequence of textual and intellectual events. It is the example especially of Lawrence Buell's interpretation of Emerson in a cosmopolitan setting and of Jan Stievermann's insistence that Emerson envisioned and wrote an American world literature in Goethe's sense of the term that I would like to invoke as an implicit orientation and guideline of my own readings of the history of reading Emerson in the German-speaking world.[9] The transnational perspective is, however, not simply a more recent event in the history of critical theories understood in terms of progressive sophistication. A number of the nineteenth- and early-twentieth-century German critics that I will introduce manifest a transnational awareness not only because they deal with the work of a thinker and writer from the other side of the Atlantic; writers like Curtius, Federn, Francke, Friedell, Grimm, Gundolf, and Schönbach realized that Emerson would best be understood not simply as an American thinker but as an outstanding and exemplary member either of a North Atlantic culture or as a true cosmopolitan intellectually embedded in a global literary, philosophical, and religious reality. The North American culture evoked and envisioned by some of these writers was either defined by productive tensions and differences between Europe and America, or, in the more conservative fashion of, for example, Kuno Francke's reading of Emerson, as dominated by the hegemonic claims of nineteenth-century German cultural imperialism. "Global culture" is not a unified concept or vision for these writers either: Friedrich Gundolf implies the possibility of a future transnational and universal realm foreshadowed in Emerson's modernist gestures, whereas Ernst Robert Curtius thinks of mystically grounded monism as the proper global dimension of Emerson's achievement. Thus, in their own special way, major aspects of the history of the "second narrative" of German Emerson reception between 1850 and 1933 are a significant anticipation of the transnational ethics of contemporary critical endeavors.

Beginnings: Setting the Tone

The son and nephew of the two great early-nineteenth-century philologists Wilhelm and Jacob Grimm, the art historian and essayist Herman Friedrich Grimm (1828–1901) is in a sense the 'onlie begetter,' the highly influential initiator of the impressive line of German Emerson criticism through 1933. This is why later critics again and again refer to Grimm with respect, even when their evaluation of Emerson's achievement radically differs from his vision. Before Grimm, we know of occasional and passing responses to Emerson in the diaries of the public intellectual and cultural critic Varnhagen von Ense in the 1840s and by the German-English Orientalist F. Max Müller in the early 1850s, and we may assume that a wider readership knew of Emerson through the 1854–55 German translations of the Swedish liberal and feminist writer Frederika Bremer's *The Homes of the New World: Impressions of America*, which contains a mostly sympathetic but not unreservedly appreciative report of her visit with Emerson in 1850.[10]

In his three early essays, published in 1857, 1859, and 1865, respectively, Grimm set the tone for numerous German responses to Emerson in the years to come. His appreciations foreshadowed and inspired positive evaluations of Emerson's writing and thinking by later critics, provoked disagreements, and set up a series of observations and comments deemed indispensable in the following decades. Grimm also provided key arguments for an appropriation of Emerson by some critics as an essentially German or Germanic thinker heavily indebted to German thought and literature. An Emerson understood as an heir of Luther or Leibniz or Kant or Goethe and the German idealists made it possible for critics to see him as returning and restoring in innovative form the spiritual and intellectual heritage of Germany when the country was in most dire need of it—during a time of cultural and political as well as moral decadence, of materialism, and of rampant scientism—a view shared by many cultural critics and literary historians of the second half of the nineteenth century. In Emerson, a later and impoverished German culture could collectively "recognize [its] own rejected thoughts . . . come back . . . with a certain alienated majesty"—as Emerson himself had described the individual experience of a defectively or insufficiently self-reliant perspective (CW 2:27).[11]

The afterword to Grimm's translation of the Shakespeare and the Goethe essays in *Representative Men* (1857) introduces Emerson primarily as a poet.[12] Grimm emphasizes the multiplicity, the pluralism of points of view in Emerson's writings, and he values the profusion of seeming contradictions as the hallmark of a genuinely free spirit for whom the whole world is an arsenal of suggestive ideas (93). In the early parts of Grimm's essay, Emerson is presented as the heir of all the ages in a new world unhampered by the constraints of a single traditional culture. A defining trait of Emerson's thought and moral outlook is the appreciation of the ordinary (95). *Representative Men,* the publication most often commented on in German Emerson criticism, is characterized by the implicit and explicit assumption of the exceptional not only in the intellectual, religious, and political representatives but in all people, in each and all seemingly ordinary human beings (99). Of equal moral importance is Emerson's argument and fight against what he once called a "mean egotism," the major blemish of contemporary American social life, as Grimm understands it. Here, Grimm argues, Emerson follows the ethos and thinks in the tradition represented by Channing and Parker (100). Grimm speaks approvingly of the objectivity of *English Traits,* which reminds him of the stylistic Latin discipline of Tacitus in his study of the Germanic tribes, because it shows no subjective and no nationalist prejudice or conceit. But then, and without awareness of the break in argumentative logic, Grimm praises Emerson because he accords German intellectual culture the highest rank among all nations (112). Toward the end of the afterword, Emerson, whom Grimm had introduced as free spirit and heir of all the ages, is seen as champion of the Germanic races, of Germanic culture, in their fight for supremacy against the Latin (and, implicitly, the Catholic) world of the Romance nations, a fight and competition virulent ever since the days of Martin Luther (113). In a sudden and unwarranted reversal, the sophisticated appreciation of Emerson as a cosmopolitan is complemented by a narrowly nationalistic and reductionist interpretation from a German point of view; illogically, Emerson's thinking is all at once subjected to culturally chauvinistic appropriation.

Grimm's 1859 essay "Emerson: Ein Brief" is almost completely identical with his best-known Emerson study of 1865, published in *Neue Essays über Kunst und Literatur.* The earlier version is written as a letter to an unnamed person who is not wholly convinced of Emerson's intellectual importance: it is safe to assume that Grimm was addressing and trying to convert his future wife, Gisela von Arnim, who later became an ardent admirer of Emerson and—like Herman Grimm himself—exchanged letters with him.[13] The 1865 essay begins with an important and, for later critics, consequential description of the experience of "first looking into" a volume of Emerson. Like Keats reading Chapman's Homer, Grimm encounters a new world, an authentic personality, a genuinely innovative language that at first puzzles and, at the same time, fascinates, a language that comes across as new and unprecedented with each successive reading: reading Emerson begins and always continues in astonishment and wondering, in the *thaumazein* of which Aristotle had maintained that it preceded and conditioned genuine philosophical thinking.[14] Grimm again emphasizes both the simplicity and the simultaneous intellectual challenge of Emerson's style, the importance of his celebration of "the common and the low," of the everyday (4). Reading Emerson, Grimm notes—and here he echoes Emerson himself in "Self-Reliance"—seems to make one really know one's own half-articulated thoughts, thoughts both old and familiar, yet radically innovative (5). Grimm also observes that for Emerson, as for Nietzsche, the past does not possess an unquestioned authority. This attitude and way of thinking allows one to simply articulate the inspiration of the moment without deliberately opposing or abandoning other and earlier views. From this emerges a chain of seemingly contradictory statements that nonetheless genuinely cohere because of their essential character as existentially authentic utterances (19–21). In the course of the argument, Grimm dwells on "Manners" as a celebration of a new kind of aristocracy that recruits its members, after the revolutionary upheavals of 1776 and of 1789, from all ranks (11). Grimm, however, limits the implied universal appeal of the Emerson text by insisting that this new aristocracy, or, rather, meritocracy, is, after all and essentially, an ingredient of an emerging Germanic world culture that, ominously, will subject the Slavic, the Romance, and the Asian peoples and nations to its legitimate domination (16). At the end of the essay, Grimm intensifies the nationalistic tone by insisting that German culture is, and for a long time will be, superior to American life and letters (20).

The very ambiguity of Grimm's attitude toward Emerson and America surfaced again and again in several later German readers of Emerson, as did the important insights and appreciations of Emerson's thought and writing that I have sketched above. Grimm seems unaware that he is using his reading, his reception, of Emerson to tell two irreconcilable "second narratives": one articulates the impact of an innovative global, emancipatory thinker and another, unsubstantiated by textual evidence, celebrates Emerson as champion of Germanic hegemony. It is indeed amazing that Grimm, who was Emerson's reader, admirer, and correspondent, as well as the friend and acquaintance of Ambassadors George Bancroft and Andrew D. White, was unable to abandon or at least to mitigate the prevailing nineteenth-century discourse of German cultural hegemony while, at the same time, he wrote to Emerson that he had modeled his own book on Michelangelo on Emerson's intellectual portraits in *Representative Men* and enthusiastically celebrated Emerson as a representative and incarnation of America, the first nation on this earth, "das erste Land der Erde."[15]

Expanding Circles: The International and Transnational Aspects of Reading Emerson

It was Gisela von Arnim (1827–89), daughter of Goethe's friend Bettina von Arnim, later a correspondent of Emerson and the wife of Herman Grimm, who in 1858 found the image of a circular flow of cultural achievement and excellence to describe and interpret the transnational significance of Emerson in the realm of an organically evolving, a naturally unfolding North Atlantic culture. In Emerson's writings, one sees the flowering of the seeds sown by his appropriation of German culture. His thoughts are flowers of more intense beauty because they emerged in a new, foreign, and healthy intellectual climate.[16] She adds that Emerson stylistically purifies German thinking, and, contrary to her future husband, she believes that in its very humility Emerson's vision will surpass German thought. The metaphor of circular evolution, the spiral dynamics of transnational cultural flow, will recur, implicitly or explicitly, in numerous later German analyses of Emerson's place in transatlantic relations. A different, but also formative and in a way complementary, vision of Emerson's place in intellectual and cultural history is offered by the novelist, literary theorist, and translator Friedrich Spielhagen (1829–1911) in his preface to the German translation of *English Traits,* published in 1857.[17] The remarkable and judicious objectivity of Emerson's rendering of the achievements and failures of English culture expresses a historically transcultural disposition in his approach. Like Grimm and in the same year, Spielhagen sees Emerson as a dispassionate modern

Tacitus and at the same time as a forerunner of the cultural critique of the future, because stylistically he provides a picture of England in the photographic mode in which a personal, well-defined, even if limited point of view provides an authentic image of great verisimilitude. Several later German critics will echo and expand Spielhagen's view of an Emerson who provides a connection and a transition between the cultural realms of classical antiquity and modernism. The spatial (von Arnim) and the temporal (Spielhagen) transitionality of Emerson's cultural location is the pattern that will manifest itself again and again in variations in major German attempts to understand Emerson in a geographical and historical continuum beyond the nation.

Heinrich Julian Schmidt's 1876 introduction to his translation of Emerson's *Letters and Social Aims* is an important link in the history of German Emerson interpretation between Grimm's seminal essays and the remarkable culmination of critical studies between 1890 and 1910. The influential journalist, and in his day widely acclaimed and popular literary historian, Julian Schmidt (1818–86) is one of the very small number of German critics who showed a high regard for American literary culture (the Americans buy more books and read more than we Germans, he said). In translating and introducing Emerson as the epitome of New England sophistication, he saw a possibility to provide a corrective for the distorted and negative image of America that he thought characterized Charles Sealsfield's novels and Charles Dickens's travelogues.[18]

Readers who disregard Schmidt's subtle and sympathetic interpretations of Emerson's *Essays* and of *Representative Men* in his "Einleitung" will be struck by the daring and innovative positioning of Emerson's writing and thinking in its temporal extension: Schmidt reads Emerson as a Platonist, but not as a Platonizing metaphysician. Rather, the structure and the argumentation of the essays, Schmidt maintains, are modeled on the Platonic dialogues and not, as so many contemporary and later critics would argue, on the Protestant sermon (24–25). Individual thoughts represent a variety of points of view; they assume the function of the interlocutors in a Platonic dialogue. Some of these views are uttered by a masterfully challenging voice, an implied Socrates-figure, while others, often contradictory propositions, are added or interspersed without ever being refuted or abandoned. In this way the essays assume the form of multi- rather than dia-logues (28). Emerson never resorts to the systematic Hegelian strategy of dialectical reconciliation of contradictions (41), so that the reader will hardly ever know which side in the implied dispute in an essay will prevail. Even though Schmidt derives Emerson's perspectivism and his rhetorical as well as epistemological pluralism from Plato, he nevertheless stresses the fact that this ancient method of presenting a philosophical dispute results in a modern, we might say, postmetaphysical and pragmatist vision. Emerson's idealism, Schmidt emphasizes again and again, does not position the "truth and reality of the ideal," as do the theologians, in a beyond, a transcendent realm; Emerson's ideal is found "in the continuous creative effectiveness of the world as a whole. . . . American idealism is so engaging for us because of its decisive relation to the real" (6, 8; my translations).

Schmidt provides a place for Emerson in an ongoing philosophical process extending from classical antiquity to a philosophy of the future that Schmidt characterizes as a kind of pluralist pragmatism *avant la lettre*. This modern, multiperspectivist position accords well with an open-ended and open-minded skepticism that tempers Emerson's idealist visions. Schmidt reminds his readers that in this modern age, like Emerson himself, "We all are seekers" (42). With the term "seekers," Schmidt again connects the present of Emerson's thought (the term is prominent in "Circles") with classical antiquity, where the skeptics were also called *zetetikoi* (seekers). The historically transnational arc within which Schmidt accords Emerson a position beyond any national cultural fixation, is complemented by the way he allows Emerson's thinking to relate to and differ from more contemporary modes of thinking—be it the religious affinity with Jacobi (32), the distant parallels of the visions of representative men and heroes in Emerson and Carlyle (11–20), shared interpretations of nature in Goethe and Emerson (21), or approximations and differences in the evaluation of individualism in Schleiermacher and Emerson (10). Schmidt opens one of the widest possible horizons within which Emerson finds a historically appropriate, cosmopolitan philosophical and geographically transatlantic cultural environment.[19]

Among the relatively large number of German-speaking critics who devote in-depth essayistic analyses to Emerson's achievement as a thinker between 1890 and 1910, three—Jewish-Austrian authors Karl Federn and Egon Friedell, and Jewish-German writer Friedrich Gundolf—excel because of the variety of their liberal transnational or cosmopolitan perspectives and the subtlety of their intellectual approaches and appreciation.

Karl Federn (1868–1943), the scion of a prominent Viennese family of medical doctors, psychoanalysts, and feminists, shows an in-depth knowledge of nineteenth-century American culture shared by only a few of the critics I deal with here. Federn used the Emerson biographies by James Elliot Cabot, Oliver Wendell Holmes, and Richard Garnett; he also used Franklin Benjamin Sanborn's studies of the transcendentalists, a book on Concord by Frank Preston Stearns, James Russell Lowell's works, and Edward Emerson's *Emerson in Concord* for his elegant collection of *Essays zur Amerikanischen Litteratur* (1899). For Federn the transcendentalists are the acme of American intellectual life, who—like Hawthorne or Lowell—are not sufficiently appreciated in Germany as authors who are emphatically not mere imitators and disciples of the Europeans; transcendentalism is something new and radically original, a modern and innovative mode of idealism.[20]

In his extensive 1892 introduction to his own and Thora Weigand's translation of Emerson's *Essays*, Federn begins by situating Emerson as a late and unique member of the Kantian school.[21] A few pages later, Federn becomes more specific by pointing out that Emerson follows a seminal thought of Kant's critical philosophy, which foreshadows idealism. In the first edition of the *Critique of Pure Reason*, Emerson could read a momentous and, for Kant, unique speculative statement: namely, that "it might be possible that the self and the thing-in-itself are one and the same thinking substance" (10; my translation). This sentence was omitted in the second edition of the *Critique*. Federn thus argues that Emerson in reading Kant was aware of the germ of what became idealist philosophy (*Identitätsphilosophie*) as proposed by Schelling. This idealist monism, which emerged from a suppressed layer of the Kantian critical position, makes it plausible for Federn that Emerson could be both an innovative late-Kantian idealist and a mystic in the grand tradition extending from the Neoplatonists through the medieval Christian mystics and Jakob Boehme (10). It accords well with this view that Federn thinks of Emerson's style with its lack of philosophical discursiveness as the style of a prophetic speaker, an evangelist (10). Emerson's implied vision of the perfect man in *Representative Men* is messianic (14), and even though he denies the existence of a transempirical world (12; he refers to Emerson's statement that there is "no other world"), his religious position, emerging from the long tradition of mystical speculation, approaches the stance of Tolstoy and the critique of institutionalized religion in Tolstoy's preface to his new translation of the gospels (15). One might generalize and say that Julian Schmidt reads Emerson as a member of a transnational Hellenistic cultural continuum extending from Plato to protopragmatism, while Federn, to use Matthew Arnold's well-known distinction, prefers a Hebraist version of that continuum, which goes back to the messianic and the mystical religious dimension of antiquity and reemerges in a visionary idealism encompassing Russia, central Europe, and America.

The almost cosmic reach of Emerson's cultural and religious involvement is underlined by the last sentence of Federn's introductory essay. He quotes "a learned Hindu" who had said about Emerson that he should or might have seen the light of day for the first time thousands of years ago on the banks of the Ganges.[22] The extension of Emerson's thinking into the present and the future, on the other hand, is thoroughly and at length discussed by Federn in his subtle comparison of Nietzsche and Emerson. He acknowledges literally "innumerable" parallel statements in the works of the two thinkers and yet insists that the total tendency and intent of their thought differ widely (8). Their emphasis on individualism, their celebration of an intellectual aristocracy, their turn away from the burden of historical knowledge, all this must not obscure the fact that, for example, Nietzsche's ultimate ideal is not noble but brutal, whereas Emerson's vision of the perfect man brings back the ideals of ancient Hebrew and early Christian ethics (14). Federn argues plausibly for the ultimate irreconcilability of Emerson and Nietzsche's thinking. However, like Spielhagen and Schmidt before him, Federn comes close to understanding Emerson's transnational and transhistorical reach in a way ironically and most elegantly expressed by Nietzsche himself when he observed in *The Twilight of the Idols:* "[Emerson] simply does not know how old he already is and how young he will still be."[23]

The cultural historian, philosopher, and actor Egon Friedell (1878–1938) is a remarkable exception among the Emerson critics between 1850 and 1933 because both his 1906 anthology of Emerson's aphorisms, *Emerson: Sein Charakter aus seinen Werken* [Emerson: His Character Manifest in His Works][24] and his monumental *Kulturgeschichte der Neuzeit: Die Krisis der Europäischen Seele von der Schwarzen Pest bis zum Ersten Weltkrieg* [Cultural History of the Modern Age] (3 vols., 1927–31), are in print and popular to this very day. Friedell was born Egon Friedmann to a wealthy Viennese Jewish family. He changed his name and converted to Lutheranism, lived as a free spirit, a bohemian, a theater and cabaret actor, and unconventional scholar in Berlin and Vienna. While Federn escaped persecution by the Nazis through emigration to England in 1933, where he became a critic of Marxist ideology, Friedell committed suicide in 1938, when he realized that he was under observation by the Gestapo.

In the 1906 preface of his collection of Emerson's aphorisms, Friedell reads Emerson primarily as an exemplary character, an existential, model human being.[25] Simplicity and naturalness are Emerson's prominent traits; his aversion to all theological and institutional formalisms, his indifference to the old and to cultural traditions, and his prophetic articulation of the new characterize his loosely arranged aphoristic and often lyrical statements, which do not call for analysis and interpretation (8, 16, 23). Emerson's texts arise spontaneously out of themselves like natural phenomena, like trees or landscapes. The spontaneous and contingent, the nonsystematic and at the same time authentic character of Emerson's utterances are hallmarks of a philosopher of the New World.[26] This identification of Emerson as an American thinker is manifest in his passion for emancipation and liberation, as shown in his advocacy for free trade and abolitionism, in his admiration for Lincoln, and in his professed duty as a liberator of imprisoned ideas and thoughts (19). Friedell, as a passionate free spirit himself, however, does not essentialize Emerson's Americanism. Friedell's analysis expands the horizon of Emerson's cultural and philosophical vision: a pervasive skepticism and the example of Montaigne (12–13; also *Kulturgeschichte der Neuzeit,* 1198, 1201) make Emerson a liberal citizen of the world, a cosmopolitan who is not beholden to any dogmas and established traditions (1198). Friedell admires the way in which Emerson loosely arranges truths of the moment, provisional opinions, and impressionistic and fleeting insights (1201), which are never subordinated to the demands of a comprehensive or totalizing structure or system. Emerson's aphorisms in their seemingly haphazard arrangement are characterized by a "deeply phenomenalist undertone" (1201). "Considerations by the Way," Friedell thinks, should be the proper title not just of one, but of all of Emerson's essays: the authentic moment as a fleeting phenomenal experience is the core of his transnational, skeptical, liberal, and therefore naturally cosmopolitan vision and faith (1201).

Friedrich Gundolf wrote only one essay on Emerson, a review of Friedell's 1906 Emerson anthology and of Wilhelm Miessner's 1907 translations of Emerson. This short review-essay, published in 1908 by the most profound and sophisticated of all German-speaking literary scholars of the early twentieth century, is unsurpassed in subtlety and analytical depth. Like Schmidt, Federn, and Friedell, Gundolf positions Emerson's philosophical achievement beyond the narrow enclosures of either American or German national cultures. Gundolf differs from his predecessors insofar, however, that he does not locate the Emersonian vision in an already known and defined historical or spatial environment: Gundolf sees Emerson primarily as proposing and projecting a philosophy of the future. Like Nietzsche's Zarathustra, Emerson is defined as a precursor, a prophet of a future mode of thinking.[27] Like John Dewey in his 1903 centennial essay on Emerson, Gundolf thinks of the global culture of the coming centuries as already proposed by the serene vision of Emerson.

Friedrich Leopold Gundelfinger (1880–1931) changed his name to the not-so-Jewish-sounding Gundolf when he joined the elitist, aristocratic, aestheticist circle formed and autocratically dominated by the poet Stefan George. Gundolf's greatest achievements as an intellectual historian and professor of German literature at the University of Heidelberg are *Shakespeare and the German Mind* (1911) and *Goethe* (1916). Like his great books, Gundolf's short essay on Emerson manages to create an intellectual portrait of such intensity that it should attract attention and admiration even today when compared with the Emerson criticism of our time.

The central and organizing concept of Gundolf's exegesis of Emerson is the process of transition. In a way, Gundolf foreshadows Jonathan Levin's

1999 study, *The Poetics of Transition*. Transition defines the substance of Emerson's thinking and his historical position. Emerson's philosophy moves, Gundolf says, with joyous assurance in the transitional realm, in the border region where power becomes rarefied and turns into consciousness (252). Throughout the essay, he describes Emerson's dominant mood in terms that recall Emerson's own and Nietzsche's idea of philosophy as a gay or joyous (*fröhliche*) poetic science and Nietzsche's praise of Emerson's existential serenity. Historically speaking, Emerson is, on the one hand, an heir of all the ages, especially of Platonism and German idealism, and, on the other hand, in transition toward a new and as yet unknown realm of thinking that may come to full fruition only for a future generation (252)—because Nietzsche does not yet fulfill Emerson's promise adequately, and Maeterlinck reduces the stature of Emerson's vision and renders it harmlessly moralistic (259, 258).

I would like to paraphrase a few central passages of Gundolf's interpretation that make it clear in which respect his Emerson is on the verge of a unique transnational and modern mode of thinking. Emerson does not propose new thoughts; rather, he displays a new temperament (252). Temperament, I may add, was seen by both Fichte and William James as the foundational disposition of any philosophical vision and intuition. At the same time, as Nietzsche once said about modern thinking in general, method becomes more important than material insight. For Gundolf, Emerson "plays" with concepts, and he does not allow words or statements to delimit his thinking; in this way, his essays and their arguments flow and merge into each other. The key essay "The Method of Nature" must be read as a hymn on movement and metamorphosis, on the mixture of elements, and on ecstasy (253). If we read this passage in Jamesian terms, Gundolf's Emerson is an anti-intellectualist like Bergson or James himself, a thinker whose method is defined by a creative Heraclitean flow, by a constant troping of terms, as Richard Poirier would see it decades later.[28] Emerson freely deforms and transforms the philosophical inheritance, the ideas of the great speculative age of the nineteenth century. He plays with traditions as does a child, both piously and without awe. Everything he encounters he simply uses as ciphers for the intellectual play of his joyous imagination; the history of philosophy turns into flowing nature for this serene Proteus (256–257, 258). The image of the child implies a reference, I think, to Nietzsche's vision of the utopian and ultimate existential mode of human existence in *Thus Spoke Zarathustra* and, at the same time, to its original or prototype, Heraclitus's vision of time itself as a child at play. In this way, Emerson is intuited not as a philosopher with opinions (*doxa*) (257), but rather as the event or method of thinking itself in its potentially endless transmutations.

This also explains, according to Gundolf, why Emerson manages to transform, with charmingly confounding grace, every single sentence in his essays into its opposite. This method of thinking as event, this thinking "on the way," as Stanley Cavell once said,[29] is characterized by a lively unrest that is nevertheless canopied by an overarching sunny stillness (257–58). Unlike Nietzsche, Emerson's thinking does not strive toward an ultimate goal like the overman; it does not find its fulfillment in a victory of power over fate. Emerson's intuition of the vital motion of thinking and being is not a Nietzschean striving and race toward the future; it is essentially balanced, because Emerson's is the mastery of the superior rope-dancer of philosophical meditation (258, 259). Gundolf's Emerson *is* the future itself—not the future of American or German or European thought. He is sheer, futuristic potential itself; his region is "defined" by the widest possible of the expanding circles, the ever-receding horizon of an unlimited and as yet undefined expanse of newness, of modernity.

In 1897, Anton E. Schönbach (1848–1911), professor of German philology at the University of Graz in Austria, added a major essay on Emerson and his circle ("Ralph Waldo Emerson und sein Kreis") to his immensely popular and successful 1888 collection of studies on modern literature, *Über Lesen und Bildung* [On Reading and Culture]. Through 1913 the book saw eight editions. Schönbach's Emerson interpretation may have reached more German-speaking readers than any other publication between 1850 and 1933. Compared with the Jewish-German scholars I have just discussed, Schönbach proposes more limited, more narrowly circumscribed cultural horizons and defining environments to situate and explain Emerson's achievement. He begins by comparing the transcendentalist movement with other periods of cultural flowering, with the era of medieval German courtly poetry (*Minnesang*), with the Elizabethan age in England, and the so-called classical period of German literature and philosophy (1770–1830). Emerson's first and foremost defining context is the tradition of the sermon.[30] Emerson's prose shows major hallmarks of an oral tradition. The essays were spoken as lectures before they were written.[31] The prophetic tone and the lack of philosophical argumentation indicate the manner of the pulpit (87–88). The abundance of quotations—Schönbach relies on Oliver Wendell Holmes's painstaking identifications of quotations and allusions in Emerson—are another indication of the composition of Emerson's essays as worldly sermons. As an erudite former minister, Emerson knew that proper quoting is an art, as he himself argues in "Quotation and Originality" (91).

Closely related to the religious, intellectual, and stylistic environment of the tradition of the Christian sermon is Emerson's indebtedness to colonial American theology and philosophy. Schönbach is the only German-speaking

Emerson critic who, like Perry Miller so much later, explains convincingly and with in-depth knowledge that Jonathan Edwards provides an intellectual frame and background indispensable for a proper understanding of Emerson's thinking and religious conceptions. Among the eighteenth-century colonial foreshadowings of Emerson's modern thinking, he notes the importance of the subjective idealism of Bishop Berkeley for Edwards, his deep veneration of nature, and the moral universe that Edwards encountered in Richardson's novels (98–100). Schönbach is well aware of the connections between German idealism and Emerson, as well as the importance of the relationship between Carlyle and Emerson (102–5); however, he thinks it more significant that Emerson's vision of nature and evolution is deeply rooted in English writing and thinking. Izaac Walton and Gilbert White of Selborn are as important in defining Emerson's vision as are features of his thought that seem to respond to Lamarck and to anticipate Darwin (108–9). Schönbach's Emerson belongs both to the transnational religious world defined by the Christian sermon and the intellectual and literary world of England and colonial, pre-national America. At the end of his interpretation, Schönbach argues that the period between 1840 and 1860 in America would one day be admired as a kind of golden age and that this would be due almost exclusively to Emerson's achievement (116)—a remarkable evaluation that may be said to foreshadow what F. O. Matthiessen would intend with his *American Renaissance*.

A truly intricate, in many ways knowledgeable, and, at the same time, ideologically highly problematic attempt to think of Emerson within a comprehensive cultural and philosophical horizon is Kuno Francke's "Emerson and German Personality" (1903). Francke was born in Kiel, Germany, in 1855, and in 1884 he began his academic career at Harvard, which culminated in a full professorship of history and German culture and the position of director of the Busch-Reisinger or Germanic Museum, which he held through 1929, one year before his death in Cambridge, Massachusetts. Francke's essay on Emerson, even though written in English and published in America, is an integral part of the "second narrative" of Emerson reception in Germany; its cultural presuppositions and values are indisputably German. The essay begins with the only apparently obvious statement: "Emerson was, above all, an American" and continues to list a few biographical facts that seem to indicate Emerson's distance from all things German.[32] The opening sentence of the third and last section of Francke's text states dogmatically: "Emerson belongs to the world" (13). This insinuates that a widening circle, originating in the nation and extending to a global circumference, properly defines the reach, quality, and the essence of Emerson's achievement as cosmopolitan. The argument of the essay, however, radically subverts this evaluation.

I would summarize Francke's interpretation of the "expanding circle" of Emerson's cultural identity in this unwritten final sentence to complement his opening statement: "Emerson was, above all, a German."

Francke begins with the highly dubious assertion that the very pressures of German authoritarian political culture "tended to force to light the life within" and therefore facilitated "a decidedly greater variety of individual views, convictions, principles, modes of life, ideals, in other words, of individual character than in America" where, under democratic conditions, conformity prevails (2). This somewhat simplified Tocquevillean view of the effects of egalitarianism and democracy in America is contrasted with Germany, where the thinker in his interiority "is his own master, . . . builds his own world" (2). But it is not only the Emersonian self-reliant individual building his own world who is an authentic German; the idea that "man thinking . . . is an essentially German conception" is exemplified in a long line of German culture heroes from Luther to Lessing to Fichte, Schopenhauer, and Nietzsche (2). On this basis, Francke lists four major aspects as "evidence of temperamental affinity between German character and Emerson" (6). These four aspects are: (1) "an implicit trust in the supreme value of the inner life"; (2) an appreciation of the "fullness of the inner life in the humblest and most circumscribed spheres of society"; (3) "a strongly developed sense of the spiritual unity of things," as in the German mystical and monistic tradition from Tauler to Goethe; and (4) "courage of personal conviction and disdain of intellectual compromises" (3–6). Emerson is then characterized as a representative of the German ideal of the academic who displays the "intellectual courage which has made Germany, in spite of state omnipotence and clerical supremacy, the home of free thought" (7). Germans of the twenty-first century shake their heads in disbelief when they read this.

Finally, in terms of cultural politics, Emerson is seen as an intellectually inferior version of Fichte in his role as moral and political preceptor of his nation. I do not hesitate to question Francke's assertion that there "is no greater or more inspiring figure in intellectual history than Fichte," but the emphasis on Fichte is plausible and obvious in the context of Francke's vision. Fichte, the propagandist of German nationalism during the war of liberation against Napoleon, provides the image of the German prototype that makes Emerson as *praeceptor Americae* appear as a minor copy of the powerful German original (10–12). At the end of his relentless Germanizing of Emerson, Francke laments the current state of German culture around 1900, the prevalent materialism, the scientism, the loss of a genuine religious life, the general decline into a mindless positivism (13). He concludes: "Now the time has come for Emerson to pay back to Germany what he owes her" (14). Francke intensifies the nationalist aspects of Grimm's interpretation of Emerson. He differs from Gisela von Arnim's view of Emerson's indebtedness to Germany because he does not, as she does, allow for the growth and refinement of the German idealist heritage in the new American environment. All value judgments in Francke's essay imply an inescapable American cultural inferiority and dependency. In spite of a few weak disclaimers applauding Emerson's American democratic disposition, in Francke's view Emerson's national identity is, culturally speaking, not really American; it is German to the core. The cosmopolitan aspect of an Emerson who is supposed to belong to the world turns out to be German after all—since in Francke's cultural obsession with the fatherland, there seems to be nothing beyond the ever-widening circle of German cultural hegemony. A reader of Francke's essay today cannot but understand his version of America and its culture—represented by the person and achievement of Emerson—as a mere German colony that preserved the best that was thought in the parent nation as an antidote for the ills of a decadent present.

The positioning of Emerson in a transnational realm proposed by Ernst Robert Curtius (1886–1956) is the exact opposite of Francke's attempt to define all of North Atlantic culture as essentially German or Germanic. Francke's paradoxical nationalist transnationalism imagines a hegemonic unity that, in the end, would obliterate all significant difference. The great Romance literary scholar Curtius imagines a unified world, a monistic totality, which preserves and supports difference. Curtius grew up in Alsace and received his doctorate from the University of Strasbourg: early on, he became familiar with and appreciated a realm defined by the—often troubled—coexistence of two cultures, German and French. In his most important work, *European Literature and the Latin Middles Ages* (1948), he characteristically argues for continuity encompassing both spatial and temporal differences between cultures and cultural epochs. In his impressive 1924 essay, "Emerson," Curtius displays an internationalist tolerance and transnational generosity of vision that would become increasingly rare as the Weimar Republic began to unravel and the nationalism of the fascist movement became threateningly prominent, even in academic circles, from the late 1920s onward. Curtius's courageous position remained one of a small number of notable exceptions.

Curtius admires Emerson's thinking as one of the most valuable legacies of the post-Goethean nineteenth century, a legacy in danger of being forgotten in present-day Germany after it had been so powerfully effective in the work of Herman Grimm and Friedrich Nietzsche. Emerson's beautiful essays provide a desperately needed corrective in a world that has abandoned Goethe's vision of a literary world culture, in a world that is increasingly dominated by historicist criticism, by positivism, and anarchism.[33] Emerson and Balzac, Curtius argues somewhat surprisingly, are two related visionaries who share what he calls an "All-Einheits-Lehre" (190), an intuitional and dynamist, a vitalist monism, in which the cosmos shows as a unified and unceasing evolutionary upward movement (191). In Balzac, this vision manifests itself as a cosmos of persons in a comprehensive system of novels; in Emerson it appears as a cosmos of ideas, a symphony of profound thoughts (194). This monism is a primordial intuition that precedes and informs philosophy, religion, literature, and science without being fully and exhaustively present in any single one of these cultural manifestations, because it will transcend and outlast all specific philosophies or religions and other systems of thought (190). The constant reemergence of this foundational monism implicitly present in all cultures begins in Asia and Mesopotamia and finds its way through Neoplatonism, medieval mysticism, and the hermetic thinking of the Renaissance, through Swedenborg and through international Romanticism into nineteenth-century spiritual syncretism (191).

Emerson is one of the latest and most important representatives of this global and transhistorical phenomenon. Curtius's interpretation of global monism is closely related to the idea of a *philosophia perennis* as Martin Buber had presented it in his anthology of mystical texts, *Ecstatic Confessions* (1909), which foreshadows the equally famous collection, *The Perennial Philosophy* by Aldous Huxley (1945). The monist intuition tends to use the circle and the ball as recurring symbols to express the essence of reality as self-enclosed infinity: "if existence is spherical, thinking has to be cyclical" (192; my translation). Emerson's "Circles" is a central text for Curtius's argument. The Platonism of Plato, the specific and historically identifiable teaching of the fourth century BCE that critics have attributed to Emerson in order to express their sense of his foundational monist philosophical intuition, this Platonism, however, is not the proper and adequate intellectual and spiritual background to elucidate Emerson's powerful renewal of the global monist tradition. Emerson's Platonism has left the temple and the cloister behind and entered unappropriated nature (196–98). It is not at home in the context of a historicist nostalgia for the past or in a messianic, future-oriented prophecy. Emerson's powerful sense of true Being is beholden to the energetic celebration of a "*strong present tense*" (202, where he uses the English phrase). Curtius argues against all those Emerson critics who saw strong parallels in his and Nietzsche's philosophies: as Curtius sees it, while Nietzsche's thought moves forward, Emerson's is directed upward. Rooted in the present, Nietzsche anticipates and projects the future; equally rooted in the present, Emerson is aware of the all-encompassing eternal day (201). Emerson's ideal of conduct in and for a global world monistically constituted is that kind of self-reliance and individualism that grounds all genuine ethics and overcomes conventional, regional, national, and historical moralities by abandoning culturally specific virtues in favor of virtue (202). The ultimate secret in this, as in all other facets of Emerson's thinking is: he is as multifarious and varied and as simple and unitary as the world itself (203).

Coda

By a conservative estimate, between 1850 and 1933, close to 150 German texts, mostly essays, articles in journals and major newspapers, introductions to translations, and a very small number of books, were published on Emerson. I have focused on ten intellectually outstanding critics and scholars whose interpretations of Emerson's position in national, transnational, and historical contexts form the outline of one possible "second narrative" of reception, the necessary complement of all histories of primary works. The conflict of the liberal imagination and a nationalist agenda in Herman Grimm's seminal essays defines the field within which his successors place Emerson. The appropriation of Emerson by Kuno Francke and his cultural nationalism is balanced by the North Atlantic perspective of Julian Schmidt and Anton Schönbach and especially by the exemplary cosmopolitan openness and liberalism of Ernst Robert Curtius and the Jewish-German intellectuals Karl Federn, Egon Friedell, and Friedrich Gundolf. It is their critical ethos that foreshadows and may inspire our transnational readings of Emerson even today.

Notes

1. In this chapter, the terms "German" and "Germany" are not used in a narrow sense designating the present or late-nineteenth-century nation-state; rather, they are intended to refer to the cultural space defined by the use of the German language, which includes Austria and German-speaking Switzerland.

2. Karl Brunnemann, *Geschichte der nordamericanischen Literatur: Eine literarhistorische Studie* (Leipzig: Friedrich Wilhelm Grunow, 1866). Eduard Engel, "Die nordamerikanische Literatur," in *Geschichte der englischen Literatur von den Anfängen bis zur Gegenwart,* 8th ed. (1883; Leipzig: Friedrich Brandstetter, 1915), 523–86. Karl Knortz, *Geschichte der nordamerikanischen Literatur,* 2 vols. (Berlin: Verlag von Hans Lüstenöder, 1891). Leon Kellner, *Geschichte der nordamerikanischen Literatur,* 2 vols., 2nd ed. (1913; Berlin: Walter de Gruyter, 1927).

3. Heinrich Brömse, "Ralph Waldo Emerson (Zu seinem 100. Geburtstag)," *Hamburgischer Correspondent* 171, no. 239 (May 24, 1903): 1–2. Josef Sauer, "Ralph Waldo Emerson, ein Dichterphilosoph," *Hochland* 3, no. 2 (May 1906): 146–60. Johannes Her-

zog, *Ralf Waldo Emerson: Die Religion der Klassiker,* vol. 4 (Berlin-Schöneberg: Protestantischer Schriftenvertrieb G.m.b.H., 1913), 23, 45.

4. Paul Sakmann, *Ralph Waldo Emerson's Geisteswelt nach den Werken und Tagebüchern* (Stuttgart: Fr. Fromanns Verlag [H. Kurtz], 1927), 156–66.

5. I was able to acquire Ralph L. Rusk's copy of Simon's dissertation: its importance for Emerson studies is impressively demonstrated by Rusk's thorough annotations and markings, especially those concerning Simon's analysis of Nietzsche's reading of Emerson.

6. The best overview, textual information, and historical orientation concerning the reception of Emerson worldwide, even though American responses predominate, are provided by Sarah Ann Wider, *The Critical Reception of Emerson: Unsettling All Things* (Rochester, NY: Camden House, 2000); and David LaRocca, introduction to *Estimating Emerson: An Anthology of Criticism from Carlyle to Cavell* (New York: Bloomsbury, 2013), 1–25.

7. I use the terms "positioning" and "field" somewhat loosely, in the sense suggested by Pierre Bourdieu in his essay "The Field of Cultural Production." See Pierre Bourdieu, "The Field of Cultural Production, or: The Economic World Reversed," in *The Field of Cultural Production: Essays on Art and Literature*, ed. Randal Johnson (New York: Columbia University Press, 1993), 29–73.

8. Winfried Fluck, "The Imaginary and the Second Narrative: Reading as Transfer," in Laura Bieger, Ramón Saldívar, and Johannes Voelz, eds., *The Imaginary and Its Worlds* (Hanover, NH: Dartmouth College Press, 2013), 257.

9. Lawrence Buell, *Emerson* (Cambridge, MA: Harvard University Press, 2003), 3ff. Jan Stievermann, "Ralph Waldo Emerson's Vision of An American World Literature," in Barry Tharaud, ed., *Emerson in the Twenty-First Century: Global Perspectives on an American Icon* (Newark: University of Delaware Press, 2010), 174ff.

10. Julius Simon, *Ralph Waldo Emerson in Deutschland (1851–1932)* (Berlin: Juncker und Dünnhaupt Verlag, 1937), 109–11.

11. It is interesting to note that Jennifer Ratner-Rosenhagen's impressive study of the American response to Nietzsche justly uses a similar argument: she reads the American fascination with Nietzsche as a persistent and often unacknowledged concern with his antifoundationalist antecedents in the thought of Emerson. America reading Nietzsche thus provides a variation on the idea of the magnified return of the culturally forgotten or repressed in an alien form. See Jennifer Ratner-Rosenhagen, *American Nietzsche: A History of an Icon and His Ideas* (Chicago: University of Chicago Press, 2012).

12. Herman Friedrich Grimm, "Emerson," in *Ralph Waldo Emerson über Goethe und Shakespeare: Aus dem Englischen nebst einer Critik der Schriften Emerson's*, ed. and trans. Herman Grimm (Hanover: Carl Rümpler, 1857), 93. Subsequent references to this work will be cited parenthetically in the text by page number.

13. Frederick William Holls, ed., *Correspondence between Ralph Waldo Emerson and Herman Grimm* (Boston: Houghton, Mifflin and Co., 1903), passim.

14. Herman Friedrich Grimm, "Ralph Waldo Emerson," in *Neue Essays über Kunst*

und Literatur (Berlin: Ferdinand Dümmler's Verlagsbuchhandlung, 1865), 1–2. Subsequent references to this work will be cited parenthetically in the text by page number.

15. Holls, *Correspondence*, 50.

16. Anon., "Vorwort," in Ralph Waldo Emerson, *Versuche*, trans. G. Fabricius (Hanover: Carl Meyer, 1858), iii. Julius Simon argues convincingly that the anonymous writer of the preface of this translation must have been Gisela von Arnim. See Simon, *Ralph Waldo Emerson in Deutschland*, 113.

17. Friedrich Spielhagen, "Vorwort des Uebersetzers," in *Ralph Waldo Emerson: Englische Charakterzüge,* trans. Friedrich Spielhagen (Hanover: Carl Meyer, 1857), iii–vii.

18. Julian Schmidt, "Einleitung," in *Neue Essays (Letters and Social Aims)*, Autorisirte Uebersetzung (Stuttgart: August Berthold Auerbach, 1876), 7. Subsequent references to this work will be cited parenthetically in the text by page number.

19. The 1876 edition of Schmidt's translation contains the facsimile of a letter by Emerson (dated February 24, 1876) in which he expresses his gratitude to the publisher August Auerbach for the opportunity to address his "village thoughts to the most intellectual of nations" and the chance to thus repay to the German reader "my *limited* [my emphasis] but precious debt to his countrymen" (Schmidt, "Einleitung," facsimile insert after p. 42). The implications of the word "limited" for Emerson's philosophy were rarely noticed by more nationalist-minded German critics of the time and later.

20. Karl Federn, *Essays zur Amerikanischen Litteratur* (Halle a.d.S.: Otto Hendel, 1899), v.

21. Karl Federn, "R. W. Emerson," in *Essays von Ralph Waldo Emerson*, trans. Karl Federn and Thora Weigand (Halle a.d. S.: Verlag von Otto Hendel, n.d. [1892]), 1. Subsequent references to this work will be cited parenthetically in the text by page number.

22. This seems to be a quotation from or, more precisely, an allusion to Protap Chunder Mozoomdar, "Emerson as Seen from India," ed. F. B. Sanborn (Boston: James R. Osgood and Co., 1885), 365–71: "[Emerson] seems to some of us to have been a geographical mistake. He ought to have been born in India" (367).

23. Friedrich Nietzsche, *Twilight of the Idols,* in David LaRocca, ed. *Estimating Emerson: An Anthology of Criticism from Carlyle to Cavell* (New York: Bloomsbury, 2013), 284.

24. This book is now available as *Emerson: Von der Schönheit des Guten; Betrachtungen und Beobachtungen* [Emerson: On the Beauty of the Good; Meditations and Observations], ed. Egon Friedell (Zurich: Diogenes Verlag, 1992).

25. Egon Friedell, "Vorwort," in *Emerson: Sein Charakter aus seinen Werken*, ed. and trans. Egon Friedell (Stuttgart: Robert Lutz, n.d. [1906]), 7–8. Subsequent references to this work are to this edition and will be cited parenthetically in the text by page number.

26. Egon Friedell, *Kulturgeschichte der Neuzeit: Die Krisis der Europäischen Seele von der Schwarzen Pest bis zum Ersten Weltkrieg* (1927–31; rpt., Munich: C. H. Beck, 2008), 1199. Subsequent references to this work are to this edition and will be cited parenthetically in the text by page number.

27. Friedrich Gundelfinger [Friedrich Gundolf], "Emerson," ed. Hans Delbrück, *Preussische Jahrbücher* 131 (Berlin: Georg Stilke, 1908), 252. Subsequent references to this work will be cited parenthetically in the text by page number.

28. Richard Poirier, *The Renewal of Literature: Emersonian Reflections* (New York: Random House, 1987), 13–19 and passim.

29. Stanley Cavell, "Thinking of Emerson," in *Emerson's Transcendental Etudes*, ed. David Justin Hodge (Stanford, CA: Stanford University Press, 2003), 18.

30. Schönbach's primary field of research was medieval German literature. In addition to several studies of major Middle High German authors, he published a critical edition of late medieval sermons in 1879.

31. Anton E. Schönbach, "Ralph Waldo Emerson und sein Kreis" (1897), in *Über Lesen und Bildung: Umschau und Ratschläge* (1888; rpt., Graz: Leuschner & Lubenskys Universitätsbuchhandlung, 1905), 86–87. Subsequent references to this work are to this edition and will be cited parenthetically in the text by page number.

32. Kuno Francke, "Emerson and German Personality," *International Quarterly* (September 1903): 1–15; also in Francke, *German Ideals of To-Day and Other Essays on German Culture* (Boston: Houghton, Mifflin, 1907), 93–125. Subsequent references to this work are to the 1903 version and will be cited parenthetically in the text by page number.

33. Ernst Robert Curtius, "Emerson" (1924), in *Kritische Essays zur Europäischen Literatur* (Bern: Francke Verlag, 1958), 189. Subsequent references to this work will be cited parenthetically in the text by page number.

[8]

RICARDO MIGUEL-ALFONSO

TRANSCENDENTAL MODERNISM: VICENTE HUIDOBRO'S EMERSONIAN POETICS

THE MUTUAL INFLUENCE BETWEEN American Renaissance writers and Latin American intellectuals and poets has been pervasive since at least the late nineteenth century and has already been subjected to specialized studies of different kinds. Emerson and Martí, Whitman and Neruda, Cortázar and Poe, and other similar pairings rank among the best known and most frequently cited examples in what is today called "hemispheric studies." There is, or so it seems, a very fruitful conversation between writers of both subcontinents that is commonly associated with their respective processes of independence from imperial powers and the ensuing literature of freedom and democracy they have produced. Perhaps because this relationship emerges and becomes stronger in the age of independence, the nineteenth century plays a particularly decisive role in terms of the consolidation of this influence. The Revolutionary War and the process leading to U.S. independence was a powerful inspiration for similar movements throughout the world.

Despite its typically Eurocentric inspiration, we can say that transcendentalist philosophy and aesthetics are also crucial in the constitution of modernist Latin American poetry,[1] especially when it comes to formal questions such as the use of free verse or, more important, substantive matters such as the liberating and democratic aspects of poetry as a form of art. Artistic conversations between North and South America were frequent throughout the nineteenth and twentieth centuries, and they continue to be so at many levels.

Although this is an important and celebrated exchange, not all lines of influence have received the same attention. Hardly any literary critic has paid attention to one of the most relevant and productive associations—for both North and South American literary culture—between poetry and philosophy in this context. Leaving aside the playful and formally disruptive character of modernist Latin American poetry (with obvious exceptions), the aesthetic vision of transcendentalist idealism, especially that of Ralph

Waldo Emerson, was a fundamental inspiration for the emergence of certain brands of early-twentieth-century poetry in South America. My interest here is to explore the role that Emerson played in the formation of the poetic movement known as *creacionismo* as well as in the poetic vocation of its creator, Vicente Huidobro. Such an intellectual alliance, which has gone unnoticed in even some of the most relevant critical studies on the subject, is especially striking because Huidobro mentioned Emerson several times in his writings on poetic theory and openly acknowledged his influence as a philosopher and a visionary. In fact, as we will see, the term *creacionismo* is intended to underscore the importance of the creative powers of the human mind in our apprehension of reality, an idea Emerson repeated throughout his career, from *Nature* to his later lectures.

Vicente Huidobro (1893–1948) first mentioned Emerson in the preface to his 1916 poem "Adán" [Adam], in which he sought to regenerate the classical conception of poetry as imitation and the Romantic idea of the poem as a reflection of the poet's subjective vision. The biblical resonance of the title seems to reveal a certain exceptionalist attitude, as well as a nod in the direction of poets such as Whitman, but that would be misleading. Tired of the classical requirements, especially when it came to the formal construction of verse, Huidobro conceived poetry as the expression of a new Adamic mind, free from the constraints of traditional poetics and increasingly closer to science in its search for the hidden mysteries and principles of nature. Here "Adamic" means not so much "newborn" or "pristine" as "original," and even this distinction has its problems. The idea of originality in Huidobro, as we will see later, has more to do with the radical newness of the result—the object that a poem ultimately *is*—than with finding a different topic for a composition. And even in that case, the new result must somehow remind the reader where it came from, what part of nature engendered it. To put it in other words, Huidobro's aim is parallel to Robert Frost's claim that the artist "snatches a thing from some previous order in time and space into a new order with not so much as a ligature clinging to it of the old place where it was organic."[2]

"My Adam," Huidobro declares, "is not the biblical Adam . . . ; it is the scientific Adam. It is the first being that understands Nature, the first in which real intelligence emerges and admiration flourishes."[3] This being who deeply comprehends Nature for the first time is the subject (in both senses of the word) of Huidobro's poem, and he must necessarily express himself in free verse, since only that kind of verse can convey the primitive impulses of the work and symbolize the absolute freedom that the author was trying to find. It is not difficult to see here Emerson's view of poetry as "metre-making argument" (CW 3:6), that is, as a discourse in which intuition and vision prescribe rhetoric and structure. Huidobro agrees with Emerson that the ultimate subject of poetry is freedom and inspiration, and in that sense the Chilean poet argues that his desire to write a great poem demanded "greater freedom, absolute amplitude" (*P* 323).

"Adán" is therefore an Adamic poem in a new sense. However, it retains certain characteristics of the Adamic myths in its American (that is, Emersonian-Whitmanian) version. The most important one is probably its idealistic tone. Huidobro was familiar with Emerson through Spanish and French translations,[4] and of the two different phases in Emersonian thinking, he chose as a poetic source the earlier, Platonic one, even if for a short period. Most of Huidobro's references—in the preface to "Adán" and later in his famous *Manifiestos*—are taken from *Nature,* "The Poet," and "Self-Reliance," some of Emerson's most idealistic texts. His vision of beauty as the creator of the universe and of poetry as a revelation of the architecture of the world is the basis of Huidobro's poetry and his creacionismo. Huidobro himself confesses in the preface to the poem that Emerson saved him in a period of crisis in which he was struggling against what he calls a "spiritual confusion," when his innermost values and poetic skills were shifting (*P* 325). In his own words, Emerson opened up "another world of beauty" (*P* 325) that appeased his tragic uncertainty and led him to the sort of poetry he was seeking. Huidobro found this new orientation in Emerson's essay "The Poet," particularly in two of its central ideas: first, that a poem has "an architecture of its own, and adorns nature with a new thing" (CW 3:6); and second, that "the poet is the Namer, or Language-maker, naming things sometimes after their appearance, sometimes after their essence" (CW 3:13). In other words, Huidobro assumed that the principle for his poetic creation was both the organic relation between poetry and the natural world and the ability of the true poet to renew language and to dismantle the traditional, fossilized conventions of figurative speech.

This is not to say that Huidobro followed, or even enjoyed, the philosophy and poetics of idealism. Although Emerson had saved him from a crisis of inspiration, there are differences between them, especially as Huidobro's thinking gradually moved toward less Romantic positions. For example, early in his famous *Manifiestos* (published between 1916 and 1935), he insisted that the object of poetry was to create artifacts, not to find "arguments," as had Emerson had said. The creative powers of the poet and the imagination were for him absolute powers, to the extent that the poetic experience was not just a "metre-making argument" but rather a total reconfiguration of some part of the real world and its transfiguration into a different object. It was not the role of a poet to seek new ways of saying the same old truths, but rather "to create a poem just as nature creates a tree."[5]

Still, there is a strong Emersonian strain in this line of thinking. The overriding importance of the imagination, which places vision above context and topic, reminds us of *Nature,* especially the chapter on "Beauty," in which Emerson claims that the human eye has a "plastic power" and "is the best of artists" (CW 1:12). The power of the imagination lies in its ability to construct something *new* out of what Nature provides. The poet, Emerson will argue years later, is "emperor in his own right" (CW 3:5), and in that sense he provides a renewed vision of the world that nobody else can. This conception of poetry as a radically creative—and not merely mimetic—endeavor lies at the heart of creacionismo, the movement originated by Huidobro's and Gerardo Diego's poetry, and possibly the most important contribution of the Spanish-speaking world to international modernism.[6] In Huidobro's words, creacionismo is intended to renovate and modernize art by revising its main categories and principles. More specifically, it attempts to regenerate poetry by making it rhetorically simple and creatively sublime.

Huidobro's most famous manifesto, also called "Creacionismo," opens with a renowned quotation from Emerson's "The Poet," in which he claims that the origin of a poem is "a thought so passionate and alive, that, like the spirit of a plant or an animal, it has an architecture of its own, and adorns nature with a new thing" (CW 3:6). To "adorn Nature with a new thing" means to bring a new object into the world, to create in the most material—even physical—sense of the word. The poet's work is not simply to replicate the world, but to produce an artifact that forces us to look at the world with different eyes. "Man no longer imitates," Huidobro would maintain in another manifesto (1923). "He invents, he adds to the facts of the world, which are born in Nature, other facts that are born in his head: a poem, a painting, a statue, a steamboat, a car, an airplane. . . ."[7] Therefore, to create is to separate oneself from Nature while at the same time remembering that Nature is the only basis of creation because it provides the objects that art recreates. "Art is one thing, Nature is another. I love Art as much as I love Nature. But to accept the representations that a man makes of Nature means that you love neither Nature nor Art" (*M* 76).

It may appear that Huidobro chose his opening quotation from "The Poet" in order to distance himself from the more Neoplatonic inclination of the younger Emerson, which he considered outdated and artificial. However, the creative process of creacionismo is analogous to the Emersonian ideal of beauty as it appears in the third chapter of *Nature,* where beauty starts in the contemplation of natural forms, continues with the perception of a spiritual element, and ends when it becomes an object of the intellect, thereby transfiguring the vision of the original forms into a universal and divine experience (CW 1:13–16). In this sense, Huidobro's poetic thinking remains under the influence of Emersonian Romanticism, even in its most idealist version.[8]

Beyond "Adán" and its first reference to Emerson, Huidobro's earliest ideas about poetry appear in a 1919 poem called "Ars poética" [Poetic Art], in which he provides a summary of what we may call his "theoretical" thinking, and outlines the basis of his poetic vision. The poem retains Romantic visionary ideas while at the same time it advances modernist notions of objectivism and rhetorical simplicity:

Let verse be as a key
That opens a thousand doors.
A leaf falls; something flies by;
Let anything your eyes see be created,
And let the hearer's soul shiver.

Invent new worlds and be careful with your words;
Any adjective that doesn't give life annihilates it.
We dwell in the cycle of nerves.
Like a memory,
The muscle hangs in the museums;
Still we have no less strength:
True vigor
Dwells in the head.

Why do you sing the rose, oh Poets!
Just let it blossom in the poem;

Only for us
all things live under the Sun.

The Poet is a small God.[9]

Several Emersonian echoes are clear even in such a brief poem. From the shivering listener who perceives the vibrating chord that the poem strikes to the more general vision of the poet as a "small God," "Ars Poética" reminds us again of Emerson, who conceived poetry as a way of revealing the hidden harmony of nature and considered poets as "liberating gods" (*CW* 3:18) because of their prophetic spirit. Especially prominent is Huidobro's recourse to the example of the rose, which Emerson had famously used in "Self-Reliance" when he claimed, "These roses under my window make no reference to former roses or to better ones; they are for what they are; they exist with God to-day. There is no time to them" (*CW* 2:38). In both cases the example is intended to suggest that natural objects are unmediated, that they exist in the present and can never be *re*produced, and therefore the artist must create his own roses. Emerson used this example to prove that "man is timid and apologetic" (*CW* 2:38); Huidobro used it to show that poets were generally timid and apologetic in their recurrence to stale forms of creativity.

Understood in this way, "Ars poética" provides a late Romantic—almost Symbolist—conception of poetry as a creative power that reveals and embellishes reality and that "opens doors" to a new perception of things. The poem also reiterates the imperative of subjectivism—according to which "Only for us all things live"—and maintains the visionary impulse of Romantic poetics to the point of making the poetic experience one of intense intuition ("A leaf falls; something flies by"). This sense of discovery is one of the principles of Huidobro's poetry and of creacionismo in general.

However, the poem also advances the tendency toward a certain rationalism ("poetic objectivity" would be T. S. Eliot's word) and immediacy that Huidobro's poetry (and modernism in general) would many times take to its limits. In this sense, the poem confronts the vigor of "muscle" against the "true vigor" that stems from the head in an attempt to replace sentimentality and rhetorical intensity with objective vision. Huidobro later defined poetry as "intelligent originality" (*M* 15) and the poetic experience as that which makes us readers "look inward" (*M* 16), not so much as a process of self-discovery but rather as a way of unveiling the analogies at play between the work of art and the natural world we inhabit.

As I have said, "Ars poética" was Huidobro's first attempt at defining poetry, even in the context of a short poem, an effort he continued to make throughout his work. However, his most overt statements on the art of poetry are to be found in his manifestos, many of which were originally speeches and addresses he gave in the first three decades of the twentieth century. From the aforementioned "Creacionismo" to his later declarations, *Manifiestos* articulated in prose the development of his poetry, while at the same time it provides keys to understanding his work and where it came from. The source of Huidobro's poetry was, as we have seen, an Emersonian ideal of creating objects anew, but it was in these prose pieces where he started to "modernize" his Romantic influence and turn it into a more innovative poetics.

The *Manifiestos* is a compendium of propositions that often takes the form of criticisms of past poetry as well as commentaries, sometimes derisive, on several modernist movements, especially Futurism and Ultraism. These new tendencies, as well as others, attempt to turn poetry into a discourse of absolute contemporaneity by worshipping technology—rather than transfiguring it poetically—and therefore undermine their goals *as* poetic movements. In a letter to his friend Gerardo Diego, Huidobro complained that "even a bullfighter could become an Ultraist poet in three days."[10] Beyond the obvious irony of this claim, Huidobro was criticizing the interest in radical immediacy of many of his contemporaries, especially their fascination with velocity, machinery, and presentness. Unlike many poets at the time, he was looking for a more visionary strategy that would force readers to "reconstitute" the meaning of the poem (*M* 14) rather than leaving them as mere spectators to the speed of modern life. "I am exactly the opposite," he assured Diego in another letter. In his poetry there are "no anecdotes, no descriptions."[11] Even though they correspond to different occasions, works in the *Manifiestos* are meant to explain how this new poetry emerges and what its main principles are. There are four different steps to be taken in order to achieve this transformation.

First, poets need to understand that Nature is not their object, but only the source of materials. Nature is an inspiration because it is a creative force, because it brings objects and facts to life. For the poet to create must also mean to produce, not to reproduce, and such creation must necessarily entail an independence from the natural world. In other words, instead of representing nature, the poet must act as nature does.

Second, the role of language in poetry has to be reexamined and must be understood as a sublime one. Huidobro distinguishes between literal and poetic language, but he does so in terms that remind us of the Symbolist movements of the late nineteenth century. Beyond the literal language that we employ to name things as if they were in an inventory, there is another, latent language that reveals the mysterious aura of objects and elevates the reader into a sort of "enchanted world" (*M* 27). This is the appropriate language of creation because it defies and subverts the grammatical order and the factual meaning of words. Poetry is in fact the kind of discourse that, because it takes language to its limit, establishes the last horizon of the imagination.

Next, if poetry is a discourse of limits, the poet thereby acquires a unique place in the social world. Echoing the Emersonian definition of the poet as a "liberating god," Huidobro declares that the emergence of the new poetry also signals the shift from the age of the Man-Mirror to that of the Man-God. If poets can create—that is, if they can actually produce new objects—then they have been able to appropriate the skill of the gods and have become one of them. Judging by this standard, the whole history of art can be divided into three eras: *reproductive* art (in which art is inferior to its medium), *adaptative* art (in which art is in harmony with its medium), and *creative* art (in which art becomes superior to its medium).

Ultimately, if poets have been able to develop the truly creative power, their work becomes universal. Presenting a new fact or creating a new object is a faculty that arises out of what Huidobro calls a "superconsciousness" (an idea similar to Emerson's Over-soul), and this makes poetry "translatable and universal, since new facts remain identical in all languages" (*M* 49, 69).

However, in spite of the redemptive and inspirational role that Emerson played in his career, Huidobro complained that Emerson had not been scientific enough to become an authentic "poet of reality" (*P* 325). Although aware of the latter's scientific interests, Huidobro lamented that Emerson did not write with a truly scientific mind—that is, that his texts are many times a symbol rather than a transfiguration of facts. In other words, Emerson was a contemplative rather than a prophetic writer. The Chilean poet had set as his poetic task the revelation of the "pantheistic nature of my soul, limiting myself to scientific truths but without renouncing the rights of poetry" (*P* 323). One of his aims as a writer was, he admits, "to write an Aesthetics of the Future, of a time that is approaching in which Art and Science will be unified" (*P* 323).[12] Huidobro understood that poetry was the discourse that would bridge the gap between science and art, but in order to make the two cohere it was necessary to get rid of certain old habits, especially to abandon the Romantic sensibility and to merge poetry with the rest of the human plastic forces.[13] This is the point at which Huidobro separates himself more consciously from Emerson, that is, by leaving aside the role of the spiritual element in art (the second step Emerson had formulated in *Nature*) and replacing it with technique. This alone can provide the renewal of vision that art requires without surrendering the necessity of being "scientific."

The best way to understand this move away from Romanticism and into a "transcendental" modernism is to look at how Huidobro himself described his poetic theory. In a 1921 manifesto titled "Creación pura" [Pure Creation], he summarized his ideas in the following way:

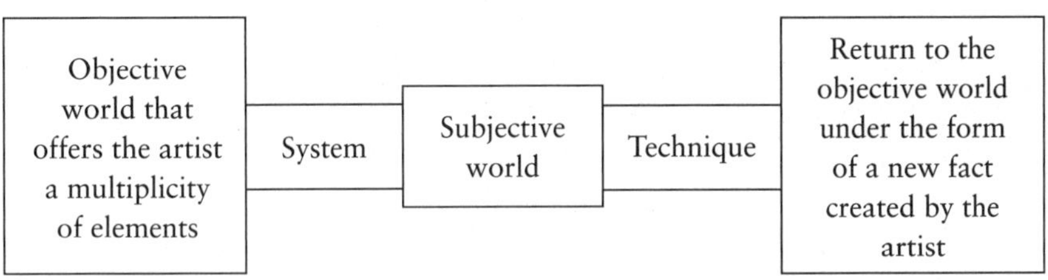

This schematic description contains both the Emersonian and the modernist visions that coexist in Huidobro's poetry and poetics. The creative process starts from the objective world and ultimately returns to it transfigured into a different object, which at the same time provides readers with a different (aesthetic) experience of the objects they already know. Between source and product, there are three mediating stages: the System, which means the set of experiences and preferences that the artist uses to select materials for the work; the Subjective World, which involves the author's self and functions as the intellectually transformative agent that generates the work; and Technique, which comprehends the means of expression that will be employed in the creation of the new fact.[14] The three intermediate elements are properly personal, but the origin and end of poetry are objective artifacts that should be measured only by the power of the vision they present and the skill of the poet who created them. T. S. Eliot famously formulated this separation as the gap between "the man who suffers and the mind which creates."[15]

This reconfiguration (or modernization) of Huidobro's poetic ideas reemerges in his most celebrated poem, "Altazor" (1931), where he returned to the idea of poetry as connected intimately with nature but radically different from it. This time, however, he did so while at the same moving consciously toward a modernist ideology that favors language experimentation and attempts to liquidate traditional mimesis. Here is one representative example:

> Cut off all the moorings
> Of river, sea and mountain
>
> Of spirit and memory
> Of agonizing law and feverish dream
>
> It is just the world that spins, that goes on and whirls
> It is just another pupil
> . . . .
> The poet is but the manicurist of language
> Not the magician who turns off and on
> Stellar words and the cherries of wandering farewells
> Far removed from the hands of the earth
> And everything he says is his own invention
> Things that happen outside the ordinary world
> Let us kill the poet who has fed us up
> . . . .
> The last poet agonizes
> The bells of the continents chime
> The moon dies with the night on its back
> The sun pulls the day out of its pocket
> The solemn new landscape opens its eyes
> And moves from earth to the stars
> The burial of poetry

All languages are dead
Dead in the hands of the tragic neighbor
We must resuscitate the languages
With a resonant smile
With wagons filled with laughter
With short-circuits in the sentences
And grammatical cataclysms
Rise and walk.[16]

The religious resonances of the last line ("rise and walk") are at once serious and ironic. They convey an impression of being at the end of an era and the beginning of another, and in that sense "Altazor" stands on the brink of a new poetic age and calls for radical renewal. Huidobro again resorts to the separation from Nature by calling poets (and readers) to "cut off all the moorings" to a reality that appears bleak at best. The poet's role is also redefined: from the magician who "turns off and on / Stellar words" to the "manicurist of language" who must be concerned with expressive accuracy (since the resurrection of poetry cannot be realized unless language itself resuscitates). The last images of the poem are typical of Huidobro's poetics and poetry: the "wagons filled with laughter" (an image that also resonates in Whitman's poem "O Me! O Life!"), the "short-circuits in the sentences" and the "grammatical cataclysms" are in themselves examples of the theoretical modes of renewal that poetry requires. As images, they provide fresh and surprising ways of looking at poetry, ones in which the reader has to participate actively in the construction of its (self-referential) meaning. As he did in "Ars poética," Huidobro constructs "Altazor" as a poem about poetry, in which form and meaning become so intertwined that we cannot separate one from the other. The poem appeals to itself as a theory and a practice of how to renew poetic language.

This passage from "Altazor" also illustrates the Emersonian and the modernist strains in Huidobro's poetic thinking. From Emerson, Huidobro retains the idea of poetic creativity as the ability to contribute a new vision of and to the world, a task in which poets grow increasingly powerful until they become "liberating god[s]." And although he also believed, as Emerson did, that in order to do so, poets must de-fossilize words, strip them of their conventional meaning, this task required a more radical experimentation than the sage of Concord could have imagined. Whether in his early, idealist phase or in his later, more naturalist one, Emerson never considered reading poetry as *only* a revelatory experience, and even in his later work, he conceived of the contemplation of beauty as having "a moral element in it" (CW 6:163). For Huidobro, this moral element was a remnant of old-fashioned conceptions of poetry and an obstacle for the overcoming of both classical and Romantic poetics. He replaced it with (or, rather, included it in) the Subjective World of the poet, but in his scheme about creation he confined this world to the role of a medium for what is really relevant: the selection of materials, and the originality of the final product after Technique has acted upon them. Still, Huidobro remains an Emersonian thinker in his emphasis on creativity and poetic immanence. In other words, his creacionismo is a transcendental version of modernism.

Notes

1. Bruce Dean Willis, *Aesthetics of Equilibrium: The Vanguard Poetics of Vicente Huidobro and Mário de Andrade* (West Lafayette, IN: Purdue University Press, 2010), x–xv.

2. Robert Frost, "The Figure a Poem Makes," in *Collected Poems, Prose, and Plays*, ed. Richard Poirier and Mark Richardson (New York: Library of America, 1995), 778.

3. Vicente Huidobro, prefacio a *Adán*, in *Obra poética*, ed. Cedomil Goic (Madrid: A.L.L.C.A., 2003), 323. Hereafter cited parenthetically in the text as *P*. All translations are mine.

4. Mireya Camurati, *Poesía y poética de Vicente Huidobro* (Buenos Aires: Fernando García Cambeiro, 1980), 14–34.

5. Huidobro, *Horizon carré*, in *Obra poética*, 417.

6. See Pedro Aullón de Haro, "La teoría poética vanguardista: El creacionismo," in his *La modernidad poética, la vanguardia y el creacionismo* (Málaga: Analecta Malacitana, 2000), 177–224.

7. Vicente Huidobro, *Manifiestos* (Santiago de Chile: Mago, 2009), 97. Hereafter cited parenthetically in the text as *M*.

8. On Huidobro and Romanticism in general, see George Yúdice, *Vicente Huidobro y la motivación del lenguaje* (Buenos Aires: Galerna, 1978), 259–78.

9. Huidobro, "Ars poética," in *Obra poética*, 391.

10. Vicente Huidobro, *Epistolario: Correspondencia con Gerardo Diego, Juan Larrea y Guillermo de Torre, 1918–1947*, ed. Gabriele Morelli and Carlos García (Madrid: Publicaciones de la Residencia de Estudiantes, 2008), 72.

11. Ibid., 55.

12. In this sense, it is important to remember that what Huidobro understands as "scientific truth" is not, at least not formally, what we now understand as such. By this term Huidobro means any natural fact that can be scientifically studied and explained.

13. According to the essayist and translator Rafael Cansino-Assens, this is the greatest "modernization" that Huidobro effected on the poetry of his time. See Rafael Cansinos-Assens, "Un gran poeta chileno: Vicente Huidobro y el creacionismo (1919)," in René de Costa, ed., *Vicente Huidobro y el creacionismo* (Madrid: Taurus, 1975), 122.

14. For an interpretation of these elements and their relation to both Kant's and Coleridge's theories of art, see Aullón de Haro, "La teoría poética vanguardista," 203ff.

15. T. S. Eliot, "Tradition and the Individual Talent," in *Selected Essays* (London: Faber and Faber, 1951), 18.

16. Huidobro, *Altazor*, in *Obra poética*, 765–68.

[9]

RICHARD DEMING

RILKE AND EMERSON: THE CASE AGAINST INFLUENCE AS SUCH

The Poets light but Lamps—
Themselves—go out—
The Wicks they stimulate,
If vital Light

Inhere as do the Suns—
Each Age a Lens
Disseminating their
Circumference—
—Emily Dickinson

IT IS AN OPEN yet still largely unexplored secret that Emerson's essays played some relatively early and possibly telling role in the thinking of Rainer Maria Rilke, one of the twentieth century's most highly regarded and influential poets. In a letter posted in June 1898, just a year before the period of time that Rilke began undertaking his first significant collection of poems, *The Book of Hours*, the youthful poet reveals to Helene Woronin, a young Russian friend of Lou Andreas-Salomé with whom he had become acquainted during a trip to Italy: "Besides, the American philosopher Ralph Waldo Emerson, who has so much influence, came to hand. I am just beginning to devote myself to him."[1] With this gesture, Rilke implies what he estimates as Emerson's prodigious impact on German arts and letters, an estimate that seems supported by others (the extent of which is detailed in Julius Simon's foundational study *Ralph Waldo Emerson in Deutschland, 1851–1932*, published in 1937). As is well documented, Friedrich Nietzsche, for instance, found himself quite sympathetic to Emersonian ideals, not the least of which is the belief that subjectivity is not a given, that any individual's perpetual process of becoming a moral agent and an empowered figure stands ever against the encroachments of social conformity and the dictates of cultural as well as institutional authoritarianism.[2] Not only was Nietzsche a committed reader of Emerson (though his devotion would wax and wane over the years), he was among the first wave of those in the German-speaking world to take so eagerly to the American philosopher. As Julius Simon shows, the high point of German interest in Emerson does not occur until the late 1890s and lasts well into the middle of the following decade. The interest is fueled in large part by a burgeoning disillusionment with materialism and the premium put on rationalism, and by a frustration with perceived pessimism so prevalent across Europe at that time. Emerson's philosophical idealism and optimism provided a welcome counterbalance for fin de siècle German-language writers.[3]

Yet Rilke's comment goes beyond acknowledging a widespread presence of Emerson's essays in turn-of-the-century Germany. What he says about his incipient devotion to Emerson also offers some enticement for looking for traces of Emersonian thinking in Rilke's own sense of the link between ethics and poetics. Such a hunt may, however, be ultimately unsatisfying if we are trying to gauge a direct transmission of Emersonian ideals to Rilke, given the paucity of comprehensive evidence. Rilke gives us little to go on. What may prove more fruitful is to investigate how Rilke invites readers to see him as taking up a conversation with Emerson in order to discover through that conversation a mutually conceived aesthetics. Within this frame we are apt to see how both writers make a case against influence as such, so as to dismantle a value structure that valorizes tradition for its own sake. Instead, the model culled from the interaction between these two describes one's intellectual, artistic, and spiritual predecessors as exemplars or catalysts for the imagination rather than forces for authenticating intellectual legitimacy.

For these reasons, it is seductive to want to see Emerson as a formative and foundational influence on Rilke. Such a desire runs up against the problem that the actual extent of a continuous exchange is far short of what, for instance, Nietzsche derived from the American philosopher. There are clearly some elective affinities between Rilke and Emerson, however, and since the respective authors similarly drew upon a Romantic conception of the interconnection of ethics and aesthetics, there is room to start to discern a genealogy flowing from Emerson to Rilke, although the limitations are evident.

Both writers insist on Romantic genius and its concomitant spontaneity as emphasizing the imagination's role in shaping how reality is conceptualized. This goes along with their respective beliefs that the model for a spiritual life in the face of what each perceived as increasing dependence on dehumanizing technology and ideology (terms, of course, neither writer would ever actually use) is manifested through attempts at attaining a complex transcendental perspective. Years later, for instance, Rilke describes the threat of technology in the tenth poem in the second sequence of the *Sonnets to Orpheus:*

> Every advance the machine threatens, as long as
> it dares, instead of obedience, to be in the mind.[4]

Technology, if it does not obey us, threatens everything we have gained. Instead of moving us forward, machines can set us back, spiritually. Only a belief in the mystery of the world can help advance our humanity.

Aside from the question of influence, both writers have foundational intellectual affinities. To begin with, a wellspring common to both exists in the form of some shared referents in intellectual history. Emerson himself acknowledges his own uses of German idealist philosophy, however idiosyncratic and creative his readings of Kant, Hegel, Herder, and Schlegel tend to be. It would be easy to suggest that Emerson's versions of German Romanticism are the result of his shaky grasp on the language, yet it is an Emersonian ideal to be a "strong reader," if we borrow Harold Bloom's characterization of the poet who deforms a precursor not intentionally, but so as to translate the work in such a way that it creates the conditions for the writer's coming into his or her own authority and abilities.[5] To put things in Emerson's own words, from "The American Scholar": "There is then creative reading as well as creative writing. When the mind is braced by labor and invention, the page of whatever book we read becomes luminous with manifold allusion" (*cw* 1:58). And to this idea we could also add Emerson's further belief, in "Nominalist and Realist," that a process of reading is not merely the acquisition of information but also the activation of the imagination in response to the consciousness of others: "I am faithful again to the whole over the members in my use of books. I find the most pleasure in reading a book in a manner least flattering to the author. I read Proclus, and sometimes Plato, as I might read a dictionary, for a mechanical help to the fancy and the imagination. I read for the lusters, as if one should use a fine picture in a chromatic experiment, for its rich colors. 'Tis not Proclus, but a piece of nature and fate that I explore. It is a greater joy to see the author's author, than himself" (*cw* 3:137). In this context, "nature" refers to both human nature and the largest order of being itself. Thus, Emerson generatively torques English-language writers and thinkers just as he does German ones. In Emerson's view, one reads not for what the *author* says, but rather to find in any text that measure of a common, recognizable humanity revealed by the way of negotiating the materials that authors use to compose. The commensurate actions of imagination and interpretation are brought into play by literary texts. Our responses are expressive of the tension between our individual subjectivity and a claim to a universal humanity.

Emerson comes to these German thinkers in large part by way of Samuel Taylor Coleridge, an early and foundational force in Emerson's development. Yet, it is Goethe, a writer whose range of talents—from the poetic to the philosophical—provided compelling permission to push past divisions of discourse and discipline. Emerson describes Goethe as "the philosopher of this multiplicity [of modern life], hundred-handed, Argus-eyed, able and happy to cope with this rolling miscellany of facts and sciences, and, by his own versatility, to dispose of them with ease; a manly mind unembarrassed by the variety of coats of convention with which life had got encrusted, easily able by his subtlety to pierce these, and to draw his strength from nature with which he lived in full communion" (CW 4:156). Undoubtedly, such a description extends also to Emerson. The length of the sentence seems to be a means for representing, rather than merely describing, the "rolling miscellany of facts" that Emerson sees as being the condition of modern life, as well as suggesting the breadth of Goethe's imagination in his essay meditating on this German author. The sentence gathers elements, accruing detail as it develops a description of Goethe, and thereby enacts what Emerson sees as the German author's estimable qualities. In this way, the subject of the essay evokes the qualities he represents.

The book in which that essay appears, titled *Representative Men,* is a collection of meditative engagements with various exemplars drawn from throughout history; however, these are not exactly biographies, psychological portraits, or sketches of great men accomplishing great deeds. Instead, Emerson sees each of the six men he writes about—from Plato to Shakespeare to Montaigne—as catalysts for thinking about what constitutes greatness or genius in regard to what he elsewhere calls "intellect constructive" (CW 2:198). They are not chosen for any intellectual capital that they might grant. One key element of genius is that it is revelatory in ways that go beyond regional, national, and even cultural boundaries. Emerson therefore specifies that in Goethe, "there is no trace of provincial limitation in his muse." Limitation is, for Emerson, something to be overcome. As he insists in "Circles," "Men cease to interest us when we find their limitations. The only sin is limitation. As soon as you once come up with a man's limitations, it is all over with him" (CW 2:182–83).

If limitation is a sin, then there must be hope for redemption, and this lies in the pursuit of overcoming one's self. Goethe may be an author who writes in German, but his thought is not merely a German's. Emerson argues there is in Goethe a cosmopolitan, searching dimension to his way of thinking that saves him from the situational limitation derived from an undue focus on the forms of education at hand. It is not what is German in Goethe's thinking that makes him so profound, but what is in him despite being formed by a given culture and within the boundaries of its history. The fact that he resists being a mouthpiece for received ideas is why Emerson believes Goethe is exceptional, and the ideas he makes available to others across time and space pushes him past the strictures of a specific and particular culture. Goethe does not teach readers how to be exceptional, but rather that exceptions can and do exist. These exceptions are manifestations of the resistance to social conformism and the acknowledgment of one's own genius. In this way, Goethe enacts a heroic principle. The question then is how Emerson might inherit such a principle and put it into practice authentically. Emerson's *use* of Goethe is therefore not merely rhetorical—employed to legitimate Emerson's thinking. His ideas are places to begin.

If German thinking exercises an influence on Emerson, it manifests itself in what Emerson takes to be concerns touching on a fundamental humanity. In that sense Emerson would be giving German-language philosophy and literature back to Rilke, but in a transformed state. Such a transformation would have been useful to the Prague-born Rilke, whose relationship to Germany was ever vexed. This return of a German Romanticism, channeled through another thinker, takes on some elements of Emerson's contention, "In every work of genius we recognize our own rejected thoughts: they come back to us with a certain alienated majesty" (*CW* 2:27). In this case, Rilke possibly recognized those Germanic tendencies, such as the interdependence of poetry and philosophy and the sense that aesthetic experiences offer insights into ethical and epistemological realities, which Emerson himself had drawn from figures such as Hegel, Kant, Goethe, and others.[6] And by "recognized" (Emerson's preferred term) I do not mean to suggest that Rilke could perceive possibly shared literary and intellectual origins, though that is likely. Instead, we might say that in encountering these family resemblances in Emerson's essays and outside the nationalized dimensions of German literature and philosophy, Rilke had the opportunity to think through these same ideas anew (and therefore "re-cognize" them—literally think them again); and in its having been transformed by Emerson and his context, the thinking would not have been overwhelmed by the determinations of an inherited Germanic intellectual tradition. This freedom from the familiarity (though we need not go so far as to call it an estrangement) of a nationalized literary inheritance might give the ideas an "alienated majesty."

If that claim feels speculative in regard to Rilke—however valid it is for Europe's reception of Emerson—it is because in all actuality there is too little information to know just what Rilke responded to in Emerson. A few scholars have tried to discern evidence for the impact that Emerson's thinking had on Rilke (Marilyn Vogler Urion and Jan Wojcik to name but two), and yet the results are, at best, limited. Critics and literary historians have pushed the connections and mapped the influence flowing between the two only tentatively, because Rilke himself, though acknowledging his "devotion," does not articulate any conscious debt to the American philosopher.[7] However, Rilke's silence on that front might in part serve as tacit acknowledgment of Emerson and may be a way of thinking about the problems of measuring influence at all. Instead, looking for influences is actually contrary to the way that Rilke and Emerson conceive of not only what artists and writers do, but also the way they construct their models of subjectivity. This is not to say that influence necessarily does not occur, but that trying to delineate that inheritance is a methodology that is neither Emersonian nor Rilkean. Both writers press against inheritance so as to insist on the primacy and spontaneity of an often-spiritualized subjectivity. Emerson argues for and Rilke demonstrates a desire to transform tradition by insisting on the way that each individual fashions an authorial self by resisting influence and yet drawing out the kind of intensity and potentiality exemplary thinkers enact. "Yet vigor is contagious," Emerson insists, "and whatever makes us either think or feel strongly, adds to our power and enlarges our field of action" (*CW* 6:131). The greatness of great figures, then, lies in the extent to which they resist transmitting a continuous line of tradition and instead offer examples of dynamic, generative action that spur people to their own actions and decisions.

Rilke, like Nietzsche, read Emerson in translation, and yet there is little evidence that Rilke's investment in Emerson was as strong as Nietzsche's had been—with the German philosopher going as far as incorporating passages of Emerson's texts into his own essays.[8] Wolfgang Leppmann, one of Rilke's most respected biographers, notes however that Emerson was, at least just at the turn of the twentieth century, one of Rilke's favorite authors.[9] This interest is reflected periodically in moments throughout Rilke's work, particularly in passages drawn from Emerson that appear in Rilke's notebooks. For instance, at the opening of his Florentine notebook from 1898, Rilke copied out in translation Emerson's self-descriptive claim: "Ich stelle einfach Versuche an, ein endlos Suchender mit keiner Vergangenheit hinter mir."[10] Or, as it appears in "Circles": "I simply experiment, an endless seeker with no Past at my back" (*CW* 3:188). It is hard to miss the irony that by quoting a precursor, Rilke is not disavowing the past, though we may see him as using the past in order to move forward, which would be an Emersonian tendency.

As I have mentioned, the echoes between the two are fleeting. In his article charting the parameters for discerning the extent of Rilke's connection to Emerson, Jan Wojcik has noted, for example, the parallels between Emerson's essay "Circles" and the second poem of Rilke's *The Book of Hours*, published in 1905.[11] "Ich lebe mein Leben in wachsenden Ringen" [I live my life in growing circles], begins the poem, which does suggest an allusion to Emerson's own claim that "[t]he life of man is a self-evolving circle, which, from a ring imperceptibly small, rushes on all sides outwards to new and larger circles, and that without end" (CW 2:180).[12] What remains to be seen is whether or not what sits at the center of the circle is the same for both writers. In Rilke's poem, the speaker circles around God or an ancient tower, and he does not know whether he is a falcon, a storm, or a "great song." Emerson, on the other hand, suggests that the movements of a self are marked by—and even marked *as*—those circles that emanate from a starting point of one's own subjectivity. That suggests something closer to waveforms than a circular path created by a falcon. Of course, the latter tropes in Rilke's list of possibilities—the storm and the song—offer more complex views of the center. With a storm, the center would be the still point of the dynamic climate patterns, and so would provide a balance that holds the storm's structure together. The "great song" does perhaps suggest that the center produces a series of resonating sounds that build outward from the origin. Still, it is clear that while the two texts share a primary trope, and although what they signify becomes quite different upon inspection, both authors point toward the center and consider what effect the growing rings have for a figure moving outward. As I want to suggest, the idea of a center that remains stable and pushes outward rather than gathering material and pulling it inward is what they both hold in terms of an ideal for aesthetic and even moral agency.

As I mentioned earlier, Rilke did include lines from Emerson in his notebooks, which indicates, however subtly, that the American's thinking was insinuating itself behind the scenes, acting as a *vis a tergo* pushing Rilke's still-burgeoning poetics. Perhaps the most telling gesture Rilke makes toward Emerson is the use of a sentence from Emerson's "Considerations by the Way," an essay included in *The Conduct of Life* (1860): "The hero is he who is immovably centered" (CW 6:147). The quotation comes at a crucial moment in Rilke's development. In 1902, at the age of twenty-six and prompted by Clara Westhoff, briefly his wife (though divorce was imminent), Rilke traveled to Paris in order to meet the great French sculptor, Auguste Rodin, and to begin to write a monograph about the artist. I would add, too, that Westhoff had been Rodin's student just two years before. But this was an especially fecund period in Rilke's life. He would soon publish his first major book of poems and would serve as Rodin's secretary for a brief time, less than four years. Bearing in mind the proximity of the date between Rilke's appearance in France and the statement in his letter to Helene Woronin that he had begun to wrestle with Emerson, the American philosopher still loomed large in his mind throughout this period.

For that reason, it may come as no surprise that as an epigraph for his meditation on the sculptor, Rilke positions as the book's initiating gesture an aphorism drawn from Emerson's essay "Considerations by the Way": "The hero is he who is immovably centered," sits at the opening of Rilke's monograph, whose first part was published in 1903, with a second part appearing in 1907. Interestingly, Rilke did not translate the line from Emerson, but kept it in English, despite the fact that the poet had no real facility with the language. We can take this as a telling nod of respect to the American, but keeping the line in English also insists on the specific context of Emerson's work, because it does not translate the words into a new milieu. That the aphorism remains in English further emphasizes the sentence's connection to its source, and it becomes something more than a sly employment of a cleverly articulated idea to quickly import some outside authority to establish the tone of what follows. It is more than ornamentation—it becomes an inheritance.

It is very likely that Rilke first came upon the aphorism in "The Work and Life of Eugène Delacroix," an essay by the French poet and critic Charles Baudelaire, initially published in 1863. Baudelaire's essay holds that the painter was "one of the rare geniuses of [an] unhappy age—an age at once so poor and so rich, an age at times too exacting, at times too indulgent—and too often unjust."[13] Discussing the painter in order to put forth what for Baudelaire were essential tenets of a Romanticism that offers a tonic for contemporary imagination, the essay makes Delacroix a figure set outside the ebb and flow of time. While it is just as possible that Rilke had encountered the sentence in his own reading of Emerson's text, the correspondence between Rilke's writing about Rodin and Baudelaire's writing about the French Romantic painter is too great to ignore. This transmission of Emerson also becomes itself a kind of circle moving outward across Europe and throughout Romanticism. We can, in any event, settle on the notion that even if Rilke had read Emerson's line in the late 1890s, it was Baudelaire's essay that lodged the sentence, and the implication of its claims, in the Bohemian-Austrian poet's mind in regard to imagining a great artist as a hero and, therefore, a particular kind of immovable node. Still, what are we to make of the fact that the sentence moves from essay to essay to essay, with all three writers being poets who write essays about precursors? The parallel gestures suggest some deeper signification in the movement of the maxim among these writers and the way they construct those figures of a prior generation that stand as initiatory models by which Emerson, Baudelaire, and Rilke can articulate their own value systems. The sentence itself becomes a tool that each writer uses in a different way.

Baudelaire, within his essay about Delacroix, cites Emerson's line as a way of characterizing the precision of the writing in Delacroix's literary fragments—somewhat surprisingly, as Delacroix has no evident connection to Emerson beyond the shared investment in Romantic sensibilities and a reliance on an aphoristic literary style. The French poet evidently was rather mixed in his feelings about Emerson, however. Identifying Emerson as the "leader of the wearisome Boston school," Baudelaire allows that the American has "the flavor of Seneca" about him, and this "effectively stimulates meditation." Furthermore, the French poet/critic indicates that Emerson has in mind the hero in conjunction with "the conduct of life" and the "sphere of business," but feels that the hero could just as well be "the hero of literature, or the true writer." Interestingly, Baudelaire cites *en passant* the title of the collection of Emerson's essays from which the quotation is drawn—*The Conduct of Life*—and places it within the flow of his sentence, blurring a distinction between the words used as title of a text and the words used to name a concept belonging to the realm of ethics. At the linguistic level, Emerson's ideas and one's comportment become one and the same rather than separate. Furthermore, by transforming the title, Baudelaire, while never dissipating the whole range of Emerson's thinking, is in essence absorbing Emerson even more fully than the way that citation usually does. By using Emerson, and in a sense translating him into Baudelaire's conceptual framework, rather than deferring to him, Baudelaire becomes Emersonian. Baudelaire is inspired by Emerson to use what he feels is most compelling and transform it into his own thinking.[14]

With that adjustment in place, Emerson's maxim applies to Delacroix, Baudelaire insists, because the painter's literary precision marked an intensity of composition directed by the entirety of the artist/hero's spiritual force and concentrated toward a single, focused point. Of course, Emerson would have felt that the distinction that Baudelaire implies is no real distinction, because between how one conducts one's life and how one creates art there is no distance. Art, just like life, is the expression of the individual's values, beliefs, and commitments. These pursuits—living, making art—rather than existing in separate, discontinuous spheres, are all expressions of one's choices, and these measure the integrity of a self set against external social pressures. The hero is a hero across all fields.

It is worth thinking about the fact that Baudelaire cites Emerson twice in his essay. The second citation sees Baudelaire quoting from "Power," also in *The Conduct of Life:* "The one prudence in life is concentration; the one evil is dissipation" (CW 6:59). It means that the reference is not a passing effect and that Baudelaire is concentrating his work with the references rather than dissipating it. The meaning of these references gets complex when we realize that Baudelaire uses Emerson to provide a context for reading Delacroix, and he uses Seneca to give a context for Emerson. As Baudelaire does this to describe the effect of style upon the reader, it becomes difficult to avoid recognizing how Baudelaire sees his own essay as extending the conditions he is describing. Baudelaire stands at the center as he uses his text to bind together disparate authors and artists that come before him. In arranging these figures, Baudelaire places himself at the center. If Emerson's "flavor of Seneca" is what prompts meditation, a heightened state of attention and the necessary condition for creative thought—or what Emerson would call "the intellect constructive"—then perhaps Baudelaire's importing "a taste" of Emerson—a taste that is Senecan in the brevity of his apothegm about the hero's being an immovable center—is designed to create the possibility of meditation within Baudelaire's readers as well. Baudelaire's essay is not just an exercise in art criticism but is itself a text that seeks to stimulate the imagination through its compositional choices. By importing provocative sentences from Emerson, Baudelaire weaves their effects into the texture of his own essay; the poet guides a reader's response to Delacroix and elicits experience and response rather than simply imparting information.

To ask such questions about what Baudelaire's use of Emerson contributes to his essay is to open just such a query in considering what Rilke does with the American philosopher when he uses the same maxim as the epigraph to *Auguste Rodin*. This approach is to move away from gauging influence, so as to see Emerson and his work as materials to be employed by those who come after him. They use his work to make their own statements.

At first glance, one would likely take Rilke's use of Emerson's sentence, "The hero is he who is immovably centered," as epigraph to suggest a description of Rodin, the subject of Rilke's book. The suggestion would be that Rodin is a hero as well as an immovable center. Of course, Rilke does make such a case for the sculptor. Yet, for Emerson, at some level such a characterization is true not just of "great men," but is potentially true of everyone. Thus, the epigraph can and ought to be taken as self-reflexive. Rather than being drawn into Rodin's gravity, Rilke places an Emersonian reminder to his readers as well as to himself that one ought to be inspired by Rodin, but one needs to resist being captured by the pull of gravity of the great artist's influence. It is this idea of "using" great men as models for the self that Rilke may learn from Emerson. At the very least, we see Rilke undertaking a similar process, using the epigraph as a signal that activates the presence of Emerson as himself a "mechanical help to the fancy and the imagination" by which Rilke regards Rodin.

Of course, as any good paratext will do, the epigraph does affect the main text. In this case, the quotation is in conversation with the opening sentences of Rilke's essay: "Rodin was lonely before his fame. And the fame that came perhaps made him even lonelier. Because fame is finally only the epitome of all the misunderstandings that collect around a new name."[15] We can hear in this passage the ways that Rilke fashions Rodin as an Emersonian figure. Before his fame, Rilke tells the reader, Rodin was isolated and that fame, or the public version of Rodin, is not really Rodin; it is a collection of misunderstandings that gather about his name. In this way, the authentic Rodin stands unmoved at the center of the activity and the misunderstandings that gather because of fame. Behind this description of Rodin, we might catch Rilke borrowing on Emerson's insistence in "Self-Reliance," "To be great is to be misunderstood."

There might be room to discern a divergence from Emerson when we note that in this description Rilke portrays Rodin as standing at the center while around him, yet separate, are all the misapprehensions that attach to fame. One could see that cluster of forces as being what circles around the hero—other people and perceptions deformed by fame. Yet it would be closer to the mark to see Rodin as standing apart from those opinions engineered by social forces. He is not in opposition to those forces because that would entail his being susceptible to them. Even an active, conscious resistance demonstrates a reaction guided by the masses.

I mentioned that Rilke portrays Rodin and that only signals the irony that Rodin is the subject rather than the creator of a portrait. This means that whatever Rilke says about Rodin's representations of others reflects back on Rilke's meditation as well. If Rodin is heroic, that is, an exemplar, then Rilke must work in concert in order to enact what Rodin shows an artist to be. Rodin's drawings and sculptures are generated in response to people, things, and experiences, but rather than maintaining a slavish fidelity to mimeticism, he seeks to create contemplation in the viewer.

Rilke writes:

> Where the initial inspiration runs out from subject matter, where an ancient legend, the verses of a poem, a historical scene, or the great accomplishment of a real person was, there, when Rodin begins, the material translates itself during the work more and more into objectivity and anonymity; communicated in the language of the hands, the needs that arise, all have a new meaning wholly in regard to its plastic realization.
>
> In Rodin's drawings this preliminary forgetting and transformation of the material inspiration advances before itself. In this art, he has developed his own means of expression, and that makes these pages (there are many hundreds) into a self-reliant and original revelation of his personality.[16]

In this passage, Rilke asserts that the exact time when whatever provides the catalyst for Rodin's initial engagement and kindles his desire to create a representation runs out of its inspirational potential is also the very moment that the work loses its debt to the past and becomes something other than a testament. It becomes the means by which Rodin's personality asserts itself. The work expresses not similitude concerning a prior event, person, or myth, but rather it expresses Rodin's imagination and interpretation of such material. The further removed they are from adherence to capturing reality, the more the sculpture becomes the expression of Rodin's struggles with the material reality of the stone to present through that medium the way he experiences memory, thought. It holds enough representation so that others can recognize the subject, but that familiarity also lets the audience know that the imagination is not mere fancy but is how the artist or writer processes materials. As Rilke indicates, it is the process of transforming and forgetting that we witness when experiencing the work of art and its struggle to assert itself in the face of what brings it into the artist's consciousness. The sculptures show how Rodin's imagination shoots through his whole sense of reality. This understanding of Rodin offered by Rilke's essay is then self-reflexive. What he develops in his essay is a meditation that also exhausts its dependency on its source material. The very claim that the work of the artist-hero determines his own personality through its ability to break free of the influence and determination provided by precursors shapes Rilke's own thinking. He eschews a strictly biographical context for discussing the sculptor, writes more about his impressions, and states these interpretations as fact. Emerson describes a similar idea when in the essay "Art" he writes, "art is the path of the creator to his work." Not participation in a tradition but rather the act of creation is the purpose of art, an idea Rilke shares with Emerson, and he presents Rodin as a living symbol for this principle. Rilke ends the first section of his monograph by writing this about the sculptor and his belief in the role of work as a means of expressing the self:

> With this development Rodin has given to all the arts a sign in this baffled time. One will recognize what this great artist has made so great: that he was a worker who, with all his power, desired nothing more than to enter into the humble and hard being of his tools. Therein lay a type of abandonment of life; but with this patience he gained it: then the world came unto his tool.[17]

Instead of offering a whole view of the sculptor, Rilke concentrates on those aspects that do separate him from others, and yet these heroic aspects are ones that stimulate people's own possibilities. As Rilke indicates, Rodin becomes a sign to others. Part of what Rodin signifies is the role of patience and its fostering of the attention that allows the world to express itself through the artist's tool. In Emerson's thinking, such a sign brings people to their own ideas and the divine spark that motivates them, a spark that we ultimately all share. Rodin's attention can be practiced in any form or craft since it is the manifestation of attention—and thus becomes a text to which others can apply their own attention. And this is why in this passage from Rilke, the heroic qualities include patience and humility before the world. We can call this attention, if art is a form of developing an attentiveness to things. Rilke essentially characterizes Rodin as a "creative reader" of people, things, and ideas and thereby places the artist's authority over the authority of an intractable material world or a prior "great man." Rodin's genius is not what makes Rodin exceptional, it is what makes him fully human, attuned to his own decisive power to make choices, to read the world actively, and to articulate his experience of it as he lives it every day. Rilke therefore uses Rodin to articulate what he wants to say, what he feels he needs to articulate.

Can we say this understanding of Rodin as hero shows an Emersonian influence? Again, this becomes impossible to gauge because of the difficulty in discerning where Emerson leaves off and where Rilke begins. However, the shared ideal is that the artist creates something new by drawing what he or she can from the subject and then transforming that into an expression of the art's own subjectivity. Rilke does just that by transforming Rodin into a kind of aesthetic allegory. The more that readers can trace influence, the less successful the artist has been in terms of being a spontaneous and generative force of Romantic genius. Influence is, finally, what needs to be overcome, especially just where one is most employed in describing a great figure that casts a long and imposing shadow. Only in that way is the artist able to see the world and articulate it, not the way someone else might, but how any of us may.

Notes

I would like to thank Ilan Ben-Meir for his invaluable research assistance on this project.

1. Vladimir Boutchik, Ernst L. Stahl, and Stephen Mitchell, "Texts of Rilke's Letters to Helene," in *Oxford Slavonic Papers* 9 (London: Oxford University Press, 1960), 148: "Außerdem kam mir der Amerikanische Philosoph Ralph Waldo Emerson zu Händen, der so viel Einfluß hat. Ich beginne erst, mich mit ihm zu beschäftigen." Except where indicated otherwise, all translations from the German are my own.

2. Relevant to this particular discussion would also be the overlap between Emerson's "representative men" and Nietzsche's discussion of exemplars and *der Übermensch*. See especially Friedrich Nietzsche, "Schopenhauer as Educator" in *Untimely Meditations*, trans. R. J. Hollingdale (Cambridge: Cambridge University Press, 1997), 127–94.

3. Julius Simon, *Emerson in Deutschland, 1851–1932* (Berlin: Junker und Dünnhaupt, 1937), 146–65.

4. "Alles Erworbne bedroht die Maschine, solange / sie sich erdreistet, im Geist, statt im Gehorchen, zu sein." *Die Sonette an Orpheus*, in *Gesammelte Gedichte* (Frankfurt: Insel, 1962), 513.

5. The implicit reference here is to Harold Bloom, *The Anxiety of Influence* (London: Oxford University Press, 1975). Bloom is a persuasive voice in the field of Emerson studies, and we can see the ways that Bloom's theories are adaptions of certain things Emerson says about reading. Emerson is less *worried* about influence, though, because for him, a creative intellect, or genius, is simply (but not merely) indicated by a reader's showing fealty mostly to him- or herself.

6. There is no shortage of scholarship detailing Emerson's interest in German thought and particularly Romanticism, but I would suggest as a place to begin Robert D. Richardson's magisterial intellectual biography, *Emerson: The Mind on Fire* (Berkeley: University of California Press, 1995). Richardson comprehensively traces Emerson's readings and creative misreadings of German arts and letters.

7. See Jan Wojcik, "Emerson and Rilke: A Significant Influence?," *Modern Language Notes* 91, no. 3 (1976): 565–74; and Marilyn Vogler Urion, "Emerson's Presence in Rilke's Imagery: Shadows of Early Influence," *Monatshefte* 85, no. 2 (1993): 153–69.

8. Interest in Nietzsche's link to Emerson has been steadily growing over the past decade and a half. The main force behind this has been Stanley Cavell; see especially his essay, "Aversive Thinking," in *Emerson's Transcendental Etudes*, ed. David Justin Hodge (Stanford, CA: Stanford University Press, 2003), 141–70. A useful place to begin surveying the field is a special issue of *ESQ: A Journal of the American Renaissance* devoted to Emerson and Nietzsche, which appeared as volume 43, nos. 1–4 in 1997. This collection includes persuasive readings by such key scholars as Herwig Friedl, Michael Lopez, George Stack, James Conant, Russell Goodman, and others.

9. Wolfgang Leppmann, *Rilke: A Life*, trans. Russell M. Stockman (New York: Fromm, 1984).

10. Ranier Maria Rilke, *Tagebücher aus der Frühzeit* (Frankfurt on the Main: Insel Verlag, 1973), 7.

11. Wojcik, "Emerson and Rilke," 568–70.

12. The German "Ringen" can be translated either as "circles" or "rings," with the latter providing the suggestion of the rings that indicate the age of trees (specifically called *Jahresringe*).

13. Charles Baudelaire, "The Life and Work of Eugene Delacroix," in *The Painter of Modern Life and Other Essays*, trans. Jonathan Mayne (New York: Phaidon, 1995), 53. One reason to think that Rilke took the sentence from Baudelaire's essay is because Baudelaire also kept the maxim in English rather than translating it into French.

14. Though there are a few scholars who discuss at length Baudelaire's engagement with Emerson, two studies stand as particularly useful. In *Baudelaire, Emerson, and the*

French-American Connection: Contrary Affinities (New York: Peter Lang, 2011), Dudley Marchi lays out the affinities and divergences between the two authors, with a particularly valuable argument about the differences in the political contexts each author had to negotiate. Bernard Howells, in his article "On the Meaning of Great Men: Baudelaire and Emerson Revisited," *Romanic Review* 78, no. 4 (November 1987): 471–90, reveals that the French poet had a stronger debt to Emerson than many Baudelaire scholars generally are prepared to acknowledge. Howells does contend (in an argument similar to the one I am making about Rilke) that in his later phase, Baudelaire pushes against the influence, but that only reveals how Baudelaire enacts Emersonian ideas about how influence needs to be overcome. One hears in this, of course, an inflection of Harold Bloom's ideas about the anxiety of influence (or, in this case, we might say the influence of anxiety).

15. Rainer Maria Rilke, *Auguste Rodin* (Frankfurt on the Main: Insel Verlag, 1955), 9. "Rodin war einsam vor seinem Ruhme. Und der Ruhm, der kam, hat ihn vielleicht noch einsamer gemacht. Denn Ruhm ist schließlich nur der Inbegriff aller Mißverständnisse, die sich um einen neuen Namen sammeln."

16. Ibid., 24–25. "Wo die erste Anregung vom Stofflichen ausging, wo eine antike Sage, die Stelle eines Gedichtes, eine historische szene oder eine wirkliche Person Schaffens-Anlaß war, da übersetzt sich, wenn Rodin beginnt, während der Arbet das Stoffliche immer mehr in Sachliches und Namenloses: in der Sprache der Hände übertragen, haben di Anforderungen, die sich, ergeben, alle einen neuen, ganz auf die plastische Erfüllung bezüglichen Sinn.

In den Zeichnungen Rodins geht, vorbereitend, dieses Vergessen und Verwandeln der stofflichen Angerung vor sich. Er hat auch in dieser Kunst seine eigenen Ausdrucksmittel sich erzogen, und das macht diese Blätter (es sind viele Hunderte) zu einer selbständigen und originellen Offenbarung seiner Persönlichkeit."

17. Ibid., 41. "Mit dieser Entwickelung hat Rodin allen Künsten ein Zeichen / gegeben in dieser ratlosen Zeit. Man wird einmal erkennen, was diesen großen Künstler so groß gemacht hat: daß er ein Arbeiter war, der nichts ersehnte, als ganz, mit allen seinen Kräften, in das niedrige und harte Dasein seines Werkzeuges einzugehen. Darin lag eine Art von Verzicht auf das Leben; aber gerade mit dieser Geduld gewann er es: denn zu seinem Werkzeug kam die Welt."

[10]

K. L. EVANS

EMERSON; OR, THE CRITIC—THE ARNOLDIAN IDEAL

HOW IS IT THAT after not placing Emerson among the great poets (for his poetry "lacks directness; it lacks concreteness; it lacks energy") or the great writers, the great men of letters (for he knows not how to work into a literary composition his materials—how to "subdue them for the purposes of literary effect") or the great philosophers (for "he cannot build; his arrangement of philosophical ideas has no progress in it, no evolution") or the great markers and recorders of the traits of human life (for Emerson's observation has not the disinterested quality of Montaigne or Addison, but "is the observation of a man systematically benevolent"), Matthew Arnold can coolly announce that in his own century, Emerson's *Essays* were "the most important work done in prose"?

Giving rise to Arnold's astonishing praise is Emerson's power as a critic. It is the figure of the critic that Arnold names as the "friend and aider" of great writers and great philosophy-makers, and consequently "the especial friend and comforter of all scrupulous and difficult, yet pure and upward-striving souls"—the critic whose portrait Arnold draws in his essay, "Emerson."[1] Arnold thus finds in Emerson the truest example of his own type. He names as Emerson's real service to culture his critical power, the vital line of work that "tends, at last, to create an intellectual situation of which the creative power can profitably avail itself."[2] As Arnold had reasoned in his most influential essay, "The Function of Criticism at the Present Time," the critic's role in culture is vital because a grand work of genius "must have the atmosphere, it must find itself amidst the order of ideas, in order to work freely; and these it is not so easy to command." It is because the creative power cannot manufacture this atmosphere *by itself* that "great creative epochs in literature are so rare," says Arnold—why there is "so much that is unsatisfactory in the productions of many men of real genius."

And to the creation of such atmospheres, Arnold submits, one can scarcely overrate the significance of Emerson.

Having tied Emerson's fate and his own to the fate of criticism, of lower rank than creative work but indispensable to it, Arnold affords Emerson his best chance for posterity—unless, of course, the Arnoldian understanding of "criticism" falls out of favor, and with it, our contented view of Emerson's inestimable importance.

This it has. As some critics worriedly observe, Matthew Arnold's name has become a kind of shorthand for a much-discredited form of cultural conservatism.[3] He is generally believed to have instigated a bourgeois agenda in literary studies predicated on the ability to recognize "the best that is thought or said."[4] His estimation of books' highest value, whether antiquated or shrewd, has fallen into disrepute. But perhaps that is because what Arnold knew as the business of the critical power has in our own age become synonymous with the critic's power to *pass judgment.* Arnold's notion of literary criticism (in relation to which the modern English department arose in the late nineteenth century, and whereby it has been sustained ever since) is characterized by Herbert F. Tucker, for example, as "the habit of capitalizing on the critic's power to discriminate and—at the right hand of the judgment seat, or its executive arm—to reject."[5] To the professional literary critic Tucker ascribes "the nay-saying Mephistophelean authority that every English Department heir of Arnold claims, the authority to pronounce: That is not it, at all." For Tucker and many equally wary inheritors of Arnold's legacy, the weakness of the position Arnold stakes out for criticism lies in what they see as his competing allegiance to, on the one hand, the critic's power to discriminate, and on the other, criticism's necessary adherence to what Arnold calls "disinterestedness."[6] And while discrimination is a faculty on which professional critics still rely, in their own disinterestedness they have no confidence whatsoever. The worry about Arnold, then, is that he lays great stress on the principle of critical judgment, but that in his writing this appears as a standard or criterion about which, apart from its importance, Arnold "discloses next to nothing."[7] Or as Tucker writes, "Arnold's all but self-parodic disavowal of critical principle and method conjures a charmed space for the privacy of literary response," in this way opening the door to the "authoritarianism of a cult of personality."[8]

In short, what Arnold says about Emerson, his view of Emerson's significance, means very little if the grounds for his criticism—and for criticism—are so easily undermined. I want therefore to use Arnold's remarks on Emerson to think again about his portrayal of the critic's task. How might the usual estimation of Arnold be troubled by his having chosen *Emerson* (in the age of Coleridge and Carlyle!) to represent the true operation of the critical power? How different does Arnold's characterization of criticism sound when played against his remarks on Emerson, specifically his admiration of Emerson's "sanguinity" or the secret effect of his "hopeful, serene, beautiful temper"?[9] Given that Emerson's best-known characteristic, his good will, is not in our own age considered the critic's distinguishing trait, how strange is the contrast between Emerson's style of criticism and the one presently employed, the business of assessment and interpretation that Arnold would likely call "too willful, too turbid, too vehement?"[10] For as should become clear, Arnold's choice of Emerson as criticism's representative does not square with what we have come to think of as criticism's function at the present time. Realigning Arnold's view of Emerson with his view of criticism, then, may do better than recover the Emersonian attributes of Arnold's critical legacy (what we might call, with much more to be said, its "optimistic" bent); it may well establish a more happy direction for the professional discipline to which Arnold's energies gave rise.

Lest my own critical effort appear too vague or abstract, I mean to look back from Arnold's late published address "Emerson" to some of his earlier and more enigmatic remarks on the surrounding conditions for great creation—the formation of which required the practical services of the critic, as Arnold understood them. My purpose here is to show how, for Arnold, what chiefly contributed to creative work's necessary "atmosphere" was not the critic's *discernment* so much as his *sanguinity.* Sanguinity—or what it signifies—is for Arnold the critic's most irreplaceable trait, and in "Emerson" he says why.

In this deceivingly forthright address, Arnold first notes that Emerson *is* sanguine, despite the fact that "no misanthropical satirist ever saw shortcomings and absurdities more clearly than he did, or exposed them more courageously" (E 208). Arnold in this way economically counters the charge that Emerson was *over*-sanguine, or that what is also called Emerson's "optimism" was profligate or excessive. For when practiced on the right grounds—when it is not easy, or when a man has eyes for what actually goes on in the world around him—it is this capacity for "holding fast to happiness and hope" that gives him an "invaluable virtue" (E 209). In calling Emerson's hopefulness or cheerfulness *virtuous,* Arnold converts what might otherwise be taken for a passing humor or mood into the expression of a deep satisfaction, a mode of living associated with the enhanced life, what Arnold in *Culture and Anarchy* calls "our *best* self."[11]

Giving emphasis to Emerson's "sanguinity" is thus how Arnold marks Emerson's attachment to "the true life of the spirit." He links Emerson's desire to maximize human happiness to the same desire in Plato and Augustine, or in other words, he shows how Emerson's confidence in man's power to realize his aspirations—and consequently his "tone of cheerful, forward-looking hope"—is part and parcel of his idealism. Needless to say, "idealism" is not a term I use here in the colloquial sense, for Arnold's Emerson is not a man living by high ideals, naively and impractically, but in the rather more formal sense of our anticipated ascent to the real world, available to the intellect but not to the senses. Looking forward in *this* way—"holding fast to happiness and hope"—is the Emersonian virtue that Arnold argues "one can scarcely overrate the importance of," and he offers as evidence for it Emerson's sanguinity. "I hear it said that Emerson was too sanguine," Arnold writes, "but by his conviction that in the life of the spirit is happiness, and by his hope that this life of the spirit will come more and more to be sanely understood, and to prevail, and to work for happiness,—by this conviction and hope Emerson was great, and he will surely prove in the end to have been right in them" (*E* 210–11).

Of course, with praise like this Arnold runs the risk of seeming too well satisfied with his subject or his own view of him, but to adopt that line of objection would be to miss altogether how, for Arnold, Emerson's hopefulness signals his unconquerable belief in the true life of the spirit—what we might think of as Emerson's special talent for keeping the ideal in view. And to come quickly to the point, keeping the ideal in view turns out to be of central importance to what Arnold calls "general literary criticism," the kind of criticism he wished to produce and, as in Emerson's case, promote.

And yet, what Emerson's spiritual temper practically accomplishes is not yet clear, and though Arnold introduces it as the basis for Emerson's significance, it is difficult to grasp why keeping the ideal in view is imperative to the literary critic, and how it is possible. Any uncertainty on this point, however, is not necessarily the result of Arnold's unwillingness or inability to define his key phrases—a fudging of pivotal issues that critics David G. Riede and Herbert F. Tucker associate with the thaumaturgic "emptiness" of Arnold's writing.[12]

A more formidable stumbling block to understanding Arnold is the fashion of treating what Plato says about the world of Ideas or Forms as passé. This was true even in Arnold's day, when as he says practical people would "talk with a smile of Plato and his absolute ideas."[13] The pugnacity of these opponents of Plato make it hard to speak soberly about his writing, as in addition to their amusement or condescension there is generally a tendency in those who are remonstrating against Plato's more particular lessons to think of them as weighing on us injuriously. Even critics in the humanities are as a result no longer conversant with Plato's "life and genius," as Arnold puts it—those habits of mind that, despite the fact that Plato's world was not ours, are suited to all sorts and conditions. I aim here to lodge the objection that the air Arnold's readers breathe, the intellectual and spiritual atmosphere in which his *writing* lives, is not permeated by that knowledge of Greek, Roman, and Eastern antiquity Arnold so prized, and this diminishes the strength of that hold his writing has upon us.[14] By this I do not mean to draw attention once more to Arnold's thoughts about the urgent social need to "Hellenize," as Terry Eagleton puts it;[15] my point is only that where there is the genuine desire to understand Arnold, not understanding what Plato did in the world and what is its value proves an impassible hurdle.

Nowhere does this dearth of shared beliefs prevent understanding more than in those many places in Arnold's writing where he refers to Plato's interest in the world of Ideas or Forms. Or at any rate, the bulk of criticism on Arnold provides ample evidence that all of his references to Plato's "absolute ideas" fall on deaf ears. Hence, when Arnold maintains that having some notion of a book's "absolute value" constitutes the critic's service to culture—as he argues explicitly in the essay "The Bishop and the Philosopher," for example—what he says is obscured, or made to sound absurd, by clumsy conceptions of Plato's logic. All Arnold's talk of books' "absolute value" gets recalibrated, as it were, from an unsettled and unsettling line of thought running throughout the middle dialogues to a jejune and contemptible popular idiom. The ramifications of this confusion are such that when Arnold employs the notion of a book's absolute value, we think of him as attempting to characterize for all time the book's *meaning*—to bring reading to an end by enforcing what Derridians would call the closure of its interpretive potential. We take him to regard a book as something he's duly equipped to classify, and consequently either eulogize or discard. And in this palling light there is something deeply problematic about the Arnoldian conception of the business, the purpose, of criticism. Barely any effort at all is then required to expose the false premise on which all of Arnold's convincing declarations about the critic's office rest.

But much is arguably left out of this picture—for example, the way Plato's interest in the absolute began in response to what he felt was the fruitless insistence that we must be able to answer the question, "What is *X*?" before we can say anything about *X*. In other words, the purpose of invoking the world of Ideas was to *put a stop* to inadequate attempts to classify or define things. It was, after all, Plato who laid the foundation for a more profound and at the same time more accurate perception of events when he taught us "to reflect on the presence of the Idea in the appearance of things and to yearn for it," as Erich Auerbach writes. It was Plato who "introduced philosophy into art," who first set artists the task of striving, by the imitation of an object's appearance, to arrive at its true essence, the group of properties without which it would not be what it is—and thus of showing the insufficiency of essences when measured against the beauty of Ideas.[16]

I should note that I have ventured into the arena of this old, old investigation of the logical background *against which* normatively structured judgments are made—this insistence as it comes to us through Plato that our knowledge presupposes generalities that are irreducible to any set of finite instances—for the purpose of offering some gentle resistance to the charge that Arnold believes too fully in his powers of observation. Tucker, for example, approvingly cites Riede's mention of Arnold's "exceptionally strong commitment to 'empirical rationalism'"[17]—a phrase, as I understand it, that invites consideration of the chief source of Arnold's self-deception, namely, his erroneous belief that a person can him- or herself determine something's essential qualities and in this way say what it is. Much ink has been spilled in the drafting of this poor estimation of Arnold (see, for example, George Levine's contention that Arnold is part of the subjectivist tradition in criticism and thus—as Stuart Tave claims—that he is an embarrassment to modern criticism),[18] but the charge, in brief, is that Arnold myopically grounds criticism's authority in its independence, or in the critic's ability to shun the practical interests of sect and party and see an object "as in itself it really is," as Arnold writes.

There is, however, some contrariety in this determination to denounce Arnold for referring to books' absolute value and, at the same time, for espousing trust in the critic's (or simply his own) taste and discernment. I mean that in the most general sense, reference to an object's absolute value is designed to destabilize or cast doubt on any one person's assessment of its defining qualities. In other words, Arnold's resolution to keep the ideal in view ought to make us reconsider whether we have properly understood his much-objected-to description of the critic's effort to "see the object as in itself it really is."

As noted, the thrust of Arnold's argument in "The Function of Criticism at the Present Time" is that the critic's business lies in what he or she contributes to the intellectual and spiritual atmosphere that inspires creative work; that this atmosphere is made up of ideas that do not originate with the critic but which the critic does *order;* and that to order ideas or present them in the most effective and attractive combinations, the critic must draw on his or her critical power. Ultimately, "it is the business of the critical power," Arnold argues, "in all branches of knowledge, theology, philosophy, history, art, science, to see the object as in itself it really is."[19]

Few critics will need more proof of Arnold's "empirical rationalism" than that! Even as sympathetic a reader as Timothy Peltason thinks of what he calls Arnold's "realist injunction" to "see the object as in itself it really is" as one of the "reactionary misjudgments" of which Arnold is "occasionally guilty"—the kind of "claim to have gotten things *right*" that should be separated out from a genuinely more progressive, or less embarrassing, strain in Arnold's writing.[20] As most critics see it, this most worrying catchphrase exposes Arnold's silly premise that the critical power operates without bias (or that his reason simply transcribes what is already inscribed in nature) and can in consequence support the critical edifice. My suspicion, however, is that what Peltason calls "the apparent essentialism of Arnold's position, with its reference to the fixed nature of the object 'in itself' " ("belied and counterbalanced," Peltason also argues, "by another emphasis in his writings, on process and particularity") should not be understood to signal Arnold's support for the idea that an object can be precisely defined or described—or that, when books are the objects, they might be thought of as having a single or timeless meaning, held in readiness for the literary critic to discover and express. I mean that Arnold does certainly believe that critics should attempt to say what a book *is;* however, he is perfectly clear that what makes this feasible is not the critic's power to discriminate but the possibility of differentiating between the many things that get said in a book and the purpose to which these propositions are put.

Rather than try to excuse Arnold's deployment of the offending phrase—that is, this bit about seeing an object as it really is—I want to recapture his sense of its usefulness. For when Arnold's championing of Emerson is kept in mind—Arnoldian shorthand for the intellectual and spiritual necessity of keeping the ideal in view—I think it is possible to see why, for Arnold, seeing something 'as it is' does *not* mean seeing without bias its essential qualities. It means seeing it in a way that is to be *contrasted with having opinions about it.*

The importance of this distinction is underscored in Arnold's essay "The Bishop and the Philosopher," his juxtaposition of Bishop Natal's "exploits in the field of biblical criticism" with Spinoza's *Tractatus Theologico-Politicus.* This is also the essay in which Arnold puts in the plainest terms his preference for "general literary criticism," something he contrasts with a "special professional criticism." The general literary critic's greater service to culture is something Arnold means to highlight when he shows how unlike two otherwise comparable books appear when looked at by someone like himself, someone who attempts to arrive at some notion of a book's absolute value—that is, to see the book "as in itself it really is."

For as Arnold argues, all works have "a special professional criticism to undergo: theological works that of theologians, historical works that of historians, philosophical works that of philosophers, and in this case each kind of work is tried by a separate standard. But they have also a general literary criticism to undergo, and this tries them all, as I have said, by one standard—their effect upon general culture." As Arnold frames it, the province of the general literary critic is the consideration of a book's absolute value, and in that light, its effect on general culture: the critic's ability to determine a book's effect on general culture is his or her means of bringing a work "within the sphere of everyone's interest." The critic's facility or talent for this work also accounts for why "literary criticism has exercised so much power."[21]

Intriguingly, a detail about which Arnold is emphatic is that trying books in respect of their influence on culture requires "abandoning a thousand special questions which may be raised about any book."[22] For it is precisely when these are not at some point abandoned that literary critics forget their task and begin instead to air their feelings about a work. And while a critic's expressed feelings may help to try works by that separate standard to which each of them is subject—theological, historical, philosophical, etc.—they *do not* help to try them by the one standard that affects all culture, namely, a work's rationale, its reason for being.[23] Moreover, by giving the professional critic jurisdiction over those "thousand special questions" any book raises, and limiting the general literary critic's authority to the question of the book's rationale, Arnold intimates that what the critic chooses to focus on determines whether a book will be seen as interesting in itself—a judgment that invariably has as much to do with the critic's preferences as the book's merit—or interesting (significant, influential) to general culture. Only the latter compels Arnold, since as he has said, what he is after is a book's absolute value, and the way to reflect on a book's value is to think in terms of its impact on culture.

The great surprise in reading Arnold, that is to say, is to discover how *little* he associates the critic's work with what Tucker calls "the habit of capitalizing on the critic's power to discriminate and . . . to reject." Because while Arnold has what many writers of powerfully surpassing expression have—what Emerson admiringly names the "devouring eyes and portraying hand" of Carlyle, "those portrait-eating, portrait-painting eyes . . . those fatal perceptions"—what Arnold likes about criticism and what he wishes to exhibit in his own writing is that "more practical, more positive direction" that only the general literary critic provides (*E* 203–7). That is why, in essay after essay, Arnold offers concrete instances of the general literary critic at work: illustrations of how criticism can sound when a critic leaves off agreeing or disagreeing with the various statements he or she finds in a book, or contextualizing them, or speculating about what they mean, and turns rather more propitiously to a book's rationale—the logical basis for an author's course of action.

Arnold's "The Bishop and the Philosopher" offers a case in point. In this essay, Arnold introduces the bishop of Natal's book on the Pentateuch by noting that it "has been judged from a theological point of view by members of his own profession," by which Arnold means it has undergone a special professional criticism, and also that critics who were not members of that profession have judged it "from the same point of view," by which he means that critics like himself, general literary critics, have considered the book in the same manner the theologians have, that is, by examining the work in light of what gets said in it.[24]

What the bishop has to say, it turns out, is that there are numerous instances in the first five books of the Bible that damage beyond repair its historical credit. In other words, the bishop is "an excellent mathematician," as Arnold puts it, "and has published an admirable Manual of Arithmetic." Caustically, Arnold cites the bishop's appraisal of what he has done: "'I tremble,' he says, 'at the results of my own inquiry—the momentous results' (he elsewhere calls them) 'to which it leads.'"[25] But what Arnold highlights is the inconsequentiality of all the bishop's "arithmetical demonstrations" on the higher culture of his nation. Arnold very humorously suggests that if the bishop's goal was to highlight "a series of problems, the solution of each of which is meant to be the *reduction ad absurdum* of the Book of the Pentateuch which supplied its terms," he need not have given his readers so many examples! He might have done away with each book more simply—by, for example, taking the number of lambs slain at the Sanctuary, as compared with the space for slaying them, and in this way disposing of Deuteronomy: "'*In an area of 1,692 square yards, how many lambs per minute can 150,000 persons kill in two hours?*' Certainly not 1,250, the number required."[26] Arnold's sardonic impression of the bishop's calculations adds levity to his more important point that the book fails to consider the question, "*What then?* What follows from all this? What change is it, if true, to produce in the relations of mankind to the Christian religion? If the old theory of Scripture Inspiration is to be abandoned, what place is the Bible henceforth to hold among books?"[27]

Arnold then makes his frustration with the bishop's book clearer by contrasting it with a newly published English translation of Spinoza's *Tractatus Theologico-Politicus*. Spinoza's book is "not so easy to summarize" as the bishop of Natal's, but unlike that book, it is of interest to the general literary critic for the reason that in it Spinoza "does attempt to answer the crucial question, '*What then?*' and by the attempt, successful or unsuccessful, he interests the higher culture of Europe."[28] What Arnold means is that it is possible to glean from the book's many details some sense of the author's overall purpose; namely, that having been struck with the contrast between the precepts of Christianity and the common practice of Christians, he "sought the cause of this contrast and found it in their erroneous conception of their own religion." If only for the instructed few, Spinoza hoped his work might prove informing; or as Arnold enthuses, Spinoza was moved to write, "not by admiration at the magnitude of his own sudden discoveries, not by desire for notoriety, not by a transport of excitement, not because he 'had launched his bark on the flood and was carried along by the waters'; but because, grave as was the task to be attempted, and slight as the hope of succeeding, the end seemed to him worth all the labor and all the risk."[29]

That there *is* an end to this author's labor is what makes Arnold admire Spinoza's book, irrespective of whether or not he admires Spinoza's way of reckoning. This is a significant point, because while it is the case that Arnold finds much to esteem in Spinoza and very little in the bishop, Arnold is wise enough to understand how immaterial his own preferences are to the business of the general literary critic. For literary criticism "must not blame the Bishop of Natal because his personal position is false, nor praise Spinoza because his personal position is sound." Rather, it must grasp that of the two, only Spinoza's book can have what Arnold calls an "informing influence" on culture, and that is because cultural influence is not decided by a book's quality, but by what Arnold names its "philosophic scope"—what with Deleuze's help we might understand as a book's ability to achieve the form of a concept by engaging or responding to the problem of its own creation.[30] Thus Arnold identifies as the most important feature of Spinoza's writing his capacity to turn a collection of propositions into something else; something thought or grasped; some way of perceiving something; what Deleuze would call a concept. As Arnold continues:

> Many and many are the propositions in Spinoza's work, which, brought by him to us out of the sphere of his unaccepted philosophy, and presented with all the calm inflexibility of his manner, are startling, repellent, questionable. Criticism may take many and many objections to the facts and arguments of his Treatise. But, by the whole scope and drift of its argument, by the spirit in which the subject is throughout treated, his work undeniably becomes interesting and stimulating to the general culture of Europe. There are alleged contradictions in Scripture; and the question which the general culture of Europe, informed of this, asks with real interest is, as I have said,—*What then?* To this question Spinoza returns an answer, and the Bishop of Natal returns none. The Bishop of Natal keeps going round for ever within the barren sphere of these contradictions themselves; he treats them as if they were supremely interesting in themselves, as if we had never heard of them before, and could never hear enough of them now. Spinoza touches these verbal matters with all possible brevity, and presses on to the more important.[31]

To Arnold, Spinoza is a "philosopher" because his genius principally shows itself in the discovery of new ideas. But his work has *philosophic scope* or is of interest to the general literary critic because the critic is able to justify his book's existence, able to point to its underlying logic—a kind of grounds for writing that, as Arnold conceived it, authors are obliged to sustain and critics to observe.

With this illustration from "The Bishop and the Philosopher" in mind—this instance of how a book might transcend the "barren sphere" of an author's various propositions, the influence of which on culture is negligible, and also how a critic might transcend the equally trifling sphere of his own preferences—I want to return to Arnold's inciting mantra that it is the business of the critical power to "see the object as in itself it really is." Coming thus to Arnold's slogan, it stands to reason that to Arnold, seeing a book "as in itself it really is" means something like attending to an author's *object* rather than to his *propositions*. For as Arnold writes in another essay on Spinoza, "Spinoza and the Bible," it is an author's object that "is most important," that "sets all his work in motion," and that is "the secret of his attraction for other minds."[32] An author's propositions, conversely, "pass by mankind at large like the idle wind, which mankind regards not; it will not even listen to a word about these propositions, unless it first learns what their author was driving at with them, and finds that this object of his is one with which it sympathizes, one, at any rate, which commands its attention."[33] What any work "really is" is determined by its author's object, what emerges as the book's underlying logic. That is why literary criticism "must deny to the Bishop's book the right of existing."[34] For in that work there is no motivating logic to be found, and consequently none of the work's minutiae, none of the author's finer points, are enlisted to any lasting effect.

There is for Arnold a related point, which is that focusing on an author's object is what gives the critic's judgment and style restraint. For when an author's *propositions* are his subject, the critic feels called upon to give his own informed opinions about them, to declare them true or false or expound on them in other ways—Arnold calls such demonstration of the critic's acuity "the learned man's vagaries"—so that in the end it is the critic's willingness to exercise his discernment that gives his criticism a "provincial tone."[35] Criticism with a provincial tone, Arnold explains, "is hurried away by fancies; it likes and dislikes too passionately, too exclusively," or "seems to aim rather at the effect upon the blood and senses than upon the spirit and intellect." Or, what means the same, the critic who serves a profession before general culture, or who looks to an author's propositions and not his object, is apt to produce "extravagant prose; prose too much suffered to indulge its caprices." For even when his writing is rich and imaginative, or interesting and affecting, the critic who loses sight of a book's effect on culture in his haste to evaluate its quality is prone to forget "all moderation and proportion" or throw the reins to whim. In "The Literary Influence of the Academies," Arnold points out how such liberties are taken even when a critic such as John Ruskin exercises his intelligence or genius.[36] Or as another example of a critic who "relies on the strength of his lungs," Arnold offers "Mr. Palgrave," who "feels no pressure constraining him either to try his dislike closely or to express it moderately; he does not mince matters, he gives his dislike all his own way." In such cases "the fitness, the measure, the centrality, which is the soul of all good criticism, is lost, and the note of provinciality shows itself."

Times are changed, in short, since Spinoza wrote, or as Arnold was already worrying, "The reserve which [Spinoza] recommended and practiced is being repudiated by all the world. Speculation is to be made popular, all reticence is to be abandoned, every difficulty is to be canvassed publically, every doubt is to be proclaimed; information which, to have any value at all, must have it as part of a series not yet complete, is to be flung broadcast, in the crudest shape, amidst the undisciplined, ignorant, passionate, captious multitude."[37] The result of this lack of restraint in expression or presentation is that the critic is distracted from producing what Arnold calls his "best spiritual work."[38] For the critic's best spiritual work is the result of dwelling upon a book "as in itself it really is." It is the result, that is to say, of investigating an author's *object,* what he or she is driving at, and through it the book's effect on *culture,* which is all that saves the critic from getting stuck in his judgment of a book's *qualities* or *appearance.* For no matter how intelligent, the critic who concerns himself merely with addressing an author's propositions will inevitably indulge that "self-satisfaction which is retarding and vulgarizing,"[39] while the critic who concerns himself with an author's object may contribute to that "order of ideas, if not absolutely true, yet true by comparison with that which it displaces." Presently "these new ideas reach society, the touch of truth is the touch of life, and there is a stir and a growth everywhere."[40]

In "The Function of Criticism at the Present Time," Arnold is confident that "out of this stir and growth" come the great creative epochs. But more far-reaching is his perception that literary critics contribute to the current of fresh ideas *not* by laying stress on the principle of critical judgment (a criterion about which, Arnold's critics rightly note, Arnold stays mum) but by replacing their desire to speculate about a book's outward aspects with attentiveness to the target toward which all the book's specified action or feeling is directed.

And finally, Arnold's overriding interest in the purpose for which books are created, what he thinks of as their absolute value, is the reason he chooses Emerson as his representative nineteenth-century critic—why in addition he models his own prose style on the prose of a man who, as he suggests, is no great poet, no great writer, no great philosophy-maker. As Arnold notes, Emerson's sentences do very well as they stand ("like 'boulders,' as he says;—in 'paragraphs incompressible, each sentence an infinitely repellent particle'"), for it is in such sentences that Emerson's "main points recur again and again, and become fixed in the memory" (*E* 206). Only on the strength of these boulders "could he break through the hard and fast barrier of narrow, fixed ideas, which he found confronting him."[41] In the same way, and whether his readers are averse to it or not, a phrase like "the object as in itself it really is" becomes fixed in the memory, from whence it may be retrieved when a change of conditions have improved its chances for taking hold. In other words, the fact that Arnold knew he had generated the kinds of propositions to which it is easy to object is suggested by his decision to not only repeat himself but to call attention to this repetition,[42] and thus that rather than be made too well satisfied with Arnold's catchphrases, or too *little* satisfied with them, the right thing to do is to try and understand them in "the high sense" (*E* 208). Understanding an author's sayings "in a certain high sense," Arnold makes clear in "Emerson," requires sanguinity, rather than discernment, since it depends on attending steadily to an author's object in lieu of some sample of his propositions.

Reading in a high sense Arnold's recommendation that literary critics try to see a book "as in itself it really is" is in any case what I have attempted here—aware, all the while, that perhaps it is too late in the day for such work, or that certain prejudices have saturated the market on subjects such as Emersonian hope or Arnoldian criticism. But if we are ever to return to the days when literary criticism "exercised so much power," as Arnold writes in "The Bishop and the Philosopher," reading our most provocative authors in a high sense seems to be our likeliest route. I mean simply that rather than deriving pleasure from finding out how authors undermine or contradict themselves, we should seize the deeper pleasure of discovering what they think they have to say.[43]

Challenged to explain the number of times Arnold repeats his most provocative or memorable phrases, critics such as J. Hillis Miller or W. David Shaw have suggested that his famous phrases are "empty signifiers," devoid of meaning. David Riede has concluded that, "empty language occurs throughout all of Arnold's writings, and tends to undermine him at his most impassioned moments"—that Arnold's "magically full language" is "sadly empty."[44] For Herbert Tucker, the problem "is not that Arnold's elegant sentences state and restate the obvious, because they hardly do even that.

Rather, they offer a set of permutations, full to the point of redundancy. . . . The circularity of this stupefying non-explanation can feel like mere filibustering, but it is, in effect, the circularity of the prayer-wheel or hypnotic mantra."[45] And yet what are the cumulative effects of such "exploits in the field of literary criticism"? Or as Arnold might have asked, *what follows* from all these disavowals of the Arnoldian posture? For Arnold, like Emerson, invites his readers to extend and amplify our understanding in the most positive way, whereas the dyspeptic, insistent, highly charged manner of the professional critic would appear to have the opposite effect. Thus what we want to know is, if the Arnoldian idea of criticism is to be abandoned, how is the critic *not* thrown ruinously back upon charismatic authority or "the cult of personality"? And what place is the ranking of books henceforth to hold in culture? And if criticism is no more than a matter of speculation —"a game," as Tucker describes it, "of spontaneous response and lucky hunch"—will it not cease to be a legitimate vocation? It is questions like these that Arnold prepared us to ask with respectful interest. And it is these questions that Arnold's critics never touch.

Notes

1. Arnold delivered the lecture "Emerson" in Boston as part of his four-month speaking series in the United States in 1883, the year after Emerson's death and only a few years before his own. His lectures and remarks during that period culminated in the appearance of *Discourses in America* (1885), composed of three sections: "Numbers, or the Majority and the Remnant," "Literature and Science," and "Emerson." In the essay "Emerson," Arnold likens Emerson to Marcus Aurelius, and in the earlier essay "Marcus Aurelius," he describes the Roman emperor as "the especial friend and comforter of all scrupulous and difficult, yet pure and upward-striving souls." "Emerson" can be found in David LaRocca, ed., *Estimating Emerson: An Anthology of Criticism from Carlyle to Cavell* (New York: Bloomsbury, 2013), 198–211; and "Marcus Aurelius" can be found in Matthew Arnold, *Lectures and Essays in Criticism*, vol. 3 of *The Complete Prose Works of Matthew Arnold*, ed. R. H. Super (Ann Arbor: University of Michigan Press, 1962), 156.

2. Matthew Arnold, "The Function of Criticism at the Present Time," in *Lectures and Essays in Criticism*, 261.

3. Timothy Peltason, "The Function of Matthew Arnold at the Present Time," *College English* 56, no. 7 (November 1994): 749–65. Peltason's project in his essay is to show how and why Arnold should be recuperated.

4. So notes Rhian Williams, in her encapsulation of the view of Arnold found, as she says, in the first four issues of the Oxford English Limited's journal, *News from Nowhere*, and particularly the special issue, *Matthew Arnold and the Fate of Critical Humanism, 1888–1988* (no. 5, 1988). Also Stefan Collini, "Afterword to the Clarendon Paperback

Edition," in Collini, ed., *Matthew Arnold* (Oxford: Oxford University Press, 1988), 125–38. In Williams's own writing, the view of Arnold as easily dismissible is eclipsed by her much more fruitful, finely drawn depiction of a figure through whom we can take some measure of the critical turn to the aesthetics of form as well as the newly emerging reconsideration of religion by the critical left. See her "'Divine Liquidness of Diction . . . Divine Fluidity of Movement': Reading Poetry after Matthew Arnold and the Higher Biblical Criticism," in *Literature and Theology* (Oxford: Oxford University Press, 2013), 1–17.

5. H. F. Tucker, "Arnold and the Authorization of Criticism," in Suzy Anger, ed., *Knowing the Past: Victorian Literature and Culture* (Ithaca, NY: Cornell University Press, 2001), 101.

6. Ibid., 113.

7. Tucker, "Arnold and the Authorization of Criticism," 115.

8. Ibid., 117.

9. Arnold, "Emerson," 209. Hereafter cited parenthetically in the text as E.

10. This is how Arnold describes Carlyle when noting his preference for Emerson—despite the fact that Carlyle has "surpassingly powerful qualities of expression, far more powerful than Emerson's" (E 203).

11. Arnold, *Culture and Anarchy*, ed. Stefan Collini (Cambridge: University of Cambridge Press, 1993), 100.

12. See David. G. Riede, *Matthew Arnold and the Betrayal of Language* (Charlottesville: University Press of Virginia, 1988). Riede is convinced that "empty language occurs throughout all Arnold's writings, and tends to undermine him at his most impassioned moments"—that his "magically full language" is "sadly empty" (3–4). Following Riede, one of Herbert F. Tucker's main criticisms in "Arnold and the Authorization of Criticism" is that in his discussion of sacralized terms (such as the matter of the critic's "disinterestedness") Arnold's discourse is "either tautologically circular or negatively prophylactic" (113). Thus for Riede and Tucker, it is on the basis of Arnold's refusal to ground his language or make transparent his criteria that Arnold derives criticism's authority—thereby making it "authoritarian."

13. Matthew Arnold, "Literature and Science," in *The Works of Matthew Arnold* (London: Macmillan, 1903), 4:317.

14. Arnold talks of knowing Greek and Roman antiquity as "the knowledge people have called the humanities." And he notes, "When I speak of knowing Greek and Roman antiquity . . . as a help to knowing ourselves and the world, I mean more than a knowledge of so much vocabulary, so much grammar, so many portions of authors in the Greek and Latin languages. I mean knowing the Greeks and Romans, and their life and genius, and what they were and did in the world; what we get from them, and what is its value" ("Literature and Science," 324–25).

15. Terry Eagleton, *Literary Theory: An Introduction* (1983; rpt., Oxford: Blackwell, 2008), 26.

16. Erich Auerbach, *Dante: Poet of the Secular World* (New York: New York Review

of Books, 2007), 5. Plato insists on the logical necessity of the world of Ideas or Forms because he has found that *a background of certain agreement is logically necessary for the possibility of genuine disagreement*. Because as Wittgenstein also argues, "All testing, all confirmation and disconfirmation of a hypothesis takes place already within a system." Because as the philosopher Meredith Williams explains, "Without some things being taken for granted, as beyond dispute, there is no logical space for making a substantive claim, forming a desire or intention, entering a challenge, citing evidence, and the like. This is not a psychological claim about us. It is a logical claim about what is required for the concepts of 'claim,' 'desire,' and the rest to have an application." *Wittgenstein, Mind and Meaning* (London: Routledge, 1999), 7. See also Ludwig Wittgenstein, *On Certainty*, trans. G.E.M. Anscombe and G. H. von Wright (New York: Harper, 1969), 16.

17. Tucker, "Arnold and the Authorization of Criticism," 110; Riede, *Matthew Arnold and the Betrayal of Language*, 27.

18. This summary can be found in Laurence W. Mazzeno's excellent history of Arnold criticism, *Matthew Arnold: The Critical Legacy* (Rochester, NY: Camden House, 1999), 98.

19. Arnold, "The Function of Criticism at the Present Time," 258.

20. Peltason, "The Function of Matthew Arnold at the Present Time," 751–52. Peltason goes some way toward excusing Arnold's "realist injunction" by pointing out, reasonably, that "it is hard to find an interpreter of texts or events who does not at some point ground his or her authority in the claim to have gotten things *right*," and that even "when the claim is downgraded to one of provisional rightness, a standard of accuracy has been invoked" (751). More generally, though, or as a rule, Peltason is careful not to be misled by the kind of Arnoldian remark that "threatens to freeze into a slogan, a phrase to have and to rest in, rather than an act of the writer's and the reader's mind" (750), since, after all, Peltason's objective is "to illustrate the dangers of literary and cultural misunderstanding that arise when a major literary figure is invoked in the culture wars, but not actually read with precision and care" (749).

21. Arnold, "The Bishop and the Philosopher," in *Lectures and Essays in Criticism*, 41.

22. Ibid.

23. In "The Bishop and the Philosopher," Arnold defines being "uncritical" as being little occupied "with the *rationale* of things," and thus uninterested in giving things "their due place in the world of thought"(40). The distinction is one Arnold says Goethe invites between the Englishman and the German (to Goethe, the English seem "uncritical"), but Arnold calls on it in the essay in order to distinguish a "special professional criticism" from his preferred "general literary criticism."

24. Arnold, "The Bishop and the Philosopher," 40.

25. Ibid., 45.

26. Ibid., 48.

27. Ibid., 49.

28. Ibid., 52–53.

29. Ibid., 50.

30. Deleuze's writings on the form of the concept in literature are many—see, for example, Gilles Deleuze, *Essays Critical and Clinical*, trans. Daniel W. Smith and Michael A. Greco (Minneapolis: University of Minnesota Press, 1997)—but a wonderful summary of this interest can be found in Anthony Larson's essay "First Lessons: Gilles Deleuze and the Concept of Literature," in David Rudrum, ed., *Literature and Philosophy: A Guide to Contemporary Debate* (New York: Palgrave Macmillan, 2006).

31. Arnold, "The Bishop and the Philosopher," 52.

32. Arnold, "Spinoza and the Bible," in *Lectures and Essays in Criticism*, 175.

33. Ibid.

34. Arnold, "The Bishop and the Philosopher," 52.

35. Arnold writes explicitly about the observable "note of provinciality" that characterizes much professional criticism in his essay "The Literary Influence of the Academies," in *Lectures and Essays in Criticism*, 232–57.

36. "The Literary Influence of the Academies," in *Lectures and Essays in Criticism*, 251–53.

37. Arnold, "The Bishop and the Philosopher," 54.

38. Arnold, "The Function of Criticism at the Present Time," 271.

39. Ibid.

40. Ibid., 261.

41. Ibid., 208.

42. For example, Arnold first commented on the critical power of seeing "the object as in itself it really is" in his remarks on translating Homer, as he notes in the first lines of "The Function of Criticism at the Present Time." It is at this point too—the very beginning of the essay most explicitly devoted to the critic's purpose—that Arnold calls attention to the way his turn of phrase did not sit well with audiences.

43. By this I mean to indicate an alternative to the practice of critics like Riede. For Riede's work is not unusual in light of the disdain many critics display toward Arnold, and as Laurence Mazzeno rightly notes, the joy for such a critic "is in finding out how Arnold contradicts himself, not in discovering what he thought he had to say" (*Matthew Arnold: The Critical Legacy*, 103).

44. Or as Riede bewilderingly explains, Arnold's language is self-referential; it "refers only to other words, not to things."

45. Tucker, "Arnold and the Authorization of Criticism," 117.

[11]

DANIEL ROSENBERG NUTTERS

"THE WHOLE CONDUCT OF LIFE": EMERSON AND HENRY JAMES

IT WAS WILLIAM JAMES, not Henry, who was born in the shadow of Emerson's aura. Yet it was Henry who, in his first memoir, *A Small Boy and Others,* narrates this American scene of instruction:

> Clearly—or should I perhaps rather say dimly—recourse to that hospitality was again occasionally had by our parents; who had originally had it to such a happy end that on January 9th, 1842, my elder brother had come into the world there. It remained a tradition with him that our father's friend from an early time, R. W. Emerson, then happening to be in New York and under that convenient roof, was proudly and pressingly "taken upstairs" to admire and give his blessing to the lately-born babe who was to become the second American William James. The blessing was to be renewed, I may mention, in the sense that among the impressions of the next early years I easily distinguish that of the great and urbane Emerson's occasional presence in Fourteenth Street, a centre of many images, where the parental tent was before long to pitch itself and rest awhile. I am interested for the moment, however, in identifying the scene of our very first perceptions—of my very own at least, which I can here best speak for.[1]

Such a scene foreshadows a canonical tradition of American intellectual culture from the point of view of an expatriate man of letters who did not find the literary milieu of his native land suitable for his imagination. While James describes "that convenient roof" of the "paternal tent" where the founder of American transcendentalism stands over the infant philosopher, this scene also shifts the memoir's focus away from William onto his narrating brother. Like the title of his second memoir, *Notes of a Son and Brother,* James initially positions himself as an outsider in relation to his family; reducing himself to "a small boy" in the background, perceiving the world of these "others." The opening paragraph of the first memoir corroborates the book's goal "to place together some particulars of the early life of William James"[2] but, as the excerpt above shows, Henry James can only speak for himself as his "very first perceptions" necessarily mediate those of his brother.

More than simply presaging the development of one line of American thought, however, this scene also anticipates the shape and future direction of scholarship on Emerson and the Jameses.[3] Just as Henry appears as an outsider with respect to his father and brother, scholarly discussions of him and Emerson usually assume their relationship to be biographical anecdote or merely an afterthought.[4] While his father was Emerson's friend and contemporary, and William's work blatantly shows an Emersonian influence, Henry seems to have much less in common with the transcendentalist.[5] But despite living his adult life abroad and cultivating a European sensibility, Emersonianism continued to bear upon Henry James Jr.'s thought. Subsequently, this chapter represents an attempt to recuperate the novelist's relationship to the essayist and poet by briefly looking at the two reviews he wrote on Emerson and, in turn, situating those writings in relation to what might otherwise seem to be two disparate texts. More specifically, the first half of this chapter revisits the dominant understanding of the James-Emerson relationship in order to set the stage for the second half, where I offer a revised and more nuanced portrait. By reading Emerson's "Fate" alongside James's preface to *The Golden Bowl,* I want to demonstrate, beyond their historical and biographical relationship, the subtle imaginative continuity between the Master and the Sage.

Henry James's lengthiest discussions of Emerson appear in book reviews of *The Correspondence of Thomas Carlyle and Ralph Waldo Emerson: 1834–1872* and James Elliot Cabot's *A Memoir of Ralph Waldo Emerson.*[6] Though these reviews do not exhaust the range of allusions and references to Emerson in James's collected writings, they represent *Partial Portraits,* the title of the book of criticism that reprinted James's review of Cabot's biography. For instance, the second essay, the review of Cabot, best exemplifies the overarching understanding of James's opinion of Emerson. By contrasting "the transcendentalist movement—that remarkable outburst of Romanticism on Puritan ground"[7]—with European culture, James sets up a dichotomy between Old World sophistication and American naïveté. Europe, James recalls, "introduced [Emerson] to a more complicated world; but his spirit, his moral taste, as it were, abode always with the undecorated walls of his youth. There he could dwell with that ripe unconsciousness of evil" (254); if Europe exposed him to the "vices of the place and times," then his return to New England "offered . . . [him] a kind of achromatic picture, without particular intensifications" (254). This unadorned and bare "picture," for James, helps to explain why Emerson's "direct, intimate vision of the soul" would lack insight into "its emotions, its contortions and perversions" and only emphasize its "passive, exposed, yet healthy form" (254).

According to James, the "achromatic picture" of New England results in Emerson's oblique vision, but, of course, this description does more to tell us about his own relationship with America than that of the subject of his review. For example, James believes that Emerson's restricted view is a result of "the world in which he grew up and lived," a world lacking "bribes and lures . . . beguilements and prizes" (255). But several pages later he contrasts Emerson with Nathaniel Hawthorne to reveal the absurdity of his own position. Responding to Cabot's assertion that Emerson was unable to read Hawthorne's novels, James writes:

> This is a judgment odd almost to fascination . . . it contains so elusive an ambiguity. How highly he must have esteemed the man of whose genius *The House of Seven Gables* and *The Scarlet Letter* gave imperfectly the measure, and how strange that he should not have been eager to read almost anything that such a gifted being might have let fall! It was a rare accident that made them live almost side by side in the same small New England town, each a fruit of a long Puritan stem, yet with such a different taste. Hawthorne's vision was all for the evil and sin of the world; a side of life as to which Emerson's eyes were thickly bandaged. There were points as to which the latter's conception of right could be violated, but he had no great sense of wrong—a strangely limited one, indeed, for a moralist—no sense of the dark, the foul, the base. (269)

One can only laugh as James mocks the Oedipal Emerson. The abundance of Adamic allusions to the Fall suggest that Hawthorne was only too willing to bite the apple, while Emerson remained ensconced in his innocence. But then again, James's reduction of Emerson to his native habitat cannot account for the anomalous Hawthorne; if they both inhabited the Edenic Concord, what accounts for the difference?

James believes that Cabot's biography neglects the antebellum New England context that shaped Emerson's "strangely limited" perspective, and his own attempt to fill in that context makes his accusation of Emerson's provinciality only seem to be the more provincial. We cannot attribute all of Hawthorne's insight to his trials in the Custom House or the burden of his name, and such a partial reading of Emerson's relation to his surroundings makes it clear that James is no New Historicist. Yet simply labeling James's reading as "thickly bandaged" in its own right would also be premature. Just prior to his discussion of Hawthorne, he reflects on an encounter with Emerson that lacks any bad faith remarks about nationality:

> The truth was that, sparely constructed as he was and formed not wastefully, not with material left over, as it were, for a special function, there were certain chords in Emerson that did not vibrate at all. I well remember my impression of this on walking with him in the autumn of 1872 through the galleries of the Louvre and, later that winter, through those of the Vatican: his perception of the objects contained in these collections was of the most general order. I was struck with the anomaly of a man so refined and intelligent being so little spoken to by works of art. It would be more exact to say that certain chords were wholly absent; the tune was played, the tune of life and literature, altogether on those that remained. (269)

This is James at his finest. In both reviews he lauds Emerson's genius just as he reduces him to a caricature of America, but I highlight this Paterian impression because it seems to be a rare moment where James shifts his accusatory register: it is the missing "chords," not the cultural context, that accounts for the discrepancy between Hawthorne and Emerson.

How we are to evaluate this instrumental Emerson is a matter for our own readings, our own impressions. What James gives us, however, is an impression more concerned with rebuking America than with prying into the status and composition of those "chords." In this manner, the review of Cabot's biography lays out the canonical narrative of Emerson's relation to Henry James, which could be summarized as follows: While James knew Emerson and deeply revered him, he read his frustration with America into the transcendentalist. James, as the story goes, was a cosmopolitan thinker, and, in turn, virtually all of his fictions tell the story of an encounter between an idealist Emersonian America with a more experienced, sophisticated, and conniving Europe.[8] Simply put: Ralph Waldo Emerson and Henry James stand in for the culture clash that constitutes James's famous "international theme."[9] Yet, turning to the first review, the review of the Emerson-Carlyle correspondence, allows us to see James still in the process of constructing his authorial personae or international cosmopolitan mask. In other words, if the review of Cabot's biography reads Emerson from within the mindset of the international theme, the first review seems to catch a glimpse of James letting down that mask and peering through the bandages erected by his willful expatriotism.

That is not to say that the international theme does not pervade the first review as well. In fact, just the opposite is true, as James repeatedly contrasts the "thinness of the New England atmosphere" with the "dense, warm life of London," whose aura gave "Carlyle's philosophy [an] aristocratic premise."[10] But instead of traversing already covered ground, I want to focus on the review's final lines: "As one finds a little of everything in a man of genius, we find a great deal of tenderness even in the grimness of Carlyle; so that we may say . . . his tenderness was never greater than when, in spite of the local limitation, he stretched across the ocean, in gratitude for early sympathy, for early services, and held fast to the friendship of Emerson. His family was predominant for him, as we say, and he cleaved to his relations, to his brothers. But it was as a brother that he addressed Emerson" (249).

Throughout the review, James contrasts the optimist Emerson with Carlyle, "the pessimist of pessimists" (242), yet, as we see, the review concludes on a note of warmth, compassion, and empathy. What I would like to suggest, however briefly, is that in these remarks James comes to see himself as a Carlyle figure and that the depiction of each thinker nicely allegorizes James's own relationship with William in America. The initial hyperbolic descriptions of Emerson and Carlyle transform into a relationship of necessary dependence, where the European, "stretched across the ocean," "cleav[es] to his relations, to his brothe[r]" in the New World. What James sees in Carlyle, in other words, is the necessity of drawing upon one's opposite to enhance one's genius. Although he left America, he refused to forsake the "Romanticism on Puritan ground." His espousal of Browning, Tennyson, Eliot, and Arnold does not come without equal admiration for his American brethren beyond Hawthorne. If Emerson sought to inaugurate a new tradition of American letters by expunging the noxious elements of his European contemporaries, then James might represent the dialectical sublimation of a common literary tradition that at some point became severed. This sublimation becomes clearer if we turn to an allusion to Emerson's "Experience" that appears in the preface to *The Wings of the Dove.*

In "Experience" Emerson writes: "We live amid surfaces, and the true art of life is to skate well on them" (CW 3:35). This aphorism suggests that living encompasses blithely touching upon a range of experiences, but never pushing too hard for fear of cracking the surface or the facade that makes life tolerable. Such a philosophy, we can speculate, calls for loose attachments so that, in the face of tragedy, one does not fall victim to the perils of Emerson's response to the death of Waldo.[11] Conversely, James, discussing the formal qualities of the novel, revises Emerson: "[The work of art] is greatest, it is delightfully, divinely great, when we feel the surface, like the thick of the ice of the skater's pond, bear without cracking the strongest pressure we throw on it."[12] Neither James nor Emerson wants to crack the ice, yet James, unlike his predecessor, chooses to heap as much upon it as possible instead of blithely skating across the surface.

Though the question of whether or not James heeds this advice is a matter for another study, at this juncture we can safely assume that his unique international sensibility, his desire to absorb the rich traditions of the Old

World and not abandon his "brothers" at home, is an attempt to place a very heavy weight on the surface of his art. That life, however, is purely imaginative; James acts as a sponge, soaking up the entire tradition of Western literature and allowing it to flow back out as his consciousness re-presents it to the world. Emersonianism is merely one tradition that James's ice bears, but it is a significant one, as we will see in the preface to *The Golden Bowl.*

Reflecting on the revisions made to his oeuvre, James concludes his final critical preface to the New York Edition with another allusion to Emerson. He remarks that his "literary deeds" reflect "the whole conduct of life" because "our expression of them, and the terms on which we understand [them] belong as nearly to our conduct and our life as every other feature of freedom" (*Art* 347). How are we to understand such a remark in light of James's somewhat dismissive opinion of Emerson? Why the turn to Emerson as the culminating gesture in his expansive and prolific career? To begin working toward an answer to such questions, I will offer a limited reading of "Fate," the opening essay of *The Conduct of Life,* in relation to the above allusion to invite and anticipate what would be a more authoritative study. The choice of "Fate" and the preface to *The Golden Bowl* is not arbitrary, moreover, because, like "Experience," it offers a rare glimpse of the tragic Emerson, as we see in the following famous remark: "No picture of life can have any veracity that does not admit the odious acts" (*CW* 6:11). Such a melancholic tone combined with the usual paean to the powers of human individuality might have resonated with James as he reminisced over his life's work. It is this combination of two competing visions that makes "Fate," I believe, an essay that can help us make sense of Emerson's place in James's final preface.

Fate represents, for Emerson, the limits nature imposes on the individual; the "weight of the universe" (*CW* 6:3) that stifles human development. While "universe" overtly refers to the physical conditions of a "world [that] is roughly and surly" (*CW* 6:3), Emerson's language tacitly implies a quasi-sociological sensibility where biological and physical constraints combine with a "moral or . . . material bias" (*CW* 6:6) to make up the "tyrannical Circumstance[s]" (*CW* 6:8) limiting what the human can achieve. In other words, Emerson seems to acknowledge how real-world conditions, both innate and imposed, dilute the unadulterated philosophical idealism of which James accuses him. Yet despite the realization of man's fated condition, Emerson remains closer to an American Kant than a Marx, since it is the abstract, transcendental "eternal laws" (*CW* 6:11) of Fate that preoccupy him, not, for example, man-made limitations.

Nonetheless, if Emerson's eyes are bandaged, the layers are not as thick as James would assume. In "Fate," Emerson seems preoccupied with revising Emersonianism to account for life's "odious facts," and, in turn, we see such revision through an elaborated account of the ice-skating metaphor from "Experience." Emerson writes: "But every jet of chaos which threatens to exterminate us, is convertible by intellect into wholesome force. . . . The cold is inconsiderate of persons, tingles your blood, freezes man like a dew-drop. But learn to skate, and the ice will give you graceful, sweet, poetic motion" (*CW* 6:17). No longer simply encouraging the individual to "skate well," Emerson realizes that such skating is difficult. "The cold" represents all the impediments that prevent an ideal form of skating, the limitations the skater encounters. But because Emerson is now able to fathom those limits, he is able to explain how humans might overcome them. That is, the skater must utilize "the cold [so that it can] brace your limbs and brains to genius, make you [a] foremost m[a]n of time" (*CW* 6:17). By transforming life's barriers into enabling conditions that can trigger and channel the power of the creative human spirit, individuals realize their "genius" through the knowledge of that which seeks to limit and confine them.

"Power, which is the other act in the dual world, immense" (*CW* 6:12) is the name for this process of overcoming or transformation. To counteract Fate's restricting influence, Emerson extols humanity's ability to draw upon each person's innate self-reliance and to emerge from its fated condition: "If Fate follows and limits power, power attends and antagonizes Fate" (*CW* 6:12). The antagonizing powers that Emerson has in mind are the "noble creative forces" that allow "the revelation of Thought [to take] man out of servitude [and] into freedom" (*CW* 6:14). In an example similar to the ice-skating metaphor, he remarks that "Steam was, till the other day, the devil which we dreaded" because of its terrorizing and menacing capacity, as he puts it, to "carry the house away" (*CW* 6:18). However, ingenuity or "the revelation of Thought" enables us to harness the power of steam for our own purposes. Rather than allow it, like the cold, to strike fear into humankind, one must learn that "where was power, was not devil, but was God; that [the danger of steam] must be availed of, and not by any means let off and wasted" (*CW* 6:18). While it would be premature to suggest that this example reflects Emerson's enthusiasm for the burgeoning modernity he saw transpire over the course of his lifetime, his brazen championing of human cunning sets up the idea that "Fate slides into freedom, and freedom into Fate" (*CW* 6:20). Imaginatively transforming previously recognized human limitations into productive means for human ends might, Emerson seems to imply, engender further limitations, as we are only too aware from our current historical vantage point. Steam power can productively benefit society, but as with technological development in general, human control over nature can equally lead to deleterious consequences. The goal is not simply an opportunistic transformation of previous limitations into newfound strengths, but rather to "build altars to the Blessed Unity which holds nature and souls in perfect solution and compels every atom to serve an universal end" (*CW* 6:26). That is, the dialectic of Fate and Power is the ability to recognize one's natural limitations and, through the creative will and human intellect, revise the self's relation to them while, at the same time, being wary of not bringing about further impediments in that act of revision. Henry James, as we will see, exemplifies this dialectic through his idiosyncratic understanding of the literary imagination.

The "tyrannical Circumstance[s]" that James repeatedly encounters in his prefaces to the New York Edition are specific to the practice of writing. Namely, the prefaces focus on, among other things, the boundaries of the novel as a literary form or, more abstractly, the confrontation between the artist's need to represent an unbounded and limitless imaginative idea within the confines of a restricted textual economy. Or, put differently, the act of representing the imagination within the demarcated space of the text, using the medium of language. James begins the preface to *The Golden Bowl* by celebrating the novel's successful use of narrative point of view as a specific manifestation of this larger theoretical problem. Because a central task of the novel is to give a full "account of somebody's impression" of the "affair in hand" (*Art* 327), James realizes that that account must be represented from some particular point of view that fits into a novel's formal structure. For example, the events of *The Ambassadors,* the first of James's so-called major phase novels, are filtered through the mind of its protagonist, and he, Lambert Strether, is our only guide to the book's "affair." In his next novel, *The Wings of the Dove,* James uses several characters to shed light on each other and that "affair," but as he re-reads this work and remarks in its preface, the endeavor to utilize several points of view or narrative centers results in an unbalanced, uneven work. Too many perspectives piled onto the surface of the ice lead to cracks.

James describes the failure of *Wings* in terms of an "economy of composition" (*Art* 302), where the "affair" envisioned by the writer must be organized and represented as fully as possible without disrupting the novel's aesthetic integrity. *The Golden Bowl* seems to succeed where *Wings* fails by containing its subject in two distinct halves, each representing a different character's perspective. James is able to expand on the technical achievement of *The Ambassadors,* but not succumb to the pitfalls of *Wings,* by going beyond a sole narrative center without upsetting the novel's balance:

> I am naturally brought up against the fact of the fundamental fewness of these [characters]—of the fact that my large demand is made for a group of agents

> who may be counted on the finger of one hand. We see very few persons in "The Golden Bowl," but the scheme of the book, to make up for that, is that we shall really see about as much of them as a coherent literary form permits. That was my problem, so to speak, and my *gageure*—to play the small handful of values really for all they were worth—and to work my system, my particular propriety of appeal, particular degree of pressure on the spring of interest, for all that this specific ingenuity itself might be. (*Art* 330–31)

This passage might seem unremarkable, but it shows James acknowledging the same kind of limitations Emerson foresees in "Fate," albeit in a different context. More specifically, he realizes that "a coherent literary form" restricts the "large demand" of the artist's imagination. While he wants to present an accurate, full, robust, and complex representation of his central characters and their "affair," he does not want to limit that representation to a sole narrative voice, nor does he want to sacrifice the decorum of "a coherent literary form." James is known for experimentation, but he is no avant-garde modernist. The "system" to which *The Golden Bowl* conforms allows the reader "to see about as much of [the Prince and Princess]" as is possible because the "very few persons"—Adam, Charlotte, Fanny, and Bob—exist within the Prince and Princess's representative halves, serving to shape our understanding of the novel's subject and protagonists without exploding its "form" or placing too much "pressure" on the ice. *The Golden Bowl,* and James's work in general, must acknowledge and capitulate to the limits of form because any attempt to exceed them results in, as James famously remarks, "large, loose baggy monsters" (*Art* 84).

However, if the opening of the preface suggests one way in which James fathoms the novel's "Fate," the rest of the preface discusses how the act of reading and revising, or re-reading, correlates to a kind of Emersonian Power that allows James to transcend those limits. As I have argued elsewhere, James's revisions enable him to see that the act of writing—or containing the literary idea, image, or the novel's "affair" in a text—is an act of compression that necessarily truncates much of the imagination's initial idea.[13] Nonetheless, by reflecting on his process of revision, James comes to see how the act of reading allows him to reconstruct that which was previously condensed. When James reads with his "maturer mind" (*Art* 339), he discovers aspects of his characters and his novel's "affair" that he did not see before or that were previously truncated and lost as he forced his subject to fit into the novel's form. Every time he reads a text and reconstructs the compressed representation it contains, he sees more than what the words allowed him originally to express. Reading, in other words, makes lucid "the growth of the immense array of terms, perceptional and expressional, that, . . . simply looked over the heads of the standing terms . . . like alert winged creatures, perched on those diminished summits and aspired to a clearer air" (*Art* 339). A novel's "standing terms" only permit a portion of the novelistic idea to exist; they are the terms that stand in for the parts of the imagination that language represents. When James reads, however, he notices aspects of that representation trying to escape their textual prison "like alert winged creatures"; he notices that his imaginative idea of the novel is buried beneath its literary representation and seeks liberation.[14]

This ability to see the "alert winged creatures" suggests a latent Emersonian Power that James begins to realize. He wants to bring those "creatures" to the surface, but he yields to his formalist sense of literary decorum. Yet, by defining revision as the ability "to see, or to look over again" (*Art* 338), James finds a solution to his problem in the creative will or the Power of the human intellect that Emerson extols. As the preface reaches its pinnacle, James equates re-vision with poetic vision à la Milton's "fields of light" (*Art* 341) and begins to understand literature as "a *living* affair" (342) that depends upon "the play of *representational* values" (346) engendered by the power of reading. If reading allows James to see the "alert winged creatures," his play on re-vision helps him to fathom a way for them to escape:

> It is scarce necessary to note that the highest test of any literary form conceived in light of "poetry"—to apply that term in its largest literary sense—hangs back unpardonably from its office when it fails to lend itself to a *vivâ-voce* treatment. We talk here, naturally, not of non-poetic forms, but of those whose highest bid is addressed to the imagination, to the spiritual and aesthetic vision, the mind led captive by the charm and a spell, an incalculable art. The essential property of such a form as that is to give out its finest and most numerous secrets, and to give them out most gratefully, under the closest pressure—which is of course the pressure of the attention articulately *sounded.* (*Art* 346–47)

Adding the previously unseen "winged creatures" to a novel still relies on a restricted textual economy of "coherent literary form." But in order for the literary idea to present itself fully to the imagination, James literally brings that image out of the text by giving it what he calls the "*vivâ-voce* treatment." The only way to access the "finest and most numerous secrets" of "incalculable art" is to repudiate the calculations of textuality and sound out the words so that their "essential property" can speak directly to the imagination, so that the novelist's unbound imagination can obviate linguistic mediation.[15]

In order to make James's connection between reading out loud and Emersonian Power explicit, I want to turn to the central allusion that appears in the preface's final paragraph:

> All of which amounts doubtless but to saying that as the whole conduct of life consists of things done, which do other things in their turn, just so our behaviour and its fruits are essentially one and continuous and persistent and unquenchable, so the act has its way of abiding and showing and testifying, and so, among our innumerable acts, are no arbitrary, no senseless separations. The more we are capable of acting the less gropingly we plead such differences; whereby, with any capability, we recognize betimes that to "put" things is very exactly and responsibly and interminably to do them. Our expression of them, and the terms on which we understand that, belong as nearly to our conduct and our life as every other feature of our freedom. (*Art* 347)

What James sees in Emerson is the ability to make literature come alive. He turns to this precursor because reading out loud—or reading in general—entails an active use of the imagination that is not only a way of escaping the restricted, fated, limits of a text, but a form of Power that leads to our "freedom." Emerson's essay "Fate" is a meditation on worldly structures of authority and restrictions that James, in the prefaces and elsewhere, describes in terms of his literary vocation and textuality. James's obsession with centers of consciousness, narrative point of view, "economy of composition" (*Art* 302), "economy of treatment" (*Art* 302), or "economic representation" (*Art* 87) suggests a quarrel with the demands made on the imagination by the publishing world, literary propriety, and simply the fact that a novel must begin and end. Yet by re-reading, re-seeing, revising or re-visioning and, moreover, reading aloud, James discovers a form of imaginative power that emancipates him from all that Emerson labels "Fate."

It should come as no surprise that James's espousal of the "*vivâ-voce* treatment" makes him think of a lecturer known for his eloquence. Both men realize that the Power of writing rests in its oral quality: "any imaged prose that fails to be richly rewarding in return for a competent utterance ranks itself as wrong through not being 'in the conditions of life'" (*Art* 347). What Emerson calls the "human intellect," James describes as "our literary deeds," which, he continues, "enjoy this marked advantage over many of our acts, that, though they go forth into the world and stray even in the desert, they don't to the same extent lose themselves; their attachment and reference . . . need not necessarily lapse—while of the tie that binds us to *them* we may make almost anything we like" (*Art* 347–48). If Emerson describes our human ability to overcome our fated condition as the Power latent in the intellect, James provides an account of the visionary imagination, that central mark of genius innate to great writers such as Emerson or

Nietzsche, that locates such a Power in the act of reading and re-reading. For all their differences, Emerson and James were both committed to the Power that allows us to transform our imaginative experience of a work of art into an emancipating endeavor that frees us from our specific "attachment and reference" and, finally, enables us to en-vision change, or hope, in all arenas of life.

Notes

1. Henry James, *A Small Boy and Others*, ed. Peter Collister (1913; rpt., Charlottesville: University Press of Virginia, 2011), 11.

2. Ibid., 5.

3. The best biographical study of the James family remains R. W. B. Lewis's *The Jameses: A Family Narrative* (New York: Anchor Books, 1991), but readers should also consult Paul Fisher's more recent *House of Wits: An Intimate Portrait of the James Family* (New York: Henry Holt, 2008). Moreover, F. O. Matthiessen's *The James Family* (New York: Alfred A. Knopf, 1947) contains important family documents featuring a section devoted to Emerson (428–58). Finally, Frederic I. Carpenter's "William James and Emerson" (1939; rpt. in Edwin H. Cady and Louis J. Budd, eds., *On Emerson: The Best from American Literature* [Durham, NC: Duke University Press, 1988], 43–61); and William T. Stafford's "Emerson and the James Family" (ibid., 81–109) represent two early essays that provide excellent overviews.

4. There are two noted exceptions: first, Jonathan Levin's *The Poetics of Transition: Emerson, Pragmatism, and American Literary Modernism* (Durham, NC: Duke University Press, 1999) aligns Emerson with American pragmatist philosophy and reads that tradition's influence on literary modernism. Second, Daniel T. O'Hara's *Visions of Global America* (Columbus: Ohio State University Press, 2009) contrasts two competing "logics of vision" contained in Emerson's "Experience" and James's "The Beast in the Jungle" to suggest their lasting influence on what O'Hara calls "global America" (73–96).

5. While it would be an impossible task to survey the plethora of scholarship on Emerson and William James, I will single out a recent essay by Gregg Crane that provides an excellent critical overview as well as an exhaustive and authoritative reading of William James's annotations to Emerson's writings. See Gregg Crane, "Intuition: The 'Unseen Thread' Connecting Emerson and James," *Modern Intellectual History* 10, no. 1 (2013): 57–86.

6. The two reviews were published in 1883 and 1887, respectively. Moreover, James's *Hawthorne* (1879; rpt. in *Literary Criticism: Essays on Literature, American Writers, English Writers*, ed. Leon Edel [New York: Library of America, 1984], 315–457) also contains a brief but worthwhile discussion of Emerson (381–84).

7. Henry James, review of *A Memoir of Ralph Waldo Emerson*, by James Elliot Cabot (1887), in Edel, *Literary Criticism*, 265. Subsequent references to this work will be cited parenthetically in the text by page number.

8. Articles and entries from scholarly reference books on Emerson and James corroborate this view. Though they contain many important nuances and insights into these thinkers' differing opinions on American identity, idealist philosophy, and individuality, the larger structure of this overarching narrative holds true. See Amanda Adams, "Ralph Waldo Emerson," in Eric Haralson and Kendall Johnson, eds., *A Critical Companion to Henry James* (New York: Facts on File, 2009), 386–87; Bill Scalia, "Henry James Jr.," in Tiffany K. Wayne, ed., *A Critical Companion to Ralph Waldo Emerson* (New York: Facts on File, 2010), 350–51; and Andrew Taylor, "Nineteenth-Century America (1843–1870)," in David McWhirter, ed., *Henry James in Context* (Cambridge: Cambridge University Press, 2010), 3–13. Moreover, the article by Stafford previously cited contains the most detailed and authoritative reading of both book reviews (91–98).

9. Two novels are worth mentioning: *The American* (1877) and *The Bostonians* (1886). The former book epitomizes James's international theme, and one might contrast Christopher Newman's experience in the Louvre with James and Emerson's encounter at the same locale five years prior to the novel's publication. *The Bostonians*, on the other hand, is less of an international novel but most clearly depicts James's critique of New England's transcendentalist reformers.

10. Henry James, review of *The Correspondence of Thomas Carlyle and Ralph Waldo Emerson, 1834–1872* (1883; rpt. in Edel, *Literary Criticism*, 244–45). Subsequent references to this work will be cited parenthetically in the text by page number.

11. See O'Hara's *Visions*, 73–80. For a contrasting take on "Experience," see Donald E. Pease's "'Experience,' Antislavery, and the Crisis of Emersonianism," in Branka Arsić and Cary Wolfe, eds., *The Other Emerson* (Minneapolis: University of Minnesota Press, 2010), 131–66.

12. Henry James, *The Art of the Novel*, ed. Richard P. Blackmur (Chicago: University of Chicago Press, 1934), 304–5. Hereafter cited parenthetically in the text as *Art*.

13. See my essay "Between the Romance and the Real: Experiencing Jamesian Reading," *Henry James Review* 35, no. 1 (Winter 2014): 12–22.

14. Julie Rivkin provides an excellent account of this passage in relation to Platonic theories of representation and Derrida's notion of supplementarity. See Julie Rivkin, "Doctoring the Text: Henry James and Revision," in David McWhiter, ed., *Henry James's New York Edition: The Construction of Authorship* (Stanford, CA: Stanford University Press, 1995), 142–63.

15. This reading revises J. Hillis Miller's authoritative account of this preface, which, for reasons of space, I cannot address. See *The Ethics of Reading* (New York: Columbia University Press, 1987), 101–22; *Versions of Pygmalion* (Cambridge, MA: Harvard University Press, 1990), 1–23; and *Literature as Conduct* (New York: Fordham University Press, 2005), 157–60, for three of Miller's different yet interconnected takes on James. Moreover, my divergence from Miller appears in "Between the Romance and the Real." In that article I corroborate the notion that the literary idea or image contained in the novelist's unbound imagination is prelinguistic.

[III]

EMERSON AND THE FAR EAST

[12]

NAOKO SAITO

EMERSON AND JAPAN: FINDING A WAY OF CULTURAL CRITICISM

> He then learns that in going down into the secrets of his own mind he has descended into the secrets of all minds. He learns that he who has mastered any law in his private thoughts, is master to that extent of all men whose language he speaks, and of all into whose language his own can be translated. . . . The deeper he dives into his privatest, secretest presentiment, to his wonder he finds this is the most acceptable, most public, and universally true. —Emerson, "The American Scholar" (CW 1:63)

What Does It Mean to Read Emerson from a Cross-Cultural *Perspective?*

WRITING IN 1903, JOHN Dewey called Emerson the "Philosopher of Democracy."[1] In the light of his visits to Japan in 1919 and 1920, it would scarcely come as a surprise to Dewey that, in the century since then, Emerson has not been well appreciated in that country—at least philosophically. The historical acceptance of Emerson by one Japanese poet and thinker, Tokoku Kitamura (1868–94), in the Meiji period (1868–1912), when Japan's phase of modernization was initiated, is discussed by Megumi Sakabe in his "'Freedom' as the Experience of the West."[2] Certainly, it seems that Emerson has been recognized in Japan more as a writer than as a philosopher, and hence he is read and referred to within literary studies, not within philosophy. In the twenty-first century, especially after what has come to be known as "3/11" (the Fukushima incident), Japan's democracy has been newly questioned, and questioned in a more penetrating way. Can democracy be separated from our personal ways of living and from deeper existential questions concerning how to recover from disastrous loss? Confronted with the present national crisis, democracy is tested in Japan, for each of us, and not simply as a political mechanism, but as a "way of life," as John Dewey once remarked.[3] Now is the time when Emerson's "inmost" to the "outmost" can perhaps be understood anew, with its global ramifications.

Centering on a broad topic—Emerson and Japan—this chapter thematizes Emerson as a philosopher in response to crisis in life, whose voice is still to be heard in Japan. It extends this to a more philosophical consideration concerning a *cross-cultural* dimension of Emerson's thought: what it means to "appreciate" Emerson's "influence" "across" "borders"—questions internal to Emerson's thought. By so doing, it attempts to explore another path in the appreciation of Emerson's global significance today, a path that enters uncharted territory and makes its way across cultural borders. Such a reading necessitates a release from any capture of Emerson in dichotomies of East and West. Following Stanley Cavell's reading of Emerson, I present Emerson's idea of "onward thinking" as a distinctive mode of antifoundationalist thinking—one that places the moment of conversion in sharp focus and that serves as a key to the reconfiguration of the criticism of culture.[4] I reclaim cultural criticism by "Man Thinking" as the most significant and beneficial way of reading Emerson from a cross-cultural perspective. Within an entangled relationship of language, subjectivity, and culture, this directs us beyond the schema of universalism and parochialism, be it American or Japanese. To this end, I argue for the global importance of Emerson as *the American* philosopher who provides an alternative concept of the human subject and who thus reveals a way of *becoming* cosmopolitan in the age of globalization: a transcendence of borders from within. This, I conclude, is the Emerson who is urgently needed today in Japan—in a Japan still to be achieved.

Emerson and Japan

What, if Emerson's global importance is to be seen, is the most beneficial way of reading him? What does it mean to read Emerson? Emerson is a writer who opens diverse entrances into his text. Japan's encounter with Emerson is itself a good illustration. In the Meiji period, the era of modernization and industrialization in Japan, Kitamura was at one time in the 1880s engaged in the civil rights and freedom movement. He dropped out of this, however, and took an inward, literary turn, which the Japanese philosopher Sakabe has called a "romanticist turn towards the inner."[5] As a typically literary figure, bruised by the challenge of modernity in Japan, Kitamura found a vision of "inner freedom"—freedom not in the outer, the political, but in the inner, the spiritual (73). In the year when Kitamura died, he published a book titled *Emerson* (1894) (75). Sakabe describes Kitamura's idea of inner freedom as a "theory of higher freedom" (78), evoking the kind of Emersonian spirituality and religiousness that Sakabe thinks underlies Kitamura's idea.[6] Sakabe's discussion of Emerson and Japan centers on the question of modernity, which Japan had to confront and, despite its technological sophistication, still is confronting. Thus, the Emerson who was received and represented by Kitamura is a figure who is inward-looking, whose spiritual realm is separated from the outer, from the political. Indicating a sharp boundary that circumscribes the inner spirituality as an isolated realm, Sakabe raises the question: "After Kitamura, has Japan ever reached the point where it can discover the way to return to the outer again, starting with inner insight?" (73).

As a thinker who writes under the influences of various cultures, including Asian influences, Emerson can be read in such a way as to show his transcultural, global orientation. Lawrence Buell proposes such a reading of Emerson: "Emerson's vision of 'Man Thinking' itself needs to be seen both as arising within a particular cultural context and also as articulating much broader western concerns to define the impediments, prospects, and scenarios for individual self-realization for whatever culture, whatever gender, at a moment when cultural flux and uncertainty threatened to confuse or even paralyze a serious-minded thinking person."[7] As an example of a contact point between Emerson and Japan, Buell refers to the Zen Buddhism of Daisetsu Suzuki, who in 1896 had published an "Essay on Emerson," and says that "some tenets of Suzuki's version of Zen seem strongly Emersonian" (E 196).[8] Buell also considers the admiration expressed by Naibu Kanda (1859–1923), who was "enchanted by the later Emerson's persona, rhetoric, and message of temperate simplicity," to be an illustration of the fact that "the sage effect had little to do with nationality" (E 147). Such a transnational and transcultural reading echoes throughout Buell's cosmopolitan interpretation of Emerson (E 188).[9] This is reiterated in the way he accounts for the reception of Emerson in Japan: "the abstractness of Emerson's theories of nature, liberal individualism, and voluntary simplicity seemingly facilitated their appropriation by reformist intellectuals like Tokoku Kitamura, author of the first critical book on Emerson in Japanese" (E 329). All this is tied up with his understanding of Emerson's *Americanness*. In Buell's view, for Emerson, "Americanness was less an object of conscious concern than his participation in an international realm of great ideas, great books, great men" (E 272).[10]

If as Buell says, Emerson embodies a "spiritual transcendence across improbable sectarian and national borders" and reclaims the "common grounds of ethico-religious understanding across cultures" (which Buell calls a "moral or spiritual universalism," no less [E 197–98]), then boundaries, whether cultural, national, or spiritual, are supposed to be transcended (E 154). If Emerson is a universal figure who embodies the common knowledge of diverse cultures, the imperative today must be to absorb such knowledge from his writings and to apply it to our particular contexts. Is this way of reading the trajectory from the "inmost" to the "outmost" able to respond to what may be a newly rising dimension of democracy as a way of life in Japan?

Let us then turn our eyes to contemporary Japan, now faced with the Fukushima disaster—a Japan that perhaps calls for a different reading of Emerson, the possibilities of which are still to be disclosed. There is a need to address the question of human subjectivity in a way different from Kitamura's struggle. In the documentary film *No Man's Zone: Fukushima—The Day After,* the forbidding silence, the ominous lack of sound evokes a horizon of life beyond accountability, transparency, and articulation through reason. Its images of debris and ubiquitous destruction embody invisible fears about what cannot be said.[11] Asked by a reporter, "What do you think?," a man who has lost his livelihood and his home answers: "I do not know what to do." Another says: "We are falling apart."

"Where do we find ourselves?" is the question with which Emerson begins his essay "Experience" (*CW* 3:27). Reading Emerson's "Fate," "Experience," and "Nature" in the context of the post-Fukushima era in Japan, Masaki Horiuchi finds in Emerson a call for moving forward after loss, pain, and disaster—from within the very state in which we do not know where to begin and where we shall arrive. This is a work of affirmation toward an opening of the new.[12] Emerson's writing might be called not only a philosophy of life but also philosophy in response to crisis—a kind of crisis that is a part of our ordinary lives. In discussing Emerson and Japan, where do we find ourselves when we are confronted with loss? What is *the* Japanese culture, if such there be, and who are the "we," those who are called "Japanese"? How, in the wake of Emerson, are we to cross borders—national and cultural, and, say, existential borders? Emerson's thesis, from the "inmost" to the "outmost," is tested once again in response to crisis in Japan, at personal, cultural, and social levels.

More philosophically, we need, along with Emerson, to find a way from loss toward recovery, a way that engages us with a boundary. Can this be the kind of boundary that is perceived to define and contain the inner spiritual self, as Kitamura expressed in the nineteenth century? Or would it be a boundary that is to be dissolved? Are we to draw a line to distinguish the inner from the outer? Or shall we challenge the limit as something to be dismantled or overcome? Pursing the enquiry in these apparently contrary directions—the outer toward the inner, the inner toward the outer—may diffuse the sense of resistance that can be posed by a limit. It is through these philosophical channels that I reconsider and reevaluate the significance of Emerson in our times, and I do this to reveal his work's cross-cultural implications.

Polarities: Finding Emerson's Way

A foolish consistency is the hobgoblin of little minds, adored by little statesmen and philosophers and divines. —*CW* 2:33

In order to unpack the implications of Emerson's statement, "the inmost in due time becomes the outmost," and to find an alternative way of crossing boundaries, let us examine his two essays "The American Scholar" (1837) and "Fate" (1860). Emerson declares the role of the American scholar as "Man Thinking" (*CW* 1:53)—as one who thinks for life and in life. The scholar must be, Emerson says, "strong to live, as well as strong to think" (*CW* 1:61). The scholar's role is to feel and translate the "force of his constitution in the doings and passages of the day" (*CW* 1:61). This movement of "transition" he defines as "action" (*CW* 1:59), action as a "resource" (*CW* 1:61). This is what Emerson calls the "philosophy of life" (*CW* 1:68). It is in this essay, along with "Self-Reliance," that Emerson explicitly presents the theme of from the "inmost" to the "outmost": "He is one who raises himself from private considerations and breathes and lives on public and illustrious thoughts" (*CW* 1:62). Emerson manifests his hope for the power of the great man, whom he calls "Man Thinking."

The passage from within, however, has the ground of Emerson's hope—"the doctrine that man is one" (*CW* 1:65). The sense of oneness is paraphrased elsewhere as "some preestablished harmony" (*CW* 1:58). The reader is puzzled over the relationship between the two—the private and the public, the one and the many, the power of a single individual and that of "one soul." Indeed, in Emerson's text, we often encounter a kind of polarity—two extremes set side by side. In his later essay "Fate," in *The Conduct of Life* (1860), we are confronted with polarity—or in Emerson's word, "oppositions" (*CW* 6:19)—in a particularly strikingly way. The essay works with a strange mixture of the ideas of fate and freedom. On the one hand, we are limited, and he calls this limit "Fate," suggesting this image of the telos: "The ulterior aim, the purpose beyond itself, the correlation by which planets subside and crystalize, then animate beasts and men,—will not stop but will work into finer particulars, and from finer to finest" (*CW* 6:21). On the other hand, there is a power that "attends and antagonizes Fate."[13] Echoing the voice of "Man Thinking," Emerson says: "So far as a man thinks, he is free" (*CW* 6:13); and, "Life is freedom,—life in the direct ratio of its amount" (*CW* 6:21). This, however, is not freedom as contingency, he writes, "a part of Fate" is "the freedom of man" (*CW* 6:12).

Stephen E. Whicher notes about Emerson, "The closer we approach him, in fact, the more we realize how entirely his thought was controlled by a shifting, complex dialectic of opposites."[14] Indeed the bipolar images and apparent paradoxes that destabilize our thought make it difficult to "explain" them in a clear-cut manner. Emerson asserts, "The secret of the world is the tie between person and event. Person makes event, and event person" (*CW* 6:21). We should begin neither with person nor event. Also, when he says that the law of our existence is "intelligence," which is "not personal nor impersonal" (*CW* 6:27), how should we interpret this, the state that is neither personal nor impersonal, "not mine or thine, but the will of all mind" (*CW* 6:15)? The challenging question that Emerson poses is: How should we live amid the polarities of life, the life of "double consciousness"—private and public; freedom and necessity; impersonality and personhood; attachment and detachment; passivity and activity; courage and fear; inward and outward; and action and reaction?

Scholarship on Emerson tends to give what might be called a *causal answer* to Emerson's apparent paradox, attributing the ultimate cause to an aboriginal oneness. Buell calls this the "spirit that potentially includes the whole world," and he draws attention to "a common spirituality behind the veils of difference" (*E* 188). With regard to the relationship between the inmost and the outmost, Buell also divides Emerson into the "Pragmatist Emerson" (in the public domain) and the "Nietzschean Emerson" (in the private domain) (*E* 223). Likewise, Japanese Emersonian scholar Masayuki Sakamoto says that we can be self-reliant *because* we are embraced by oneness.[15]

In contrast to these interpretations that tend to overshadow the transitory nature of the passage from the inmost to the outmost, and hence, to fix (and fixate on) boundaries, Branka Arsić's reading offers us another entrance into Emerson's text, into an *antifoundationalist* aspect of his work, inviting us to release our thought into Emerson's apparent polarity instead of resolving it. "Siding with" the recent scholarship on Emerson, including that of Barbara Packer, Stanley Cavell, George Kateb, Sharon Cameron, and Lawrence Buell, Arsić's reading takes its force from "Emerson's ontology as one of flux" and from a notion of "being he describes to be in becoming, the over-soul as watery, the way of natural life as by abandonment."[16] More particularly, she highlights the idea of change as "harboring a dialectics of departing-arriving or ending-beginning," and here she places a sharper focus on the act of leaving and departing (*OL* 9). Through this approach, Arsić simultaneously overturns the relationship between the active and the passive as a mode of our thought, and more broadly, of our life. By so doing, she resolves the apparent paradox of the personal and the impersonal in Emerson's thought: "The 'I' is not only relational—conditioned by impersonal otherness—but also the power to respond to this otherness, hence, quite literally, the force of responsibility. The activity of responsibility is not severed from the passivity of impersonal receptivity; to the contrary, it is conditioned by it" (*OL* 212).

In her view, the poles of the personal and the impersonal do not contradict each other: Emerson's impersonal is not to be seen as "the negation of the person, but rather as an assemblage of forces and power": our identities are as if improvised and medial. This is the image of "a personal identity contrived of tensions, divides, and gaps that make it permanently 'tremble'" (*OL* 14). Through leaving, we become "different persons" (*OL* 148), "somebody else" (*OL* 138). Coming back to the theme of from the "inmost" to the "outmost," and the question of boundaries, Arsić's recounting of Emerson's antifoundationalism opens a way beyond both the inward closure of the self and its assimilation into a total, predetermined wholeness.

There are, however, some limits to Arsić's representation of Emerson. First, in her antifoundationalist reading ("[p]ersons are always translational and transitional" [*OL* 137]), leaving is itself, as it were, reified. Her text gives the impression that we leave for the sake of leaving; that we become "someone else" for the sake of becoming, for nothing else.[17] As a result of this emphasis on releasing our mind from fixity, the idea of leaving involves no sense of direction—except the ethical vision of what she calls Emerson's "cosmopolitics" (*OL* 15, 250). Second, and in relation to the first point, in her interpretation of Emerson's idea of the impersonal, the way a person is understood is equally devoid of position, proclivity, directionality. ("[W]hat reliance relies on here is the impersonal, nonpositioned life, a *life*" [*OL* 162]). In the state of "overleaping" in which the self loses itself, "stepping out of itself" (*OL* 127), there is a muffling of the undeniable sense of innerness that permeates "The American Scholar" and "Self-Reliance." The kind of self that Arsić draws out from Emerson is not individualist but a quasi-Eastern self that is passive and receptive (*OL* 7) and that abandons itself. This is what she calls the "fragile self" (*OL* 7, 148, 213), the self that will "tremble with restlessness" (*OL* 17). The self is not the "agent" but the "patient" of overcoming (*OL* 146): the self is "*passively* exposed" (*OL* 95). If, as she says, "the 'I'—in its innermost identity—is already relational and unstable" (*OL* 52), what happens to one's responsibility toward what has happened in the past, to what one's culture has been and has caused?

Third, a question arises over Arsić's "cosmopolitan" reading of Emerson:[18] "He formulated a remarkable theory of cosmopolitics that was intrinsically related to his theory of universal departing" (*OL* 15). She takes even an extreme position in opposition to nationalism: "a person is never born into a nation" (*OL* 249).[19] When she goes on to say, "because all men can become great through self-bettering, to become cosmopolitan is revealed as the highest ethical task of an improved identitarian politics" (*OL* 258), her thesis about leaving takes on an evangelical tone. It blurs the boundaries between cultures; and the boundaries between the inner and the outer, between the private and the public, are fused. This is similar to Buell's espousal of Emerson's "cosmopolitan detachment" (*OL* 51).[20]

In Arsić's representation and account of Emerson, it is hard to capture what happens in the very moment when we *are crossing* borders—how it is made possible, what awaits us beyond borders, and how the power of crossing is exercised (to which Arsić's answer would be: "in the abandonment of oneself"). There is, as she says, a blurring of the sense of a border: "the personal boundaries both of our selves and our sensuality are destabilized" (*OL* 211). The sense of struggle, of hardship, in attaining the outmost from the inmost in Emerson's text disappears. In response to Emerson's voice in "Fate"—"we can afford to allow the limitation, if we know it is the meter of the growing man" (*CW* 6:16)—we want to know how the power of recovery is exercised at the time when we face limitations, how we can live our lives so that "[p]ower attends and antagonizes Fate" (*CW* 6:12).

To reconsider the way we are engaged in the limit, the boundary between the inner and the outer, and to elucidate the passage from the inmost to the outmost, we need to recount the losses and gains of Emerson's antifoundationalism. In fact, it is Arsić's occasional reference to Cavell that helps us reorient our way. Arsić's focus on leaving is in tune with Cavell when it comes to "transfiguration" (*OL* 88). She also endorses Cavell's Emersonian moral perfectionism, if only to the extent that it echoes (her sense of) Emerson's "opening a possibility for each of us to become somebody else, renewed and better" (*OL* 138).[21] When it comes, however, to the point where Cavell (in her eyes) seems to sound a note of stability and activity, Arsić immediately distances and differentiates her position. She writes, for example: "Cavell reads the argument of 'Self-Reliance' as seeking to ensure the stability of the 'I.' . . . Moodiness and consistent leaving would thus suggest the person's inability to exist, the radical impoverishment of the 'I,' to the point of its negation." The self is abandoned, Arsić continues, in "self-dissolution" (*OL* 147). Arsić's reaction to Cavell can be seen in what she takes to be his shifting to an emphasis on the active: "It seems that Cavell sees intuition as a kind of irrational knowing to which more rational (tuition) is opposed. But Emerson . . . in fact . . . saw intuition as the highest form of rational knowing" (*OL* 153).

The points of divergence between Arsić and Cavell (as she understands him) are not only a matter of scholarly difference in the reading of Emerson: more generally they have a bearing on how we are to understand our engagement in culture, especially when we are confronted with its limits. Arsić says, "It seems that Cavell offers the thesis about standing and sitting in specific relation to 'Self-Reliance' only, for it is clear that elsewhere he sees

Emerson as a philosopher of departure. Ever since his seminal essay 'Thinking of Emerson,' which ends in a long meditation on abandonment and leaving, Cavell has understood Emerson to be a philosopher of the way" (*OL* 352). Is it true that Cavell switches his mood from one to another in different writings? To say no to this question requires us to unpack and elucidate the thoroughly radical nature of Cavell's antifoundationalist reading of Emerson.

Finding as Founding with Cavell

If Fate is ore and quarry, if evil is good in the making, if limitation is power that shall be, if calamities, oppositions, and weights are wings and means—we are reconciled. —*CW* 6:19

To believe your own thought, to believe that what is true for you in your private heart, is true for all men—that is genius. Speak your latent conviction and it shall be the universal sense; for always the inmost becomes the outmost. —*CW* 2:27

The substantive disagreement with Heidegger, shared by Emerson and Thoreau, is that the achievement of the human requires not inhabitation and settlement but abandonment, leaving. Then everything depends upon your realization of abandonment. For the significance of leaving lies in its discovery that you have settled something, that you have felt enthusiastically what there is to abandon yourself to, that you can treat the others there are as those to whom the inhabitation of the world can now be left. —Cavell, *SW* 138

What we have constructed is fate itself. That it never turns aside is merely what the word fate, or rather, Atropos, means. And we are not fated to it; *we* can turn. —Cavell, *SW* 97

In the first epigraph above, Emerson, in the encounter with limitations, points to a path toward recovery from loss. Cavell's rereading of Emerson helps us find an alternative way of living the life of polarity, and of living through limitations. In the third epigraph, though Cavell indeed mentions abandoning and leaving, he shifts the focus from the act of abandoning itself to that of crossing with its way beyond, considering "what there is to abandon yourself to." His reading of Emerson points us to a kind of antifoundationalism that does not dissolve boundaries.

Cavell reads Emerson from the perspective of "Emersonian Moral Perfectionism."[22] Echoing Emerson's statement from the "inmost" to the "outmost," Cavell's idea is of perfection without perfectibility—the idea that we are perfecting ourselves here and now, where this is inseparable from the perfection of society and culture. With regard to the self in perfection, Cavell writes: "'having' 'a' self is a process of moving to, and from nexts" (*CHU* 12). In this process, the way of perfecting is "not up but on," and the "goal" is decided by "nothing beyond the way of the journey itself" (*CHU* 10). As the term "perfection" connotes, however, this is still a kind of meliorism, here in tune with Emerson's American idea of forwardness.[23] This is similar to Arsić's Emersonian self in transition and in change. What matters to Cavell, however, is *the way* of perfecting and the fact that the attained self is always "a next, knotted" (CHU 12). It is at this juncture that our ways are being reoriented, by the critical point of turning (what he calls "aversion"), where we get into knots and then cut them. It is this poignant sense of going through difficulties, of wrestling with knots, and of "negation" that permeates Cavell's reading of Emerson—the sense of crossing boundaries, resisting the force posed by limits. The crucial point in Emerson's "Self-Reliance" lies in how the "attained" self relies on the "unattained/attainable" self, and in how, if we cannot manage it, we fall into a state of conformity, the "negation of the *position* [Emerson] calls for" (CHU 12). Cavell is attuned to the insistence in Emerson's remark that "[t]here is no middle way between, say, self-reliance and self-(or other-) conformity."[24] This points to a kind of dynamic oscillation, to a movement that never allows us to settle down, and hence acknowledges, perhaps broaches more directly, our deeper anxiety. Reading Emerson's "Experience," Cavell draws attention to the start of this path: our deeper condition of existence is the state of "loss"—the loss of where we stand.[25] "The recovery from loss is, in Emerson, as in Freud and in Wittgenstein, a finding of the world, a returning of it, to it" (TNUA 114). In this oscillation, we do not simply succumb to transition: we should never lose our own sense of finding where we stand. Cavell reads Emerson as inviting us to "find ourselves" and "ask where we are" (TNUA 89). This is Emerson's idea of *finding as founding* reconceived as perfectionism (CHU xxxiv). While Arsić asks us to choose between "standing" and "departing," stability and instability, Cavell says that it is not a matter of choosing one or the other: rather, it is a matter of accepting both. We need to revise our standing, our stance, the criteria of our judgment, testing them in the eyes of the other (Emerson's "friend"). The positionality of the self is the condition of its leaving. Between the sense that "you have settled something" and the sense that "you have felt enthusiastically what there is to abandon yourself to,"[26] there is a sense of standing on a border (SW 19).

What is crucial here is a certain sense of directionality in the process of perfection. What divides Cavell and Arsić in their respective readings of Emerson's idea of the person is Cavell's preservation of the idea of partiality. In the idea of the attained and the unattained self, Cavell says that we are, and our thinking is, "partial" (CHU 12). We do not simply become "somebody else": we have to be responsive and responsible to our partialness—to our not being whole and to our proclivities toward things. Self-abandonment cannot be equated with selflessness: dissolution of the self is not the disappearance of the self or the abrogation of its past. The autobiographical "I" is at stake.[27] Our growth, Cavell says, is both continuous and discontinuous (SW 135); the path of perfection is "discontinuous encirclings" (CHU xxxiv). In discussing Emerson's idea that thinking is partial and life is total, Cavell says: "In the opening two paragraphs of 'The American Scholar' it 'accepts' its topics in hope, and understands hope as a sign, in particular of 'an indestructible instinct,' yet an instinct that thinking must realize as 'something else'" (CHU 42).

It is this sense of partialness and the down-to-earth sense of instinct and taste (or Emerson's "whim")[28] that is the condition of achieving the path from the inmost to the outmost. Emerson says that if "the single man plant himself indomitably on his instincts, and there abide, the huge world will come round to him. Patience—patience" (CW 1:69). Whim is not a matter of whimsicality: rather it is a matter of authority. Anticipating Nietzsche, Emerson's idea can be reconceived as a philosophy of affirmation.[29] It is permeated by a sense of loss and despair, and by a sense of shame.[30]

Cavell also retains the sense of innerness that is pervasive in Emerson's text (and this is something that is covered over by Arsić's account of self-abandonment).[31] Emerson's text is permeated by the imagery of the inner eyes, a kind of standpoint (what Emerson calls the "private observatory" of the American Scholar [CW 1:62]) from which to observe the outer world.[32] This innerness is in a sense unapproachable: it is the singularity of the "single person" (CW 1:68), around which there hovers a sense of "solitude" (CW 1:57). While the Emerson of Buell and Arsić aspires to the cosmopolitan unity of selves (by blurring the boundary between the self and the other), Cavell detects and retains the sense of absolute separation in Emerson's text. It is this unapproachability, this sense of the knots in understanding others, that is at the heart of the idea of friendship in Emersonian perfectionism. As Cavell says of Thoreau's *Walden,* its "drift" is that "we *are* alone, *and* that we are never alone" (SW 80).

At the same time, impartiality is conditioned by partiality: there is no oneness to be achieved without partiality. This overturns the conventional reading of Emerson's idea of impartiality as a state of "selflessness" (the sense emphasized in the Japanese translation of Emerson's "impartiality").[33] And it resists Buell's view that "impersonality is 'depersonalized'" (E 169), the impersonal being associated with the "transpersonal" (E 237).[34] By contrast, in Cavell's reading, impartiality requires our own *interestedness.* Cavell interprets the idea of "unattachment," which Thoreau draws from the *Bhagavad Gita*, as inseparable from "interestedness."

> [The Bhagavad Gita's] doctrine of "unattachment," so far as I am able to make that out, is recorded in *Walden*'s concept of interestedness. (This is, to

my mind, one of Thoreau's best strokes. It suggests why "disinterestedness" has never really stabilized itself as a word meaning a state of impartial or unselfish interest, but keeps veering toward meaning the divestment of interest altogether, uninterestedness, ennui. Interestedness is already a state—perhaps the basic state—of relatedness to something beyond the self, the capacity for concern, for implication. It may be thought of as the self's capacity to mediate, to stand, between itself and the world.) (*SW* 117)

Paradoxically, the state of impartiality is conditioned by "interestedness." Emerson writes: "I see that when souls reach a certain clearness of perception they accept a knowledge and motive above selfishness" (*CW* 6:15).[35] Though he negates "selfishness," he does not say that therefore we should relinquish our own interest: it is "not personal nor impersonal."[36] In this sense alone, unity is *to be* achieved.[37]

Cavell's overturning of the relationship between partiality and impartiality, and their paradoxical coexistence, takes us further into his sense of the conversion of our thinking: thinking as passively active, or the passive force of thinking. (This Cavell calls "Emerson's most explicit reversal of Kant": it is seen in his "picturing the intellectual hemisphere of knowledge as passive or receptive and the intuitive or instinctual hemisphere as active or spontaneous" [*SW* 129].)[38] Along with Heidegger and Wittgenstein, Cavell says that the "establishing of thinking [is] knowing how to go on, being on the way, onward and onward" (*TNUA* 116). He calls this Emerson's "onward thinking" (*SW* 135)—a distinctive mode of antifoundationalist thinking, in which we are encouraged to ride on two horses on the way, the private and the public.[39] In reference to Emerson's remark, "A man must ride alternately on the horses of his private and his public nature" (*CW* 6:25), Cavell writes: "the human being is the being who *can* take a representative—public—stance, knows the (moral, objective) imperative," and also, "anyone can *claim* to be speaking on the part and interest of the universe and on the side of the Deity."[40] The representative, however, is not a priori: it is to be achieved on the way. Such onward movement requires thinking as suffering and patience (*PP* 115), not the negation of thinking. In order to live the polarity of life on the way, we need a dimension of *exceeding thought*—a way of thinking that exceeds any binary and that crosses borders. Redrawing the boundary between the inner and the outer, Cavell's idea of finding as founding shows us a different route to rebirth through cross*ing* and indicates a kind of radical power of recovery from within.

Change (call it self-transcendence) is a matter neither of the spiritual nor of the natural tout court: it is rather a distinctively *human* crisis (*SW* 43). Arsić writes that "[Cavell] tends to understand transfiguration in question as 'rhetorical.' . . . My interpretation differs from Cavell's in that instead of interpreting 'transfiguration' as a rhetorical gesture, I tend to see it as existential" (*OL* 336). It is this very binary thinking that divides language and existence that Cavell asks us to transcend. Cavell says that the transcendentalism of Emerson and Thoreau is underwritten by ordinary language philosophy (and, by implication, that language plays a crucial role in transcendence).[41] The way of transcendence is not immediate: it is mediated by language. A strong sense of interiority in Emerson's text is not an isolated individualism but a singularity of the self, different from solipsism. This is an innerness that is not enclosure (of the kind that Kitamura found in Emerson). Secrecy and privacy are already a part of linguistic practice, and in that sense alone they are *already* public. The interiority of the self is not a priori, but is something to be achieved, paradoxically, in participation in the language community. Emerson's way of confronting fate, his recoil from fate, is his writing, in every word (*PP* 25). Cavell is alert to the fact that it is the performative aspect of language—the way that to say something is to do something—that conversion takes place. And it is his idea of the projective nature of language that shows how language helps break through the limit.[42] Paul Standish explains this as follows: "there is something *projective* about language because the rule-following of language does not finally determine future usage but is always open to new development."[43] It is this risk-taking language that is at the heart of Cavell's and Thoreau's antifoundationalism. This is language that enables us to take a risk in uncertainty. It is through words that the prophetic drive of instinct and whim is to be tested by and experimented with. This is another aspect of Emerson's "onward thinking."

Taking a Chance: Cultural Criticism from Within

> Free should the scholar be—free and brave. Free even to the definition of freedom, "without any hindrance that does not arise out of his own constitution."
> —*CW* 1:63–64

> To say, "Follow me and you will be saved," you must be sure you are of God. But to say, "Follow in yourself what I follow in mine and you will be saved," you merely have to be sure you are following yourself. This frightens and cheers me.
> —Cavell, *SW* 160

Coming back to the original question concerning Emerson's aphorism, "the inmost in due time becomes the outmost," and to its cross-cultural implications: in what way is one to relate oneself to one's own culture, especially to one's relation with its boundary? Cavell's antifoundationalist reading of Emerson points us toward an idiosyncratic mode of cultural criticism: to think, to suffer, standing "on tiptoe" (*CW* 6:18) on a border between the inner and the outer. This is a way of living with limitations, without blurring or fusing boundaries, and it is the way of living in the polarity of fate and freedom. It requires one to respond to one's culture *from within.* One's own taste is a resource for the criticism of culture—*re*source as a source to be worked on, to be tested, and to be reoriented. (This is the relationship between Intuition and Tuition in Emerson's thought.) Our own partiality, our own taste, which is already embedded in culture, never dissipates.[44] There is no "cosmopolitan detachment," if by that is meant loss of interest, no withholding of one's stake in things. We are called upon to trust our own taste, with a hope that "in due time" it becomes the outmost, finding *some* "preestablished harmony." Here is the poignant sense, then, that there is no guarantee: it is only you who can achieve this. This is a hope for one's culture, where that culture is always still to be achieved.

America is "this new yet unapproachable" land: and this opens the thought of a Japan that is also still to be achieved, always with a rift within itself—between whim, on the one hand, and inheritance from the past and the limitations given by culture, on the other—a rift that can never be entirely closed. Emersonian perfectionism takes us away from the idea of *an* authentic culture and of *a* common humanity, understood as somehow preestablished. The common in Emersonian perfectionism is to be achieved "in due time," through encountering the uncommon within the common, and, that is, most importantly, encountering it within the inmost. In this sense, Emerson is more than anything—before being a cosmopolite[45]—*the American* Scholar, "Man Thinking," who is thoroughly engaged in cultural criticism from within, who confronts the fate of his culture. This is a cross-cultural reading of Emerson that is different from the one that is presented by Buell's "cross-cultural applicability of the individual" in his attempt to move beyond "Americanist readings of Emerson" (*E* 56): Buell emphasizes "Emerson's will to thrust beyond local, provincial, national contexts toward a mode of expression that could speak across the borders of place and time" (*E* 156). Cavell disturbs the very dichotomy of patriotism and cosmopolitanism. His is a search for a more thorough antifoundationalist idea of *becoming* cosmopolitan. Without a thorough criticism from within, without a confrontation with the cultures in which one finds oneself, there is no oneness to be achieved in this world. There is no "absolute hospitality" to others before we learn how to confront ourselves and our own cultures. Understanding *other* cultures, and for that matter, one's own, begins at home. There is no immediate fusion with the other, but only a gradual approaching, with endless gaps and mishaps on the way. This is why understanding another culture is always already mediated by language and why it is accompanied by the experience of translating one's mother tongue to what Thoreau calls the "father tongue."[46] Reengagement with language from within opens to this idea of translation. Translation here signifies more than the linguistic, more than the inter- or intralingual: it involves the translation of the human subject, understood now as inseparable from language and culture.

The idea of translation is crucially related to an antifoundationalist, transitional concept of the self, espoused by Cavell and Emerson—of ourselves always in translation. In Cavell's and Emerson's way of finding as founding, what is at stake is the moment of crossing borders and of conversion from negativity to affirmation (or, to borrow Cavell's reading of Thoreau, "from mourning to morning" [*TOS* 54]): this is a passage through crisis. One may wonder how such conversion can take place. Cavell, with Emerson, would reply that while criticism of culture is to be conducted from within, the test of its success cannot be known in advance: "power seems to be the result of rising, not the cause" (*SW* 136). Power is discovered on the way, perhaps after the event. In this provocative overturning of causal relationships, we need to expose ourselves to chance. To take a chance, however, does not mean to be at the mercy of contingency and to leave culture behind: rather it is to find culture's resourcefulness. Cultural criticism requires us "to confront the culture with itself, along the lines in which it meets in me" (*CR* 125). To take a chance is not to abrogate rules but to resuscitate the practice of rule-following, in a revision of the criteria for judgment. While placing in sharp focus the critical moment of departure, Cavell's Emersonian "onward thinking" highlights the critical moment of conversion, at the "threshold" and at the "crossroads" (*CR* 19), moving "from darkness to light" (*CR* 102).[47] Emersonian perfectionism is "a perspective from which it may be seen that with a small alteration of its structure, the world might be taken a small step—a half step—toward perfection."[48] There is no absolutely new beginning; we always begin anew, taking a chance. We need to learn to take risks in speaking, where risk implies not so much adventurous forward movement but rather a humble receptivity in action, involving suffering and patience. This is what Cavell means by the "power of passiveness—a power to demand the change of the world as a whole" (*TNUA* 115).

"One key, one solution," Emerson writes, "to the mysteries of human condition, one solution to the old knots of fate, freedom, and foreknowledge exists: the propounding, namely, of the double consciousness. A man must ride alternately on the horses of his private and his public nature" (*CW* 6:25). These birth-knots of new departure that I have considered suggest a way of reading and living with Emerson that is urgently needed today in Japan—the power of "Man Thinking," the person who is not fragile, but rather is resilient, who can exercise the power of thinking for recovery from loss.[49] This is also an alternative way of regaining a kind of innerness that is not seclusion, and of reclaiming the outer that does not dissolve the boundary. This is Cavell's American response to the question Sakabe raises about Emerson and Japan: "has Japan ever reached the point where it can discover the way to return to the outer again, starting with inner insight?" (73).[50]

Notes

1. John Dewey, "Emerson—The Philosopher of Democracy," in *The Middle Works of John Dewey*, 15 vols., ed. Jo Ann Boydston (Carbondale: Southern Illinois University Press, 1977), 3:184–92.

2. Megumi Sakabe, *Philosophy in the Turning Period: Japanese Modernity in the Turning Period* [in Japanese, my translation] (Tokyo: Minerva Sho-bo, 1999). Subsequent references to this work will be cited parenthetically in the text by page number.

3. John Dewey, "Creative Democracy—The Task before Us," in *The Later Works of John Dewey*, 17 vols., ed. Jo Ann Boydston (Carbondale: Southern Illinois University Press, 1988), 14:224–30.

4. Stanley Cavell, *The Senses of Walden* (Chicago: University of Chicago Press, 1992). Hereafter cited parenthetically in the text as SW.

5. Sakabe, *Philosophy in the Turning Period*, 68.

6. Yoshio Takanashi, an Emerson scholar, also points out that in the Meiji period and the Taisho period (1912–1926) Emerson was one of the most influential figures from the West who was read by the Japanese. Takanashi also points out that Kitamura shed light on the idealistic and transcendental aspects of Emerson as a poet. See Yoshio Takanashi, *The Formation of Emerson's Thought and Its Development: In Comparison with Zhu Xi's Confucius Doctrine* [in Japanese, my translation] (Tokyo: Kinseido, 2011), 50.

7. Lawrence Buell, *Emerson* (Cambridge, MA: Harvard University Press, 2003), 55. Hereafter cited parenthetically in the text as E.

8. Buell continues: "Suzuki's feeling for Emerson as a kindred spirit makes sense in terms of Suzuki's vision of Buddhism as taking different forms in different cultures but emerging in its highest form when 'the spirit and not the letter of the Buddha' is made central" (E 197).

9. Buell says: "a national ideology of personal or collective particularism suppresses Emerson's cosmic monism" (E 195).

10. In an exercise in comparative philosophy, Steve Odin discusses common ground between Stanley Cavell's Emersonian moral perfectionism, on the one hand, and Zen and Kitaro Nishida's ideas, on the other. See Steve Odin, "The Ordinary as Sublime in Cavell, Zen, and Nishida: Cavell's Philosophy of Education in East-West Perspective," in Naoko Saito and Paul Standish, eds., *Stanley Cavell and the Education of Grownups* (New York: Fordham University Press, 2012), 188–99.

11. Toshi Fujiwara, *No Man's Zone: Fukushima—The Day After* (Switzerland: Trigon-Film, 2012).

12. Masaki Horiuchi, "Looking Obliquely: 'Fate,' 'Nature,' 'Experience.'" *Studies in Henry David Thoreau* 38 (2012): 21–29.

13. "For though Fate is immense, so is Power, which is the other fact in the dual world, immense" (CW 6:12). "The revelation of Thought takes man out of servitude into freedom" (CW 6:14).

14. Stephen E. Whicher, introduction to *Selections from Ralph Waldo Emerson: An Organic Anthology* (Boston: Houghton Mifflin, 1957), xviii.

15. Sakamoto writes: "The private realm, as it is, is connected with the public, and to be true to one's own mind, as it is, is provided with universality." Masayuki Sakamoto, trans., *Collected Essays of Ralph Waldo Emerson* [in Japanese, my translation] (Tokyo: Iwanami, 1973), 376.

16. Branka Arsić, *On Leaving: A Reading in Emerson* (Cambridge, MA: Harvard University Press, 2010), 7–9. Hereafter cited parenthetically in the text as OL.

17. "As a stepping out of oneself, overleaping is about intense becomings or elevation" (OL 127).

18. "Emerson consistently advocated a cosmopolitics" (OL 250). She takes the view that "[c]osmopolitanism thus requires a process of existential transformations reflecting Emerson's ontology of becoming and psychology of a fluctuating personal identity" (OL 253).

19. "Emerson's politics were—certainly until 1850 but, as Buell persuasively argues, also after that—'decidedly antinationalist'" (OL 249).

20. "The point of [Emerson's] cross-border appeal in and beyond his own time is to underscore that his vision and standing were not reducicle to his 'Americanness'" (E 48).

21. "Similarly, because the self is the ethical response to its openness and receptivity, the idea of the impersonal doesn't contradict Stanley Cavell's understanding of moral perfectionism in Emerson as departing from and arriving to a self, thus as an activity essential to the 'criticism of democracy from within'" (OL 213).

22. Stanley Cavell, *Conditions Handsome and Unhandsome: The Constitution of Emersonian Perfectionism* (Chicago: University of Chicago Press, 1990). Hereafter cited parenthetically in the text as CHU.

23. "Fate involves the melioration. No statement of the Universe can have any soundness which does not admit its ascending effort. The direction of the whole and of the parts is toward benefit, and in proportion to the health. Behind every individual closes organization; before him opens liberty,—the Better, the Best" (CW 6:19).

24. Stanley Cavell, *Emerson's Transcendental Etudes*, ed. David Justin Hodge (Stanford, CA: Stanford University Press, 2003), 9.

25. Stanley Cavell, *This New Yet Unapproachable America: Lectures after Emerson after Wittgenstein* (Albuquerque, NM: Living Batch Press, 1989), 90; hereafter cited parenthetically in the text as TNUA. Cavell writes: "In a new world everything is to be lost and everything is to be found" (95); and "Emerson's notation of time that is necessary to contemporary experience . . . is the stepping from Old to New, matters of successions

that require conversion, and the aspiration of freedom, and discovery (arrivals, hence departures, abandonings)" (102).

26. This remark by Cavell echoes the following words of Emerson: "Every solid in the universe is ready to become fluid on the approach of the mind, and the power to flux it is the measure of the mind" (CW 6:23).

27. Stanley Cavell, *Little Did I Know: Excerpts from Memory* (Stanford, CA: Stanford University Press, 2010).

28. "I shun father and mother and wife and brother when my genius calls me. I would write on the lintels of the door-post, *Whim*. I hope it is somewhat better than whim at last, but we cannot spend the day in explanation" (CW 2:30).

29. Paul Standish, "Europe and Continental Philosophy," *Comparative Education* 40 (November 2004): 485–501.

30. Stanley Cavell, "Stanley Cavell in Conversation with Paul Standish," *Journal of Philosophy of Education* 46, no. 2 (2012): 155–76.

31. In his earlier writing on Emerson, Cavell is rather critical of Emerson's innerness in comparison to Thoreau's. In his view, Emerson "locates [an Over-soul], among other places, *within* the self, as a unity, or *the* Unity; and he leaves me the habitual spectator of my world. That is where Emerson is always stuck, with his sense, not his achievement, of outsideness, the yearning for the thing to happen to him" (SW 102).

32. "[T]he inward eye opens to the Unity in things, to the omnipresence of law" (CW 6:14).

33. Sakamoto, *Collected Essays of Ralph Waldo Emerson*, 209.

34. Buell sides with Kateb's interpretation of Emerson's "impersonal individuality" as meaning the individual devoid of personhood (E 65).

35. "'Tis the majesty into which we have suddenly mounted, the impersonality, the scorn of egotisms, the sphere of laws, that engage us" (CW 6:14). "Each pulse from that heart is an oath from the Most High" (CW 6:16).

36. "Let us build to the Beautiful Necessity, which makes man brave in believing that he cannot shun a danger that is appointed, nor incur one that is not; to the Necessity which rudely or softly educates him to the perception that there are no contingencies; that Law rules throughout existence; a Law which is not intelligent by intelligence;—not personal nor impersonal—it disdains words and passes understanding; it dissolves persons; it vivifies nature; yet solicits the pure in heart to draw on all its omnipotence" (CW 6:27).

37. "Let us build altars to the Blessed Unity which holds nature and souls in perfect solution, and compels every atom to serve an universal end" (CW 6:26).

38. "The power of passiveness—a power to demand the change of the world as a whole" (CHU 115).

39. This is from Emerson: "Man moves in all modes, by legs of horses, by wings of wind, by steam, by gas of balloon, by electricity, and stands on tiptoe threatening to hunt the eagle in his own element: There is nothing he will not make his carrier" (CW 6:18).

40. Stanley Cavell, *Philosophical Passages: Wittgenstein, Emerson, Austin, Derrida* (Oxford: Blackwell, 1995), 20, 22. Hereafter cited parenthetically in the text as PP.

41. Stanley Cavell, *Themes out of School: Effects and Causes* (Chicago: University of Chicago Press, 1984), 32. Hereafter cited parenthetically in the text as TOS.

42. Stanley Cavell, *The Claim of Reason: Wittgenstein, Skepticism, Morality, and Tragedy* (New York: Oxford University Press, 1979), 180–90. Hereafter cited parenthetically in the text as CR.

43. Paul Standish, "Education for Grown-Ups, a Religion for Adults: Skepticism and Alterity in Cavell and Levinas," *Ethics and Education* 2, no. 1 (March 2007): 85 (my italics).

44. In Emerson's words: "Let him hold his purpose as with the tug of gravitation. No power, no persuasion, no bribe shall make him give up his point" (CW 6:13).

45. Here is Arsić misreading the Cavellian idea of hospitality: "Emerson's idea of friendship is thus not only the 'the prize of democracy,' as Cavell suggested but is intrinsically organized by the values of radical democracy in the form of an absolute hospitality" (OL 191).

46. Henry David Thoreau, *Walden and Resistance to Civil Government*, ed. William Rossi (New York: Norton, 1992), 69.

47. Cavell's idea of taking a chance is different from Arsić's "take the leap," as the latter involves a complete destruction of the self (OL 127).

48. Stanley Cavell, *A Pitch of Philosophy: Autobiographical Exercises* (Cambridge, MA: Harvard University Press), 50.

49. "Of two men, each obeying his own thought, he whose thought is deepest will be the strongest character" (CW 6:15).

50. I thank Paul Standish for invaluable suggestions and help in the preparation of this chapter.

[13]

NEAL DOLAN AND LAURA JANE WEY

EMERSON AND CHINA

IT IS A MEASURE of the spiritual breadth of Emerson's writing that it overlaps significantly with no fewer than four major strains of Chinese culture and history. Scholars have already established resonances between Emerson's work and each of the three major Chinese religio-cultural traditions—Taoism, Buddhism, and Confucianism. And in ways as yet unexplored, Emerson's writing also bears on the lurching course of Chinese political and social history in the twentieth and twenty-first centuries. In the pages that follow we will first briefly revisit the three broad religio-cultural connections in the order of their increasing importance to Emerson, drawing in part on others' published scholarship. We will then take up the modern political-historical links at more length, drawing on Dolan's work on Emerson's liberalism[1] and Wey's research on Chinese consumption of Western literature in the Republican era. In conclusion, we will reflect on all of these connections together, asking what they may tell us about the international reach and limitations of Emersonian liberal culture.

Ironically, the Chinese religio-cultural tradition about which Emerson knew least was the one with which his work had most in common.[2] Taoism is the oldest of China's three great traditions, but its principal text, the *Tao Te Ching,* was not published in English until 1891, almost a decade after Emerson's death. There is nonetheless a striking range of broad similarities between the major emphases of Taoism and Emersonian thought. Both are fundamentally characterized by a privatistic inward turn away from public, political, institutional spheres of activity. "Your inner being guard and keep it free," Lao Tze wrote—words that could serve as a coda to Emerson's opus as a whole.[3] Both Taoists and Emersonians give clear priority to the individual over society and established authority. Both emphasize simplicity and naturalness of behavior over the formalities of social deference or condescension. Both find in nature an imminent source of ecstatic self-renewal and transformation—inner metamorphoses that they verbally enact in evocative and sometimes cryptic poetic language. And both take nature's organic, unforced, seemingly effortless doing as a model for noncoercive but efficacious human endeavor. In *The Tao of Emerson* Richard Grossman goes so far as to correlate each verse of the *Tao Te Ching* with lines taken from Emerson's works, and the resonances are many, and striking. "The highest excellence is like that of water," wrote Lao Tze in the sixth century BC. "The true order of nature," Emerson wrote almost 2,500 years later, "beholds the visible as proceeding from the invisible. The rushing stream will not stop to be observed."[4]

Emerson's relationship to Buddhism was not so uniformly affirmative. He never counseled radical asceticism or complete withdrawal from the world. He overtly rejected what he regarded as Buddhist pessimism, and in his journals he confessed fear in relation to the Buddhistic concept of cosmic emptiness.[5] But one need only recall the famous "transparent eye-ball" passage from *Nature*—"I am nothing; I see all; . . . I am part or particle of God" (*CW* 1:10)—to recognize that there is an important place in Emerson's work for a conception of self-emptying as a means to intimate contact with a universe understood as divine. In *Emerson and Zen Buddhism,* John G. Rudy provides a powerful account of "the meditative dynamics of spiritual emptiness" in numerous Emerson writings stretching from "The Lord's Supper" (1832), to *Nature* (1836), "Literary Ethics" (1838), "Experience" (1844), "The Poet" (1844), "Nominalist and Realist" (1844), "Fate" (1860), and "Worship" (1860).[6] Like the Zen masters, Rudy points out, Emerson taught reliance on one's own consciousness as a means to a kind of spiritual enlightenment. But like the Zen masters, Rudy stresses, Emerson also taught that the full realization of the capacities of the individual consciousness required the repeated breaking down of the ever-ossifying formation most conventionally equated with individual selfhood—the calculating, controlling ego. Rudy illustrates by close readings how reiterated variants of this process of self-dissolution frequently provided the principal subject of Emerson's best enraptured prose. The result, he suggests, for Emerson as for the Zennists, was the transcendence of conventional binaries and dualities in favor of an all-embracing apprehension and acceptance of a vast reality. Thus, although equally focused on the individual, neither Zen nor Emerson aimed at the consolidation of a stable selfhood defensively set off against the mutable world. Both sought rather a radically open, alert, flexible and fluid consciousness joyfully immersed in the "stream of Being."[7]

By contrast to Taoism and Buddhism, Confucianism has an explicit and substantial presence both in Emerson's notebooks and in his published writing. It has long been accepted that this presence was initially established in

1836, when Emerson first read Joshua Marshman's translation of Confucius's voluminous *Lun-gnee*.[8] Clearly taken with Marshman's terse epigrammatic renderings, Emerson copied many into his journals, and they regularly found their way into his writings from *Essays: Second Series* (1844) forward. But Frederic Carpenter, in his *Emerson and Asia* (1930), does not give these Confucian motifs in the later work formative importance, suggesting that Emerson used them "externally"—as illustrations of his own already-established moral emphases.[9] Certainly Emerson found the Confucian sense of a moral law discernible in nature directly compatible with his own similar Christian/Platonic conception. And in part he seems to have employed corroborating Confucian formulations in a strategy of rhetorical refreshment by estrangement: he hoped that readers overly familiar with classical and Christian strictures regarding obedience to the moral law might pay more attention to the same basic idea as voiced or embodied by a storied pagan sage.[10] Indeed, the persistent presence of Confucius in Emerson's later writing should serve to remind contemporary scholars of the centrality and pervasiveness of the idea of virtue in Emerson's work as a whole—a fact easy to overlook in part because Emerson himself seems to take the concept so much for granted. Whatever else he may have meant to Emerson, Confucius undoubtedly symbolized a secular devotion to virtue. Emerson was also clearly powerfully drawn to the Confucian ideal of the scholar as engaged in moral no less than in intellectual self-cultivation. And he shared with Confucius a sense that the scholar's personally exemplary ethical refinement provided the best model for the moral renovation of the state.

Such threefold resonances between Emersonian thought and Chinese tradition inevitably raise the question of influence. Surely these parallels cannot be entirely fortuitous and contingent. Surely the later Western writer derived some of his thinking from the earlier Eastern texts. But with regard to Taoism, the translation of the *Tao Te Ching* after Emerson's death rules out the possibility of direct influence. With regard to Buddhism, it is true that Emerson had acquired some historical knowledge from reading Eugene Burnouf's *Introduction a l'histoire du Buddhism indien* (1844). But he had already begun his remarkable verbal enactments of self-emptying in *Nature* some eight years before, and the dynamics of meditative consciousness traced by Rudy throughout Emerson's opus run too deep to have been derived in any way from Bernouf's historical overview.

Only in the case of Confucianism is there any possibility of consequential influence, but even here it is doubtful. Very recently Kyle Simmons has argued that Emerson encountered and seriously engaged Confucius much earlier than hitherto believed—in 1830, in Rémusat's *L'invariable milieu*, a French translation of the Confucian work *Chung Yeng* (usually translated in

English as "The Golden Medium" or "The Doctrine of the Mean").[11] Simmons attributes decisive importance to this encounter for the development of Emerson's thought as a whole. He claims that Emerson derived from Confucius the idea of virtue as action in accordance with the order of nature—a core notion of *Nature* (1836), "The American Scholar" (1837), and "The Divinity School Address" (1838). And thereafter, Simmons asserts, this and other Confucian ideas "operate[d] within the fabric of Emerson's writing and thought process."[12] Simmons is certainly correct about the importance of this idea of virtue to Emerson's thought as a whole: it is foundational and pervasive. But he fails to consider other more likely sources. The idea is central, for one, to Platonic ethics, and the presumption must go to Plato not only because of Emerson's early and extensive reading of works such as *The Republic*, but also because of Emerson's immersion in a long tradition of Western moral philosophy shaped by the same Platonic conception. This is not entirely to dismiss the importance to Emerson of Confucius's vivid formulations, but rather to suggest that they functioned, more or less as Carpenter suggested, as a valuable non-Western reinforcement of an idea Emerson had already absorbed from Western sources.

But the question then remains: how does one account for the broader congruencies between Emerson and the Chinese traditions? The absence of direct influence only makes the question more intriguing. Pure coincidence seems unlikely, given the extent of agreement. And yet in this postmetaphysical moment, one is also reluctant to go to the opposite extreme and accept the metaphysical answer that Lao Tze, Confucius, Plato, and Emerson himself would all readily have given: their ideas overlap because they are all equally accurately grounded in an absolute and unitary transhistorical truth accessible by reason properly understood.

A more pragmatic middle ground is offered in a different but pertinent context by John Rawls's conception of the "overlapping consensus." In an effort to explain how a contemporary multicultural liberal polity may accommodate a variety of "comprehensive doctrines" (religious or philosophical teachings about the nature of reality and concomitant human values), Rawls suggests that at a very high level of abstraction it will be possible to identify a small set of common or "overlapping" values or norms on which members of all particular cultural traditions might reasonably agree for the purposes of peaceable and fair coexistence. There need be no comprehensive claim for the ultimate validity of these values, Rawls stresses, but rather only a pragmatic political agreement that they satisfactorily express and protect the fundamental rights and interests of a large and diverse group of human beings with a variety of metaphysical commitments.[13] With Rawls's idea in mind, it becomes possible to suggest that the broad confluences we have noted between Emerson and the three strains of Chinese tradition indicate not metaphysical equivalence but rather a possible site of what one might call global overlapping consensus. It might test our historical optimism, but it need not flout our skepticism to entertain the possibility that thinkers so searching and expressive as Lao Tze, the Buddha, the Zen masters, Confucius, and Emerson happened separately upon what turn out to be overlapping human needs for inner freedom, disciplined self-cultivation, and some form of ecstatic contact with being.

For Emerson himself, in any case, such a historically and geographically far-flung consensus was not impossible to imagine. As early as 1830 and 1831, he had encountered ambitious semi-systematic attempts to construct such syntheses in the works of Joseph de Gerando and Victor Cousin. "[W]ith Gerando and with all of his reading henceforward," Robert Richardson notes, "[Emerson] was looking for traces of the momentary outbreaks of reason—these flashings forth of the intuitive truth, as Melville called them—down through history. And already he was recognizing his own ideas reflected back to him in the ideas of Confucius, Pythagoras, and Heraclitus."[14] Twelve years later, Emerson and Thoreau conceived the "Ethnical Scriptures" section of *The Dial* in a similarly ecumenical liberal spirit. They published excerpted translations from foundational religio-cultural texts from around the globe, including works such as the Hindu *Laws of Menu,* the Persian *Desatir,* and, to be sure, the teachings of Confucius (April 1843), the *Chinese Four Books* (October 1843), and the sayings of Buddha (January 1844).[15] Of course, Emerson did not himself use Rawls's term "overlapping consensus" in providing a rationale for this feature, but he evoked a strikingly analogous procedure of gathering, abstracting, and discovering common ground: "Each nation has its bible more or less pure. . . . None has yet been willing or able in a wise and devout spirit to collate its own worth with those of other nations, and sinking the civil-historical and ritual portions, to bring together the grand expressions of the moral sentiment in different ages and races."[16] It is worth recalling here that it was the prompting of this same universal moral sentiment that led Emerson just two years later, in 1844, to begin to speak out publicly against slavery. In this case such pragmatic historical "collation" provided sufficient foundation for the vision of a liberal culture at once morally principled and inclusive.

For Emerson, the global overlapping consensus had a temporal dimension as well. His earliest notebooks from his time as an undergraduate at Harvard show him absorbing chapter and verse of the Whig sense of history that was standard fare at American universities in the nineteenth century until the Civil War. On this view, human history as a whole was unfolding in the direction of universal freedom. Freedom was conceived in liberal terms as the individual right to think, speak, publish one's ideas, travel, worship, work, trade, participate in self-governance, congregate socially, and own property as one chose. The relative security of these freedoms (for white males) in the Western world was understood to be the result of an epic sequence of historical events that in various ways helped to establish and preserve boundaries between the individual and the state—events as remote in time as the emergence of Hebrew prophecy and the advent of classical Greek rationalism, or as relatively recent as the Protestant Reformation and the English, American, and French Revolutions.

There remained a providential cast and a decidedly Western bias to this narrative, from neither of which Emerson was entirely free, even as it became increasingly secularized over the course of the nineteenth century. But in editorial efforts such as the excerpting of "Ethnical Scriptures" in *The Dial* or in the many instances in his writing where Emerson makes reference to non-Western sages such as Confucius or Zoroaster, it becomes clear that he had adapted the Whig metanarrative to a form more global in scope and ecumenical in spirit. For Emerson, the ineluctable advance of freedom and reason in history, as signaled by the ancient wisdom literature of all cultures no less than by democratic revolutions or recently proliferating scientific discoveries, was, in principle, carrying all peoples forward in its tide.

"The revolution is the work of no man," Emerson declared of the American Civil War in "Fortune of the Republic" (1863), "but the eternal effervescence of nature. It never did not work. . . . It is elemental. It is the old gravitation" (*AW* 153). There is undoubtedly an element of cosmic determinism in these sentences, as if Emerson, like Hegel, saw progress as somehow providentially built into the nature of things. But it is also not insignificant that the force Emerson evokes here moves up from the depths rather than down from on high. He goes on to say that "a revolution is a volcano, and from under everybody's feet flings its sheet of fire into the sky" (*AW* 153). It is true that here as elsewhere in his work, Emerson writes about progress in part as if it were determined from beyond, from a metaphysical point beyond human agency. But the language of eruption and effervescence also opens to the more secular possibility that progress might push its way up democratically from below. "In each new threat of faction," Emerson notes in these paragraphs, "the ballot of the people has been beyond expectation right and decisive" (*AW* 152). Thus, he raises the possibility that progress may work more in the manner of Lao Tze's waters wearing away the stone—that the gradual democratic emancipation of universally legitimate human interests must in time undermine long-entrenched structures of ignorance, exploitation and subjugation.

Emerson's commitment to a liberal sense of history initially bred hostility in his mind toward China. "Hang the Celestial Empire! I hate Pekin [*sic*]," the twenty-one-year-old Emerson wrote in one of his first notebooks—at the same time as he was transcribing his undergraduate teachers' accounts of the classic episodes of the history of liberty (*JMN* 2:228). To this progressive outlook China was principally an antithetical, conservative other—collectively locked since time immemorial in an exploitative feudal-aristocratic system rendered unchangeable by elaborate culturally inculcated rituals of deference. In time, as we have seen, Emerson's antipathy was counterbalanced to some extent by his interest in Confucius, though some aversion remained with Emerson throughout his life. Even in the very late 1863 speech "Fortune of the Republic," quoted immediately above, Emerson refers disparagingly to "Chinese conservatism" and "Chinese . . . servility to wealth" (*AW* 147, 141). But things have changed dramatically in "Pekin" since 1863—indeed, even since 1963. Evidence of significant interest in Emerson in contemporary China raises questions not only as to how Emerson's work has generally been received there in the twentieth century, but also as to how Emerson might have regarded twentieth- and twenty-first-century China in turn.[17] To essay some preliminary answers to those questions, we will turn first to two important figures from the Republican period before concluding with an Emersonian-Whig comment on the contemporary, post-Mao moment.

The writings of two important thinkers from the Chinese Republican period, Hu Shi (1891–1962) and Li Dazhao (1888–1927), clearly indicate that they read and thought about the works of Emerson. Both wielded considerable influence over the intellectual life of the young nation during the early years of the Republic as it attempted to navigate its way through a sea of turmoil, uncertainty, and opportunity. Li was one of the founding figures of Chinese communism; Hu was the preeminent scholar-thinker of the liberal-leaning elite. Despite their clashing philosophies, perhaps in part owing to the shared but unconscious influence of Taoism, both men seemed to have found inspiration in Emerson's insistence on the individual's prerogative—and, indeed, duty—to forge his or her own path forward, rather than follow the dictates of social norms, arcane traditions, and other such human institutions.

Hu Shi's reflections about Emerson appear in the journal he kept during the years he studied in the United States. In several scattered entries between spring of 1911—half a year before China became a republic—and fall of 1915, we learn that Hu read Emerson's essays[18] and "some dozen pages" of his 1836–38 journals.[19] Because of the informal and often fragmentary nature of these entries, we have to cobble them together to get a picture of what Hu thought of Emerson. There is no doubt that Hu held Emerson in the highest estimation: he regards Emerson as "the greatest thinker of this nation [America],"[20] and, in a poem written for a friend beginning his studies at Harvard, Hu asks his friend to visit Concord to pay homage to Emerson on Hu's behalf.[21] But exactly what does Hu find admirable about Emerson? We will look at several passages that give us some insight into how Hu read Emerson's work.

With the exception of his brief commentary on several quotes from Confucius's *Analects* that Emerson recorded in his journals,[22] as well as non-specific praise for the "insightfulness" of Emerson's essay "Friendship,"[23] Hu does not address any particular piece of Emerson's writing; instead, he writes about what he perceives to be the overarching tenets of Emerson's philosophy as a whole. According to Hu, Emerson held the lifelong belief that "between heaven and earth, everywhere there is truth; in each hill and valley, each flower and bird, natural law resides." Here we find ourselves again at a site of overlapping consensus, as it is entirely unclear whether Hu is in fact characterizing Emerson here or merely projecting Confucius. That either could be the case confirms the degree of commonality between the two sages. From whichever source it is derived, Hu's evocation of "truth" and "natural law" is significant in that it implies the existence of a moral order independent of human laws and traditions, an order as permanent, immutable, and "true" as the universe itself. Such an order, although in itself neither in favor of nor against tradition, offers ample justification for breaking away from entrenched practices and institutions—a point the Whig historians regularly made regarding the liberal implications of Stoicism and Christian natural law. It is thus no surprise that the young Hu, with his progressive agenda, might find such a concept appealing. Whether he in fact derived the idea from Emerson, Confucius, Taoism or some overlap thereof, Hu was able to use the critical leverage afforded by the idea of natural law to denounce positive laws promoting widow suicide as "barbaric and cruel,"[24] to advocate a total overhaul of traditional funereal ritual,[25] and to spearhead a literary revolution that transformed writing style from the classical to the vernacular.[26]

What is left unexplained in Hu's redaction of Emerson's thought in the previous quotation is: how does one access this "natural law"? Hu explains this in a separate journal entry: "The gist of [Emerson's] philosophy is that everything between heaven and earth exists within the self; the self is the source of both good and evil. If [good and evil] lie within, why seek them without? All that a human being should seek is self-knowledge. Heaven (God) is in the hearts of men; why search for Him elsewhere?"[27] Here Hu iterates a key facet of Emersonian philosophy: namely, the central, absolute, and irreplaceable role played by the individual in accessing natural law.

"Heaven," traditionally the highest authority in Chinese cosmology, and one that Hu identifies with the Judeo-Christian God, becomes as it were subsumed in "the hearts of men," thus making the latter, rather than the former, the custodians of the universe and its incorruptible principles. This placement of the individual ahead of all traditional forms of authority further empowers the individual to discover new ways of navigating his or her circumstances and makes independent thought not merely a choice, but a necessity.

What Hu has omitted in his formulation of the relationship between the individual and natural law is that for Emerson, reason is the faculty by which every individual has access to natural law. Emerson conceives of reason as intuitive and holistic rather than purely scientific and empirical. It is impossible to tell whether Hu grasped Emerson's concept of reason and, if so, what he thought of it. But we do know that Hu, even as he passionately advocates a "scientific" (as opposed to a superstitious or mythical) approach to the world, understands the limitations of science in the realm of human affairs: "We tried to answer everything through science; but how should we unravel [the question of] life now? . . . Each person has his or her own approach; but one must be scientific in one's method, spirit and attitude," he writes in his essay "A Scientific View of Life."[28] Implicit in the statement is the acknowledgment that, while one should use one's reason in searching out the meaning of life (assuming that there is one), one cannot expect science to empirically provide an answer. While Hu in all likelihood derived this notion from his mentor, the pragmatist John Dewey, rather than Emerson, a parallel can be traced between it and Emerson's idea of reason. Yet again Hu's formulations carry overlapping resonances from Taoism and Confucius as well as Emerson.

If one sees little incongruity between Hu Shi's broadly liberal outlook and Emerson's philosophy, the same cannot be said of Li Dazhao. Emerson's influence on the future Communist was passing, occurring during a time when Li was sifting through the ideas of dozens of Western thinkers in search of his own creed;[29] it is nevertheless worth investigating which aspects of Emerson's thought appealed to Li.

In his well-known 1916 essay, "Spring," and again in a much shorter 1918 essay titled "Today," Li borrows identical lines that he attributes to Emerson: "If you love eternity, then you should love the present. Yesterday can no longer be recalled, and tomorrow is yet uncertain; today is the only thing you have a sure grasp on. One today is worth two tomorrows."[30] Li is almost certainly paraphrasing Emerson here, or translating from a Japanese version of the text, as we are unaware of the existence of a passage resembling it in Emerson's works. The unapologetic celebration of the present over both the past and the future is certainly plausibly Emersonian, echoing lines such as, "Whenever a mind is simple, and receives a divine wisdom, old things pass away,—means, teachers, texts, temples fall; it lives now, and absorbs past and future into the present hour" (*CW* 2:38). But the contexts in which each author expresses this celebration of the present are vastly different; indeed, the ultimate point of "Spring" could not be more antithetical to Emerson's core beliefs.

The title of "Spring" plays on the double entendre of nature's annual rebirth and youth. Li cleverly manages a series of equations and interchanges to align the fortunes of a new ("young") China reborn from its eons-old, "decaying" self with the actions of a new generation of Chinese "youths." In the essay, Li makes use of affective inspiration far more than rational discourse to make the argument that the individual can achieve a sort of never-ending life through committing oneself to an ever-evolving, ever-rebirthing greater self; this greater self is often figured as a nation or a people, but at moments expands to include all humanity: "Youths . . . upon the basis of reason further bolstered by hard work, should forge forward without a backward glance, turning their backs on darkness and looking instead toward the light to advance the civilization of the world and forge the happiness of humankind. Out of one's own youth [one should] build a youthful family, a youthful country, a youthful people, a youthful humankind, a youthful Earth, a youthful Universe, through which one enjoys boundless life."[31]

The youthful "now" (as opposed to the ancient past) is infinitely important in Li's estimation because the inspired labors of the present moment are what make it possible for one to yoke one's individual self to the greater self; it is the all-too-fleeting opportunity to win immortality—"boundless life"—for both selves. The final goal of Li's affirmation of the value of the present is therefore political; "now" is the best moment to mobilize, to strive toward the building of a better society, or country, or universal brotherhood—a community for sure, whatever the scale. The contrast with Emerson could not be greater, as in Emerson's philosophy, the "present hour" signifies the individual's extreme freedom from all dependencies past and future, including freedom even from the obligation to adhere to one's past selves. That Li's endgame in "Spring" is ultimately collective betterment rather than individual realization puts him starkly at odds with Emerson, whose view of social solidarity is at best skeptical: "Society everywhere is in conspiracy against the manhood of every one of its members" (*CW* 2:29).

There are certainly moments in Li's writing where he stresses the importance of individual thought and action, typically in discussions about the notion of truth. For example, in a 1917 essay, "The Authority of Truth," Li writes: "If my words correspond to truth, then even though the society of the time wouldn't listen to my words, and offers me no place in it, because of my love for truth I would not dare mince my words in order to please such a society. If my words are a betrayal of truth, then even though the society of the time welcomes my words, and holds me in esteem, because of my love for truth I would not dare to endorse and flatter in order to cater to such a society."[32] The main point—that individuals must hold fast to the "truth" they have determined for themselves without allowing society to sway them—can certainly be construed as a strong statement about the individualistic basis of free thought. Both Maurice Meisner and Wu Hanquan identify Emerson as the source of Li's thought here.[33] While that may be the case, it is nevertheless worth pointing out that Li has made his own adaptations to Emerson's concept of individual thought. There is, once again, little sense that Li perceives society as being fundamentally detrimental to the independence of individual thought. The individual's perception of truth is never for one moment threatened in Li's hypothetical scenario; what is at risk is merely his advancement in a potentially hostile environment.

To sum up, for Li Dazhao, Emerson's celebration of individualism is a powerful tool for making a break with the problem-ridden institutions and traditions of the past. But Li has little interest in pursuing Emerson's thought anywhere beyond that. He does not share Emerson's mistrust of human aggregates; for him, there are institutions that do not work, and those that do, and his goal is simply to build one that does, with whatever tools are at his disposal.

In the short run of twentieth-century Chinese history one might say that Li's misreading of Emerson prevailed over Hu's more accurate one. The horrifying details of Mao's catastrophic programs of economic and cultural collectivization are familiar and need not be spelled out at length here. It is sufficient to quote John King Fairbank on "The Great Leap Forward": "In 1958–1960 some 20 to 30 million people lost their lives because of the policies imposed upon them by the Chinese Communist Party. Measured by the statistics showing an increase of mortality, this was one of the greatest of human disasters."[34] And on "The Cultural Revolution": "So pervasive was the cataclysm, directly involving something like 100 million people, that its full history is still far from known or written."[35] But in the longer run, some preliminary liberal regard for the individual has emerged in Chinese economic life, with beneficial effects almost as astounding as the negative effects of Maoism. "Official government estimates," Fairbank reports, "indicate that China had 250 million people living in poverty in 1978; the figure had declined to around 30 million by 2005."[36] In all the annals of history there is perhaps no starker illustration of the validity of the liberal preference for individual liberty and spontaneous order over centralized governmental planning and control than the story of China since 1949. As Emerson put it in "Experience," which is in part an account of his own emancipation from his personal psycho-epistemological compulsion to try to dominate the world, "Nature hates calculators; her methods are saltatory and impulsive . . . for practical success, there must not be too much design" (CW 3:39). But as inheritors of Taoism, Buddhism, and of aspects of Confucianism, the Chinese need not take such wisdom from Emerson. They will find it in the spaces of an emerging global culture in which the truths of liberalism and the truths of their own great traditions will overlap, counterbalance, and correct one another.

Notes

1. Neal Dolan, *Emerson's Liberalism* (Madison: University of Wisconsin Press, 2009).

2. Frederic Ives Carpenter confirms this in an early book-length study of Emerson's work in relation to Asia: *Emerson and Asia* (Cambridge, MA: Harvard University Press, 1930): " . . . it is striking that he never seems to have come in contact with Taoism—a philosophy which would doubtless have been more congenial to him than that of Confucius"; and Qian Mansu makes the same point in "Emerson and China: Reflections on Individualism" (Ph.D. diss., Harvard University, 1992): "It is unfortunate that we shall never have Emerson's response to Taoism, a philosophy much closer to Transcendentalism than Confucianism" (81).

3. Quoted in Lao Tze and Richard Grossman, *The Tao of Emerson: The Wisdom of the Tao Te Ching as Found in the Works of Ralph Waldo Emerson* (New York: Modern Library, 2007), 12.

4. Ibid., 18, 31.

5. "This remorseless Buddhism lies all around, threatening with death and night. . . . Every thought, every enterprise, every sentiment, has its ruin in this horrid infinite which circles us and awaits our dropping into it" (JMN 7:474).

6. John G. Rudy, *Emerson and Zen Buddhism* (Lewiston, NY: Edwin Mellen Press, 2001), 18.

7. Ibid.

8. Carpenter, *Emerson and Asia,* 233; Robert D. Richardson, Jr., *Emerson: The Mind on Fire* (Berkeley: University of California Press, 1995), 220.

9. Carpenter, *Emerson and Asia,* 234.

10. Qian Mansu makes this point in "Emerson and China: Reflections on Individualism."

11. Kyle Bryant Simmons, "Emerson, the American Confucius: A Consideration of Confucian Motifs in the Early Writings of Ralph Waldo Emerson (1830–43)" (Ph.D. diss., University of Texas at Dallas, 2013), http://gradworks.umi.com.

12. Ibid., 19.

13. See John Rawls, *Political Liberalism* (New York: Columbia University Press, 1993), 131–72.

14. Richardson, *Emerson,* 104–5.

15. Ibid., 378–79.

16. *Dial* (July 1842): 82; quoted in Richardson, *Emerson,* 379.

17. A search under "Emerson, Ralph Waldo" on Project Yao, a database jointly administered by Iowa State University, Arizona State University, and Sichuan University that keeps track of Chinese translations of American works of literature, turns up some sixty different editions of Emerson's works, nearly forty of them published since 2000; China Academic Journals, the largest online database of liberal arts and social sciences publications in China, lists more than four hundred journal articles on the subject of Emerson, more than three hundred of them published since 2000.

18. Hu Shi, *Hu Shi liuxue riji*, 2nd ed. (Taipei: Taiwan Commercial Press, 1969) 28, 66 (April 30 and August 17, 1911).

19. Ibid., 280–81 (July 5, 1914).

20. Ibid., 383 (September 13, 1914).

21. Ibid., 783–85 (September 17, 1915).

22. Ibid., 280–81 (July 5, 1914).

23. Ibid., 28 (April 30, 1911).

24. Hu Shi, *Da yuzhou zhong tan boai*, ed. Qiu Sang (Beijing: Dongfang chubanshe, 1998), 89.

25. Ibid., 92–104.

26. Ibid., 218–29.

27. Hu, *Liuxue riji*, 383 (September 13, 1914).

28. Hu, *Da yuzhou*, 188.

29. Maurice Meisner, *Li Ta-chao and the Origins of Chinese Marxism* (Cambridge, MA: Harvard University Press, 1967), 20–21.

30. Li Dazhao, "Qingchun," in *Li Dazhao xuanji* (Beijing: Renmin chubanshe, 1959), 74; also "'Jin,'" *Li Dazhao xuanji*, 93.

31. Li, "Qingchun," 76.

32. Li Dazhao, "Zhenli zhi quanwei," in *Li Dazhao xuanji*, 86–87.

33. Meisner, *Li Ta-chao and the Origins of Chinese Marxism,* 36–37; Wu Hanquan, "Shilun Aimosheng dui Li Dazhao zaoqi sixiang de yingxiang," *Guizhou jiaoyu xueyuan xuebao* 3 (1998): 75–76.

34. John King Fairbank and Merle Goldman, *China: A New History* (Cambridge, MA: Harvard University Press, 2006), 368.

35. Ibid., 383.

36. Ibid., 406.

[14]

MATHEW A. FOUST

CONFUCIUS AND EMERSON ON THE VIRTUE OF SELF-RELIANCE

Was there ever a thinker more at odds with Confucius? Self-reliance! What an idea.

—Gish Jen[1]

RECORDS FROM THE BOSTON ATHENAEUM show that R.W. Emerson borrowed Joshua Marshman's *The Works of Confucius: Containing the Original Text with a Translation* from February 16 to March 1, 1836.[2] Excerpts from Emerson's journals, written days later, reveal the impression that Confucius made on Emerson, with dozens of "Sentences of Confucius" quoted. In 1843, upon further contact with Confucius via David Collie's complete translation of *The Four Books*, Emerson again quoted Confucius prolifically in his journals, professing his admiration of the great sage.[3] In 1863, Emerson continued his study of the Confucian classics, reading James Legge's translation of the *Confucian Analects, the Great Learning, and the Doctrine of the Mean*, again extensively excerpting sayings from Confucius in his journals.[4] Despite this clear connection, only passing attention has been paid to the Confucian influence on Emerson's thought.[5] This chapter is an effort to remedy this deficiency in the scholarship.

To set the stage for this comparative analysis, I echo the observation of Egbert S. Oliver: "The United States in the 1830s and 1840s, after a generation of friendly and extended trade relations with the Orient, gradually became aware of the intellectual, spiritual, and literary values of the ancient cultures of Asia. Ralph Waldo Emerson, a young minister, lecturer, and thinker, who was settling in the 1830s in Concord, Massachusetts, to devote himself to a life as 'man-thinking,' is probably the most important American illustrating that impact."[6] In Oliver's estimation, "Emerson came at a momentous time in world history, when the East and the West were awakening to a realization that each needed the other, when the old nations of the Orient were opening their doors to commerce in materials of usefulness and beauty and to the intercommunication of intellect and spirit. Emerson was one of the first Americans to venture into the literature of Asia and absorb it sufficiently to be an early interpreter."[7] While Emerson's interest in Asian thought germinated with his engagement of Indian Hindu texts in the 1820s, as David Weir recently corroborates, "the 1840s is the decade when Emerson's Asiatic enthusiasms seem to have been most intense."[8]

The best-known book-length treatment of Emerson's venturing, absorption, and interpretation of the literature of Asia is Frederic Ives Carpenter's *Emerson and Asia* (1930). While much is to be gleaned from Carpenter's study, especially concerning Emerson's contact with sacred texts of India, I challenge Carpenter's assertion that with respect to Chinese philosophers, Emerson "never actually incorporated their thought into his own writing, but merely quoted the sayings of Confucius, Mencius, and the rest, externally, as illustrations of his ideas."[9] I am thus more aligned with Arthur Christy, who writes in *The Orient in American Transcendentalism* (1963), "The Confucian, or Chinese, parallel is to be found in Emerson's ethical writings."[10] I contend that Emerson's conception of self-reliance as a virtue in the essay "Self-Reliance" (1841) bears striking resemblance to the ways in which self-reliance is conceived and emphasized in the *Analects*. I thus recommend as plausible the thesis that the development of this notion in Emerson's philosophy was shaped in part by his contact with Confucius through Marshman's early translation.[11] Given the importance of self-reliance as a virtue in the thought of Confucius and Emerson, the possibility of further areas of conceptual overlap between the two must be considered.

Marshman's Self-Reliant Confucius

If Emerson first learned of Confucius via Marshman's *The Works of Confucius,* it is likely that Emerson's true introduction to Confucius came in the form of the short biographical sketch found at the front of the volume. Among the details of Confucius's life that Emerson would have first learned is this description of his adolescence:

> When quite a child, Confucius was modest, grave, and courteous in his deportment, and delighted in imitating, in his puerile way, the ceremonies of worship used in the temples. He was also exceedingly fond of enquiring into the nature of things, which inquisitive temper is said, in the following work, to have exposed him on a certain occasion to censure, when inquiring about the nature of things in his paternal temple. At the age of fifteen he gave himself up to more serious studies, making the maxims and examples of the ancient sages, the constant subjects of his contemplation. He acknowledges in this volume, that in his youth he was reduced to great straits, and that this gave occasion for his acquiring skill in horsemanship, archery, and other arts.[12]

On this account, the young Confucius was modest and imitative, but at the same time, inquisitive and independent. There is no doubt that these qualities stuck with Confucius into adulthood and old age. The Confucius of the *Analects*—the text translated in Marshman's volume—is certainly describable in these terms.

Another great figure of philosophy characterized in similar terms is Socrates. The coincidence was likely not lost on Emerson,[13] though he would have been reminded of the connection by Marshman's calling it "somewhat singular" that "this era of Chinese literature (which includes about eighty years) should so nearly synchronize with that in which the most celebrated Greek writers flourished."[14] Still, Marshman believed, there was an important difference between ancient Chinese and ancient Greek thought: "The pursuits of the latter . . . differed considerably from those of the Chinese sages, as the attention of these was restricted almost entirely to morals and manners. If the pursuits and labors of the Chinese sages were less splendid however, than those of the Greek philosophers, they were perhaps superior in point of utility; as, with respect to civilization and political order, they have shed a salutary influence over nearly a third part of mankind for probably two thousand years."[15] Although it is not clear whether Emerson took Marshman's word concerning the scope of ancient Chinese philosophical reflection, it is clear enough that Emerson would have been interested in learning of the "morals and manners"—the character or virtue—of Chinese sages, especially one of such far-reaching influence as Confucius.[16] Emerson admired "great" figures, as illustrated in *Representative Men* (1850), in which he devotes lecture-length discussions to the greatness of Plato (the Philosopher), Swedenborg (the Mystic), Montaigne (the Skeptic), Shakespeare (the Poet), Napoleon (Man of the World), and Goethe (the Writer). "Confucius (the Sage)" would have been a coherent addition.[17]

There is, therefore, something beguiling about the epigraph to "Self-Reliance"—"Ne te quaesiveris extra" (Do not seek for things outside of yourself [CW 2:25])—for Emerson continually sought outside of himself and celebrated the things he found upon having done so! Thus, we must be careful when considering a remark such as the following, found early in "Self-Reliance": "Familiar as the voice of the mind is to each, the highest merit we ascribe to Moses, Plato, and Milton is, that they set at naught books and traditions, and spoke not what men but they thought" (CW 2:27). Emerson's meaning is that we should value Moses, Plato, and Milton less for the content of their particular ideas and more for their having formulated and expressed these ideas (rather than going along with what was popular in their given contexts).

Returning to the example of Socrates, Emerson would have us appreciate his practice of questioning, of always desiring to learn, of challenging popular ideas and assumptions, and of never taking for granted that he had any sort of wisdom, great or small. To the extent that Emerson was familiar with the character of Confucius, he would have seen him exhibiting a very similar attitude.[18] Although it would be the height of scholarly error to claim that Confucius "set at naught books and traditions," as we will see, Confucius is nevertheless representative of the qualities that Emerson advocates in "Self-Reliance."

Whoso Would Be a Jūnzǐ *Must Be a Nonconformist*

Emerson's central claims in "Self-Reliance" might be distilled to the following: Sacrificing independence and critical reflection is anathema to virtue. In the project of self-cultivation, one is best served by resisting the forces of social conformity and misplaced insistence on consistency. An individual who goes with the flow, and who refuses to consider the merits of alternative ways of doing and being, is hardly worthy of being called an "individual" at all. "Whoso would be a man must be a nonconformist" (CW 2:29) and "a foolish consistency is the hobgoblin of little minds" (CW 2:33).

Early in "Self-Reliance," Emerson laments the tendency of individuals to absorb the thoughts and ideas of great authors while jettisoning their own. This is a theme to which Emerson devoted an entire essay, "The American Scholar" (1837), four years prior. In each place, Emerson insists that merely parroting another's thinking—even when the other is someone who is, on all accounts, wise—is not equivalent to, and indeed, is much worse than thinking on one's own. One must move past ideas from bygone eras to form new ideas to put to use in the present. Only then can one truly be called a scholar; only then can one truly be deemed self-reliant. As he puts the point in "Self-Reliance": "A man should learn to detect and watch that gleam of light which flashes across his mind from within more than the lustre of the firmament of the bards and sages" (CW 2:27). Assuming that Emerson's use of "firmament" is meant to conjure images of the skies or heavens, the point is that brilliance does not reside exclusively in unreachable places (e.g., with *those* great thinkers whose minds we cannot inhabit) but may be found, if intermittently, within ourselves. So, Emerson thinks, it is time to stop looking outward and start looking inward.

This prescription is one that Confucius would at least apparently *not* endorse. Consider the following passages from the *Analects*:[19]

> 2.2 The Master said, "The *Odes* number several hundred, and yet can be judged with a single phrase: 'Oh, they will not lead you astray.'"

> 17.9 The Master said, "Little Ones, why do none of you learn the *Odes*? The *Odes* can be a source of inspiration and a basis for evaluation; they can help you to come together with others, as well as to properly express complaints. In the home, they teach you about how to serve your father, and in public life they teach you about how to serve your lord. They also broadly acquaint you with the names of a [*sic*] various birds, beasts, plants, and trees."

> 7.18 The Master used the classical pronunciation when reciting the *Odes* and the *History,* and when conducting ritual. In all of these cases, he used the classical pronunciation.

In *Analects* 2.2 and 17.9, Confucius extols the great value of studying the *Odes* and expresses frustration with his disciples who apparently refuse to do so. In 7.18, we find that Confucius practices what he preaches, and moreover, recites the *Odes* (and the *History*) in a classical way, refusing to deviate from classical pronunciation.[20]

Before drawing too sharp a contrast between Confucius and Emerson on this point, however, it is prudent to acknowledge that Confucius laments his disciples' not learning the *Odes* because they are failing to tap into the rich resources contained therein, one of which is the capacity of the *Odes* to inspire. There is no doubt that Emerson endorses the learning of great texts for much the same purposes. The problem comes when in the midst of great texts, one abandons one's own capacity for original or inspirational thought—when the individual "dismisses without notice his thought, because it is his" (CW 2:27). In fact, this position of Emerson's echoes that of Confucius. While Confucius may take disciples to task for having not "mastered the *Odes*," he is also liable to do so for their having done nothing but mastered them:

> 17.10 The Master said to Boyu, "Have you mastered the *Odes* from the 'South of Zhou' and 'South of Shao'? A man who has not mastered the 'South of Zhou' and 'South of Shao' is like someone standing with his face to the wall, is he not?"

> 13.5 The Master said, "Imagine a person who can recite the several hundred odes by heart but, when delegated a governmental task, is unable to carry it out, or when sent abroad as an envoy, is unable to engage in repartee. No matter how many odes he might have memorized, what good are they to him?"

Confucius and Emerson appear to be closely aligned, then, when it comes to how they conceive of the proper relationship between individuals and classic texts. It is important to engage them, to learn them, and to know them—but this is all for naught if they inspire nothing from us as thinking individuals relationally situated, inhabiting a world that quite often requires active response with no recourse to a script or record of precedents.

The relation one ought to have to classic texts is part and parcel of that which we ought to have to society in general. Emerson describes the problem in these words: "Society is a wave. The wave moves onward, but the water of which it is composed does not" (*CW* 2:37). Emerson would prefer, of course, for the water of which it is composed (individuals) to chart their own course. Instead, "Our housekeeping is mendicant, our arts, our occupations, our marriages, our religion, we have not chosen but society has chosen for us" (*CW* 2:32). Contrary to what might be the common perception of Confucianism as calling for conformity at all costs, Emerson's view of things finds a forerunner in the ideas of Confucius. Consider these comments about the Way (*dào*):

> 8.9 The Master said, "The common people can be made to follow it, but they cannot be made to understand it."
>
> 16.9 Confucius said, "Those who are born understanding it are best; those who come to understand it through learning are second. Those who find it difficult to understand and yet persist in their studies come next. People who find it difficult to understand but do not even try to learn are the worst of all."
>
> 15.29 The Master said, "Human beings can broaden the Way—it is not the Way that broadens humans."

While there is no question that Confucius wishes for "the common people" to follow the Way, it is also true that he would prefer that people understand the Way, or at the very least, attempt to. Rather than merely acting in a fashion consistent with virtue by accepting direction and engaging in imitation,[21] one is more virtuous (or authentically virtuous) if one understands the virtue of one's behavior and chooses to act virtuously over and against the alternatives.[22] Moreover, virtuous individuals do not simply allow for their character to be shaped by the Way; in harmonizing with the Way, the Way is able to manifest itself in the world more broadly than it could without such individuals.

"For nonconformity," Emerson writes, "the world whips you with its displeasure" (*CW* 2:32). One might imagine Emerson addressing this line to Confucius. Take, for instance, an episode recounted in the *Analects*:

> 5.1 The Master said of Gongye Chang, "He is marriageable. Although he was once imprisoned as a criminal, he was in fact innocent of any crime." The Master gave him his daughter in marriage.

As Edward Slingerland comments, "The social stigma attached to former criminals in early China was enormous and inescapable, since criminals were prominently branded, tattooed, or physically mutilated. In giving his daughter in marriage to a former criminal, Confucius is flouting conventional mores and making a powerful statement concerning the independence of true morality from conventional social judgments."[23] Slingerland's commentary is consistent with that of Fan Ning, who writes, "In giving his daughter in marriage to Gongye Chang, Confucius' intention was to make quite clear the corruptive and excessive manner in which punishments were administered in his fallen age, and to provide future encouragement to those who truly held fast to rectitude."[24]

In response to such social stigma—in response to being whipped by the world with its displeasure—one can only imagine Confucius saying, as he does in the *Analects*:

> 4.10 The Master said, "With regard to the world, the gentleman [*jūnzǐ*] has no predispositions for or against any person. He merely associates with those he considers right."

One should hope that Confucius's daughter was in agreement with her father on this point. If not, perhaps this arrangement was an especially vivid—and unconventional—way of imparting the lesson.

Additional examples abound of Confucius's bucking convention, approving of those who buck convention, and advising others to buck convention. Consider these examples:

> 9.3 The Master said, "A ceremonial cap made of linen is prescribed by the rites, but these days people use silk. This is frugal, and I follow the majority. To bow before ascending the stairs is what is prescribed by the rites, but these days people bow after ascending. This is arrogant, and—though it goes against the majority—I continue to bow before ascending."

> 5.6 The Master gave Qidiao Kai permission to take office. Qidiao Kai replied, "I cannot yet be trusted with such a responsibility." The Master was pleased.

> 15.36 The Master said, "When it comes to being Good, defer to no one, not even your teacher."

In the first passage, Confucius embraces a practice veering away from *lǐ* (rites, ritual), in using a silk ceremonial cap rather than one made of linen. It is significant, of course, that the concern occasioning the alteration is worthy (frugality), and the alteration itself (from one fabric to another) is somewhat minor. The matter of bowing before ascending the stairs rather than after is one that carries more weight for Confucius, and with there being no apparent good reason for the change, Confucius refuses to go along with the crowd. With respect to each incident, it seems that Confucius embodies the trait of self-reliance promoted by Emerson.[25] In the second passage, Confucius is pleased with Qidiao Kai's critical self-appraisal. Whereas most people given the chance to take office would do so, even if they felt that they were not adequately qualified, Qidiao Kai resists this tendency, exhibiting rectitude, and indeed responsibility—the very quality that he perceives himself as lacking. In the third passage, Confucius would seem to upend the entire master-disciple dynamic, if not for the qualification that *when it comes to being Good,* one should defer to no one, even one's teacher. While Confucius does not appear to ever guide his students toward bad action, one can conceive of being directed by one's teacher in such a direction and knowing that it is best to defy the direction and act otherwise. In such a case, one exhibits self-reliance, a quality that Confucius clearly underscores in his teachings.

A Foolish Consistency Is the Hobgoblin of Xiǎo *Minds*

Following his discussion of conformity as an impediment to self-reliance, Emerson introduces his discussion of the problem of foolish consistency with these words: "The other terror that scares us from self-trust is our consistency; a reverence from our past act or word, because the eyes of others have no data for computing our orbit than our past acts, and we are loath to disappoint them" (*CW* 2:33). The reason we are frightened of being inconsistent is that we will be viewed as muddled in our thinking, or otherwise misunderstood.[26] In familiar style, Emerson cites examples of "great men" describable in precisely these terms: "Pythagoras was misunderstood, and Socrates, and Jesus, and Luther, and Copernicus, and Galileo, and Newton, and every pure and wise spirit that ever took flesh. To be great is to be misunderstood" (*CW* 2:34). Once again, Confucius could have easily been included.

Confucius's antipathy toward foolish consistency is shown succinctly in the *Analects*:

> 17.3 The Master said, "Only the very wise and the very stupid do not change."

If one is very wise, then one knows better than to change from being very wise to not being very wise! If one is very stupid, one does not know of one's need to improve, or does not know how to improve, or is unable to improve, or simply chooses not to improve. These behaviors typify the *xiǎorén* (small or petty person), with whom Confucius frequently contrasts the *jūnzǐ*.

Confucius offers a specific example of a lack of foolish consistency–what perhaps we could call a wise inconsistency—in the *Analects*:

> 15.37 The Master said, "The gentleman [*jūnzǐ*] is true, but not rigidly trustworthy."

As commentator Huang Kan remarks, "The gentleman [*jūnzǐ*] uses discretion to respond to changing circumstances and does not have any single, constant way of doing things. In his handling of affairs he must sometimes bend the rules in order to harmonize with the Way and properly realize principle."[27] It is quite likely, then, that Confucius would appreciate Emerson's claim that "a foolish consistency is the hobgoblin of little minds," and would perhaps share Emerson's observation that it is "adored by little statesmen and philosophers and divines" (CW 2:33).

Conclusion

Despite the similarity between Confucius's and Emerson's conceptions of the virtue of self-reliance, it should be acknowledged that the two views are not identical. Emerson is more insistent on moving past tradition and custom, whereas rites simply mean too much to Confucius to allow for the injunction to fly away from tradition that Emerson appears to endorse.[28] Still, Confucius would approve of the spirit, and much of the letter, of the arguments Emerson advances for the need of self-reliance in a virtuous life. The level of compatibility between the two may be brought into sharper relief with consideration of the following entries in the *Analects*:

> 2.11 The Master said, "Both keeping past teachings alive and understanding the present—someone able to do this is worthy of being a teacher."

> 4.17 The Master said, "When you see someone who is worthy, concentrate upon becoming their equal; when you see someone who is unworthy, use this as an opportunity to look within yourself."

> 11.20 Zizhang asked about the Way of the excellent person. The Master replied, "If he does not personally follow in the footsteps [of the ancients], he will be unable to enter the inner chamber."

> 12.1 Yan Hui asked about Goodness. The Master said, "Restraining yourself and returning to the rites constitutes Goodness. If for one day you managed to restrain yourself and return to the rites, in this way you could lead the entire world back to Goodness. The key to achieving Goodness lies within yourself —how could it come from others?"

Taking each of these passages into account, we see clearly that Confucius adheres to the value of tradition and conformity, while simultaneously believing that tradition and conformity are nurturing forces, developing disciples into teachers; turning individuals wholly dependent on others for guidance into individuals who are virtuous and capable of guiding others; creating individuals who are self-reliant. Given Emerson's proclivity for "great men" and his fascination with Confucius leading up to the composition of "Self-Reliance," it is plausible to think that Confucius's thought and personage were influential on Emerson as he developed what is considered one of the most distinctively American philosophical essays and outlooks.

Notes

1. Quoted in "The Living Legacy of Ralph Waldo Emerson: Emerson and Literature," Harvard Square Library, http://www.harvardsquarelibrary.org. Gish Jen originally wrote this in an e-mail to Susan Wilson (August 11, 1999), for inclusion in a Boston literary guide. I thank Gish Jen for help with tracking down the origin of her quote (e-mail from Gish Jen to author, September 13, 2012).

2. Joshua Marshman, trans., *The Works of Confucius: Containing the Original Text with a Translation* (Serampore: Mission Press, 1809). Marshman apparently intended two volumes, but produced only this one.

3. The Four Books are: *Great Learning, Doctrine of the Mean, Analects, Mencius*. Emerson read these in David Collie, trans., *The Chinese Classical Work Commonly Called the Four Books* (Malacca: Mission Press, 1828). Emerson mentions his engagement with this text in correspondence to Margaret Fuller: "I have the best of Chinese Confucian books lately, an octavo published at Malacca, in English" (*L* 3:179).

4. James Legge, trans., *Confucian Analects, the Great Learning, and the Doctrine of the Mean, The Chinese Classics I* (London: Trübner, 1861). In a letter to Charles H. Glover, dated October 16, 1863, Emerson "apologizes for his delay in returning a stately edition of Confucius and adds that he many years ago knew the substance of this work not only in Marshman" but also "in *The Chinese Classical Work*, published at Malacca." As Ralph L. Rusk correctly infers, "The book Emerson was returning was no doubt James Legge's translation" (*L* 5:338).

5. Arthur Christy's discussion of the Confucian influence on Emerson is a notable exception. See Arthur Christy, *The Orient in American Transcendentalism: A Study of Emerson, Thoreau, and Alcott* (New York: Octagon Books, 1963), 123–37.

6. Egbert S. Oliver, "The Asia in Emerson's Mind," *Korean Survey* 2 (May 1953): 11.

7. Ibid., 12.

8. David Weir, *American Orient: Imagining the East from the Colonial Era through the Twentieth Century* (Amherst: University of Massachusetts Press, 2011), 58.

9. Frederic Ives Carpenter, *Emerson and Asia* (Cambridge, MA: Harvard University

Press, 1930), 234. While Carpenter claims that Emerson *did not* incorporate Confucian thought into his own writing, more recently, Richard Grossman asserts that Emerson *could not* have done so: "[I]n practice, Confucianism was not a philosophy to which Emerson could have wholly subscribed, since it was almost exclusively concerned with societal structure, worldly transactions, codified rules of behavior, and what might be called patriarchal politics. While many of these themes interested Emerson, they all fall into the realm of 'Society,' which for him was only a part of human reality, needing always to be counterpoised with 'Solitude,' wherein the richness of the spiritual life becomes possible." See Richard Grossman, *The Tao of Emerson* (New York: Modern Library, 2007), xxiv. While I concur that Emerson does not wholly subscribe to Confucianism, Emerson's thought is much more Confucian than Grossman allows.

10. Christy, *The Orient in American Transcendentalism*, 123.

11. Because there is no record of Emerson's having read Collie's translation until 1843, I limit the scope of this speculation to Marshman's translation.

12. Marshman, *Works of Confucius,* ii.

13. Emerson makes just this connection (and adds one of Confucius with Jesus) in his speech at the banquet in honor of the Chinese Embassy in Boston in 1868: "Confucius has not yet gathered all his fame. When Socrates heard that the oracle declared that he was the wisest of men, he said, it must mean that other men held that they were wise, but that he knew nothing. Confucius had already affirmed this of himself: and what we call the GOLDEN RULE of Jesus, Confucius had uttered in the same terms five hundred years before" (*CW* 10:491).

14. Marshman, *Works of Confucius,* xxii.

15. Ibid., xxiii.

16. It would seem as though Marshman had Emerson in mind when writing, "To the curious admirer of antiquity, this work recommends itself by exhibiting to him the celebrated Chinese Sage, exactly as he appeared in the eyes of his disciples, both in public and private life. It may also serve to convey some idea of Chinese Manners, nearly as unvarying in their nature as those of the Hindoos, and which we have here an opportunity of contemplating in their origin" (xxxiv).

17. Emerson included Confucius in such lists a number of times. Carpenter mentions the following, noting that Confucius appears sometimes in strange company, but always with great men: "Socrates, Menu, Confucius, Zerthust"; "Moses, Confucius, Montaigne and Leibnitz"; "Zoroaster, Confucius, and the Indian Scriptures." In a journal entry of 1847, Emerson writes, "Ah we must have some gift of transcending time also, as we do space, & collecting our club from a wider brotherhood. Crier[,] call Pythagoras, Plato, Socrates, Aristotle, Proclus, Plotinus, Spinoza, Confucius & Menu, Kepler, Friar Bacon" (*JMN* 10:110). In a notebook entry of 1855, Emerson writes, "Judges rest on 'Laws of Menu, Laws of Moses, Laws of Confucius, Laws of Jesus, Laws Code of Justinian'" (*JMN* 14:397). In addition to these lists, in his essay "Books," he emphasized the importance of single books to great nations, "as Hafiz was the eminent genius of the Persians, Confucius

of the Chinese, Cervantes of the Spaniards" (Carpenter, *Emerson and Asia*, 242). Moreover, in a notebook entry of April 6, 1824, Emerson states, "the light of Confucius goes out in translation into the language of Shakespear & Bacon" (*JMN* 2:378).

18. See *Analects* 9.8: "The Master said, 'Do I possess wisdom? No, I do not. [For example, recently] a common fellow asked a question of me, and I came up completely empty. But I discussed the problem with him from beginning to end until we finally got to the bottom of it.'"

19. Because the Marshman translation of the *Analects* is decidedly outdated, I will henceforth quote from a more recent translation (viz., Edward Slingerland's). The integrity of the comparative analysis does not suffer from this transition, however, as the two do not impart substantively different philosophical interpretations as concerns the themes addressed in this chapter. Edward Slingerland, trans., *Confucius: Analects* (Indianapolis, IN: Hackett, 2003).

20. A related remark, not explicitly tied to the *Odes*, is found in *Analects* 7.1: "The Master said, 'I transmit rather than innovate. I trust in and love the ancient ways.'" Confucius's reverence for the *Odes* is consistent with this avowed trust in and love of the ancient ways. At the same time that Confucius is committed to transmitting the ancient ways, he does so in an innovative fashion—including, as we will see, sometimes seeing fit to stray from the letter of the ways.

21. For an example of Confucius's distinguishing between actions that pass for virtue and actions that truly are virtuous—in the case of filial piety (*xiào*)—see *Analects* 2.7: "Ziyou asked about filial piety. The Master said, 'Nowadays "filial" means simply being able to provide one's parents with nourishment. But even dogs and horses are provided with nourishment. If you are not respectful, wherein lies the difference?'"

22. This way of conceiving of the virtuous agent is strikingly similar to that of Aristotle.

23. Slingerland, *Confucius: Analects,* 39.

24. Quoted in ibid.

25. Compare the spirit of this portion of *Analects* 9.3 with *Analects* 19.11: "Zixia said, 'As long as one does not transgress the bounds when it comes to important Virtues, it is permissible to cross the line here and there when it comes to minor Virtues.'"

26. In today's political climate, the fear is that one will be accused of "flip-flopping" as opposed to "staying the course" and "showing resolve." In short, inconsistency is viewed as symptomatic of a lack of integrity, when as Confucius and Emerson understand, integrity may be expressed via inconsistency!

27. Quoted in Slingerland, *Confucius: Analects,* 188.

28. For Confucius's more conservative stance, see *Analects* 3.17: "Zigong wanted to do away with the practice of sacrificing a lamb to announce the beginning of the month. The Master said, 'Zigong! You regret the loss of the lamb, whereas I regret the loss of the rite.'" See also *Analects* 4.20: "The Master said, 'One who makes no changes to the ways of his father for three years after his father has passed away may be called a filial

son.'" I can only see Confucius regarding as bombastic, pretentious, and off-putting the following excerpt from "Self-Reliance": "I hope these days we have heard the last of conformity and consistency. Let the words be gazetted and ridiculous henceforward. Instead of the gong for dinner, let us hear a whistle from the Spartan fife. Let us never bow and apologize more. A great man is coming to eat at my house. I do not wish to please him; I wish that he should wish to please me" (CW 2:35).

[IV]

EMERSON AND THE NEAR EAST

[15]

KENNETH S. SACKS

EMERSON AND SOME JEWISH QUESTIONS

NEAR THE END OF "Perpetual Forces," a Civil War talk he gave often in behalf of the Union, Ralph Waldo Emerson looked forward to the aftermath and posed the question: "How then to reconstruct?" He answered himself this way:

> Leave slavery out. Since nothing satisfies men but justice, let us have that, and let us stifle our prejudices against commonsense and humanity, and agree that every man shall have what he honestly earns, and, if he is a sane and innocent man, have an equal vote in the state, and a fair chance at society. Ernest Renan, the first living writer in France, speaking of the Jews, says, that "they everywhere in the world at this day form a society apart, except only in France, which has exhibited in the world the principle of a civilization purely ideal, ignoring all thought of differences in races." Well, the day will come here of an equal glory. (*LL* 2:300)

For more than a century after his death, scholars condemned Emerson for being slow to embrace the cause of abolition. Certainly, in his early public talks of the 1830s and into the 1840s, Emerson shockingly skirts the subject, and in his journals he sometimes offers judgments of black Americans that even in his day would have made many uncomfortable. But following Len Gougeon and Joel Myerson's publications of Emerson's previously little-known antislavery talks from the mid-1840s, it has become startlingly evident that Emerson undertook a personal reevaluation of the position of Africans and African Americans among peoples of the world. Indeed, we now appreciate that in his own lifetime Emerson was widely honored as a moral leader for abolition and racial justice.[1] And, as "Perpetual Forces" makes clear, he spoke out, not just for legal justice, but as well for social equality.

When it comes to the far less pressing issue of Emerson's attitude toward Jews, a similar pattern appears. Viewed through various categories of antisemitism, both those of the premodern period and those emerging out of late-nineteenth-century Germany, historians consistently label Emerson an antisemite.[2] But within the decade of the 1830s, Emerson metamorphosed from a somewhat desultory student and conventional Unitarian minister into America's most acclaimed public intellectual. Closer study will reveal that during that transformation Emerson became a strong public supporter of contemporary Jews and Judaism.

Beyond the somewhat simplistic binary of whether he was actively "antisemitic" or "philosemitic" lie more interesting questions. That in 1862 Emerson could rely on Ernest Renan to frame an opinion reflects the complications. European intellectuals such as Renan and Matthew Arnold were then wrestling with issues of race and culture arising as the industrialized nation-state developed simultaneously with Jewish emancipation. Characteristic of the intellectual turmoil, both Renan and Arnold saw themselves as philosemitic (as have many Jewish intellectuals since), and yet their categories of thinking are now often viewed as helping validate the antisemitism that resulted in the twentieth-century catastrophe. One need only attempt to work through modern criticism of Marx's *On the Jewish Question* (1843) to appreciate how contested is the terrain.[3] It is during this very period that Emerson also navigated the same issues of race and culture.

As a practicing Christian minister, Emerson naturally evoked biblical Judaism in his sermons. How Emerson characterized ancient Judaism in relation to its "successor" religion—*his* religion—raises concern among historians. Later, as a secular writer who had resigned from the active ministry (in 1832, although he infrequently preached until 1839), Emerson employed contemporary categories of the incipient fields of ethnography and historical linguistics in describing cultures as "Hellenic" or "Hebraic."[4] What Emerson meant by "Hebraic" also troubles scholars. Even if he did not actively humiliate or exclude contemporary Jews, it remains to be determined whether his positioning of ancient Judaism to Christianity or his employing the cultural signifier of Hebraism implies its fundamental inferiority. And, finally, because he lived within one of the country's most intensively self-reflective communities during a time of tremendous social change, Emerson was among the first American intellectuals, not only to have extensive interaction with Jews, but to exert significant influence on Jewish theology, a consideration hitherto largely unexplored. These are the more complex of Emerson's "Jewish Questions." But the first issue to address is his explicit attitude toward contemporary Jews.

Virtually every survey of antisemitism in America concludes, usually categorically, that Emerson was lifelong an antisemite.[5] Here's why. In correspondence with older brother William, in 1828–31, the young Waldo (born

1803) three times evokes Jews as synonyms for vulgar businessmen and as real or metaphorical Shylocks:

> "[I] know little of you more than to suspect you are sunk into the vulgarest man of business who has no correspondence for any but the Jews with whom you have dealings—as ye aforesaid [brother] Edward."
>
> "Do you not die of the Jews to whom you pay usance? What is your debt? I dare not yet promise you any help because I do not know what I am worth."
>
> "I have not paid [brother] C[harles].C[hauncy].E[merson]. but will as quick as I can find a banker or a Jew that will trust me.—"[6]

There has also recently (2011) been published an obscure, but securely identified Emersonian poem, "William Rufus and the Jew." Based on a story he found in David Hume's *History of England,* Emerson submitted the poem in 1829 to a collection assembled by his Harvard teacher Andrews Norton.[7] According to Hume and poeticized by Emerson, a Jew approached King William II (died 1100 CE), also known as William Rufus, offering fifty marks if the monarch could win back the Jew's son, Isaac, from conversion to Christianity. William failed, but kept thirty marks for his effort. Hume maintains that William was blamed by the clergy for his impiety. And while in the poem King William is certainly put in worse light, Emerson used Jews as comic props, characterizing them as obdurate ("But Isaac the Jew was so hard and stiff-necked, / That by no means could the king come to any effect") and avaricious ("My lord the king! I do as Moses bids; / Eschewing all evil, I shut my coffer lids"). Chronologically, the poem falls within the same period as the letters Emerson wrote to his brother William.

Emerson's mockery could hardly have been based on personal experience. Near the beginning of the nineteenth century, there were no known Jews in Massachusetts; as late as 1840, there were perhaps fewer than forty Jews even in Boston,[8] and these seem to have been peddlers and artisans, rather than bankers.[9] Not having personal knowledge did not stop writers from characterizing Jews. Emily Dickinson, who almost certainly never knew any Jews, three times attributes to them the qualities of Shylock.[10] And, Thoreau, who also probably never met a Jew, remarks in his journals about their eternal sadness.[11] Despite the lack of familiarity, this is the time when the verb, "to Jew," was popularized.[12] As John Higham notes, "Until the mid-nineteenth century the average American seemed to think of Jews primarily as ancient patriarchs in flowing robes, smelling of frankincense and myrrh."[13] Derivative of medieval European stereotypes, Emerson's characterizations carried no social consequence for offending or despising the "other," because there was then effectively no "other" to offend or despise.

It is generally assumed that the first Jew Emerson actually met was Gustave d'Eichthal, a member of a prominent French banking family, at a party in Rome in 1833.[14] The next day, d'Eichthal, on his own initiative, delivered to him a letter for John Stuart Mill requesting that the English philosopher introduce Emerson to the individual who would become his lodestar, Thomas Carlyle (*L* 9:185).[15] The association with d'Eichthal, then, was life-changing for Emerson. But was d'Eichthal a Jew? He was born into a family of Jewish heritage, but almost all its members, including Gustave, had long since converted to Catholicism. Emerson wrote retrospectively in 1848: "I met Gustave D'Eichthal . . . in Rome. He was then what was called a Saint Simeon" (*JMN* 10:522). D'Eichthal had already progressed through Judaism, Catholicism, Comptism, and, by then, the utopian socialism of Saint-Simeonism. To Emerson, d'Eichthal was remarkable for his political ideology, not his religion. Despite having ceased worshipping as a Jew, however, d'Eichthal remained, lifelong, highly visible in his efforts to improve the social and political conditions of European Jews.[16] And yet, although referring to him several times in his correspondence and journals, Emerson never notes d'Eichthal's religious heritage.[17] Other New Englanders might label Jews: while Harvard instructor in Hebrew, Judah Monis, publicly embraced Christianity in 1722, suspicions about the sincerity of his conversion followed him to his grave.[18] But always honoring individual accomplishment, Emerson never tried to unearth religious heritage to explain character and pointedly criticized those who did.[19]

While in Rome, Emerson did at least *see* people he identified as Jews, and these were the disadvantaged and persecuted for whom he expressed sympathy. He records in his journals: "I did not go to the baptism of the Jew today. Usually it is a weary farce. 'Tis said they buy the Jews at 150 scudes the head to be sprinkled. This man was respectable." And during the same Italian trip at Ferrara: "Thence to the Campo Santo passing through the Jews' quarter of whom there are 2800 who are shut up every night as in Rome like dogs" (*JMN* 4:156, 181–82; similarly *JMN* 11:264). It was perhaps at this time that Emerson came to understand a living reality that he could distinguish from his earlier stereotypical characterizations.

Scholars point to later Emersonian observations to prove lifelong antisemitism when, in fact, careful reading demonstrates the opposite. Most often cited is this journal entry of 1839: "the Polish Jews are an offense to me, they degrade & animalize." In isolation, as it is nearly always quoted, it seems a telling admission. But the full passage turns out to be an attack on these very stereotypes: "In the Allston gallery the [paintings of] Polish Jews are an offense to me, they degrade & animalize. As soon as a beard becomes any thing but an accident, we have not a man but a Turk, a Jew, a satyr, a dandy, a goat." Emerson is not offended by Polish Jews (or Turks), *but by how they are being portrayed* (JMN 7:221–22).[20]

The object of Emerson's ire was Washington Allston's *Sketch of a Polish Jew.* Allston produced several studies of the subject for his show, one of which is currently in the Corcoran Gallery of Art, Washington, DC, and viewable online. It is, in fact, a portrait of a proud and handsome man emitting an inner light. Although transcendentalists praised the work of this contemporary Romantic painter and poet, Emerson expresses in his journals that Allston's stereotypical representations deprive his subjects of individuality: "Allston's pictures are Elysian; fair, serene, but unreal" (JMN 7:200).[21]

Another frequently noted example, from toward the end of Emerson's life, involves the poet Emma Lazarus (whose "The New Colossus" was to be inscribed on the Statue of Liberty). In return for Emerson's well-documented mentoring, Lazarus dedicated "To My Friend, Ralph Waldo Emerson" her poem "Admetus." When she later voiced anger that none of her poems were included in his collection *Parnassus,* he invited her to his home in 1876. There were almost certainly no Jews yet living in Concord,[22] and about the visit Emerson's elder daughter, Ellen, wrote her sister, Edith: "Then think of what nuts it was to me, old S[unday] S[chool] teacher that I am, to get a real unconverted Jew (who had no objection to calling herself one, and talked freely about 'Our Church' and 'we Jews')."[23] Although it was Ellen, temperamentally very different from her father, who wrote the letter, this is usually construed as reflecting Waldo's own distain for Jews.

Yet Lazarus herself told others of Ellen's kindness during her visit,[24] and, in a note to Edith upon Lazarus's arrival, Ellen brims with delight: "[Lazarus] is very pleasant and has plain natural manners."[25] Even in the letter where she mentions Lazarus's religion, Ellen admits: "The interior view [of Lazarus's description of Jewish practice] was more interesting than I could have imagined."[26] A recently discovered Lazarus letter describes a second visit to Concord in 1879, the invitation for which came directly from Ellen.[27] This is Ellen's own later recollection of that second visit: "It seems to me that we had this summer another visit from Emma Lazarus who talked with Mother very interestingly, she had begun to care for her co.s as she called the Jews. She explained that this meant co-religionists. When she came the first time she did not love her nation, but now, she said, now, that Hotels would not receive them, and that they were persecuted in Russia, she was wholly & earnestly a Jew herself."[28] Although it was always a stretch to ascribe to Waldo his daughter's isolated sentiment, Ellen had a far more interested and positive relationship with the poet and her religion than one phrase might suggest.

Thomas Wentworth Higginson, among the most politically radical of transcendentalists, was an essential patron of aspiring writers (her "Preceptor" was what Emily Dickinson called him). Although equally supportive of Lazarus's career, Higginson wrote to his sisters that Lazarus "is a Jewess; they are very rich and in fashionable society in New York."[29] While not critical of her heritage, he did, as did Ellen Emerson, make note of it. But Waldo Emerson, whose relationship with Lazarus was both intimate and yet at times trying, not in his journals nor in any letter to her or to anyone else ever mentions her religion.[30] As always, he shows no interest in labeling others by their religious traditions.

Transcendentalists, Emerson certainly among them, worked hard to achieve a liberal temperament. Contemporary with Emerson was transcendentalist colleague John Weiss, widely respected for his spiritual devotion and commitment to abolition. A Unitarian minister of Jewish heritage, Weiss was a central figure in the most liberal wing of the church and a founder of the Free Religious Association (see below), of which Emerson was titular leader. Although his religious heritage went unmentioned while alive, at his death, two friends include it in their published obituaries. "His father, I have understood, was a barber in the town of Worcester, a German by blood and by race a Jew,—to which last I have sometimes ascribed the singular fervor of his religious genius," eulogized Joseph Henry Allen.[31] And Cyrus Augustus Bartol, at the conservative end of transcendentalism, also connects Weiss's heritage to his religiosity: "Anti-supernatural in faith, yet how supernatural and preternatural he was in fact! How he opposed spiritualism, yet what a medium he was, as if this modern Jew had descended from those old Hebrews that dealt with similar spirits!"[32] In the official memorial of Harvard College, Class of 1837, there is quoted from Weiss's notebooks—the same ones on which the other obituary writers drew—details about his grandparents' emigration from Germany, but no mention of his Jewish heritage.[33] It was the transcendentalists, praising Weiss equally as Jew and Unitarian, who acknowledged the complicated issues of race and culture during the emerging years of American nation building.

There is early reflection of these concerns in Bronson Alcott's *Conversations with Children on the Gospels* (1836), as recorded by Elizabeth Peabody. Constructing a school around the Pestalozzian philosophy of education, in a short segment titled "Prejudice," Alcott purports to demonstrate how children uncover inherent truth through discussion:

EDWARD B. Why are Jews held in such contempt, when Jesus was born a Jew?
FRANKLIN. Because they killed Jesus, and said, "his blood be on us and our children."

EDWARD B. And Jews are mean, avaricious. (*Mr. Alcott explained the last characteristics by the oppressions they had suffered.*)
MR. ALCOTT. Who think it is a wicked prejudice?
WELLES. It is a right prejudice.
ALL. There are no right prejudices.[34]

With almost no Jews in Boston then, student prejudice reflected medieval stereotypes that Alcott attempted to undo. Alcott was, of course, Emerson's closest friend, and Emerson was particularly involved in supporting Alcott during his public humiliation following the publication of *Conversations*.[35] Emerson also knew well Alcott's in-laws, the Mays, who helped convince Emerson to speak out against slavery.[36] In the late eighteenth century, the Mays had encouraged their children to socialize with what might have then been the only Jewish family in Boston: "If the children of my day were taught, among other foolish things to dread, if not despite Jews, a very different lesson was impressed upon my young heart," recalled abolitionist Samuel Joseph May.[37]

By the 1840s, transcendentalists were becoming increasingly aware of Jews through contact with New York. In 1843, Lydia Maria Child, sister of sometime transcendentalist Convers Francis, published one of her many best-selling works, *Letters from New-York*, in which she offered impressions of her visit to a New York synagogue. A traditional Christian, Child emphasized the artifactual nature of Judaism. Even though "[t]here is something deeply impressive in this remnant of a scattered people, coming down to us in continuous links through the long vista of recorded time . . . I could not escape the conclusion that the ceremonies were shuffled through in a cold, mechanical style."[38]

Moving to New York to work for Horace Greeley in 1844, Margaret Fuller began a romantic involvement with a German Jew, James Nathan. Soon after, she wrote an essay, "The Modern Jews," that was printed as the lead column on the front page of the April 21, 1845, *New York Daily Tribune*. She and Lydia Maria Child were close acquaintances and commented on each other's work.[39] Perhaps motivated by her new romantic relationship and wanting to counter Child's impression of them as living fossils, the woman who would ignite American first-wave feminism celebrates the political virility of emancipated Jews with an odd metaphor: "The girdle which so tightly repressed the vital energies of the nation is broken, and the form and proportions of the Jewish man are expanding and approximating to the modern European standard.—Nay, more! The Jew who is thoroughly 'emancipated,' inclines to join or even to head the extreme radical party."[40] It is possible that Emerson read that column (*JMN* 8:499, 517n94;

9:371 suggest he had access to the *Tribune*), and he, too, grew progressively sensitized to the position of Jews. During his first European trip in 1833, he already expressed sympathy for the low status and lack of civil liberties of Italian Jews. In the following decade, stimulated by his second trip to Great Britain in 1847–48 and motivated by abolition, Emerson became vocal in support, culminating at the time of the Civil War when he was a public champion.

Soon after the start of this second trip abroad, Emerson mused: "Dr. B[rown], I think, must be a Jew; his manners are of Monmouth street" (*JMN* 10:181). Because Monmouth Street in London was known for its used-clothes shops owned by Jews, historians suggest that Emerson was either delving into Brown's heritage or characterizing him by the coarse behavior of lower-class Jews. A closer look helps us understand instead Emerson's increasing appreciation of Jews while in Great Britain. Dr. Brown was Samuel Morison Brown, a prominent scientist and Emerson's week-long host in Edinburgh.[41] Emerson was not actually wondering whether he was Jewish, for Brown was descended from the noted theologian of the Scottish church, John Brown, and was known to other transcendentalists through Carlyle. Nor was Emerson being critical. Writing to his wife, Lidian, he refers to "my friend Dr Brown . . . he is a head & heart of the chiefest interest to me . . ." and writing to Margaret Fuller: "Samuel Brown . . . certainly inspired me with great respect & confidence. . . ." Contemporaries confirm their warm relationship (*L* 4:18, 19, 23, 26; *JMN* 10:180).[42]

The allusion to Monmouth Street Jews, too, has a benign interpretation. After disembarking at Liverpool, Emerson spent just four days in London and then went on his speaking tour of Great Britain during which, in Edinburgh, he made this journal entry. There is no record of his earlier (or ever) visiting Monmouth Street.[43] For his information, Emerson may have been drawing on Charles Dickens's "Meditations in Monmouth-Street," included in *Sketches by Boz* (1836). Emerson had access to Dickens's works,[44] and later on in this visit was to become friendly with him.[45] The sketch begins: "We have always entertained a particular attachment towards Monmouth-street, as the only true and real emporium for second-hand wearing apparel. . . . The [Jewish] inhabitants of Monmouth-street are . . . a peaceable and retiring race . . . and their habitations are distinguished by that disregard of outward appearance . . . so common among people who are constantly immersed in profound speculations."[46] Perhaps Brown the scientist reminded Emerson of Dickens's Monmouth Street Jews who are "constantly immersed in profound speculations." Or, as a few weeks later Emerson contrasts to somber British attire "a mere carnival or kaleidoscope or Monmouth street of clothes" (*JMN* 10:296), perhaps Brown dressed colorfully. Whatever the association, Emerson intends his comparison of Brown to Monmouth Street Jews playfully.

After completing his speaking tour, Emerson spent altogether four months in London and had a chance to learn the city firsthand. Among the enclaves of ethnic communities he observed and noted in his journals are the French at Spitalfields and the Germans at Whitechapel (*JMN* 10:237). But there is no indication that he also visited Monmouth Street. Following his return home, Emerson lectured on "London" (1849) and near the beginning states: "There are in London several little nations; a Jew's quarter in Monmouth Street and Holywell, a German quarter in Whitechapel; a French quarter in Spitalfields . . ." (*LL* 1:211). Perhaps still depending on Dickens for knowledge of Monmouth Street, he lists the Jewish quarter first and alongside those of the French Huguenots and Germans to illustrate the cosmopolitanism of London. Could he have demonstrated a greater presumption of equality?

In fact, his British trip appears to have sensitized Emerson to contemporary Judaism precisely at a time when he was most open to its issues. If there is no reason to think he was staying with a Jew in Edinburgh, in Nottingham Emerson was the house guest of probably the first publicly identified Jew he ever knew well. Emerson described Joseph Neuberg to others as "our good friend" (*L* 7:168, 146), and he later highly recommended him to Carlyle to serve as his secretary. Neuberg was both an industrialist and a labor advocate, as were the Schwanns of Huddersfield, another publicly identified Jewish family that Emerson mentioned in a letter to home. He praised those manufacturers who provided schools and other means of support for their workers and families (*L* 3:460).

Later in the trip and just a few weeks before having dinner with Lionel Rothschild (*L* 4:46–51), Emerson read a book in which Rothschild was quoted, and this sparked him to recall a recent discussion: "Mr Neuberg said that the Rothschilds make great fortunes, but they really do a certain important service to society; they are the cashiers of the world: and it is a public mischief when any calamity befals them. People at Nottingham are carried into crime, because Rothschild does not accept bills at Paris; it is quite obvious to him: he can trace it all the way. So when a bank discounts freely in any district, immediately an impulse is given to population, & new men are born" (*JMN* 10:305). Already in 1836, Emerson expressed admiration for Rothschild because his wealth was a manifestation of his self-reliance. Praise goes to "[t]he man that takes up the world into his proper being. The two oared boat may be swamped in a squall. The vessels of Rothschild every wind blows to port. He insures himself" (*JMN* 5:126). The theme he recalled from his conversation with Neuberg was expanded: here, wealth produces broad social utility.

Although there were then only about thirty-five thousand Jews in England,[47] their legal status finds a place in *English Traits,* a set of essays emerging from Emerson's visit (published in 1856 but evolving since 1852). Jewish emancipation occurred in stages, and Emerson, witness to some of those struggles, reflected his impatience. In "Race," he relates, "The Jews have been the favorite victims of royal and popular persecution," thereby treating with gravity what he ridiculed in his youthful "William Rufus and the Jew" (CW 5:35).[48] Probably in doing research for this essay, he notes in the journals the "ferocity/the persecution of the Jews" (JMN 13:222). In "Religion," he observes that "The bill for the naturalization of the Jews (in 1753) was resisted by petitions from all parts of the kingdom" and quotes the official reason why: it was "'tending extremely to the dishonor of the Christian religion, and extremely injurious to the interests and commerce of the kingdom in general.'" The remark about dishonor is obviously sarcastic, as he there also voices contempt for the Church of England (CW 5:127, 129). In the concluding essay, "Result," he laments of England that: "There is a drag of inertia which resists reform in every shape;—law-reform, army-reform, extension of suffrage, Jewish franchise, Catholic emancipation,—the abolition of slavery, of impressment, penal code, and entails" (CW 5:172).[49]

In "Fate" (published in 1860 as part of *The Conduct of Life,* but versions of the lecture existed since 1851), a contemporary individual's Jewish faith is, for the first time in Emerson's extant writings, an essential consideration. Emerson observes, "The sufferance, which is the badge of the Jew, has made him, in these days, the ruler of the rulers of the earth" (CW 6:19). He is referring, of course, to the Rothschilds. Although scholars suggest that Emerson is antisemitic in alluding to a grand Jewish cabal akin to the Elders of Zion, since 1836 in his journals, Emerson was expressing unalloyed admiration for the Rothschilds (JMN 5:126).[50] Similarly, in "Power," the essay in *The Conduct of Life* paired with "Fate," Emerson links Rothschild with Newton (science) and Pericles (politics) as positive examples that "[c]oncentration is the secret of strength in politics, in war, in trade, in short, in all management of human affairs" (CW 6:40). When he esteems the Jewish banker alongside Isaac Newton and Pericles, we can precisely measure just how far Emerson has come from his earliest, unreflective references to Shylocks. And it is no coincidence that Emerson exalts a British Jew as "ruler of the rulers." "Fate" was published just two years after the first Jew, following half a century and fourteen failed attempts at altering the law, was admitted to Parliament. That first Jewish MP was the very same Lionel Rothschild. Emerson was in England during one of the previous times in which Rothschild, although elected to Parliament, was denied his seat, and that may have spurred Emerson's indignation.

That indignation became manifest when Emerson returned home. Jews were at least somewhat on Emerson's mind when giving his 1849 talk "London," as he named first the Jewish enclave in demonstrating the vitality of England's metropolis. And in 1858, Emerson appeared to go out of his way to rebut supposed racial distinctions. Referring to those who proclaimed, "Let there be no commerce between that Gentile and these Jews," Emerson rejoined: "Now, we are reconciling them in phrenology, the new German physiology, and in the new unproven sciences" (*LL* 2:97).

In the Civil War speech "Perpetual Forces," quoted at the beginning of this chapter, Emerson spoke boldly against the marginalization of the Jew in America, and there may be an historical context for this. On December 17, 1862, Ulysses S. Grant issued Order No. 11, expelling all Jews from parts of Mississippi, Tennessee, and Kentucky (an order rescinded immediately by Lincoln). Less than a month earlier, Emerson had given his "Perpetual Forces" speech for the first time, but we cannot be sure that his reference to Jews was not added to a subsequent version, in response to Order No. 11.[51] In fact, a week before Emerson gave the talk for the first time, Grant had already ordered that: "[N]o Jews are to be permitted to travel on the railroad southward from any point. . . . [T]hey are such an intolerable nuisance that the department, must be purged of them."[52] And earlier that year, after a long and bitter public struggle, Lincoln convinced Congress to permit Jewish clergy to serve as military chaplains.[53] The war that emancipated African Americans also touched on the civil rights of Jews.

Indeed, in April 1867, Emerson scolds an imagined audience: "You complain that the negroes are a base class. Who makes & keeps the jew or the negro base, who but you, who exclude them from the rights which others enjoy?" (*JMN* 16:55). Within a few years, Emerson would address the newly formed Free Religious Association (see below): "you cannot bring me too good a word, too dazzling a hope, too penetrating an insight from the Jews. I hail every one with delight, as showing the riches of my brother, my fellow soul, who could thus think and thus greatly feel."[54]

Why did Emerson speak in support of Jews? Certainly, his actual experience in England sensitized him, but, as well, he wrote *English Traits* while he was increasingly incensed by the Fugitive Slave Law of 1850 and its consequences. Although he had privately long held antislavery views, part of his decision to risk what he saw as his philosophical self-reliance and to embrace publicly the cause of abolition was how profoundly moved he was by stories of the Middle Passage.[55] When in "Fate" he refers to "[t]he sufferance, which is the badge of the Jew," and reflects that "[w]e see how much will has been expended to extinguish the Jew, in vain" (*CW* 6:9), Emerson's empathy is at least partly motivated by his sensibilities toward the suffering of blacks.

Despite scholarly opinion to the contrary, then, Emerson spoke out for the civil rights and social acceptance of contemporary Jews. But there remain essential questions involving how he saw biblical Judaism in its religious relationship to Christianity and how he employed the idea of the Jewish mentality as metaphor. These are complex issues, for it may be easier to support the rights of contemporary people than to give up long-held views about their culture (a problem Emerson struggled with regarding African Americans). Despite inevitable ambiguities, what seems likeliest is that there is a similar broad arc of development: from traditional expressions emerging out of conventional ministerial training, to an amalgamation of emerging beliefs, and, finally, to a radicalized transformation that included support of Jews.

Within Emerson's 175 surviving sermons (out of the 177 he composed), there are few attacks on ancient Jews. Only once does he invoke a blood libel: "The Jew and the Pagan cried Blood! . . . Paul of Tarsus died triumphing at Rome, his head being severed from his body by the command of Nero" (*CS* 1:231). Emerson also charges, similarly in three sermons, that Jews, in expecting a more martial messiah, were contemptuous of Jesus. "Jesus came a Jew to the Jews, to the bigoted selfish oppressed sanctimonious Jews. So depraved and barbarous that they expected for the Messiah such a person as Attila or Napoleon who should conquer and grind and kill their enemies and therefore when a poor peasant presented himself . . . this was not the Messiah they wanted: they hated him for calling himself so" (*CS* 3:250, CXXXII).[56] The harsh rhetoric reflects a Puritanical strategy meant to associate ancient Jews with contemporary and sinful Christian parishioners.[57] Nowhere in his secular, post-ministerial life does he express anything remotely similar.

But subtler questions remain. Fundamental to Christianity is the belief that Jesus came to offer a new spiritual message. Supersessionism, denoting that Christianity supersedes Judaism in some essential way, is, of course, as old as the faith itself. Even as it honored Judaism, as in the Puritan tradition from which eventually evolved American transcendentalism,[58] contemporary Christianity perforce claimed supersessionist status. For much of his ministry, Emerson preached Christianity.[59]

Supersessionism is evident when Emerson observed in a sermon, "To lead men from this earthly to a heavenly worship . . . seems to have been the wise and merciful end of the Jewish economy" (*CS* 4:173). Emerson suggests that Judaism was limited to a mission of leading people from paganism to monotheism. And, in a number of sermons, he indicates that Judaism was the first stage in monotheism, while earliest Christianity produced a greater godliness (*CS* 2:56, 4:211). But although Christianity "faithfully preached" had been an improvement, Emerson told his congregation, "it has not been preached" (*CS* 4:195).[60] Returning from Europe in 1832, he proclaimed that, while Christianity was "the most emphatic affirmation of spiritual nature . . . [i]t is not the *only* or the last affirmation. There shall be a thousand more" (*CS* 4:195; my emphasis). From then on, *Emerson consistently attacks all institutionally based, supernatural religions.* In the last three sermons he ever composed and delivered in a church, Emerson mentions Christianity only once—to criticize it—and never refers to Jesus (*CS* 4:229–50, criticism at 246–47).

During the early part of the nineteenth century, which was Emerson's formative period, belief in individual perfectionism invigorated New England,[61] and the period of his full maturity, after the Civil War, was marked by idealisms that eventuated in social gospel and progressivism. Emerson's life spanned the development of ideologies of secular improvement, and he grew to understand supersessionism, not as the replacing of an older body of religious practice and dogma with another, but as the privileging of individual human potential over all supernatural religion. Historically based religion was for him merely a spiritual stop along the way to some greater transformation. "Christian, Jew, Pagan, leave all behind you & rush," he urges in 1838 (*JMN* 7:151, 3:61–62, and 4:8).

Connected closely to his evolving understanding of supersessionism is Emerson's use of ancient Judaism as typology. In midlife, when writing *Representative Men* (1850) and *English Traits* (1856), Emerson drew on the rapidly developing fields of anthropology and sociology to describe cultural characteristics and qualities of mind. (Similarly, Emerson dichotomizes the essential social and intellectual qualities of women and men in his 1855 speech "Woman.") When he divides civilizations and individuals into those that are "Hebraic" and those that are "Hellenic," some see Emerson stereotyping, and thus disparaging, Judaism.

For Emerson, Hebraism is the privileging of the exterior moral voice of God over individual spiritual autonomy (which he sometimes called the "Hellenic idea") (*EL* 2:187; *JMN* 5:434, 11:402, 13:280; *CW* 7:35, 99). But, just as he complicates supersessionism by seeing the same failings in contemporary Christianity as in earlier Judaism, so, too, he creates a Hebraism of both Judaism and Christianity.[62] In *Representative Men,* Emerson judges Swedenborg to have an excess of the "Hebraic muse, which taught the lore of right and wrong to men . . . ," adding that "Swedenborg and Behmen both failed by attaching themselves to the Christian symbol, instead of to the moral sentiment, which carries innumerable christianities, humanities, divinities, in its bosom." Jewish and Christian symbols that reflect a judgmental deity whose moral authority burrows into the soul of humanity are the same (CW 6:75–76, 67–68, 71–72, and 10:346),[63] an inevitable identification for an intellectual emerging from the Calvinist tradition.

Emerson applies this broader Hebraism to *English Traits,* for "[t]he doctrine of the Old Testament is the religion of England." In their prayer for Queen Victoria the English ask God to "'grant her in health and wealth long to live.' And one traces this Jewish prayer in all English private history" (CW 5:126–27). Indeed, "There is no country in which so absolute a homage is paid to wealth [as England]. . . . They are under the Jewish law, and read with sonorous emphasis that their days shall be long in the land, they shall have sons and daughters, flocks and herds, wine and oil" (CW 5:87).[64]

Because Emerson also reminds readers there of the Jewish struggle for civil rights, he is hardly antisemitic. The point is that the English, who spawned American Puritanism, are a materially covenantal people. They believe that in return for moral piety, they will prosper; and, mutually, it is that materialistic success which affirms that they are in the moral right. Nor did this Hebraist England choose badly. In the concluding essay of *English Traits,* Emerson begins, "England is the best of actual nations" (CW 5:169). Earlier, he says with sincerity, "The wonderful power of that Jewish idea which has so written itself on the nations, has its full force in the Saxon race" (LL 1:10).

The dichotomy between Hebraism and Hellenism was first expressed in the third century, when the Christian apologist Tertullian asked plaintively, "What has Athens to do with Jerusalem?"[65] But with the Jewish emancipation after the French Revolution,[66] Herder, Heine, and Renan expanded the categories,[67] and the distinctions became forever delineated by Matthew Arnold in *Culture and Anarchy* (1869): "The aim and end of both Hebraism and Hellenism is, as I have said, one and the same, and this aim and end is august and admirable. Still . . . [a]s Hellenism speaks of thinking clearly, seeing things in their essence and beauty, as a grand and precious feat for man to achieve, so Hebraism speaks of becoming conscious of sin, of awakening to a sense of sin, as a feat of this kind."[68] Arnold met Emerson during the 1847–48 visit and subsequently both in private and publicly acknowledged an intellectual debt to him.[69] But although Emerson applied the typologies of Hellenism and Hebraism to English culture earlier than did Arnold, the Oxford poet attributed his own understanding especially to Heine,[70] while it is likely that Emerson was most directly influenced by Herder, whom he read extensively.[71]

Herder was well-disposed to Jews, and for him Hebraism was certainly a virtue. But Emerson's Hebraism became intertwined with his own critique of Christian supersessionism. Near the end of his ministry, Emerson's religion was transitioning from the euphemistic label of "liberal Christianity" to Unitarianism, a name with significant Christological implications. In an 1832 sermon just before he resigned, Emerson explained that Jesus could not assure followers of personal resurrection, because his purpose "was to redeem us from a formal religion, and teach us to seek our wellbeing in the reformation of the soul" (*CS* 4:193). Rather than it superseding Judaism, to Emerson the "formal religion" of Christianity, with its promise of resurrection, was artifactual and essentially the same as Second Temple messianic Judaism. This is largely what he meant by Hebraism.

In the 1840 talk "Religion," Emerson criticizes the claim of traditional Christian supersessionism: "The radical vice of the popular thought is that with the Christian era a new state of things took place." Emerson then merges this Christian supersessionism with Hebraism, pronouncing that popular thought wrong, because (inverting Tertullian's question): "With Judaea, what has the genuine life of Paris and New York to do? . . . [W]e have found out the mythical character of Christianity. . . . We are in a transition state from this Jewish idea . . . to a more human and universal and heavenly country" (*EL* 3:273–74).[72] Emerson demands that secular supersessionism of the individual replace Hebraized and supersessionist Christianity. He continues to use Hebraism as a tool of cultural analysis through *Representative Men* and *English Traits*. But then, energized by the social transformation of the Civil War, he largely ends his typological investigations of individuals and cultures and takes up the call for radical universalism and natural religion (to which I soon will turn). At the time when Arnold made Hebraism a household word in the English-speaking world, Emerson was rapidly moving beyond it.

In fact, Emerson always understood a more elemental, "purer" Judaism, as the following passages (out of many)[73] exemplify: "You cannot say God, blood, & hell too little. Always suppose God. The Jew named him not" (*JMN* 9:273, 11:67); "The boldest vision of the prophet communing with God only, is confined & coloured & expressed according to the resistless example of the Jewish" (*JMN* 5:5–6, 12:114); "[A man of courage] will come to hear God speak as audibly through his own lips as ever He did by the mouth of Moses or Isaiah or Milton" (*JMN* 4:92). In a late sermon, he refers to "the pious line of Jewish teachers whom their religion seems truly to have made wisest of men" (*CS* 4:245). In 1848, talking to a London audience, which in *English Traits* he would criticize for its resistance to Jewish emancipation, Emerson argued for inherent truths by invoking the spiritual Jew: "The history of one of these eternal Jews on the high road of eternity must supersede Malebranche, Locke, Stewart, and Hegel" (*LL* 1:160).

During the nineteenth century, serious consideration was paid to the religious identity of Jesus. Ernest Renan, for example, a distinguished New

Testament scholar and philosopher whom Emerson quotes in "Perpetual Forces," argued that Jesus was no longer a Jew, a position taken earlier as well by Kant.[74] But Emerson, a true Unitarian who views Jesus only as human, consistently calls him a Jew. In 1831, he preached on "Jesus Christ, a poor benevolent Jew" (*CS* 4:36), and in the sermon quoted above, "Jesus came a Jew to the Jews" (*CS* 3:250).[75] Emerson several times refers to Jesus as "the Blessed Jew" and in the journals sympathetically as "the poor Jewish boy" (*JMN* 11:161).[76]

Emerson's primitive Judaism—what existed prior to the creation of "the triune god" during the Second Temple—was closer to the natural order of things. Largely a Platonist, Emerson was influenced by the seventeenth-century Cambridge Neoplatonists Henry More and Ralph Cudworth (often referenced by Emerson). In following the Middle Platonist Philo of Alexandria, they saw all spiritual and religious truths originating with earliest Judaism, especially Moses, in close proximity to nature,[77] as did Jonathan Edwards,[78] often seen as an important influence on Emerson. Referring to the Old Testament as "our Jewish Bible" (*CW* 6:26), Emerson appreciated prophetic Judaism as an expression of the sublime, as Longinus had observed in the third century and which Herder later stressed.[79]

The emerging Higher Criticism enforced this respect for Jewish primitivism. In the early nineteenth century, John Gottfried Eichhorn established the framework for Julius Wellhausen's later documentary hypothesis. Emerson's Harvard teacher Edward Everett had studied with Eichhorn at Göttingen,[80] as had brother William, whose books by Eichhorn Waldo devoured on his return.[81] In disaggregating layers of the Old Testament, Eichhorn identified the "Priestly Code" or "P" tradition as reflecting an evolving rigid and legalistic society that allowed the Jews to survive the sixth-century BCE Babylonian exile. What preceded that evolution toward Second Temple legalism was a Yahwistic culture with a more direct relationship to the divine. Emerson absorbed the belief that, before Judaism ossified under the social crisis of the Babylonian exile, there had been a "purer" belief.[82] "Our age is not intelligent of the Jews. His religion was in every drop of his blood," Emerson observed (*JMN* 16:8).

In contrast to his attachment to this elemental Judaism, it is more difficult to understand Emerson's Hebraism as applied to modern cultures. As with so many of these categories inspired by the social sciences, he blurred lines, preferring impact over rigor—what Lawrence Buell describes as Emerson's "art of lobbing bombshells."[83] What probably is safest to say is that Emerson had a separate appreciation of early Judaism, whereas Hebraism, reflecting first-century Judaism, was used initially to express disappointment with contemporary Christianity and then evolved as a way of analyzing secular society. He discarded such reductive terms when he began to argue more fully for a new spiritual vision for America based on natural religion, to which I now turn.

So far, we have examined how Emerson thought about Jews, Hebraism, and ancient Judaism. We now look at his influence on contemporary Judaism. And, if he drew on available critical theory in understanding ancient Judaism and Hebraism, Emerson subsequently made his own, original mark on Jewish theology. He lived in the age of Jewish rationalism, and that drew these Jewish thinkers to Emerson and his call to open religious interpretation to the broadest possible inspection.

Emerson's own rationalism aligned with the emerging social sciences, which, by focusing on human commonalities, were laying claim to the empirical truths of the natural sciences. Long disposed to the principles of evolutionary biology,[84] Emerson read *On the Origin of Species* in 1860, the year after it appeared. That same year, in "Worship" he proclaimed the marriage of science and religion: "There will be a new church founded on moral science, at first cold and naked, a babe in the manger again, the algebra and mathematics of ethical law, the church of men to come, without shawms or psaltery, or sackbut; but it will have heaven and earth for its beams and rafters; science for symbol and illustration; it will fast enough gather beauty, music, picture, poetry" (*CW* 6:128).[85] Emerson's scientific turn was well recognized in George Santayana's 1911 talk "The Genteel Tradition in American Philosophy." Momentarily resuscitating the then-lapsed reputation of Emerson as philosopher, Santayana, then somewhat under the spell of pragmatism and its attempt to soften the objective scientism of the times, argued: "Transcendentalism is systematic subjectivism. It studies the perspectives of knowledge as they radiate from the self; it is a plan of those avenues of inference by which our ideas of things must be reached, if they are to afford any systematic or distant vistas. In other words, transcendentalism is the critical logic of science. . . . I regard it as the chief contribution made in modern times to speculation."[86]

Because for Emerson all religions come from the same essential mental impulse—what he called natural religion and what generally has come to be known as religious naturalism—religious spirit is inherent and not contingent on a supernatural power. It is simultaneously subjective to the individual and yet objective, and, therefore, observable. Identifying through scientific inquiry the common religious sentiment promised to put an end to claims of Christian supersessionism, even if it also meant putting an end to Jewish exceptionalism—a bargain some Jews were (at least momentarily) willing to make.

During Emerson's life, the Jewish population in the United States increased exponentially. With fewer than 6,000 in the United States (and virtually none in Boston) in the 1820s, the number of Jews grew to around 15,000 by 1840, and then, remarkably, to around 150,000 by 1860. Because of immigration, Jewish population during the latter part of the nineteenth century increased some fifteen times more quickly than did non-Jewish population.[87] By 1877, at the first official U.S. census to count the Jewish community and just at the start of the massive immigration from eastern Europe, there were approximately 250,000 Jews. It is during this latter part of the nineteenth century, as the Jewish population of Boston began catching up with that of other major cities, that Emerson exerted his greatest direct influence on Jewish theology through the Free Religious Association (FRA).

The FRA had intellectual antecedents stretching back to before the Civil War,[88] but it was formally founded in Boston in 1867, largely on the initiative of Octavius Frothingham, a former Unitarian minister who had an independent church in New York, and John Weiss, self-described in the FRA rolls as a "Radical."[89] The FRA came about in direct response to the divisive 1866 Unitarian National Conference in Syracuse, New York, whose attendees split between those wanting a somewhat traditionally Jesus-centered religion and those seeking more "unity of spirit than . . . uniformity of belief."[90] Reacting to "the Battle of Syracuse," FRA members declared their desire "to promote the scientific study of religious truth, not to defend the legacy of theological tradition."[91] Their purpose was later modified "to promote the practical interests of pure religion . . . and to encourage the scientific study of man's religious nature and history."[92] "Scientific study" is the recurrent phrase, and "pure religion" means identifying transcendent universal principles residing in all religions. Personal belief in a reified godhead was optional, though the presence of vocal agnostics did at times present problems.[93] The association lost a lot of its energy after 1894, when Unitarians adopted pretty much the same position on religious inclusion.

Because Emerson was neither an active organizer of the FRA nor directly engaged in its philosophical discussions, scholars do not credit him with a prominent role in the association.[94] But as a consequence of his enormous intellectual stature, Emerson was essential to its identity. He is listed at the very top of the FRA's first public announcement,[95] and eyewitnesses to the organizing meeting in 1867 reported that he was the first to deliver to the dais the requested dues of one dollar.[96] Whether urban legend or carefully designed gesture, this put the stamp of America's greatest public intellectual on the new organization. Although rarely attending meetings once they became well reported by the press,[97] for the rest of his life Emerson was a vice president and called "the patriarch of the Free Religionists."[98] He spoke at the first two meetings,[99] and reprinted in the first issue of an

FRA-affiliated publication, the *Radical,* was his "Divinity School Address" of nearly three decades past, suggesting that it was the organization's intellectual blueprint.[100] Within that first volume of the *Radical,* an anonymous reviewer of Emerson's public lectures that year concluded that "no living man has done so much as Emerson to waken this Religion."[101] A decade later in the FRA's *Index,* Francis Ellingwood Abbot, certainly not in agreement with him on all matters theological, called Emerson "the greatest legacy that God has yet bestowed on America."[102]

Around the time of the Civil War, Emerson was moving rapidly away from his more structured studies of the character of individuals (*Representative Men*) and society (*English Traits*). Though different from his initial embrace of self-reliance, his newer thinking once again put greater emphasis on philosophical transcendence—a part of what has been called "a second cycle of American Transcendentalism."[103] By the early 1860s, Emerson was talking widely about a universalistic spirituality, still based on individual belief, that transcended established religion and drew legitimacy from emerging biological and social sciences. He gave the lecture "Natural Religion" as many as five times (LL 2:177–95); "Essential Principles of Religion" in 1862 (LL 2:266–73); "Character" in 1865 (so critical of traditional religions that the *Atlantic Monthly* refused to publish it; CW 10:810–15, published the following year in the *North American Review*); and "The Rule of Life" just eighteen days before the founding of the FRA in 1867 (LL 2:376–88).

In "Natural Religion," delivered also in 1869 for the FRA lecture series, Emerson tied human spirituality to the natural impulses of the cosmos: "A religion of the simplest elements; the first duties that everywhere exist commanded by the primal sentiments, need no magnificent annunciation by ancient prophecy or special messengers attended by angels from the skies, but are born in the Indian and the Hottentot, and only need to be obeyed, in order to speak with a clearer voice, and to deliver the whole code of moral and spiritual life." Naturalism, therefore, is the end in itself: "I think we should not assail Christianity, Judaism, or Buddhism, or the *Koran,* but frankly thank each for every brave and just sentence or history they have furnished us. We should not contradict or censure these well-meant, best-meant approximations, but point out the identity of their summits with every other inspiration" (LL 2:180, 185).

Emerson's ideas on the evolution on religious thinking supported by science somewhat aligned with the *philosophie positive* of Auguste Comte, the philosopher who probably exerted the greatest influence on members of the FRA.[104] But at precisely the time when the FRA was being established in 1867, Emerson, never the philosophical formalist, explicitly rejected Comte's teleological resolution. As always for Emerson, the *act* of thinking mattered more than its outcome: "The tendency of the new time is toward a religious belief compatible with the expansion of science: And each new school of metaphysics, as Hegel or Comte, is not final or universal, but only an attempt to emphasize one of the irresistible corrections which new science has made necessary" (*JMN* 14:84). Because of his naturalistic bent, Emerson believed that science could help *explain* the religious impulse, but he did not follow Comte's argument that scientific positivism's secular ideology had *replaced* the religious sentiment. Long before John Dewey's epochal *A Common Faith* (1934), Emerson articulated the distinction between formal religion and individual religious experience. "Goethe, the surpassing intellect of modern times, is spiritual, but not a spiritualist," Emerson observed in 1848 (*LL* 1:166).

Although the idea of natural religion had been evolving over the past two centuries in Europe,[105] Emerson's public pronouncements, unfettered by the teleological secularism of Comte, drew the most attention among Jewish theologians associated with the FRA. As they became emancipated from the ghetto and other social restrictions and began integrating within European society during their own Enlightenment (or *Haskalah*), Jews generally espoused the pervasive theism of western Europe and radicalized it in America.[106] Jonathan Sarna notes: "The late 1860s and early 1870s were a period of confident optimism in American Jewish life. . . . [L]iberal Jews and Protestants spoke warmly of universalism, and rabbis and ministers even occasionally traded pulpits."[107] This exchange was facilitated by common belief, as Reform Judaism lessened its emphasis on ritual and abandoned the remaining Jewish vision of an eventual messiah. The Civil War engendered an enormous amount of Christian messianic yearning,[108] and Reform Judaism and Unitarianism became natural allies against Christian sectarianism and evangelicalism.[109]

The minutes of the first FRA meeting read: "In the chosen list of officers, while those who held or had more or less direct connection with Unitarianism had the ascendency in numbers, Liberal Universalism, Liberal Quakerism, Spiritualism, Progressive Judaism, and the Unchurched were also represented."[110] And the first issue of the FRA's publication, *Radical,* proclaimed: "Out there in Cincinnati there are societies of modern Jews, liberal Jews. We sent off a missive to them, and said, 'Come and we will give you an opportunity to speak from the inside of your own body; let us know what you think.'"[111] Two Cincinnati rabbis attended that first Boston meeting: Isaac M. Wise and Max Lilienthal.[112] These were two of the most important pioneers in promoting Judaism as a modern religion readily understood by liberal Christians. Elected a director of the FRA, Wise caught up to the early transcendentalists in rejecting a literal interpretation of the Bible and belief in miracles.[113] At the 1870 FRA meeting, "Rabbi Wise spoke for Judaism, which he conceived to be the oldest Free Religious Association. Its God had been universalized since the days of Moses, and it recognized no Messiah but Truth and Reason."[114] Aligning with Emersonian naturalism,[115] Wise wrote in 1887 that theology is "the science of the conception of Deity in the human mind."[116]

Other Jews found a place within the FRA. At its second meeting also present was a "Dr. Morris Ellinger, Hebrew."[117] It is unclear whether Ellinger, from New York, was a rabbi.[118] Along with Wise and Lilienthal, he would have heard Emerson address that meeting with the ringing pronouncement, quoted earlier, that: "you cannot bring me too good a word, too dazzling a hope, too penetrating an insight from the Jews. I hail every one with delight, as showing the riches of my brother, my fellow soul, who could thus think and thus greatly feel."[119] Although in his remarks Emerson welcomes all religions worldwide, he singles out Judaism alone for specific endorsement. Jews were likely the only participants not at least indirectly affiliated with Christian traditions, and therefore Judaism was the obvious religion to evoke in describing a universal religious sentiment. But we can well appreciate the effect of America's most honored intellectual on Jews in the audience.

Because the FRA grew quickly, holding meetings and events in numerous cities without much surviving documentation, it is impossible to track accurately subsequent Jewish participation at the local level. But a list of the national directors indicates that prominent Jews were highly visible in the organization.[120] Jews were even solicited from far afield. Invited to the first meeting was Rabbi I. Sangary Nathans. His name suggests he lived in the subcontinent of India, a supposition supported by the fact that the other absent invitee sending felicitations was the chief of the Theistic Association of India.[121]

Much closer to home, nineteenth-century Boston (unlike, say, Philadelphia or New York City) had a relatively homogeneous population, famous even then for its tightly bound religious and social strata. At the time of the establishment of the FRA, Boston had three synagogues, all Orthodox—and therefore none of its religious leaders attended early meetings of the FRA. But just a few years later, in 1874, the most important of the synagogues, Congregation Adath Israel (later Temple Israel),[122] chose for its new rabbi Solomon Schindler. German born, the type of Reform Judaism he fashioned within this previously Orthodox synagogue was entirely American. A vice president of the FRA by 1892,[123] Schindler preached that the Jewish God was evolving "from a household god into a tribal god, then into a national divinity, finally into the god of the Universe"[124] and that Unitarians had more in common with Judaism than with orthodox Christianity.[125] Although Judaism remained exceptional in that its core belief was universality,[126] Schindler predicted, just as had Emerson, that: "[t]he religion of the future will be neither specifically Jewish or Christian or Mohammedan. It will be an entirely new system, in which the immortal parts of all the present religions will be represented, but at the same time so equally balanced that none will dare to claim superiority."[127]

In seeing God as an ever-evolving concept reflecting humanity's own constantly evolving state, Schindler voices the incipient notion of what is now known as process theology. Emerson had long before, in "Circles" (1841), redefined religion as "expectation," which is, as David Robinson observes, "a constant movement forward that never reaches a final destination."[128] (Although Charles Hartshorne is today widely credited with the current realization of both Christian and Jewish process theology, Hartshorne, in turn, acknowledges that "Emerson's *Essays* . . . changed my life substantially.")[129] But it is not just Emerson's anticipation of process theology that Schindler echoes. As humanity must understand God in contemporary terms, those terms are to be established by the most modern, scientific thinking. For Schindler, it is not religious figures, but scientists and scholars who are to be "the real saviors of humanity."[130]

Although Schindler helped to triple membership in Adath Israel, he was forced out in 1894 for urging intermarriage with Christians. His successor, however, proved even more determined to push Judaism along that path. A director of the FRA by 1897,[131] Rabbi Charles Fleischer proclaimed the need for an entirely new American faith: "*We need a new religion which shall express the spirit of this age, the interests of this country, and the character of this people.*"[132] The spirit of that age was, as another of his talks was titled, a natural religion.[133] At Boston's Second Church, Emerson's original pulpit, Fleischer preached that Emerson "has, since my youth, been my 'patron saint' . . . the one man and mind that has helped me to help myself."[134] And in his Jewish New Year's sermon of 1899 at Adath Israel, he invoked "New England's universal seer, Emerson."[135] When his congregation grew predictably uneasy with Fleischer's amalgam of Judaism and Christianity, Fleischer happily resigned in 1911. He went on to found the first nonsectarian congregation in Boston, proclaiming that he "preferred Emerson to Moses."[136]

Yet with the massive eastern European Jewish immigration and concomitant rise of antisemitism in the 1880s, many Jewish utopianists grew disillusioned. Solomon Schindler returned to Adath Israel to recant his earlier vision, and liberal Christians and Jews were unable to surrender the belief that their own heritage was the culmination of their civilizations. "Christianity is the natural development of Judaism; Judaism is germinal Christianity; Christianity is fructified Judaism," wrote the atheist Francis E. Abbot.

Meanwhile, his friend Rabbi Isaac Wise argued that Mosaic Law was the culmination of God's plan, and therefore Unitarians should become Jews.[137] Schools and organizations became restrictive, and many Jews were embarrassed by Christian acceptance of Felix Adler's model of a "de-Judaized Ethical Culture movement as a harbinger of Judaism's future course."[138] But Adler, too, was part of the Emersonian arc.

Before founding Ethical Culture, Felix Adler was drawn to the FRA. His presence initially proved awkward, for, unlike Wise and Lilienthal, Adler was not a religious individual in any conventional sense. In fact, in 1872 the FRA paved the way for Adler's participation by specifying that there should be no "test of speculative opinion or belief."[139] The rapid ascent within the FRA of this young (Adler was born in 1851) former rabbinical student who renounced Jewish exceptionalism and any accepted sense of a divine force sparked Rabbi Wise to resign from the association.[140] By 1879, Adler was president of the FRA, a position he surrendered in 1882,[141] when it became clear to him that the FRA was determined to limit itself to discussing matters of the spirit rather than engaging in the social activism he had urged on it.[142] Under the influence of social gospel, Adler turned to the organization he had founded in 1876—the New York Society for Ethical Culture (whose motto was "not the creed but the deed,"[143] but which traditional Jews publicly described as "a Jewish congregation that excluded the Jewish religion").[144] Yet his affiliation with the FRA brought him many friends who later also joined his Ethical Culture movement,[145] thus strengthening ties to Emerson.

It was through the FRA that Adler initially found Emerson, who, in the words of Adler's best biographer, Benny Kraut, "profoundly colored his religious and intellectual thinking."[146] Soon after joining the FRA, in 1875 Adler visited Emerson in Concord, and he befriended other Emersonians while teaching at Cornell.[147] In his 1918 reflective work, *An Ethical Philosophy of Life Presented in Its Main Outlines,* Adler acknowledges two primary intellectual influences: Kant (on whom, of course, American transcendentalism is based) and Emerson:

> "I made Emerson's acquaintance in 1875. I came into touch with the Emerson circle and read and re-read the Essays. The value of Emerson's teaching to me at that time consisted in the exalted view he takes of the self. . . . So for a time I continued to walk on air with Emerson, and had my head in the clouds,—the clouds in which Emerson enveloped me." Adler had the type of mind that needed to expunge the ambiguities on which Emerson thrived, and he ultimately condemned the use of Emersonian insights: "I soon discovered that Emerson overstresses self-affirmation at the expense of service." Emerson proved to be "an ethical guide to be accepted only with large reservations."[148]

But earlier, in his 1905 work, *The Essentials of Spirituality,* Adler appealed to an Emersonian vision in resolving his own deep ambivalence:

> How is it possible that at one moment I should be sympathetic and kind . . . should take a generous interest in public causes, and try to act justly; and that at another moment I am so selfish and base? How can there be this oscillation from one pole to the other of human character? . . . Am I, too, not "truly one but truly two"; am I, too, a Jekyll and a Hyde, both dwelling under the same skin? The answer is: You are neither the Hyde nor the Jekyll unless you elect to be. The true self is a principle in you superior to both these natural characters, a kind of oversoul, as Emerson puts it.[149]

The Emersonian Over-soul ("The Over-Soul" was published in 1841) proved helpful to Adler in understanding the tension between ego and altruism. Adler's ego represents materialism and the Kantian phenomenal world identified by transcendentalists as Understanding, whereas Adler's altruism is part of the Kantian noumenal world of innate moral sensibilities that transcendentalists (somewhat reductively) knew as Reason. For Emerson, it was a lifelong struggle to maintain an honest presence in both material and moral worlds, for which he invented the now-famous term "double consciousness" (*CW* 1:213; also *CW* 6:25).

Although Emerson actually focuses more on the soul in that essay, the Over-soul was clearly a governing authority. In the Neoplatonic schema on which it is based, Emerson's Over-soul is associated with the Mind (*nous*) and derived from the Good (Emerson's "the eternal One"). The Over-soul describes the congregation of all individual souls, providing both community and an individual relationship to the higher spirits. Belief in something akin to Emerson's Over-soul assured Adler that there was a greater attainable good than what he found in his struggle between ego and altruism, and that in turn supported his commitment to political activism.

Emerson's Over-soul also supplied insight for twentieth-century America's most influential Jewish theologian. By 1902, Felix Adler was teaching social and political ethics at Columbia, and one of his graduate students that year was Mordecai Kaplan.[150] Although Kaplan was drawn to Adler's struggle with what was demanded ethically of the individual, he was repelled, as had been Isaac Wise, by Adler's universalizing of those ethics to the point of separating himself from a Jewish past.

Judaism as a Civilization (1934) is Kaplan's most famous work, and its title informs us that for him Judaism was not defined by metaphysics. Rather, Kaplan's focus reflects his Columbia training in sociology and especially the pragmatism and religious naturalism of his teacher, John Dewey. Living a life in the present but dominated by values created in the past creates a "split mentality."[151] To navigate this double consciousness in a society moving toward ever-greater democracy and social justice, Jewish civilization, too, must evolve, and that includes a continuous reinterpretation of God.[152] "God is the *process* that makes for man's life abundant or salvation. . . . God is not apart from the world but rather the power in the world that makes for human salvation."[153] Living in the age of social science and evolutionary biology, Kaplan understood humanity, nature, and the divine as constantly evolving and, building on the work of Emerson's direct epigone, John Dewey, and Emerson's godson, William James, he identified the religious impulse as biological. "In order therefore that Judaism survive, nature must be, so to say, reinstated," Kaplan wrote in his journal in 1904.[154]

Along with those of Dewey, Henri Bergson, and Ahad Ha'am (the founder of cultural Zionism), Emerson was one of the "voices in [Kaplan's] head."[155] In 1938, Kaplan constructed a new prayer, inspired by Emerson's "Divinity School Address" (of precisely one hundred years earlier), that started: "NEEDED PROPHETS FOR OUR DAY / by Rabbi Mordecai M. Kaplan / in the name of Ralph Waldo Emerson."[156] Later, he composed another prayer, based on Emerson's "Compensation," titled "The Laws of the Soul . . . in the name of Ralph Waldo Emerson."[157] Elsewhere, he quotes from "Self-Reliance."[158]

As did Alder, Kaplan relies on Emerson's "the Over-Soul" for what Kaplan calls "the integrating influence of the communion with God." And yet also perhaps influenced as well by Adler's insistence on communal ethics, Kaplan separated himself from Emerson: "But Emerson was apparently unaware of the extent to which communion with God is dependent on the social experience of community worship," he observed in his journal.[159] Kaplan may be misreading Emerson, who is most certainly aware of the necessity of community, even in "The Over-Soul," in which he refers to "that Unity, that Over-soul, within which every man's particular being is contained *and made one with all other*" (CW 2:160; my emphasis). It may well be that Kaplan *necessarily* misreads Emerson, because the implications of Emerson's radical naturalism undermine the possibility of an intentional community defined, not merely by common sentiment, but also by historical connection.

The story does not end here. As is well known, Emerson's spiritual ideas migrated to Europe via Nietzsche. And while the main sources of influence lay elsewhere, in 1904, the great Austrian Jewish neo-Romantic, Martin Buber, acknowledged Emerson as producing "the most convincing literary expression" of "metaphysical individualism."[160] Although the fact that Jewish theologians befriended or drew inspiration from Emerson does not prove his own personal sympathies toward Judaism, it is an important part of the record that has previously gone unexplored. By offering a radical naturalism, Emerson gave Jewish theologians an original American religion within which to grow—that is, until they faced the inevitable challenge of surrendering historical exceptionalism. Emerson also had a profound effect on many Jewish novelists, poets, and academic writers. But much has already been written about the secular side of Emerson's influence, and, for now, there have been raised enough "Jewish Questions."[161]

Notes

1. See, for example, Gary Collison, "Emerson and Antislavery," in *A Historical Guide to Ralph Waldo Emerson*, ed. Joel Myerson (New York: Oxford University Press, 2000), 179–210.

2. Jacob Katz, "The Preparatory Stage of the Modern Antisemitic Movement (1873–1879)," in *Antisemitism through the Ages*, ed. Shmuel Almog (Oxford: Pergamon Press, 1988), 279–80. Current practice in Jewish studies is that "antisemitism" refers to hatred of Jews, while "anti-Semitism" denotes hatred of any Semitic peoples.

3. Miriam Leonard, *Socrates and the Jews: Hellenism and Hebraism from Moses Mendelssohn to Sigmund Freud* (Chicago: University of Chicago Press, 2012), 139–76, 217–23.

4. Ibid., 10.

5. The fullest exposition is Robert Loewenberg, *An American Idol: Emerson and the "Jewish Idea"* (Lanham, MD: University Press of America, 1984); supported by Jonathan Sarna, "American Antisemitism," in David Berger, ed., *History and Hate* (Philadelphia: Jewish Publication Society, 1968), 115–28, esp. 118–23, who cites others (though Sarna at least does include contradictory evidence); to which add more recently: Louis Harp, *Image of the Jew in American Literature: From Early Republic to Mass Immigration* (Philadelphia: Jewish Publication Society of America, 1974), 102–3; Egal Feldman, *Dual Identities: The Jewish Encounter with Protestant America* (Urbana: University of Illinois Press, 1990), 54–56; Robert Michael, *A Concise History of American Antisemitism* (New York: Rowman & Littlefield, 2005), 81–82; Robert Michael and Philip Rosen, *Dictionary of Antisemitism: From the Earliest Times to the Present* (Lanham, MD: Scarecrow Press, 2006), 145; Michael Hoberman, *New Israel/New England: Jews and Puritans in Early America* (Amherst: University of Massachusetts Press, 2011), 244–45 (qualified). Naturally, this has morphed and multiplied on the Internet, where Emerson is either criticized as an antisemite—or praised as one. See, for example, Benjamin Ivry, "Emerson, Emma Lazarus and the Jews," *Jewish Daily Forward*, December 26, 2011.

6. *L* 1:227. Also *L* 1:327 (1831) and 1:397 (1833).

7. David Hume, *History of England: The History of England from the Invasion of Julius Caesar to the Revolution in 1688* (New York: Inskeep & Bradford, 1810), 1:256 (*CW* 9:619–21).

8. Sarna, "American Antisemitism," 118–23. See also Hoberman, *New Israel/New England*, 32–43, 51–85, 202–36.

9. Stephen G. Mostov, "A Sociological Review of German Jewish Immigrants in Boston," *American Jewish Studies Review* 3 (1978): 121–52. Moses Michel Hays had been a wealthy Boston merchant, but he had died in 1805, and none of his family remained in Boston (Hoberman, *New Israel/New England*, 202–36). In some other parts of the United States, Jews were disproportionately involved in banking, and it is not impossible that Emerson had heard of them: Jay Michael Eidelman, "'In the Wilds of America': The Early Republican Origins of American Judaism, 1790–1830" (Ph.D. diss., Yale University, 1997), 32–33.

10. Michael, *Concise History of American Antisemitism*, 81. On the period generally, see ibid., 69–96; and Louis Harap, *Image of the Jew in American Literature: From Early Republic to Mass Immigration* (Syracuse, NY: Syracuse University Press, 2003), 27–81.

11. Harap, *Image of the Jew in American Literature*, 101.

12. John Higham, *Send These to Me: Jews and Other Immigrants in Urban America* (New York: Atheneum, 1975), 122–40.

13. Ibid., 140.

14. Ralph L. Rusk, *The Life of Ralph Waldo Emerson* (New York: Columbia University Press, 1957), 180 (based on *L* 1:374, not cited in his biography); also *CEC* 105 (Emerson to Carlyle, August 12, 1834).

15. The negative—even contemptuous—opinion of Emerson that Mill later formed is set out in a remarkable recent discovery: Frank Prochaska, "Mill and Emerson: Sense and Nonsense," *History Today* 63 (September 2013): 21–26.

16. Barrie M. Ratcliffe, "Crisis and Identity: Gustave d'Eichthal and Judaism in the Emancipation Period," *Jewish Social Studies* 37 (1975): 122–40.

17. Most important, Emerson's letter to Charles of April 16, 1833 (*L* 1:274).

18. Oscar Reiss, *The Jews in Colonial America* (Jefferson, NC: McFarland, 2004), 41–42. See also Holly Snyder, "A Tree with Two Different Fruits: The Jewish Encounter with German Pietists in the Eighteenth-Century Atlantic World," *William and Mary Quarterly* 58 (October 2001): 855–82, esp. 871–73, 880–82, and her "Roger Williams, English Law and Religious Tolerance: The Jewish Experience in the Southern New England Colonies, 1677–1798," in Josh B. Stein and Sargon G. Donabed, eds., *Religion and the State: Europe and North America in the Seventeenth and Eighteenth Centuries* (Lanham, MD: Lexington Books, 2012), 107–26; 115.

19. He is caustic about the attack on Benjamin Disraeli's Jewish heritage by Irish leader Daniel O'Connell (*JMN* 9:387; compare with *JMN* 9:15 and 21). Emerson generally had good things to say about Disraeli as novelist and politician (*JMN* 9:48, 118, 351, 361, 531).

20. Albert J. von Frank, "The Visual Arts," in Joel Myerson, Sandra Herbert Petrulionis, and Laura Dassow Walls, eds., *The Oxford Handbook of Transcendentalism* (Oxford: Oxford University Press, 2010), 446, virtually alone has the correct interpretation of the journal entry.

21. Emerson lifelong held a deeply ambivalent attitude toward Allston: *The Correspondence of Washington Allston*, ed. Nathalia Wright (Lexington: University Press of

Kentucky, 1993), 427–28, and esp. the note on 430; to which add: C. P. Seabrook Wilkinson, "Emerson and the 'Eminent Painter,'" *New England Quarterly* 71 (1998): 120–26. See also *JMN* 5:199–200, where Emerson admires Michelangelo's portraits of Jews as individuals. Another example of a misreading is the 1832 journal entry (*JMN* 4:6), which is often seen as denigrating Jews. But Emerson is the "wobegone friend" in mourning for Ellen. See *JMN* 4:7 and esp. *JMN* 3:244–45, where he assumes the role of a Jewish mourner just after her death.

22. John Keyes, revised by Adams Tolman and Marian Blackall Miller, "Houses & Owners or Occupants in Concord, 1885," revised 1940, (MS. Concord Free Public Library) mentioned that around the turn of the twentieth century, Bertram Louis Filene "a rather quarrelsome and noisy Hebrew" had a store there briefly (he was younger brother of Edward A. Filene, founder of the famous Boston department store). Robert Gross believes Filene was the first Jew to live in Concord. Felix Adler (see below) had visited Emerson a year earlier, in 1875, but, although a Jew by birth, by then he hardly identified as such. Gross identified several Jewish inmates in the state prison at Concord (Concord Reformatory) by the 1900 census, but the prison itself did not open until 1878.

23. Ellen Tucker Emerson to Edith Emerson Forbes, August 26, 1876, in *Letters of Ellen Tucker Emerson*, ed. Edith E. W. Gregg (Kent, OH: Kent State University Press, 1982), 2:225.

24. Bette Roth Young, *Emma Lazarus in Her World: Life and Letters* (Philadelphia: Jewish Publication Society, 1955), 194: Letter to Rose Hawthorne Lathrop, 1882; pp. 89 and 91: two letters to Helena deKay Gilder in 1881.

25. *Letters of Ellen Tucker Emerson,* 2:223

26. Ibid., 2:225; see also 220, 223, 291.

27. To Helena deKay Gilder: Young, *Emma Lazarus in Her World*, 72.

28. Ellen Tucker Emerson, *The Life of Lidian Jackson Emerson*, ed. Delores Bird Carpenter (East Lansing: Michigan State University Press, 2012), 185–86. In that work, Ellen expresses caution about Lazarus's first visit not because of her religion—which goes unmentioned there—but out of desire to protect her father, already in mental decline, from strangers (179; on the mental decline, 173).

29. *Letters and Journals of Thomas Wentworth Higginson, 1846–1906*, ed. Mary Thatcher Higginson (Privately printed, 1921), October 1872, 266.

30. Emerson also notes in his pocket diary the addresses of Lazarus and her father, whom he visited while in New York (*JMN* 16:371, 378, 473).

31. Joseph Henry Allen, *Sequel to "Our Liberal Movement"* (Boston: Roberts Brothers, 1897), 108–15.

32. Cyrus Augustus Bartol, *Principles and Portraits* (Boston: Roberts Brothers, 1880), 386–87. Elsewhere, however, neither Bartol nor Frothingham mentions in their obituaries his Jewish heritage: Cyrus Augustus Bartol, *Unitarian Review*, April 1879, 437–39; O. B. Frothingham, *Unitarian Review*, May 1888, 417–29 (rpt. in O. B. Frothingham, *Recollections and Impressions, 1820–1890* (New York: G.P. Putnam's Sons, 1891), 190–208.

33. Henry Williams, *Memorials of the Class of 1837 of Harvard University: Prepared for the Fiftieth Anniversary of Their Graduation* (Boston: G. H. Ellis, 1887), 58–63.

34. Bronson Alcott, *Record of Conversations with Children on the Gospels Held in Mr. Alcott's School, Unfolding the Doctrine and Discipline of Human Culture* (Boston: James Munroe, 1836–37), 1:66.

35. Kenneth S. Sacks, *Understanding Emerson: "The American Scholar" and His Struggle for Self-Reliance* (Princeton, NJ: Princeton University Press, 2003), 98–120.

36. Phyllis Cole, "Pain and Protest in the Emerson Family," in T. Gregory Harvey, ed., *The Emerson "Dilemma": Essays on Emerson and Social Reform* (Athens: University of Georgia Press, 2001), 67–92.

37. Samuel Joseph May, *Memoir of Samuel Joseph May* (Boston: Robert Brothers, 1873), 15–16; see also Ellen Smith, "Strangers and Sojourners: The Jews of Colonial Boston," in Jonathan D. Sarna, Ellen Smith, and Scott-Martin Kosofsky, eds., *The Jews of Boston*, 2nd ed. (New Haven, CT: Yale University Press, 2005), 21–43.

38. Lydia Maria Child, *Letters from New-York* (New York: Charles S. Frances & Co., 1843), Letter 6, "The Jews. Black Jews. Old Clothes. Reading by Lamplight in the Daytime," 25–35, quotations from 28 and 31.

39. Bell Gale Chevigny, *Margaret Fuller's Life and Writings: The Woman and the Myth* (Boston: Northeastern University Press, 1976), 500–501.

40. *New York Daily Tribune*, April 21, 1845, 1.

41. Rusk, *Life of Ralph Waldo Emerson*, 338–40; see now esp. Daniel Koch, *Ralph Waldo Emerson in Europe: Class, Race, and Revolution in the Making of an American Thinker* (London: I.B. Tauris, 2012), 102–5.

42. See also P. L., "Emerson's Meeting with De Quincey," *Blackwood's Magazine* 155 (April 1894): 480–89.

43. Rusk, *Life of Ralph Waldo Emerson*, 330–59; see *JMN* 10:409; Koch, *Ralph Waldo Emerson in Europe*, 11–27.

44. Rusk, *Life of Ralph Waldo Emerson*, 330.

45. Ibid., 346ff.

46. While Dickens praises Monmouth Street Jews, he adds: "Holywell-street we despise; the red-headed and red-whiskered Jews who forcibly haul you into their squalid houses, and thrust you into a suit of clothes, whether you will or not, we detest." Predictably, Emerson ignores this.

47. Donald S. Katz, *Jews in the History of England, 1485–1850* (Oxford: Oxford University Press, 1994), 389.

48. For the source of his information, see *CW* 5:218. Probably in preparation for *English Traits*, he asks himself in his 1852–53 journals: "What is the law touching Jewish franchise?" (*JMN* 10:568).

49. Volume 6 of Charles Knight's *London* appeared a few years earlier and contained a long, generally sympathetic historical description of Jews in Great Britain: Charles Knight, *London* (London: Charles Knight & Co., 1844) 6:34–48. While we have no

record of Emerson's reading that particular volume and there is no obvious correlation between the facts Emerson produces and what Knight wrote, we do know that he dined at Knight's home in 1848 (*L* 4:67). We only know of Emerson's reading volume 2 in 1865: Albert J. von Frank, *An Emerson Chronology* (New York: G. K. Hall, 1994), 410; he read also another Knight work: *JMN* 14:282. Emerson had in his home Henry Holt Milman, *The History of the Jews,* 3 vols. (London: John Murray, 1829); see Walter Harding, *Emerson's Library* (Charlottesville: University of Virginia Press, 1967), 190. But the volumes did not cover more recent history of British Jews.

50. See also *JMN* 10:290 and 11:217. Other references to the Rothschilds in *The Conduct of Life* appear neutral (*CW* 6:21 and 56).

51. Emerson gave the speech for the first time on November 19, 1862, and repeated it frequently over the next four months and perhaps for even as long as a year. The current printed version is Emerson's standard manuscript, but there may have been other versions, and, of course, Emerson also made notes no longer available to us (*LL* 2:287–89).

52. *The War of the Rebellion: A Compilation of the Official Records of the Union and Confederate Armies*, ed. Robert N. Scott (Washington, DC: Government Printing Office, 1887), series 1, 17:337.

53. Bertram Wallace Korn, *American Jewry and the Civil War* (Philadelphia: Jewish Publication Society, 2001), 66–115.

54. "Talk at the Second Annual Meeting of the Free Religious Association, at Tremont Temple, Friday, May 28, 1869," in *Complete Works of Ralph Waldo Emerson*, 12 vols., ed. Edward Waldo Emerson (Boston: Houghton Mifflin, 1904), 11:489–90.

55. Len Gougeon, *Virtue's Hero: Emerson, Antislavery, and Reform* (Athens: University of Georgia Press, 1990), 70–79.

56. Similarly, CXXXXIV and CLXV.

57. Charles L. Cohen, *God's Caress: The Psychology of Puritan Religious Experience* (New York: Oxford University Press, 1986), 162–200. On the Puritans as New Israel, see Sacvan Bercovitch, *The American Jeremiad* (Madison: University of Wisconsin Press, 1978), 76–80; and Harry S. Stout, *The New England Soul: Preaching and Religious Culture in Colonial New England* (Oxford: Oxford University Press, 1986), 54–56.

58. Edmund Wilson, "Notes on Gentile Pro-Semitism: New England's Good Jews," *Commentary* 22 (October 1956): 329–35, esp. 329–31. The bibliography on, and debate about, what Puritans drew from Judaism is immense: see most recently, Hoberman, *New Israel/New England*, 1–50.

59. Still fundamental to understanding Emerson's religion during his years in the ministry is David M. Robinson, "The Sermons of Ralph Waldo Emerson: An Introductory Historical Essay" (*CS* 1:1–32).

60. See also *CS* 4:161 and 4:172.

61. John L. Thomas, "Romantic Reform in America, 1815–1865," *American Quarterly* 17 (1965): 656–81.

62. Already in 1841, when eulogizing his step-grandfather, the Reverend Ezra Ripley,

Emerson evokes the image of a fading Puritanical Hebraism: "Not speculative, but affectionate; devout, but with an extreme love of order, he adopted heartily, though in its mildest forms, the creed and catechism of the fathers, and appeared a modern Israelite in his attachment to the Hebrew history and faith. . . . And now, in his old age, when all the antique Hebraism and its customs are passing away, it is fit that he too should depart, most fit that in the fall of laws a loyal man should die" (CW 10:153).

63. Similarly in 1867: "Theophilus Parsons understands Swedenborg only up to the limit of 'Hebrew symbolism.' Philosopher up to that limit, but here accepts the village-church as part of the sky" (JMN 16:54). "Village-church" is a clue that Emerson does not tether Hebraism to Judaism but applies it generally to historically based monotheisms.

64. See also CW 5:133.

65. *De praescriptione haereticorum*, 7.

66. Leonard, *Socrates and the Jews*, 7.

67. Louis H. Feldman, "Hebraism and Hellenism Reconsidered," *Judaism: A Quarterly Journal of Jewish Life and Thought* 43 (1994): 115–27; also more modern Jews, such as Mordecai Kaplan and Lionel Trilling: Seth Korelitz, "The Menorah Idea: From Religion to Culture, from Race to Ethnicity," *American Jewish History* 85 (1997): 75–100; Tessa Rajak, "Jews and Greeks," in *The Jewish Dialogue with Greece and Rome: Studies in Cultural and Social Interaction* (Leiden: E. J. Brill, 2001), 535–57.

68. "Hebraism and Hellenism" is chapter 4 of *Culture and Anarchy* (London: Smith, Elder & Co., 1869), 143–66; quotations are from 145 and 153.

69. Arnold wrote to Emerson: "I can never forget the refreshing and quickening effect your writings had upon me at a critical time of my life." *The Letters of Matthew Arnold*, 6 vols., ed. Cecil Y. Lang (Charlottesville: University Press of Virginia, 1996–2001), June 19, 1864, 5:343; cf. Francis Turner Palgrave to Thomas Arnold, April 28, 1848; Letter V1P106D1. Arnold later wrote to his brother: "Tomorrow I give my lecture on Emerson for the first time; I don't think he was ever a favourite of yours, but he was of mine" (*Letters of Matthew Arnold,* November 30, 1883, 1:106). Arnold told Moncure D. Conway that "Carlyle was the more striking figure, but I loved Emerson more because he never lost his sanity." Moncure D. Conway, "Emerson: The Teacher and the Man," *Critic: An Illustrated Monthly Review of Literature, Art & Life* 42 (1903): 411. Arnold publicly proclaimed Emerson's *Essays* the most important thing done in prose in the nineteenth century: "Emerson," in *Essays in Criticism. Second Series*, in *The Works of Matthew Arnold* (London: Macmillan, 1903–4), 4:377.

70. Leonard, *Socrates and the Jews*, 120.

71. Gene Bluestein, *Poplore: Folk and Pop in American Culture* (Amherst: University of Massachusetts Press, 1994), 48–49.

72. First at JMN 7:321; see also JMN 5:434.

73. EL 1:138, 166, 2:152, 225, 3:69, 206, 224, 299; CW 7:16; JMN 5:465 (used in CW 2:16). Some believe Emerson attacks Jews in "Self-Reliance," when, probably referencing

Leviticus 16, he mentions that "those foolish Israelites, 'Let not God speak to us, lest we die.'" But Emerson goes on to attack anyone who demands to control how people think, including Locke, Lavoisier, Fourier, and Swedenborg (CW 2:45). It is the institutionalization of any spiritual quest that Emerson is renouncing. At the very beginning of "Self-Reliance," Emerson names Moses, along with Plato and Milton, as deserving "the highest merit" (CW 2:27).

74. Rajak, "Jews and Greeks," 535–57; 547; Leonard, *Socrates and the Jews*, 70.

75. Also referring to "Jews like Jesus" (CS 4:189).

76. A phrase he uses in a poem without naming, though clearly intending, Jesus (CW 9:546; JMN 10:389); see also CS 2:192 with CS 2:361; also JMN 8:196.

77. Peter Harrison, *"Religion" and the Religions in the English Enlightenment* (Cambridge: Cambridge University Press, 1990), 130–38.

78. See, for example, Gerald R. McDermott, "Poverty, Patriotism, and National Covenant: Jonathan Edwards and Public Life," *Journal of Religious Ethics* 31 (2003): 229–52; 237.

79. The subject of Hebraism is massive. See most recently the extensive discussion in Roland Greene et al., eds., *The Princeton Encyclopedia of Poetry and Poetics*, 4th ed. (Princeton, NJ: Princeton University Press, 2012), 597–601.

80. Paul A. Varg, *Edward Everett: The Intellectual in the Turmoil of Politics* (Selinsgrove, PA: Susquehanna University Press, 1992), 19–22; also Robert D. Richardson, Jr., *Emerson: The Mind on Fire* (Berkeley: University of California Press, 1995), 11–13, 49.

81. Karen Lynn Kalinevitch, *Ralph Waldo Emerson's Older Brother: The Letters and Journal of William Emerson* (Knoxville: University of Tennessee Press, 1982), 26–29. Barbara Packer has cogently argued that Emerson was aware of Eichhorn's New Testament criticism: "Origin and Authority: Emerson and the Higher Criticism," in Sacvan Bercovitch, ed., *Reconstructing American Literary History* (Cambridge, MA: Harvard University Press, 1986), 67–92, esp. 76–82.

82. Herder, in fact, stressed the difference between pre- and post-exilic Jews. Moses made the Jews noble, but the Jews do not take advantage of their own natural resources: Rajak, "Jews and Greeks," 541.

83. Lawrence Buell, *Emerson* (Cambridge, MA: Harvard University Press, 2003), 281.

84. See, generally, Laura Dassow Walls, *Emerson's Life in Science: The Culture of Truth* (Ithaca, NY: Cornell University Press, 2003); and, now, William Rossi, "Evolutionary Theory," in *The Oxford Handbook of Transcendentalism*, 583–96.

85. Previously in an unpublished lecture of 1848 (LL 1:189); initially at JMN 10:306.

86. George Santayana, "The Genteel Tradition in American Philosophy," in *Winds of Doctrine* (New York: Scribner's, 1913), 186–215, quotation on 193–94; discussed by Charles Capper, "'A Little Beyond': The Problem of the Transcendentalist Movement in American History," *Journal of American History* 85 (1998): 502–39, on 511–15.

87. Jonathan Sarna, *American Judaism: A History* (New Haven, CT: Yale University Press, 2005), 54, 63.

88. Most recently, David M. Robinson, "The Free Religious Association," in *The Oxford Handbook of Transcendentalism*, 617–28.

89. George Willis Cooke, "Free Religious Association," *New England Magazine*, n.s., 28 (1903): 484–99; 491.

90. Cooke, "Free Religious Association," 485.

91. Ibid., 488.

92. Ibid., 489.

93. Stow Persons, *Free Religion: An American Faith* (New Haven, CT: Yale University Press, 1947), 66–68; on science in the FRA, see also Robinson, "The Free Religious Association," 621–22.

94. Emerson merits hardly a mention: Charles Cashdollar, *The Transformation of American Theology* (Princeton, NJ: Princeton University Press, 1989), 281–308; and Robinson, "The Free Religious Association," 617–28.

95. Sydney E. Ahlstrom and Robert Bruce Mullin, *The Scientific Theist: A Life of Francis Ellingwood Abbot* (Macon, GA: Mercer University Press, 1987), 72.

96. Persons, *Free Religion*, 49–50.

97. Cooke, "Free Religious Association," 499. He probably attended only two additional lunches: June 1, 1876, and June 1, 1877 (*ETE* 2:206, 254). But he had more extensive attendance at the "Radical Club," which overlapped with his purposes. See John T. Sargent, ed., *Sketches and Reminiscences of the Radical Club of Chestnut Street, Boston* (Boston: James R. Osgood & Co., 1880), index.

98. Ahlstrom and Mullin, *The Scientific Theist*, 74.

99. *The Radical: A Monthly Magazine Devoted to Religion* (Boston: A. Williams, 1866), 1:494, 540–44; also Cooke, "Free Religious Association," 490.

100. *Radical*, 1:30–44.

101. Ibid., 1:354.

102. *Index*, August 8, 1878, quoted by Ahlstrom and Mullin, *The Scientific Theist*, 96.

103. Arthur Versluis, *American Transcendentalism and Asian Religions* (New York: Oxford University Press, 1993), 326. The impact of Emerson's European visit and of his abolitionism is complex. See Koch, *Ralph Waldo Emerson in Europe*, 1–10, for the range of interpretations. Emerson's remarkable "The Powers and Laws of Thought" (LL 1:137–51) demonstrates that he was already reestablishing his idealism in the late 1840s.

104. Cashdollar, *Transformation of American Theology*, 281–308.

105. Harrison, *"Religion" and the Religions in the English Enlightenment*, 130–72.

106. Michael A. Meyer, *Response to Modernity: A History of the Reform Movement in Judaism* (New York: Oxford University Press, 1988), 226–27, noting there Emerson's influence as well.

107. Jonathan D. Sarna, "The Late Nineteenth-Century American Jewish Awakening," in Walter H. Conser, Jr., and Sumner B. Twiss, eds., *Religious Diversity and American Religious History* (Athens: University of Georgia Press, 1997), 5.

108. Mark S. Schantz, *Awaiting the Heavenly Country: The Civil War and America's Culture of Death* (Ithaca, NY: Cornell University Press, 2008).

109. Benny Kraut, "The Ambivalent Relations of American Reform Judaism with Unitarianism in the Last Third of the Nineteenth Century," *Journal of Ecumenical Studies* 23 (1986): 56–68; 60–61.

110. William J. Potter, *The Free Religious Association: Its Twenty-Five Years and Their Meaning* (Boston: Free Religious Association of America, 1892), 14–15.

111. *Radical,* 1:494.

112. Cooke, "Free Religious Association," 489.

113. Arthur Mann, *Growth and Achievement: Temple Israel, 1854–1954* (Cambridge, MA: Riverside Press, 1954), 6–7.

114. Persons, *Free Religion*, 78.

115. James G. Heller, *Isaac M. Wise: His Life, Work and Thought* (New York: Union of American Hebrew Congregations, 1965), 522–24.

116. Ibid.

117. Cooke, "Free Religious Association," 491.

118. He is frequently referred to as "brother" of the B'ne Brith lodge in *Menorah* 9 (1890), distinguishing him from rabbis mentioned there.

119. "Talk at the Second Annual Meeting of the Free Religious Association," 489–90.

120. Including prominent New York attorney Edward Lauerbach (1880), Rabbi Henry Berkowitz (1901), and Lincoln scholar Alonzo Rothschild (1907). *Proceedings of the Fortieth Annual Meeting of the Free Religious Association* 40 (Free Religious Association: Boston, 1907). See also Benny Kraut, *From Reform Judaism to Ethical Culture: The Religious Evolution of Felix Adler* (Cincinnati: Hebrew Union College Press, 1979), 218.

121. *Radical,* 1:560. Keshub Chunder Sen, chief of the Brahmo-Somaj.

122. Smith, "Strangers and Sojourners," 49.

123. *Christian Register*, January 2, 1913, 21.

124. Sermon at Adath Israel, rpt. in *Boston Daily Globe*, October 23, 1886; Arthur Mann, "Solomon Schindler: Boston Radical," *New England Quarterly* 23 (December 1950): 462.

125. Ibid., 460.

126. Meaghan Dwyer-Ryan, Susan L. Porter, and Lisa Fagin Davis, *Becoming American Jews: Temple Israel of Boston* (Waltham, MA: Brandeis University Press, 2009), 34.

127. Solomon Schindler, *Messianic Expectations and Modern Judaism* (Boston: S. E. Cassino & Co., 1886), 166.

128. David M. Robinson, *Emerson and the Conduct of Life: Pragmatism and Ethical Purpose in the Later Work* (Cambridge: Cambridge University Press, 1993), 65, on CW 3:41.

129. Charles Hartshorne, "How I Got That Way," in John B. Cobb, Jr., and Franklin I. Gamwell eds., *Existence and Actuality: Conversations with Charles Hartshorne* (Chicago: University of Chicago Press, 1984), xiii.

130. Mann, *Growth and Achievement*, 57.

131. *Christian Register*, January 2, 1913, 21.

132. Charles Fleischer, *American Aspirations* (New York: B. W. Huebsch, 1914), 8 (his italics).

133. Fleischer, *American Aspirations*, 62–63.

134. *Boston Evening Transcript*, April 12, 1900, 23. He also gave a lecture in Boston to commemorate the Emerson centennial: "Emerson, the Seer of Democracy" (*New England Magazine* 28 [1903]).

135. Mann, *Growth and Achievement*, 72.

136. James P. Wind, *Places of Worship: Exploring Their History* (Lanham, MD: Rowman & Littlefield, 1997), 81.

137. Kraut, "Ambivalent Relations of American Reform Judaism," 64–65.

138. Sarna, "The Late Nineteenth-Century American Jewish Awakening," 6.

139. Persons, *Free Religion*, 53.

140. Sefton D. Temkin, *Creating American Reform Judaism: The Life and Times of Isaac Mayer Wise* (New York: Oxford University Press, 1992), 213.

141. But he continued his membership in the FRA, even remaining as a vice president in 1892. See Potter, *The Free Religious Association*, 2.

142. Sarna, "The Late Nineteenth-Century American Jewish Awakening," 1–25.

143. Persons, *Free Religion*, 71.

144. Mel Scult, *Judaism Faces the Twentieth Century: A Biography of Mordecai M. Kaplan* (Detroit: Wayne State University Press, 1993), 79.

145. Horace L. Friess, *Felix Adler and Ethical Culture: Memories and Studies*, ed. Fannia Weingartner (New York: Columbia University Press, 1981), 69, and esp. 24.

146. Kraut, *From Reform Judaism to Ethical Culture*, 106. Emerson's influence was equally profound on the circle of cofounders of Ethical Culture: Howard B. Radest, *Felix Adler: An Ethical Culture* (New York: Peter Lang, 1998), 10.

147. Friess, *Felix Adler and Ethical Culture*, 41.

148. Felix Adler, *An Ethical Philosophy of Life Presented in Its Main Outlines* (New York: D. Appleton & Co., 1918), 27.

149. Felix Adler, *The Essentials of Spirituality* (New York: James Pott, 1905), 84–85.

150. Students' notes from that course have been preserved. Adler framed his course largely around Kant, and Emerson appears to have been mentioned only when urging students to be cultivated individuals and therefore to study Emerson, along with Goethe, Matthew Arnold, Thomas Carlyle and Ruskin, in contrasting ancient, medieval, and more modern intellectual culture. Notes of lecture of April 21, 1903, MS Coll. Adler, Columbia Lectures 100 Political and Social Ethics 1903 J, Rare Book and Manuscript Library, Columbia University, New York, NY.

151. Mordecai Kaplan, *Judaism without Supernaturalism: The Only Alternative to Orthodoxy and Secularism* (New York: Reconstructionist Press, 1958), xiv.

152. See Sheila Greeve Davaney, "Beyond Supernaturalism: Mordecai Kaplan and

the Turn to Religious Naturalism," *Jewish Social Studies*, n.s., 12, no. 2 (Winter 2006): 73–87.

153. Simon Noveck, "Kaplan and Milton Steinberg," in Emanuel S. Goldsmith, Mel Scult, and Robert M. Seltzer, eds., *The American Judaism of Mordecai M. Kaplan* (New York: New York University Press, 1990), 140–70; 154–55. Whether Kaplan believed in a purely natural religion or held some idea of a reified godhead is debated.

154. Kaplan journal, December 8, 1904, quoted by Scult, *Judaism Faces the Twentieth Century*, 61.

155. Mel Scult, "Mordecai Kaplan and Ralph Waldo Emerson: A Theology of the Individual," *Jewish Social Studies*, n.s., 12 no. 2 (Winter 2006): 206; Arnold M. Eisen, "Mordecai Kaplan's *Judaism as a Civilization* at 70: Setting the Stage for Reappraisal," *Jewish Social Studies*, n.s. 12, no. 2 (Winter 2006): 1–16.

156. Scult, "Mordecai Kaplan and Ralph Waldo Emerson," 104.

157. Mel Scult discusses the Kaplan–Emerson connection in *The Radical American Judaism of Mordecai M. Kaplan* (Bloomington: Indiana University Press, 2013).

158. Scult, "Mordecai Kaplan and Ralph Waldo Emerson," 105.

159. *Communings of the Spirit: The Journals of Mordecai M. Kaplan*, vol. 1: *1913–1934*, ed. Mel Scult (Detroit: Wayne State University Press, 2001), 258–59. Note Adler's criticism of what he saw as Kant's exclusive focus on individual ethics in the Columbia course that Kaplan took: "Notes of Lecture of March 27, 1903," MS Coll. Adler, Columbia Lectures 100 Political and Social Ethics 1903 J, Rare Book & Manuscript Library, Columbia University.

160. Gilya Gerda Schmidt, *Martin Buber's Formative Years: From German Culture to Jewish Renewal, 1897–1909* (Tuscaloosa: University of Alabama Press, 1995), 35.

161. Thanks are due to my many Brown University history colleagues; to Rabbis Eugene Borowitz, Alan Flam, and Leslie Yale Gutterman; Professors Michael Berkowitz, Robert Gross, Miriam Leonard, Mel Scult, David Sorkin, and Bruce Uhrmacher; and especially to Dr. Holly Snyder.

[16]

DAVID MIKICS

EMERSON AND JEWISH READERS

WHEN THE *New York Jewish Messenger* reported in 1880 on Concord's recent celebration of the seventy-seventh birthday of Ralph Waldo Emerson (May 25), the newspaper declared that "the Concord sage is in spirit a Hebrew. In his utterances are heard the ethics of Judaism." In Leipzig, the *Messenger*'s anonymous reporter added, he had met a "Russian Israelite who had come to purchase goods": "The man, who was of magnificent physique, spoke English, French, German and Russian with equal facility, while he had received as well the training of a rabbi, quoted Emerson, and referred to him in extravagant tones of admiration."[1]

The *Messenger*'s claim that Emerson was a Jewish thinker might well startle us. After all, Emerson is the source of all those American authors who celebrate the sublime and solitary self. How could Emerson's celebration of self-reliant individualism possibly be reconciled with family and community, which Jewish life so insistently depends on? In a 1977 essay, "Strangers," Irving Howe recalls his bewildered reaction to the Emersonian tradition when he was a young, eager reader of American literature. Emerson's line, Howe thought, had somehow missed the importance of family, so obvious to a Yiddish-speaking immigrant. "In American literature there were all these strange and homeless solitaries, motherless and fatherless creatures like Natty and Huck and Ishmael. Didn't they know where life came from and returned to?" Howe asks. He then remarks, much more pointedly,

> For most of us [immigrant Jews], individualism seemed a luxury or a deception of the Gentile world. Immigrant Jewish culture had been rich in eccentrics, cranks, and individualist display; even the synagogue accepted prayer at personal tempos. But the idea of an individual covenant with God, each man responsible for his own salvation; the claim that each man is captain of his soul . . . the notion that you not only have one but more than one chance in life, which constitutes the American version of grace; and the belief that

> you rise or fall in accord with your own merits rather than the will of alien despots—these residues of Emersonianism seemed not only strange but sometimes even a version of that brutality which our parents had warned was intrinsic to Gentile life. Perhaps our exposure to this warmed-over Emersonianism prompted us to become socialists, as if thereby to make clear our distaste for these American delusions and to affirm, instead, a heritage of communal affections and responsibilities.

In strong contrast to the traveling Emersonian merchant-rabbi described by the *Messenger,* Howe rejected Emerson as un-Jewish. "So we abandoned Emerson even before encountering him," Howe concludes, "and in later years some of us would never draw closer than to establish amiable diplomatic relations."[2]

Howe's skeptical perspective on the Emersonian tradition—a version of the familiar charge that Emerson, absorbed by the self, remains inattentive to community—stands in stark opposition to that of Alfred Kazin, Howe's fellow New York intellectual. Kazin evidently considered himself an Emersonian, and, in an imaginative way, connected his fealty to Emerson with his Jewishness. In his journals (November 15, 1958), Kazin recounts his annoyed reaction after reading an essay by Edmund Wilson on Pasternak: "Why, I thought irritably, can't *I* have the patience, the learning, above all the meticulous curiosity, to do an essay like this?" Kazin supplies the answer to his question, and in doing so identifies himself with Emerson: "I always know so well what I think, the gift of conviction is so firmly and inescapably in me, that like Emerson I build a house without thinking of the stairs; I am so concerned with the essence of things that I seem to go straight to it, and as a result my things are usually short, fragmentary and repetitive." ("I found when I had finished my new lecture that it was a very good house," Emerson remarks in his journal in 1851, "only the architect had rather unfortunately omitted the stairs" [*JMN* 11:327].)

Rather surprisingly, Kazin goes on in his journal entry to explore this Emersonian trait in the light of Judaism. He writes, "[Gershom] Scholem says in his book on medieval Jewish mysticism that the distinctively Jewish literary forms are usually short, and in my own case, too, the need to wrest the essence out of things, to get at the heart of experience, to see the spiritual identity beneath the material form of any problem, always results in this lightening trip straight to the center. Yet it is precisely this that makes for Jewish conceit, or Jewish incuriosity, for we feel that we already know the answer—and I agree that we do." Kazin adds a qualification to his championing of Emerson and, along with Emerson, the Jewish "lightening trip straight to the center." The strongly penetrating insight belonging both to

Emerson and to himself as a Jew ought to be, at times, "suspended," Kazin says: "The 'revelation of unity' that Lipschitz once spoke of is so native to the Jew that he must learn, as it were, to suspend it—to look at the radical disharmonies of life for their own sake, to learn to describe life as it exists in time instead of seeking the figures that are so easily reconciled under the aspect of eternity. . . ."[3] (It is not clear which Lipschitz Kazin refers to here; most likely is the sculptor Jacques Lipschitz, rather than a member of the rabbinical family of that name.) In this comment, Kazin touches on the risk of Emerson's stance as he sees it: the temptation to insist on pure insight and so fail to attend to the dissonances of the life lived day to day. Emerson is not, to be sure, a realist like Tolstoy, Kazin seems to be suggesting, and such realism is necessary to do full justice to life. But Kazin's caution appears in the light of the close affinity he claims with Emerson. Unlike Howe, he is a loyal Emersonian.

A few years earlier in his journal (July 27, 1955), Kazin summarizes the "Jewish-Christian feeling" in Emerson: "man as the child of God, man as image of truth, as a vessel appointed to receive him." He goes on to underline the personal element in Emerson's illuminations: "Unlike the old tradition, he had to keep saying, '*I* see it! *I* see it!' and his audience had to believe in the sight of his rapture. Otherwise, the whole system, so delicately made up of personal insights, of rapturous flights, of balances held together only in this man, and by him, fell apart." He concludes, "Nevertheless, Emerson held firm to the tradition—in the vital sense that life makes sense, that there is a design": in contrast to Melville, Kazin remarks, whose heroes cannot find the meaning they so desperately seek.[4] In these comments, Kazin places Emerson halfway between a religious tradition (seen by Kazin as both Jewish and Christian) and a despondent modernism like Melville's, for which the unifying consolation of Emerson's rapturous affirmation is no longer available. In his journals and elsewhere, Kazin usually sees himself as closer to Emerson than to Melville: an affirmer of the transcendent that shines through the everyday, rather than a frustrated quester after meaning. In "Dry Light and Hard Expressions," a tribute to Emerson and Thoreau published in the *Atlantic* in July 1957, he sees the two Concord thinkers as "holy men," masters of gnomic compression and of living what they wrote. Kazin argues:

> The writers who become our saints and sages, the wise men of our tribe, they who help us to live—there is only one way by which we can know them: their genius for compression. They are the ones who are always stripping life down to fundamentals and essentials, to aphorisms and parables and riddles, and if we ask what is holy about men whose life sayings often shock and hurt as

> much as they illuminate, the answer is that the final compression they get into their speech is a compression they have attained in their lives. The absolute in their writing is an absolute they have learned to live, and the sometimes overemphatic sharpness, the well-known intolerance by holy men, the cutting blow, the very quickness with which they sum up life and eternity in a sentence, is only the expression in words of the attempt to meet existence with the greatest possible directness.[5]

Like Kazin, Saul Bellow was another Jewish-American writer who saw that Emerson teaches us a required lesson: we must meet existence with maximum directness and insight. Near the end of Bellow's sprawling novel *The Adventures of Augie March* (1953), the book that made Bellow famous, the youthful Augie encounters a high-powered Armenian lawyer named Mintouchian. Bellow paints Mintouchian as a manly, heroic figure. "He had legs on him," Augie says, "like that statue of Clemenceau on the Champs Elysées where Clemenceau is striding against a wind and is thinking of bread and war, and the misery and grandeur, going on with last strength in his longjohns and gaiters." Mintouchian's way of acknowledging misery, and yet raising grandeur and strength, is notably Emersonian. In his sermon to Augie, Mintouchian seems to ventriloquize Emerson: "Erratic is nothing. Only system taps the will of the universe." He overtly draws on Emerson's "Fate" when he tells Augie that "the thing that kills you is the thing that you stand for": "What is the weapon? The nails and hammer of your character. What is the cross? Your own bones on which you gradually weaken. . . . The fish wills water, and the bird wills air, and you and me our dominant idea." Most of Mintouchian's talk centers on philandering husbands and untrue wives, but this subject matter is merely the occasion for his tremendous excursion into self-reliance, or, as he describes it, "how to return to simplicity." Mintouchian is superbly conscious of the human will to deceive oneself and others. Yet he tells Augie with powerful conviction, "You must take your chance on what you are."[6] Like Emerson in "Experience" and "Fate," Mintouchian is capable of seeing through our many secrets and lies and digging down to solid essence. The sublime self-trust he recommends to Augie is one of the most memorable peaks of Bellow's vast novel.

Eleven years after *The Adventures of Augie March,* Bellow again drew on Emerson, in his pained, exuberant best seller, *Herzog*. Moses Herzog, a stymied, heart-troubled academic, writhing from his ex-wife's affair with his best friend, broods both somberly and hyperactively over the disastrous history of the twentieth century. He writes a series of letters to thinkers and political leaders, from Heidegger to Eisenhower. Herzog is particularly disturbed by what he describes as the "commonplaces of the Wasteland outlook, the cheap mental stimulants of Alienation, the cant and rant of pipsqueaks about Inauthenticity and Forlornness. I can't accept this foolish dreariness." He assails the intellectuals who "deny the humanity of the industrialized, 'banalized' masses": "It was easy for the Wastelanders to be assimilated to totalitarianism," he adds.[7] And he despises the "Protestant Freudianism" of postwar America, calling it "a lousy, cringing, grudging conception of human nature."[8] Like Emerson, Herzog hates the builders of dungeons in the air, the thinkers who are determined to see the worst in humankind. Yet Herzog too wrestles, not only with his own distress, but with the mass atrocities of twentieth-century history, which he alludes to succinctly as "the black cloud of faces, souls."[9] Set against these grim recognitions is Herzog's memory of quoting Emerson's "The American Scholar" as class orator of his high school: "He didn't lose his voice then, telling the Italian mechanics, Bohemian barrel makers, Jewish tailors. *The main enterprise of the world, for splendor . . . is the upbuilding of a man. The private life of one man shall be a more illustrious monarchy . . . than any kingdom in history. Let it be granted that our life, as we lead it, is common and mean. . . . Beautiful and perfect men we are not now. . . . The community in which we live will hardly bear to be told that every man should be open to ecstasy or a divine illumination.*" The passage from Emerson is encircled by irony: it is interspersed with Herzog's wartime memory of losing contact, due to his hoarse voice, with the crew of his ship on maneuvers in the Gulf of Mexico —"the whole fleet heard him groan, 'We're lost! Fucked!'"[10] But Herzog also takes Emersonian aspiration seriously: he is "open to ecstasy or a divine illumination."

Near the conclusion of *Herzog,* Bellow's hero again alludes to Emerson, in a passage that unlocks the possibilities concealed in his suffering. In a letter to a (fictive) Professor Mermelstein, who exalts "*modern forms of Orphism*" and "*people who are not afraid of suffering,*" Herzog rebukes Mermelstein for

> such cocktail-party expressions. Why not say rather that people of powerful imagination, given to dreaming deeply and to raising up marvelous and self-sufficient fictions, turn to suffering sometimes to cut into their bliss, as people pinch themselves to feel awake. I know that my suffering, if I may speak of it, has often been like that, a more extended form of life, a striving for true wakefulness and an antidote to illusion. . . . We love apocalypses too much, and crisis ethics and florid extremism with its thrilling language. Excuse me, no. I've had all the monstrosity I want.[11]

Herzog here, in a decisive way, aligns himself with the Emerson who wrote (in "Experience"), "There are moods in which we court suffering, in the hope that here at least we shall find reality, sharp peaks and edges of truth." Instead of the false melodrama of apocalypse so popular among postwar intellectuals, Bellow's Herzog chooses a pragmatic, and Emersonian, meaning for his pain: it is a way to wake himself up, to look for reality.

A decade younger than Bellow and Kazin, the philosopher Stanley Cavell has made Emerson crucial to his writing. Early in his career, Cavell focused on Thoreau as the central American thinker, but by the 1980s he had shifted his attentions to Emerson. In his essay "Thinking of Emerson" (1979), Cavell cites Emerson's resounding credo from "Self-Reliance": "I would write on the lintels of the door-post, *Whim*." Cavell supplies a commentary:

> He says he would do this after he has said that he shuns father and mother and wife and brother when his genius calls him; and he follows it by expressing the hope that it is somewhat better than whim at last. (Something has happened; it is up to us to name it, or not to. Something is wrestling us for our blessing.) Whether his writing on the lintels—his writing as such, I gather—is thought of as having the constancy of the contents of a mezuzah or the emergency of the Passover blood, either way he is taking upon himself the mark of God, and of departure. . . . Our fatality, the determination of our fate, of whether we may hope, goes by our marking the path of whim. We hope it is better than whim at last, as we hope we may at last seem something better than blasphemers; but it is our poverty not to be final but always to be leaving (abandoning whatever we have and have known): to be initial, medial, American.[12]

In this rapid-fire midrash on Emerson, Cavell first takes up the seeming blasphemy of Emerson (who, like Jesus, shuns his family); he then moves on to his own allusion, to Jacob's struggle with the angel who gives Jacob a new name, Israel. For Cavell, by contrast with the Genesis account, "it is up to us," not a divine messenger: Can we find a name for the call of our genius? And, even more pressing, can we bless the consequences that result from that call? Cavell follows Emerson when he takes the mezuzah as a symbol of abandonment rather than a sign that, as a Jew, one has found a home by accepting a firm covenant. Instead of the binding Jewish trust in God, Cavell envisions a departure not just from Egypt, but from wherever we find ourselves. The Promised Land (in this case, America) is promising only because it makes room for abandonment: Americans are always striking out for the territories. In my rather secular neighborhood in Brooklyn, mezuzot are frequently, and mistakenly, placed pointed outward rather than inward; I have always found this practice odd, and, to be honest, rather annoying. Emerson and Cavell might help to explain the mistake. Such a resistance to the ritual requirement that mezuzot must be slanted toward the interior of a house is, to be sure, based in ignorance, but it perhaps jibes with a preference for outward-directed action, for what Cavell calls the "initial, medial, American."

In a 1980 essay, "An Emerson Mood," Cavell alludes to the Shema, one of the central Jewish prayers, a portion of which is written on the scroll hidden within the mezuzah. He writes, "So it is in obedience to Emerson's genius that he speaks of it wherever he is, showing that it speaks everywhere to him; not to acknowledge it would be not to keep faith with it. As if his essays were so many mezuzot, declarations of his faith, and his part in attempting to keep this land of milk and honey from perishing."[13] The Shema tells Jews to speak of Torah when they rise up and lie down, when they are on the road and when they are at home, and to love God with all their heart, soul, and strength. In Cavell's account, Emerson's love for his inspiration provokes a conversation like the one that the Shema imagines between the Jew and Torah. Emerson's own speaking about his genius becomes the law for him: he keeps not scripture but his own sentences close to him at all times.

In "An Emerson Mood," Cavell says offhandedly that mezuzot are sometimes worn as amulets, but "more commonly" seen on a door frame. As Cavell well knows, the occasional use of mezuzot as amulets is a purely inventive practice with no basis in Jewish law. But one can see why Cavell would want to mention it: the mezuzah worn on the chest, near the heart and the source of breath, is an imaginative displacement from the actual, ritually mandated places where excerpts from the Torah must be placed: the mezuzah on the door frame, the tefillin on the arm and head. The necklace-mezuzah represents a kind of homemade religious custom, one at home in New Age America.

Rael Meyerowitz understands Cavell's comments on Emerson's whim-inscribed doorpost as a way of reviving Jewish tradition by endorsing Americanism: "Jewish experience, losing its impact with the waning of orthodoxy and the passing of generations, is revived by being played out in a new mythic, intellectual, and historical context: the Wilderness-cum-Promised Land that is America."[14] "Transforming" might be a better word than Meyerowitz's "reviving" for Cavell's Emersonian use of Jewish tradition. Cavell remakes Jewishness in the image of Emerson-inspired, individualist America. Because so many American Jews have done the same, Cavell cannot be charged with mere idiosyncrasy; instead, he speaks from within a living culture.

Cavell's radical use of Jewish ritual in the light of Emerson brings to mind the stance of another influential Jewish Emersonian, Harold Bloom. Bloom's image of himself as a Jewish Gnostic has little place for ritual observance, but much for the idea of a divine self hidden amid the darkened world.

Bloom does to Jewish heritage what Emerson's America does to the idea of the Promised Land: makes it uncharted, perilous, and promising in new ways. But Bloom, in much of his criticism, also quietly draws a distinction between Emersonian freedom and Jewishness. Bloom sees in the religion of the Tanakh a way of thought bound to the past, and confronting that past in sublime, frighteningly personal form. Jewishness in its origins experiences the anxiety of influence more immediately than any other religion, according to Bloom: the Hebrew God is the sublime father who is always too close. (This is why Bloom sees Freud and Kafka as the definitive Jewish thinkers of modernity.) Bloom sometimes waxes Jewish and sometimes Emersonian. His *Ruin the Sacred Truths* shows us a fundamentally Jewish Bloom. Here he sees tradition as a dark, anxious struggle, and he gives a prominent place to the Jewish canon from Genesis and Jeremiah to Kafka and Freud. Emerson does not appear in *Ruin the Sacred Truths,* because Bloom knows that Emerson's wish to liberate himself and us from the burdens of the past takes a form that might seem fantastic or effortless when compared with the struggles of a Kafka (or a Milton, that Hebraizing Christian).

But there is also an Emersonian Bloom. Bloom's *The American Religion,* his pungent survey of American religious beliefs, sees Emerson as the origin of our native efforts to raise the self to divinity by blessing the spontaneous impulses of head and heart—a project unthinkable in the Jewish tradition (including the kabbalistic mysticism that Bloom has also studied intensively). Meyerowitz sees Bloom as "a fearful Jewish child—though one already old at birth, forewarned, forearmed, and burdened by the weight of inherited knowledge—who wishes to paint himself as Emerson's nonchalant American boy, disdainful of conciliation, and of the spectral past."[15] Meyerowitz's judgment is a shrewd one, but it must be amended: Bloom only sometimes aspires to be the nonchalant youth of Emerson's "Self-Reliance," who easily turns the tables on his elders. In much of his work, Bloom acknowledges the pull that inherited knowledge continues to exert. If Emerson is the antidote to this inheritance, he can be taken only in temporary doses—he is exhilarating and anything but self-deluded, yet the dark and contrary wisdom of Freud must also be faced.

In his own way, Bloom harks back to the ambivalence about Emerson that Kazin expressed. Both fear that such confirmed ecstasy as Emerson's seems to leave something out: for Kazin, it might blind us to the reality that we follow from day to day; for Bloom, it might be too self-confident to recognize the violent ironies that take place when we confront our origins. Yet Bloom perhaps shares more with Howe than with Kazin. Where Kazin, like Bellow and Cavell, establishes a solidarity between Emerson and Jewishness, Bloom, like Howe, implies a difference. Bloom shows one way for a Jew to inherit our pivotal American thinker: as a standing provocation that, instead of demanding allegiance, can sharpen the sense of the ancestral powers, dark forces that the Emersonian drive toward freedom might, in its haste to leave Egypt, fail to reckon with.

Notes

1. *New York Jewish Messenger* (June 1880), n.p. (Emerson archive, Houghton Library, Harvard University).

2. Irving Howe, "Strangers," in *Selected Writings 1950–1990* (New York: Harcourt Brace Jovanovich, 1990), 328.

3. *Alfred Kazin's Journals*, ed. Richard M. Cook (New Haven, CT: Yale University Press, 2011), 236–37.

4. Ibid., 191.

5. Alfred Kazin, "Dry Light and Hard Expressions," *Atlantic* 200, no. 1 (July 1957): 74–76.

6. Saul Bellow, *The Adventures of Augie March*, in *Novels 1944–1953* (New York: Library of America, 2003), 935–36.

7. Saul Bellow, *Herzog*, in *Novels 1956–1964* (New York: Library of America, 2007), 491–92.

8. Ibid., 474.

9. Ibid., 491.

10. Ibid., 577.

11. Ibid., 738.

12. Stanley Cavell, "Thinking of Emerson," in *The Senses of Walden: An Expanded Edition* (San Francisco: North Point Press, 1981), 137.

13. Cavell, "An Emerson Mood," in *The Senses of Walden*, 156.

14. Rael Meyerowitz, *Transferring to America: Jewish Interpretations of American Dreams* (Albany: State University of New York Press, 1995), 193.

15. Ibid., 164.

[17]

ROGER SEDARAT

MIDDLE EASTERN–AMERICAN LITERATURE: A CONTEMPORARY TURN IN EMERSON STUDIES

AS A SCHOLAR OF Arab literature importantly qualified at a conference on Ameen Rihani's *The Book of Khalid,* the first Arab-American novel published in the United States, "Middle Eastern" and "American" should always be put in quotes, as they remain especially problematic conceptual references to complicated regions and literary traditions. Insofar as they link together, first with Emerson's early appropriation of Persian poetry and then through the later return of Emerson as an influence on Middle Eastern–American writers like Rihani, the quotes on both sides of the hyphenated conflation ought to further end with curved arrows. More than referencing mere reciprocal relations, such circularity better foregrounds the emergence of an ambiguously hybrid literature that tends to resist identification owing to a critical tendency to privilege one side of the dichotomous relation over the other. Emerson's writing, underpinned in part by Persian verse that he translated through intermediary German renderings, offers perhaps the best place to begin examining the formative effects of an emerging American literary engagement with the Middle East, which in turn have come to transform early texts like Rihani's novel, as well as later Middle Eastern–American writing.

Two disparate critical approaches in this chapter attempt to more closely follow Emerson's borrowing from the Persian tradition, circling back to the origins of one of many important transnational sources for stylistic and thematic inspiration. First, Harold Bloom's *The Anxiety of Influence* allows for a conceptual framework from which to consider the formative effects of Persian poetry, both on Emerson's verse as well as his influence on later Middle Eastern–American writers. Bloom's theory, predicated on psychoanalysis, offers a way to further investigate how Emerson attempts to overcome important Persian predecessors, one of whom, Sa'di, he deems the ideal poetic father in a poem titled with his name.[1] Following Bloom by considering Emerson as the prophet of "the American Sublime" (103) under the category of "Daemonization"—which consists of a radical attempt to negate predecessors—better allows for a critical understanding of Emerson's attempt to claim a kind of "first priority" as self-appointed American Adam, even when confronting a more than one-thousand-year-old Persian tradition. To disavow the "sepulchers of the fathers" (CW 1:7) mentioned in the introduction to *Nature,* Emerson of course must reckon with several Western and Eastern influences. Bloom's theory especially helps to reveal the irreconcilable paradox of Emerson's insistence on the centrality of his vision, best exemplified by the "transparent eye-ball" in his "Nature" chapter. His textual sullying of the self-proclaimed, all-seeing transparency by his reporting on it corresponds to an essential wrestling of spirit with letter in the classical Persian poetry that he would come to discover in his later career and translate, as well as imitate, with great interest. Interrogating Emerson's trope of the all-encompassing eye that seems to obviate literary predecessors in turn allows for further consideration of hybrid Middle Eastern–American writers who attempt to follow Emerson's example, though with the added weight of their substantial foreign traditions, since the start of the twentieth century.

More than merely accounting for literary influence, Bloom's theory helps to extend a more substantial argument into Emerson's problematic linguistic rendering of Persian poetry from German intermediary texts. Translation of course resists a unifying theory, given the unique process of rendering specific source texts into another literary tradition with its own disparate qualities. Yet the author as imitator/translator, regardless of language or tradition, must surely reconcile literary influence in his or her own writing, if not in the translation as well. As Willis Barnstone has argued in response to Bloom in *The Poetics of Translation,* "the influence of translation in the work of poet translators occurs not so much because of their encounter with an extraordinary source text but through their own transformation of that source text into their own invented language."[2] For the purposes of this investigation, Bloom allows for a comparative analysis of poetics beyond close linear comparisons between Emerson and his Persian predecessors found in earlier Emerson scholarship, helping to demonstrate how Emerson had to reckon with the poetry originating in Iran that he transformed into English through German Romanticism.[3] Though following the same kind of radical breaking with tradition indicative of Bloom's American sublime, because this foreign influence remains so latent in Emerson's writing, it warrants special attention.

As productive as Bloom's theory becomes in reconciling an important transnational influence on Emerson's writing, however, it falls short in offering a means by which to interrogate the crossing of influence between two rather different worlds inhabited by vastly different literary conventions, cultural practices, and languages. The majority of examples offered in Bloom's influential book focus exclusively on Western models. The Greek terms themselves, as well as the Freudian model that informs the entire theory, demonstrate a proclivity toward Western literary and philosophic origins. Subtly, much like the way that the anglicizing of names in translations of the Bible comes to render away the importance of Jewish culture, Bloom begins to reproduce a kind of Oedipal breaking from the plethora of more foreign traditions and languages that precede and heavily inform the English literature he favors. This in turn reinforces, if not condones, the modernist move of translation as appropriation established so firmly by Ezra Pound in the early twentieth century. If only to foreground a discursive space to serve as a continual reminder that writers accommodating the work of others from different traditions do not merely attempt to reckon with the influence of foreign writing into their own rhetoric but have their own texts transformed into something new, further theoretical understanding that accommodates difference appears necessary.

To this end, this chapter juxtaposes Homi Bhabha's postcolonial concept of a "third space of enunciation" with a Bloomian analysis of influence anxiety. Applied mainly to traditional formations of hybrid literature, Bhabha's "third space" is understood as the circle embodied by the colonizer's culture and all it entails (language, tradition, etc.) that intersects with part of a circle from the colonized world. The intersection of the circles thus becomes a formative third space, embodying the synthesis of different traditions that transform into something new.[4] Such a site of meaning and stylistic reformation proves antithetical to idealized conceptions of a homogenous tradition. Though Emerson's writing engages other languages and traditions into English, insofar as it does not explicitly emerge as a hybrid transformation between disparate literatures, admittedly it fails to qualify as a "third space" according to Bhabha.[5] Nevertheless, such an approach paradoxically more closely identifies the underpinnings of world literatures in the American tendency to appropriate and render invisible much of the foreign that very much originates with Emerson's predilection to incorporate all he sees into a kind of "colonizing consciousness." Intersecting Bhabha's theory with Bloom's, as if in a new kind of third space, allows for further speculation as to how Emerson's voice, predicated on visionary language, might derive at least in part from elsewhere, outlining the presence of a formative influence that otherwise remains hidden. As such, it begins to make visible Emerson's seemingly transparent claims on a first priority that dissemble important sources outside his assumed sphere of influence. Bhabha's interpretation on the disruptive presence of postcolonial hybrid literature, which, "reimplicates its identifications in strategies of subversion that turn the gaze of the discriminated back upon the eye of power" (159–60), offers a means to interrogate both the effect of Emerson's vision on Middle Eastern–American writers and their response to it.

Though Emerson's early book *Nature* predates his deep reading, translating, and rhetorical modeling of Persian poets like Hafez and Sa'di,[6] reconsideration of arguably its most seminal passage of the invisible eyeball reveals a contained textual site that leads toward a rather unconventional yet potentially productive understanding of how he anticipated a Middle Eastern influence, as if to have subsumed it as his own. It becomes the origin of origins, alpha and omega of an American claim to an illusory first priority. Predicated on the longing for an all-seeing vision, much like the Persian verse he would come to read, his transformation into proclaimed invisibility offers the most essential and primary "first circle" in Emerson's cosmic circular view, wherein "The eye," as Emerson's "Circles" essay begins, constitutes the "first circle" through which the other circles emanate (CW 2:179). Insofar as Emerson attempts to obviate the text of its own reporting, as if the transparency occurs in real time beyond the naming of it, he of course keeps literary precursors out of sight. However, when viewing the trace or outline of the eyeball as a kind of Bhabhaian "third space," the following well-known excerpt presents a new way of understanding the latent role of unforeseen influences such as Persian verse in Emerson's first claim on literary tradition: "Crossing a bare common, in snow puddles, at twilight, under a clouded sky, without having in my thoughts any occurrence of special good fortune, I have enjoyed a perfect exhilaration. . . . Standing on the bare ground,—my head bathed by the blithe air, and uplifted into infinite space,—all mean egotism vanishes. I become a transparent eye-ball; I am nothing; I see all; the currents of the Universal Being circulate through me; I am part or particle of God" (CW 1:10).

By paradoxically foregrounding himself as a circle devoid of center, Emerson introduces a central passage for a discussion of illusory influence. Recently Lawrence Buell, partly responding to the scholarship of Wai Chee Dimock, has called for moving the discussion of Persian verse as an influence on Emerson "from the edges of discussion" and more toward "the center."[7] Quite tellingly, Paul Kane, in his comparative study of Hafez and Emerson, has expressed doubt about so positioning Persian poetry in the center, remarking, "I'm not convinced there is a center, or at least a stable one" (134). In part to extend the close correspondence of the letter in Persian verse in Emerson's writing to the spirit of Persian influence, Kane begins to show how the foreign verse remains latently elusive for the American poet-philosopher, helping to explain a problematic critical tendency to limit comparative analyses between Emerson's specific translations of Persian poetry and his own verse. Considering instead the interconnectedness of Emerson's poetry and prose to the fourteenth-century classical Persian poet, Hafez, Kane demonstrates a more subtle yet pervasive influence of the Persian tradition on Emerson's sensibility beyond a line-by-line analysis of translations or Emerson's imitations of Persian verse as offered by J. D. Yohannan. Arguing that Emerson appreciated Hafez as a bridge between the secular and the spiritual, he stresses that the American followed the Iranian in part because Hafez kept mysticism from becoming a mere static concept in his poetry. It remains "vehicular" (119), much like the functioning of metaphor. Such a de-centered literary analysis leads Kane to assert that Emerson became especially attracted to Hafez for his spirit of self-reliance, insofar as he asserted a liberating power within the confines of a religious context (119).

Kane's most original claim, which provides a point of departure for this chapter when applied to the passage above, connects Emerson's liberation through self-reduction to Leonard Lewisohn's observation of *malámati,* or self-censure, found in the Sufi mysticism that underpins much of the verse by Hafez.[8] Drawing on Lewisohn's citation from Emerson's "Self-Reliance" essay for a comparable Western analogue to explain Hafez,[9] Kane compares it with the inversion of power found in the *rend,* which diminishes self-importance in the Persian poet's attempt to challenge hypocrisy.[10] Further referencing the description of Hafez in Emerson's journals, he notes how this could easily serve as Emerson's self-reliant man: "He fears nothing, he sees too far, he sees throughout."[11] Kane's analysis astutely predicates his reading of the *rend* in the vision of both writers: "The Emersonian *rend,* like Hafiz, is fearless because he *sees;* he is a visionary in both a religious and secular sense: the clarity of his perception penetrates the world" (123).

The metaphorical or "vehicular" nature of Hafez's de-centered verse, combined with the positioning of the diminished self through the *rend*, which, like Hafez, Kane finds operating in Emerson "through a disinterested and visionary gaze" (122) offers an alternative turn in transnational Emerson studies, wherein the respective Persian and American traditions can be read as transforming, through an alternative third space, an originating and elusively emerging hybrid voice that seemingly claims complete rejection of any influence whatsoever. Arguably the greatest and most paradoxically liberating self-reduction that resists a "centering" presence for Emerson is found in his self-proclaimed transformation into transparency. Though the publication of this passage predates Emerson's close reading of Hafez by roughly five years, it seems to anticipate the Persian master's presence upon the American landscape. The *rend* for Emerson, connected to vision, occurs here, as dramatized in his own time by the publication of a famous cartoon lampooning the writer's outlandish transformative claim, depicting him as a mere eyeball on stick legs. Following Kane's analysis of the *rend*, such a caricature embodies comparable self-diminishing moves by Hafez, the Persian poet most translated by Emerson, as seen in such lines that Emerson himself brought into English from his German source: "I am: what I am / My dust will be again."[12]

The passage of the transparent eyeball can therefore be viewed as providing an outline from which to further interrogate foreign influence, wherein the foregrounding of Emerson's consciousness via invisibility as American Adam intersects by attempting to subsume all tradition he would absorb. Though a multitude of Western influences remain present here,[13] the quoted passage amalgamates a host of traditions that can be seen as including the poet Hafez, especially as it predicates the *rend* of the Sufi mystic upon vision. Significantly, Hafez was called in Arabic at the time of his death the "tongue of the invisible world," paradoxically articulating that which could not be seen. Such a metaphor that gives voice to the invisible closely resembles the function of Emerson's transparent eyeball that became a primary statement on an attempt to transcend self-identification. Emerson's personal veneration of Hafez reinforces such a comparison, especially as he references the Persian poet as a master of vision: "Hafez is not to be scared by a name, or a religion. He fears nothing. He sees too far; he sees throughout. . . . Such is the only man I wish to see and to be" (*JMN* 10:165).

Such a description closely imitates the stated function of Emerson's transparent eyeball, which, explains James Cox, involves not so much merely seeing the material world but attempting to see through it.[14] Ultimately, Hafez and Emerson rhetorically wrestle with the materiality of language itself as they seek to visually transform into something like pure agency. Ego-reduction becomes a function of metaphorical invisibility. Such is the essence of Sufi mysticism as experienced in classical Persian verse.

To exemplify this comparative analysis on Emerson's and Hafez's own metaphorical terms, consider the following lines (translated by Emerson through Joseph von Hammer's German rendering): "Take my heart in thy hand, O beautiful boy of Schiraz! / I would give for the mole on thy cheek Samarcand and Buchara!" (259). Following the spirit of the *rend*, the mystic vision of classical Persian poetry, like Emerson's transformation upon the winter New England landscape, attempts to see all through the sacrifice of self. According to legend, Tamerlane, a native of Samarkand, confronted Hafez for the blasphemy of offering his land for the mole of the beloved's face. Hafez is said to have replied, "Your Majesty, it is because of such prodigality that I have fallen into such poverty."[15] Such self-inflicted poverty for mystic vision in Sufi poetry exemplifies, through the trope of the mole, the return to the most primal source of material origins in search of the spirit. As Florence Lederer writes in the introduction to another Persian poet in the same tradition as Hafez, "The mole on the cheek is the point of indivisible Unity," adding that "the heart and soul of Adam evolved from there."[16] Syed Mumtaz Ali's description of the mole for Sufis could just as well apply to Emerson's eyeball, or at least to the reductive material foundation from which it emerges: "The mole on her face signif[ies] that when the pupil, at times, beholds the total absence of all worldly want on the part of the preceptor, he also abandons all the desires of both worlds—he perhaps even goes so far as to desire nothing else in life than his preceptor."[17]

In another poem by Hafez, the mole becomes a mirror of the perceiver's pupil: "Her cheek's a mirror of all my vision / My pupil in her mole is seen (subtly)."[18] Like the paradoxically opaque mole on the face of the beloved that opens to a seemingly infinite world for Hafez, Emerson experiences his visionary transformation to an Adamic state devoid of influence on a dirty puddle that appears to metonymically displace the pupil as part of his entry into an all-seeing transparency. The "common" landscape that Emerson crosses, as well as the smaller microcosm of space in the puddle where he stands, gets subsumed by the comprehensive vision of the eye, an inversion of his expanding "Circles" essay wherein the eye as first circle goes out to define the world.

Emerson's "first circle" in the nineteenth century of course fails to originate an all-knowing Adamic vision. Attempting to transcend predecessors, it paradoxically replicates the kind of fundamental wrestling with the materiality of language found in classical Persian verse. His attempt to embody the spirit that would overcome the letter through the metaphor of invisibility, which would obviate metaphor itself, finds a comparable analogue in Rumi's famous declaration that the poetry he recited at best became a poor metaphor for the experience of the divine. Considering the self-reducing *rend* in this visionary context, it is as though Emerson has sunk all of his "mean egotism" into that displaced puddle, much like the Sufi goes searching through the mole of the beloved via a reduction of beauty to its most reduced state. His transcendent individuation emerges from his attempt to repress his ego by burrowing, like a mole, into the earth (with its etymological origins of "humility") as an American Adam, demonstrating the Bloomian counter-sublime through his claim to see through all of creation.

Extending such a theoretically comparative reading between the Persian tradition that Emerson appears to anticipate, the transparent eyeball passage stylistically mirrors the Persian tradition at the level of pun, upon which the verse of Hafez that Emerson would come to translate and imitate thrives. Puns in classical Persian poetry, especially in the verse of Hafez, liberate as they contain, as if trying, like Emerson's attempt at transparency, to out-metaphorize the metaphor they posit. Donald Pease effectively deconstructs the essence of Emerson's punning to show how the eyeball ultimately becomes an originating metaphor from which the process of metaphor emerges: "The eyeball is trans-parent, trans-individual, trans-objective . . . undefinable as either subject or object, God or nature . . . like the living glance exchanged when God and nature look face to face."[19] Pease inadvertently offers here perhaps the best description for Persian Sufi poetry, invested in paradoxically liberating yet confining puns that frequently tend to read the book of nature as divine.

In an essay on the difficulty of translating Hafez, Dick Davis cites a representative pun from the Persian tradition by Masud Sa'd: "Nalam bedel chu nai man andar hesar-e nai." As Davis writes, "Only in Persian can this line be evocative. The pun is on the word *nai,* which means a reed flute, and also alludes to the name of a fortress used as a prison. Hence the line means, 'While I am (imprisoned) in *nai* (the fortress), I complain in my heart like a *nai* (reed flute).'"[20] The freedom in the ethereal song (which occurs, in Persian, at the level of sound in the reading of lines from contained couplets) remains predicated on physical captivity.

To take an even more essential, and perhaps more Emersonian, example from the verse of Hafez, the following ghazal couplet basically defines wine through the repetition of *ast,* meaning "is," a state-of-being verb upon which the intoxicating illusion of the jars that contain it remains predicated: "Through intoxication, all in tumult and shout are the jars / And that wine in that place true is, not illusory, is."[21] Tellingly, Emerson interpreted Hafez's use of wine, an especially ubiquitous trope in the Persian tradition that Iranian critics continue to interrogate,[22] as a claim on intellectual freedom, as evidenced by his famous imitation of Hafez's poem in his own "Bacchus."[23] Paul Kane rightly points out Emerson's suspicion of mysticism, citing his use of wine more to embody a spirit of a self-reliant "power and liberty" (119). Equally dismissive of the kind of fatalism in the Persian tradition,[24] which derives in part from a culture informed by Shia' Islam, Emerson in his own introductory essay for a collection of Persian verse in translation explicitly praises Hafez for his individual rebellion against religious strictures, his challenging of hypocrisy as he "tears off his turban and throws it at the head of the meddling dervis" (116). This tension between the exertions of a kind of self-reliance within the confines of an established system of organized morality exemplifies both the verse of Hafez as well as the philosophy of Emerson. In the previously quoted texts from both authors, the transparent eye, like the wine jars, proves illusive as well as allusive through the agency of Emerson's ego, yet through a kind of intoxicating transcendence of "eye" over "I," wherein he becomes "glad to the brink of fear," and the illusion vanishes. As Kenneth Burke reveals, for Emerson all of nature becomes a crossing of matter into spirit, wherein the "I" is lost.[25] Such a summation could easily apply to the Persian verse Emerson studied, to the extent that it functions upon a visual *rend* in relation to language through the loss of self to the beloved as metaphor for the divine.

In another context, Kane compares the ghazal, the principal lyric form of Iranian verse, consisting of disparate couplets linked through style as opposed to theme (the form in which the previously excerpted Hafez quotations were originally written), to the tension between Emerson's epigraphs and the essays to which they seem disjointedly attached (130–32). Often a given speaker in the ghazal, much like the litany of quoted voices in Emerson's essays, gets positioned with a dialogic tension between other preceding voices. The inherent nature of the ghazal invites such intertextual interjections of lines from, among many sources, the Qur'an or from other poets (via a received set of common tropes in the literary tradition, actual poetic lines, various historical allusions, etc.), much in the way that Kane shows Emerson disjointedly positing established quotations as epigraphs to which he both responds as well as thematically resists by breaking away from the originating point, often merely picking it up, like the ghazal, in a random place. Pease has tellingly observed how "Emerson turns his writing into the equivalent of quoting," an apt summation of the classical Persian masters of the ghazal form who, also like Emerson, quote themselves to increase dialogical tension as they seemingly also distance themselves from fixed subjectivity.

By calling out the ego and naming himself as an invisible presence in the early passage from "Nature," Emerson can further be seen as demonstrating the Persian ghazal's convention of "signing" a final couplet with the poet's name or persona. This stylistic predilection proves especially significant in both traditions. In the Persian form, the brief series of disjointed couplets concludes with the poet's ego (or at least the performance of it), which, like Emerson's naming of "mean egotism" paradoxically gets undercut by self-diminishment, as seen in the aforementioned translation by Emerson wherein Hafez reduces his name to dust. This common self-*rend*ing via self-referencing helps to exemplify Ricardo Miguel-Alfonso's observation of how Emerson differs from European influences "by a greater acceptance or affirmation of discontinuities of self."[26] Emerson, as a speaker foregrounding his presence in an attempt to transcend it, follows a pattern of ego-disruption through the interposition of other voices in both Emerson as well as Hafez, wherein objectifying a variety of disparate and foreign texts helps to disrupt a subjective presence. "When 'I' quote, then 'I' am speaking by another who speaks through me when I assume his word," writes Pease.[27] Such a rhetorical strategy in the ghazal as well as in Emerson's prose reflects, then, another means for the *rend*. The self literally as well as visually disappears from the text, at least at significant moments. The elision of ego in turn mirrors both Emerson's prose and the ghazal's tendency to suspend meaning as though through recurring ellipses, wherein gaps of meaning between sentences and couplets invite, if not trap, the reader into that same sense of ego-absence that relays such an inexplicable spiritual tone. This becomes yet another means of a "de-centering" rhetorical practice for Emerson. At significant turns, it coincides with the intersection of a somewhat unrecognized, as if invisible, sphere of Persian influence.

Emerson clears space in the American landscape as he stands in a dirty puddle within "the public common" not only to claim transcendence of ego as transparent eyeball, but to figuratively clear the Western canon and so make way for his own assumptive imitative practices from other literary traditions. The Bhabhaian third space between Persian and American verse thus gets subsumed in the transparency. Attempting to render the ego invisible in turn represses literary precedence, seeing as how according to Emerson, in America the poet himself is to become the poem. Insofar as "man is only half himself, the other half is his expression" (*CW* 3:4), Emerson effectively establishes a priori the means by which to interject his own appropriative practice into a seemingly original self-expression. In a poem like "Bacchus," for example, which Buell considers his finest, Emerson effectively imitates Hafez, rewriting the original that he read in German, to make it his own. That it becomes impossible to fully explicate what Emerson takes from Hafez as opposed to the German intermediary rendering supports, as if by default, a Bloomian reading of the American sublime. Emerson follows both Goethe and Hafez in calling for a wine that is more than mere wine to reach a more insightful vision.[28]

Yet Emerson's more officially translated poem out of which this poem emerged[29] (the original of which Von Hammer, the editor of the German version, cited as one of the verses that possibly earned Hafez the title of "Tongue of the Secret") references "Jamschid's glass."[30] This too could be considered a mere carryover from the German version, were it not for Emerson's grander claim on its metaphorical import in his own poem. Paradoxically, the art of literary translation often follows Emerson's attempt at transcendence, attempting to move beyond mere literal naming to better capture the spirit of the source. Considered a locus of all-knowing power held by various kings in Persian mythology, the cup of Jamshid is said to reflect the whole world and reveal the seven heavens of the universe. A frequent trope in the poetry of Hafez—one of the many rhetorical reasons that the Persian poet comes to claim the tongue of the unseen—its vehicular power carries Emerson's "Bacchus" to the throne of an atemporal place where the American makes claims on an ancient future yet to materialize: "Kings unborn shall walk with me . . ." (*CW* 9:233). The wine itself in Emerson's translation changes the lowly "Saki" or "wine boy" in the Persian court to a Western "Butler," thereby changing the very means of delivery of the all-encompassing metaphor of wine. Emerson's own history, which will get written as if for the first time, in turn links the eternity of humanity to the seven heavenly sisters of Western antiquity. The essence of Western Romantic free expression through Goethe, whose translations and adaptations from German Emerson read, surface in the same intersecting circle of influence with Emerson's own circle of latently appropriated vision. Categorizing the ecstasy-producing power of wine—which plays on a central trope of classical Persian verse under the title of the Greek god "Bacchus" in the title—follows Bloom's aforementioned Western shift in the theorizing of influence itself under Greek names. The speaker's appeal to the "remembering wine" ultimately comes down to reviving his "dazzling memory" so that he can, as he states:

> write my old adventures with the pen
> Which on the first day drew
> Upon the tablets blue,
> The dancing Pleiads and eternal men. (*CW* 9:234)

The Western universe of antiquity concludes the poem like the end of an elegy, which for Emerson becomes a beginning before the beginning in the concluding reversion to an empty blue sky, a *tabula rasa* as clear as the first day of Genesis. Ultimately, a commingling Persian influence from a source poem by Hafez transforms into Emerson's own successful poem, at least in part through his appropriative misplacement of Greek mythology.

It is no small feat that upon his deeper discovery of Persian verse Emerson continued to translate as well as appropriate a tradition of which he had little knowledge beyond the intermediary German texts from which he worked. Though beyond the scope of this chapter, it warrants emphasizing that to get to Hafez, Sa'di, and others, he also goes through the daunting influence of Goethe, a fellow Romantic writer who had responded to the Persian tradition before him. Emerson thus subverts an even more pressing German influence through his assumption of a more distant, though incredibly substantial, classical Persian tradition. The real "turn" in Emerson's studies around the Bhabhaian third space (which metaphorically can be seen in relation to Bloom as the transparent eyeball) can also be seen as occurring most profoundly, albeit still rather latently, at this intersecting point. Contrary to the common assumption that Ezra Pound was the founder, if not the discoverer, of using Eastern traditions in American poetic practices, and thereby effectively establishing what we have come to consider modern poetry, Emerson arrives as a significant, though relatively invisible, appropriative American progenitor. Steven Yao perhaps prematurely credits Pound with an unprecedented change in the history of literary translation, wherein, he explains, the modernist poet-translator "obviated intimate knowledge of the source language as a precondition for translation by demonstrating in an irrefutable way that successful . . . results could be attained without thorough . . . understanding of the original language of the text one translated."[31] Emerson can instead be seen here as protomodernist in an importantly new way, and with all the Bloomian implications, insofar as he subsumes the foreign letter to make original claims on the spirit. In so doing, he acts as harbinger to Pound's comparable claim that all literature is contemporaneous. Emerson thereby provides a foundational rhetorical model for many writers to follow, instructing how to write over the masters.

By effectively clearing the literary landscape to invite his own appropriative practices of Eastern sources, Emerson in turn lays the figurative groundwork to invite a return of the foreign into the American tradition, allowing anglophone Middle Eastern–American writers to claim their voices here in the same "third space" into which he has written himself. Having claimed a first priority predicated on transparency, however, Emerson marks the spot of ego-transcendence, so to speak. Much as the verse of Wallace Stevens moves around the transparent eyeball—sullying the preceding American romantic tradition established by his forefather through an indelible textual presence in poems like "Sailing after Lunch," wherein the speaker positions himself as "a pupil of the gorgeous wheel"—hybrid writers must come through Emerson, though with the added burden of reconciling a much deeper tradition from one of their two originating countries. Paradoxically, they attempt to replicate the transparent eyeball by outlining or writing over Emerson's example.

The Book of Khalid, the first Arab American novel by Lebanese American writer Ameen Rihani, who came to America with the poet Khalil Gibran, effectively demonstrates such a return upon Emerson's origins. Walter Dunnavent has shown how Rihani mined Emerson in his story of a young, idealistic immigrant who came to New York City in the early twentieth century with Shakib, his poet friend, by pointing out such themes as "primacy of intuition," "a mixture of the mystical and the practical," and the "individual rejection . . . of the social order."[32] Of further importance in the novel, the protagonist, Khalid, consistently inserts an Emersonian will to a first priority within the "sepulchers of the fathers" from the old country. Haunted by the metaphorical presence of the invisible eyeball of the American counter-sublime and all its implications on history as well as the Romantic ego, Khalid finds the cleared space both inviting as well as threatening to his origins. As he explains, America "makes foreigners forget their native land."[33] To this end, and very much in the spirit of following Emerson's displacing the "sepulchres of the fathers," Khalid acquires the habit of burning existing books after he reads them, as if cremating the very tradition he attempts to absorb. Emerson's brazen appropriative imitations and translations in English of ghazals by Hafez from an original source text in a language he could not even read seem inversely to drive the protagonist poet Khalid to write over, in English, the famous Arabic couplets of the classical Iraqi poet al-Mutannabi by making a Whitmanesque catalogue of all the modern American inventions (as if combining Emerson with Franklin) in imitative lines like: "O Phonograph, thou wonder of our time, / Thy tongue of wax can sink like me in rhyme" (126) and "Electricity and Steam and Compressed Air / Will carry us to heaven yet, I swear" (127). It is as though Emerson anticipated Rihani's imitation not just of himself, but his own imitation of predecessors from the Middle East.

What makes Khalid arguably most like Emerson, however, ironically involves his inability to sustain comparable self-reliant claims in New York, a failure that ultimately motivates him to transplant his American influence back in his country of origin. The all-encompassing, invisible claim on the New World makes it difficult to reconcile, especially when coming from the old one. Like other hybrid Middle Eastern–American writers who follow later in the twentieth century, Rihani reconfigures the intersecting "third space" back to his foreign origins as if to invert Emerson's latent subsuming of the old into the new by overtly positioning Emerson onto the established tradition of his home country. Rihani's protagonist, for example, rebels against the authoritative father of his beloved in Syria, leaving the patriarchal establishment of his own home to sleep in the tomb of Zeus (26), as if obviating mythical hierarchy in the way that Emerson equates himself with ancient kings of Persia through the possession of Jamshid's cup in the aforementioned appropriation of Hafez. Upon returning to his native origins, which means a direct confrontation with the old mores and tradition from which he originally fled in America, Khalid finds a more viable authority to challenge when relatively free from Emerson as predecessor. While in America he had a dream of becoming a donkey boy in his home country, his voice in his poem recording it remains silenced by a goblin—in contradistinction to Whitman, who, the narrator mentions, "would have wrung his neck, after he had ridden upon it." (51). While Emerson has created seemingly inexhaustible space across which Whitman can run his infinitely expanding lines, Khalid finds America and its verse haunted by the anxiety of a presence he cannot repress or subvert via comparable sublime power.

Such a reading barely begins to expose the way hybrid Middle Eastern–American writers see their way back to their origins through a kind of third space that exposes Emerson's vision in a foreign context. Just as the influence of the American predecessor surfaces throughout Rihani's novel, so too does it inform other transnational texts. As if in response to Emerson's appropriation of the Persian ghazal, for example, the Kashmiri poet Agha Shahid Ali would reintroduce the form to countless American poets in English through his own intertextual modeling (that also must look back to older origins to reconcile the especially pervasive Emersonian influence of the American sublime). Continued study of influence in this new direction appears warranted, especially as it helps to better explain how hybrid writers in the United States must, like their American-born counterparts, come through Emerson, though with the added weight of a substantial ancient tradition behind them. Rather than seeing them as mere outsiders responding to an all-encompassing influence, exposing the seemingly invisible first priority of Emerson's vision reveals that a comparable foreign presence has preceded them in the emerging field of American letters. They do not so much as immigrate as return the spirit of their own literary predecessors.

Notes

1. Harold Bloom, *The Anxiety of Influence: A Theory of Poetry* (London: Oxford University Press, 1975), 98–103. Subsequent references to this work will be cited parenthetically in the text by page number.

2. Willis Barnstone, *The Poetics of Translation: History, Theory, Practice* (New Haven, CT: Yale University Press, 1995), 23.

3. Thus far much has been done to establish a comparative relation between Emerson and the Persian verse tradition. J. D. Yohannan's investigation first made an exhaustive tracking of specific poems by the fourteenth-century classical Persian poet Hafez that Emerson translated through German renderings from Joseph von Hammer Purgstall (J. D. Yohannan, "Emerson's Translations of Persian Poetry from German Sources," *American Literature* 14 [January 1943]: 407–20), which was soon followed by his attempt to account for the influence of Persian poetry on Emerson in three predominant ways: an actual relation to a specific Persian source, a similarity between Emerson's translation as well as imitation of the German intermediary rendering, and a conceptualization of an ideal poet whom Emerson names after the classical Persian poet, Sa'adi. Understandably, he claims to have left out an examination of the "less tangible effect of Persian poetry on Emerson's

philosophy," noting how difficult it proves to ascertain. J. D. Yohannan, "The Influence of Persian Poetry upon Emerson's Work," *American Literature* 15 (March 1943): 25.

4. Homi K. Bhabha, *The Location of Culture* (New York: Routledge, 1994), 52–56. Subsequent references to this work will be cited parenthetically in the text by page number.

5. However, the political situation found in the early internationalist interventions of the United States beyond Emerson's New England begins to create other third spaces among marginalized people, true to Bhabha's definition, who continue to encounter various colonist interventions beyond Emerson's New England.

6. Paul Kane cites Emerson's mention of Hafez in "History" (1841) and also notes that Emerson first acquired a German translation of the Persian poet in 1846. Paul Kane, "Emerson and Hafiz: The Figure of the Religious Poet," *Religion and Literature* 41 (Spring 2009): 113–14. Subsequent references to this work will be cited parenthetically in the text by page number. Frederic Ives Carpenter cites Emerson's first introduction to the reading of Persian poets as 1841, while concluding that his reading of Asian literatures began to "bear fruit," meaning to influence his thinking, as early as 1845. Carpenter, *Emerson and Asia* (1930; rpt., New York: Haskell House, 1968), 161, 13.

7. Lawrence Buell, *Emerson* (Cambridge, MA: Harvard University Press, 2003), 151.

8. Robert Bly and Leonard Lewisohn, trans., *The Angels Knocking on the Tavern Door: Thirty Poems of Hafiz* (New York: HarperCollins, 2008).

9. "For nonconformity the world whips you with its displeasure" (Kane, "Emerson and Hafiz," 123).

10. Significantly, Kane notes in his comparison with Emerson that, for Hafez, the most important theme is challenging hypocrisy (121).

11. As cited in Emerson's journals. See "Notebook Orientalist," in *The Topical Notebooks of Ralph Waldo Emerson*, ed. Ralph H. Orth et al., 3 vols. (Columbia: University of Missouri Press, 1990–94): 2:119.

12. Ralph Waldo Emerson, *Collected Poems and Translations*, ed. Harold Bloom and Paul Kane (New York: Library of America, 1994), 258.

13. See, for example, Eric Wilson's reading of biblical influence on Emerson's passage in *Emerson's Sublime Science* (New York: St. Martin's, 1999).

14. James M. Cox, "R. W. Emerson: The Circles of the Eye," in David Levin, ed., *Emerson: Prophecy, Metamorphosis, and Influence* (New York: Columbia University Press, 1975), 78.

15. Aryanpur Kashani, *Odes of Hafiz*, trans. Abbas Aryanpur Kashani (Costa Mesa, CA: Mazda Publishers, 1984), 7.

16. Florence Lederer, *The Secret Rose Garden of Sa'd ud din Mahmud Shabistari*, trans. Florence Lederer (London: John Murray, 1920), 15, 29.

17. Syed Mumtaz Ali, "Sama (Mystical Music)." Canadian Society of Muslims, http://muslimcanada.org.

18. Ghazal 68, translated by the author.

19. Donald E. Pease, "Emerson, Nature, and the Sovereignty of Influence," *boundary 2* 8, no. 3 (1980): 59.

20. Dick Davis, "On Not Translating Hafez," *New England Review* 25, nos. 1–2 (2004): 310–18; 315.

21. Hafez, *The Divan of Hafez, Written in the Fourteenth Century, by Khwaja Shamsu-d-Di Muhammad-i-Hafiz-i-Shirazi, Otherwise Known as Lis anu-I Ghaib and Tarjum anu-I-Asrar*, trans. H. Wilberforce Clarke (Calcutta: Government of India Central Printing Office, 1891), 82. Complied and corrected by Behrouz Houmayoun Far at http://www.enel.ucalgary.ca/People/far/hobbies/iran/Gazal/hafez_ghazal_bi_p1.pdf.

22. For a good comparative discussion of the association of wine between Eastern and Western cultures, see Mahmood Karimi-Hakak and Bill Wolak, ed. and trans., introduction to *Your Lover's Beloved: 51 Ghazals by Hafez* (New York: Cross-Cultural Communications, 2009), 26–37.

23. Yohannan, "Influence," 28.

24. Carpenter, *Emerson and Asia,* 36–37.

25. Kenneth Burke, "I, Eye, Ay—Emerson's Early Essay on 'Nature': Thoughts on the Machinery of Transcendence," *Sewanee Review* 74 (1966): 875–95.

26. Ricardo Miguel-Alfonso, "The Influence of Anxiety; or, the Postmodernity of Emerson," in José Ramón Prado-Pérez and Dídac Llorens-Cubedo, eds., *New Literatures of Old: Dialogues of Tradition and Innovation in Anglophone Literature* (Newcastle: Cambridge Scholars, 2008), 55.

27. Pease, "Emerson, Nature, and the Sovereignty of Influence," 67.

28. Buell, *Emerson,* 152.

29. As cited by Emerson in his rather loose translation of a related poem from Hafez, which Buell considers relatively close in correspondence (Buell, *Emerson,* 152–53).

30. As cited in note to translation in Emerson, *Collected Poems and Translations*, 104–5.

31. Steven Yao, *Translation and the Languages of Modernism* (New York: Palgrave, 2002), 26.

32. Walter E. Dunnavent, "Rihani, Emerson, and Thoreau," in Nathan Funk and Betty Sitka, eds., *Ameen Rihani: Bridging East and West; A Pioneering Call for Arab-American Understanding* (Lanham, MD: University Press of America, 2004), 56.

33. Ameen Fares Rihani, *The Book of Khalid* (1911; rpt., New York: Melville House, 2011), 118. Subsequent references to this work will be cited parenthetically in the text by page number.

ACKNOWLEDGMENTS

From David LaRocca

I begin with pronounced thanks to the gifted and generous contributors to this volume; their critical insights—at once elastic and probing—into our shared subject have generated a remarkable, and we hope enduring, set of reflections on Emerson's impact on the thinking of his own time as well as his evolving legacy thereafter. And we all have Ricardo Miguel-Alfonso to thank for dreaming up the conditions for this fertile and fecund conversation; I, for one, am immensely grateful to Ricardo for his vision, and humbled that he reached out to me to undertake a collaborative project—his invitation was the first moment of transatlantic imagination that would lead, in time, to this bounteous and coruscating collection. Moreover, his copious skills as editor leave me in awe and feeling very lucky. I am duly and happily obliged to Ricardo.

I owe significant debts to several institutions that provided the necessary conditions—both contextual and collegial—for such work to take shape: at Cornell University, I thank Roger Stephen Gilbert, Chair, for facilitating my appointment as Visiting Scholar in the Department of English; at the College at Cortland, State University of New York, I am grateful to Andrew Fitz-Gibbon, Chair, for arranging my term as Lecturer in the Department of Philosophy; and at The New York Public Library Stephen A. Schwarzman Building, I appreciate the chance, once again, to thank Jay Barksdale of the General Research Division and Study Rooms Liaison, for retaining me—from book to book—as Writer-in-Residence in the Frederick Lewis Allen Room, and also for assisting with the Manhattan Research Libraries Initiative, thereby extending research possibilities into the Bobst Library at New York University and the Butler Library at Columbia University in the City of New York.

For many years now, the Signet Society of Harvard College has provided the space and occasion for discovering the work of passionate thinkers in the arts and humanities. On Dunster Street and elsewhere, I am thankful to the members of the Society for spirited conversations and sustaining collaborations, and to Mark Hruby for his graciousness.

For the ones whose existence inspires and cheers my days—precious Ruby and shimmering Star—I give my love.

And as ever, and with ever more affection, gratitude, and admiration, I thank my incomparably astute wife, Dr. K.L.E. LaRocca, who knows well and mercifully that "there are all degrees of proficiency in knowledge of the world."

From Ricardo Miguel-Alfonso

The contributors to this volume are the first to be warmly thanked for their effort, kindness, and patience. This project would not have been a worthy initiative without their good will, unflagging support, and generosity of spirit. It has been a pleasure to work with a group of truly *Emersonian* scholars.

I also want to thank David LaRocca for his generous attention to my ideas and his enthusiasm to carry this project forward from the very beginning. Not only is he one of the most perceptive and learned young philosophers currently at work in the United States (his recent book on Emerson's *English Traits* testifies to it), but he is also someone who gives philosophical work its best name. His expertise on Emerson's oeuvre—and modern philosophy, and editorial matters, and so many other things—have proved crucial for the successful completion of this volume, and we are all in his debt for that. This book would not exist without him.

Here in Spain, my friends and colleagues J. A. Álvarez Amorós and Pedro Aullón de Haro have helped me in ways they cannot imagine. For many years their magisterial work has been a model of what true intellectual work must be, and this collection is a small token of my appreciation for them. Other colleagues—at home and abroad—have been indispensable to my understanding of Emerson, philosophy, and modernity, and I especially want to thank David M. Robinson and Richard Eldridge for their support and patience.

For this project I also benefited from my stay at the English Department of the University of Nebraska–Lincoln in the cold spring of 2010. My hosts, Susan Belasco and Ken Price, as well as other colleagues at UNL, were very helpful in shaping some of my ideas about Emerson (and Fuller and Whitman).

I want to thank my family, who have supported me for many years now even though they didn't always understand who Emerson was, what he said and did, or what it means to be a "philologist"—an outdated word today—in the twenty-first century. My parents, my sister, and my brother-in-law have always believed in me in ways I can't even begin to describe but I'll always be thankful for. Thank you for just being there.

To my wife, Loretta, I have the strongest and most enduring debt one can ever imagine. Her unfailing support and encouragement have been a constant presence in my life, academic and otherwise. She has been especially strong whenever I was at my weakest, which unfortunately seems to happen too often. Let this volume be my modest personal tribute to her.

From Both Editors

At Dartmouth College Press of the University Press of New England, we wish to convey warm thanks to Donald E. Pease—series editor of Re-Mapping the Transnational: A Dartmouth Series in American Studies—for crucial support from submission through the publication process. Most especially, we also extend our sincere gratitude to Richard Pult, whose guidance and orientation—from first contact to final proof—has been essential to the shape and success of the manuscript. We are tremendously grateful to Amanda Dupuis for her expert production assistance and her evident care with the manuscript. Likewise, Beth Gianfagna—with her adroit and elegant copyediting—saved us from errors, improved clarity and consistency, and contributed notable improvements to the fit and finish of the pieces collected here. Lastly, we appreciate the informed and incisive comments of several anonymous outside readers for the press—both at the proposal stage and the draft stage—which prompted deeper integration of this volume's content into conversations under way across time and discipline, and also stimulated refinements of argument form and prose style.

ABBREVIATIONS

AW Ralph Waldo Emerson. *Emerson's Antislavery Writings*. Edited by Len Gougeon and Joel Myerson. New Haven, CT: Yale University Press, 1995.

CEC Ralph Waldo Emerson. *The Correspondence of Emerson and Carlyle*. Edited by Joseph Slater. New York: Columbia University Press, 1964.

CS Ralph Waldo Emerson. *The Complete Sermons of Ralph Waldo Emerson*. Edited by Albert J. von Frank, et al. 4 vols. Columbia: University of Missouri Press, 1989–92.

CW Ralph Waldo Emerson. *The Collected Works of Ralph Waldo Emerson*. Edited by Alfred R. Ferguson, et al. 10 vols. Cambridge, MA: Harvard University Press, 1971–2013.

EL Ralph Waldo Emerson. *The Early Lectures of Ralph Waldo Emerson*. Edited by Stephen E. Whicher, Robert E. Spiller, and Wallace E. Williams. 3 vols. Cambridge, MA: Harvard University Press, 1959–72.

ETE Ellen Tucker Emerson. *The Letters of Ellen Tucker Emerson*. Edited by Edith E. W. Gregg. 2 vols. Kent, OH: Kent State University Press, 1982.

JMN Ralph Waldo Emerson. *The Journals and Miscellaneous Notebooks of Ralph Waldo Emerson*. Edited by William H. Gilman, Ralph H. Orth, et al. 16 vols. Cambridge, MA: Harvard University Press, 1960–82.

L Ralph Waldo Emerson. *The Letters of Ralph Waldo Emerson*. Edited by Ralph L. Rusk and Eleanor M. Tilton. 10 vols. New York: Columbia University Press, 1939 (vols. 1–6) and 1990–95 (vols. 7–10).

LL Ralph Waldo Emerson. *The Later Lectures of Ralph Waldo Emerson*. Edited by Ronald Bosco and Joel Myerson. 2 vols. Athens: University of Georgia Press, 2001.

CONTRIBUTORS

The Editors

David LaRocca is Visiting Scholar in the Department of English at Cornell University and Lecturer in the Department of Philosophy at the College at Cortland, State University of New York. He is the author of *On Emerson* (Wadsworth, 2003) and *Emerson's English Traits and the Natural History of Metaphor* (Bloomsbury, 2013), and the editor of Stanley Cavell's *Emerson's Transcendental Etudes* (Stanford, 2003); *The Philosophy of Charlie Kaufman* (Kentucky, 2011); *Estimating Emerson: An Anthology of Criticism from Carlyle to Cavell* (Bloomsbury, 2013); and *The Philosophy of War Films* (Kentucky, 2014). His essays on Emerson are published in *Nietzsche e L'America; Ralph Waldo Emerson: Bicentenary Appraisals; Platonic Traditions in American Thought; New Morning: Emerson in the Twenty-First Century;* and *Emerson for the Twenty-First Century: Global Perspectives on an American Icon.* His articles on American philosophy, autobiography, value theory, and film have appeared in *Epoché, Afterimage, Liminalities, Transactions of the Charles S. Peirce Society, Film and Philosophy, The Midwest Quarterly, Nineteenth-Century Prose, The Journal of Business Ethics, The Journal of Aesthetics and Art Criticism,* and *The Journal of Aesthetic Education.* He was a conferee at the National Endowment for the Humanities Summer Institute on Emerson, "Emerson at 200: Literature, Philosophy, Democracy"; became Harvard's Sinclair Kennedy Traveling Fellow in the United Kingdom; and subsequently has received multiple grants from The Ralph Waldo Emerson Society, including a Community Project Award for the conference he directed, "Liberty and Necessity in Emerson and Nietzsche." Contact: DavidLaRocca@Post.Harvard.Edu. More details at www.DavidLaRocca.org.

Ricardo Miguel-Alfonso is Associate Professor of American Literature in the Department of Modern Philology at the University of Castilla–La Mancha, Spain. He is the author of *El Romanticismo americano y la idea de la literatura* (Verbum, 2014). He has published essays on Robert Coover, Ralph Waldo Emerson, Nathaniel Hawthorne, Elizabeth Palmer Peabody, and Adam Smith. He has also translated into

Spanish Emerson's two series of *Essays* (Espasa Calpe, 2001) and George Santayana's *Reason in Art* (Verbum, 2008), among other texts. He is currently at work on a book addressing Emerson's aesthetic and philosophical transformation between the 1830s and the 1870s, tentatively titled *Emerson's Aesthetic Vision and the Disenchantment with Modernity*.

The Contributors

Richard Deming is Director of Creative Writing and Lecturer in English at Yale University. He is a poet and a theorist whose work explores the intersections of poetry, philosophy, and visual culture. He is the author of *Listening on All Sides: Toward an Emersonian Ethics of Reading* (Stanford, 2007), and he contributes to such magazines as *Artforum* and the *Boston Review*. His collection of poems, *Let's Not Call It Consequence* (Shearsman, 2008), received the 2009 Norma Farber First Book Award from the Poetry Society of America. His poems have appeared in such places as *Sulfur, Field, Indiana Review,* and the *Nation*. In spring 2012, he was the John P. Birkelund Fellow of the American Academy in Berlin.

Neal Dolan is Associate Professor of English at the University of Toronto. His research concerns the conflict between individualist and communal values in liberal societies. He recently published the first full-length study of Ralph Waldo Emerson's symbolic construction of liberal culture—*Emerson's Liberalism* (Wisconsin, 2009)—and is now working on a book about class, community, and individualism in American ethnic writing.

Monika M. Elbert is Professor of English and Distinguished Scholar at Montclair State University, New Jersey, and editor of the *Nathaniel Hawthorne Review*. She has published widely on nineteenth-century American authors, especially on Hawthorne, and has recently coedited a collection, *Culinary Aesthetics and Practices in Nineteenth-Century American Literature* (Palgrave, 2009), which includes her essay on Hawthorne's nationalism and food preferences. She also recently edited the collection *Enterprising Youth: Social Values and Acculturation in Nineteenth-Century American Children's Literature* (Routledge, 2008), which includes her essay on charity in Alcott's Christmas stories. Her essay, "Transcendentalist (S)exchanges: Reconciling Difference in Julia Ward Howe's *The Hermaphrodite*," has just appeared in *Toward a Genealogy of Female Transcendentalism*, edited by Jana Argersinger and Phyllis Cole (Georgia, 2014).

K. L. Evans is Visiting Scholar in the Department of English at Cornell University. Previously she was Associate Professor of Literature and Philosophy at Yeshiva University in New York City and Assistant Professor of English at the University of Redlands in California. She teaches literature and philosophy, nineteenth-century

American literature, and film criticism. While she was a Fulbright scholar in New Zealand, she studied Melville's Pacific poetics, and this research culminated in the book *Whale!* (Minnesota, 2003). In her forthcoming book *Melvillean Mimesis,* she examines the "realism without empiricism" at large in Melville's *Moby-Dick* and Wittgenstein's *Tractatus.* She has participated in two National Endowment for the Humanities Summer Institutes, including "Emerson at 200: Literature, Philosophy, Democracy." Selected recent publications include "A Rest from Reason: Wittgenstein, Drury, and the Difference between Madness and Religion" (*Philosophy,* 2010); "While Reading Wittgenstein," in *Stanley Cavell, Literature, and Criticism* (Manchester, 2011); "How Job Begat Larry: The Present Situation in *A Serious Man,*" in *The Philosophy of the Coen Brothers* (updated ed., Kentucky, 2012); "Wittgenstein and Lessing: Why the *Tractatus,* like the Old Testament, Is 'Nothing but a Book,'" in *Wittgenstein Reading* (De Gruyter, 2013); and "The Work of Art in the Age of Embedded Journalism: Fiction versus Depiction in *Zero Dark Thirty,*" in *The Philosophy of War Films* (Kentucky, 2014).

Mathew A. Foust is Assistant Professor of Philosophy at Central Connecticut State University. Previously, he was Assistant Professor of Philosophy in the Department of History and Philosophy at Lander University in Greenwood, South Carolina, and in the General Education Office at Beijing Normal University–Hong Kong Baptist University United International College. His areas of specialization include American philosophy, ethics, and Chinese and comparative philosophy. He is the author of *Loyalty to Loyalty: Josiah Royce and the Genuine Moral Life* (Fordham, 2012). He has published articles in American philosophy and Chinese and comparative philosophy in journals such as *Transactions of the Charles S. Peirce Society, Southern Journal of Philosophy, Journal of Chinese Philosophy, Asian Philosophy, William James Studies,* and the *Pluralist.* He is the organizer and editor of a special issue of the *Journal of Chinese Philosophy* on "Classical American Philosophy and Chinese Philosophy: New Comparisons" (2012). His research on American philosophy has resulted in his being awarded grants to travel to the Harvard University Archives and the Bancroft Library at University of California–Berkeley. He has won the Douglas Greenlee Prize, awarded by the Society for the Advancement of American Philosophy, as well as the Costello Prize and the John E. Smith Memorial Essay Contest, awarded by the Josiah Royce Society.

Herwig Friedl is Professor Emeritus of American Literature and History of Ideas at Heinrich-Heine-Universität Düsseldorf. He studied American and German literatures and philosophy at the University of Heidelberg and at Cornell; he was a Postdoctoral Fellow at Yale in 1973–74, a Visiting Professor at the University of New Mexico in 1984, and a Visiting Scholar at Harvard in 2002, 2006, and 2007. His book publications include a study of Henry James's aesthetic theory (1972) and, as editor, essay collections on E. L. Doctorow (1986), on women's studies as cultural studies (2000), and on gender and conceptions of space (2006). His numerous essays focus on transcendentalism, pragmatism, modernism (Gertrude Stein), and American thinking in an international context. He continues to publish on transcendentalism and pragmatism and is presently also working on comparative analyses of American and Asian thinking and poetry.

Len Gougeon is Professor of American literature and Distinguished University Fellow at the University of Scranton (Pennsylvania). He is the author of *Virtue's Hero: Emerson, Antislavery, and Reform* (Georgia, 1993); *Emerson and Eros: The Making of a Cultural Hero* (SUNY, 2007); and *Emerson's Truth, Emerson's Wisdom* (American Transcendental Press, 2010). He is the coeditor (with Joel Myerson) of *Emerson's Antislavery Writings* (Yale, 1995). In 2008, he received the Distinguished Achievement Award from the Ralph Waldo Emerson Society. His most recent work is "Militant Abolitionism: Douglass, Emerson, and the Rise of the Anti-Slave," forthcoming in *New England Quarterly.* He is currently at work on a book dealing with the cultural warfare that occurred between America and Great Britain as a result of tensions and conflicts arising from the American Civil War and the struggle to end slavery.

Robert D. Habich is President of the Ralph Waldo Emerson Society and Professor of English at Ball State University, where he has taught American literature and literary history since 1984. His publications include *Building Their Own Waldos: Emerson's First Biographers and the Politics of Life-Writing in the Gilded Age* (Iowa, 2011); *Romanticism and Transcendentalism, 1820–1865* (coauthor, Facts on File, 2010); *Lives Out of Letters: Essays on American Literary Biography and Documentation in Honor of Robert N. Hudspeth* (editor, Fairleigh Dickinson, 2004); and *Transcendentalism and the "Western Messenger"* (Fairleigh Dickinson, 1985), as well as numerous articles and presentations on Emerson and his circle, including the chapter on biography and memoir in the *Oxford Handbook of Transcendentalism* (2010). In 2008, he was visiting scholar in American literature at the Instituto Politécnico do Porto in Portugal.

David Mikics is John and Rebecca Moores Professor of English and Fellow of the Honors College at the University of Houston. He is most recently editor of *The Annotated Emerson* (Harvard, 2012). Among his other recent books are *The Art of the Sonnet* (with Stephen Burt; Harvard, 2010); *Who Was Jacques Derrida? An Intellectual Biography* (Yale, 2009); and *A New Handbook of Literary Terms* (Yale, 2007).

Daniel Rosenberg Nutters is a Ph.D. candidate in the Department of English at Temple University. He earned a B.A from the University of Michigan and an M.A. from the State University of New York at Buffalo, both in English. For his master's thesis, he explored the relationship between Herman Melville's major novels and the cultural and aesthetic phenomena examined by Walter Benjamin in the *Arcades Project.* In his dissertation, titled "The Man of Imagination: Transformations of Romanticism in Henry James," he examines James's prefaces, memoirs, and unfinished works in relation to Romantic theories of the self and fragmentation. Additionally, he is completing a study of Wordsworth's influence on Henry Adams. His main research focus is the transatlantic reception and influence of Romantic aesthetics from the nineteenth century through the First World War.

Donald E. Pease is Professor of English, the Ted and Helen Geisel Third Century Professor in the Humanities, Chair of the Dartmouth Liberal Studies Program, and winner of the 1981 Distinguished Teaching Award at Dartmouth. In 1996, he founded the Dartmouth Institute in American Studies, and in 1997 he also served as Academic Director of the Alumni College program. A recipient of a Ph.D. from the University of Chicago, he is the author of *Visionary Compacts: American Renaissance Writings in Cultural Context* (Wisconsin, 1987), which won the Mark Ingraham Prize for the best new book in the humanities in 1987; *The New American Exceptionalism* (Minnesota, 2009); and *Theodor Seuss Geisel* (Oxford, 2010). The author of more than one hundred articles on figures in American and British literature, Pease is also the coeditor of *The American Renaissance Reconsidered* (Johns Hopkins, 1985) and the editor of seven other volumes, including *The Cultures of United States Imperialism* (Duke, 1992); *The Futures of American Studies* (Duke, 2002), and *Re-Framing the Transnational Turn* (Dartmouth, 2012). In 2010, he inaugurated Re-Mapping the Transnational Turn: A Dartmouth Series in American Studies. He has been awarded Guggenheim, Mellon, Ford, and Hewlett fellowships and has twice received an NEH Directorship to teach college teachers about nineteenth-century American literature. In 2000, he was the Drue Heinz Visiting Professor at Oxford University. Over the past five years, Pease has been Distinguished Visiting Professor at the JFK Institute in American Studies at the Freie Universitaett, Berlin; the State University of New York at Buffalo; and the University of Rome at Tor Vegata. In January 2011, Pease was awarded a Doctorate Honoris Causa by the Faculty of Languages at Sweden's Uppsala University.

David M. Robinson is Oregon Professor of English and Director of the Center for the Humanities at Oregon State University. He was educated at the University of Texas (B.A.), Harvard Divinity School (M.T.S.), and the University of Wisconsin (M.A., Ph.D.), where he studied under the Melville and Emerson scholar, Merton M. Sealts, Jr. His research has focused on Emerson, Thoreau, Fuller, and the New England transcendentalist movement, and on American liberal religion. He is author of *Apostle of Culture: Emerson as Preacher and Lecturer* (Pennsylvania, 1982); *The Unitarians and the Universalists* (Greenwood, 1985); *Emerson and the Conduct of Life* (Cambridge, 1993); and *Natural Life: Thoreau's Worldly Transcendentalism* (Cornell, 2004). From 1988 through 2008 he was author of the chapter "Emerson, Thoreau, Fuller, and Transcendentalism" in the annual *American Literary Scholarship* (Duke). He served in a Fulbright Guest Professorship at the University of

Heidelberg and has been awarded research fellowships by the American Council of Learned Societies and the National Endowment for the Humanities. From 1987 to 1996, he directed nine National Endowment for the Humanities Summer Seminars for School Teachers on the works of Emerson, Thoreau, and Fuller. In 2010, he was elected Fellow of the Massachusetts Historical Society. His current projects include a study of Margaret Fuller and her relationship with the New England transcendentalist movement, and a study of Stanley Cavell's philosophical revival of Thoreau and Emerson in the 1980s and 1990s.

Kenneth S. Sacks is Professor of History at Brown University. His major area of research is ancient Greek intellectual history, and his publications include *Polybius on the Writing of History* (California, 1981) and *Diodorus Siculus and the First Century* (Princeton, 1990). Although he continues to teach and write on ancient history, his interest in Neoplatonism led him to Emerson. *Understanding Emerson: "The American Scholar" and His Struggle for Self-Reliance* (Princeton, 2003) was reviewed in the *Times Literary Supplement* and the *New Yorker* (by John Updike), and he has also edited *The Political Writings of Ralph Waldo Emerson* for the Cambridge Texts in the History of Political Thought series (Cambridge, 2008). Sacks teaches a senior undergraduate seminar on American transcendentalism that regularly draws maximum enrollment.

Naoko Saito is Associate Professor at the Graduate School of Education, University of Kyoto, Japan. Her area of research is American philosophy and pragmatism and its implications for education. She writes in Japanese and English, with a commitment to crossing cultural borders. She is the author of *The Gleam of Light: Moral Perfectionism and Education in Dewey and Emerson* (Fordham, 2005) and *Uchinaru Hikari to Kyoiku: Pragmatism no Sai-Kochiku* (Hosei, 2009), an adaptation of *The Gleam of Light,* as well as numerous articles. In collaboration with Paul Standish, she has coauthored *Democracy and Education from Dewey to Cavell* (Blackwell, 2012) and has coedited the collections *Education and the Kyoto School of Philosophy* (Springer, 2012) and *Stanley Cavell and the Education of Grownups* (Fordham, 2012). She is translator of *The Senses of Walden* (2005), the first book of Cavell's to be published in Japanese, and of Paul Standish's *Beyond the Self: Wittgenstein, Heidegger, Levinas and the Limits of Language* (2012).

Roger Sedarat is Associate Chair of the English Department and Associate Professor of the MFA Program at Queens College, City University of New York. He is the author of *New England Landscape in American Poetry: A Lacanian View* (Cambria, 2011) and articles on Iranian and Middle Eastern–American literature. Additionally, he has published two poetry collections: *Dear Regime: Letters to the Islamic Republic* (Ohio, 2007) and *Ghazal Games* (Ohio, 2011). He teaches literary translation and courses in Middle Eastern–American Literature.

Laura Jane Wey is Lecturer in English at the University of Toronto, Scarborough. She holds a bachelor's degree in English from National Taiwan University and a Ph.D. in comparative literature from Harvard University. Her bilingual background fuels her interest in investigating linguistic and/or cultural crossings; she is currently working on a book on four twentieth-century translations of Shakespeare's *Antony and Cleopatra*. She is also an active literary translator; her translation of Taiwanese writer Egoyan Zheng's collection of short stories was long-listed for the 2007 Man Asian Literary Prize under the title *Fleeting Light* and the 2008 Frank O'Connor International Short Story Prize under the title *Urn's Bottom Village Stories*.

INDEX